ON WISCONSIN!

The History of Badger Athletics from 1896-2001

Don Kopriva

Jim Mott

Sports Publishing, L.L.C.
www.SportsPublishingLLC.com

Editor: Susan M. McKinney
Interior design: Michelle R. Dressen and Deborah M. Bellaire
Senior Project Manager: Jennifer L. Polson
Cover design: Joe Buck and Kenneth J. O'Brien
Color section design: Terry N. Hayden

ISBN: 1-58261-314-1

All photos in this book were provided by the University of Wisconsin Men's and Women's Sports information Departments.

Printed in the United States.

SPORTS PUBLISHING, L.L.C.
804 North Neil Street
Champaign, Illinois 61820

www.SportsPublishingLLC.com

To my parents, Ray and Flo, for their love and support;

To Tim, Scott, Joe, Jim, John and Cathy, Kim, Steve, Glenn and Pat, with thanks for some great track and field and continuing friendship;

and to all Badgers everywhere, thanks for the memories.

–Don Kopriva

This book is dedicated to my wife Dorothy and our three sons, Bill, Dave and Eric, all avid followers of Wisconsin's athletic program.

–Jim Mott

CONTENTS

ACKNOWLEDGMENTS

A book like this involves many people beyond those who have written the words. We're the ones whose names you see on the cover but we most assuredly couldn't do this alone.

Special thanks are due four people in particular for their extra efforts in aiding in some writing and compilation. Justin Doherty, associate men sports information director at Wisconsin, and Diane Nordstrom, women's associate SID, provided critical assistance with numerous profiles and lists. And Chris McClimon of Stoughton was of early, and valuable, assistance in compiling all-time Big Ten finishes and UW coaches throughout the years. Former Big Ten Conference communications director Dennis LaBissoniere provided important editing help.

We're also grateful to Steve Malchow, men's sports information director at the UW, and women's SID Tam Flarup for their cooperation and willingness to help, particularly in allowing Justin and Diane the necessary time to assist.

Vital in this whole process has been the great work, feedback and assistance from all the good people at Sports Publishing in Champaign. Mike Pearson has been a mainstay throughout and we've drawn heavily on his experience in writing the first of these type of books. Marketing director David Kasel deserves kudos for his work in getting the word out as does publisher Peter Bannon for his support through what can be a long and arduous process.

Not the least of all these important efforts has come from Sports Publishing design staff, past and present. Our thanks to Jennifer Polson, Debbie Bellaire, Michelle Dressen and Kenny O'Brien for remaining cool, calm and collected in the face of raging deadlines. Their patience and good humor have been important in keeping us on an even keel.

My thanks also to co-author Jim Mott, whose knowledge of and love for Wisconsin sports provided the initial impetus for this book.

And I'd be remiss if I didn't thank Jim Elsener, publisher of *The Business Ledger* in Oak Brook, Ill., where I have my real job as its editor. Jim's willingness to let me sneak away occasionally to Madison or Champaign helped keep things on track, and his interest in and advice on the book have been invaluable.

DON KOPRIVA

FOREWORD

It has been nearly 60 years since I first played football for Wisconsin and more than 30 since I had the privilege of being named athletic director.

But in many ways, those days of yesteryear seem like just yesterday, thanks to the good memories that have accumulated and kept my Badger spirit alive over the years.

Many things have changed over the decades but one thing that has stayed constant is a belief in the Wisconsin idea, which from the beginning has recognized that excellence in athletics—as in academics—is critical to the mission of the University.

We've never suffered academically at Wisconsin and have steadily maintained our reputation as one of the nation's premier institutions of higher learning. We have gone through some difficult times athletically, but we have come out the stronger and the better for it. And that in large measure is because of our many loyal fans throughout the state and around the nation who have "kept the faith."

And they've been rewarded, especially in recent years. They've been able to enjoy the sights of the Badgers in the Rose Bowl and in the NCAA basketball and volleyball tournaments and to celebrate recent NCAA championships in hockey, men's and women's cross country and men's soccer.

We are fortunate indeed to have fans such as these—current students, faculty and staff, alumni and friends—who have stuck with the Badgers through thick and thin.

I know that they've always been important to me, as a player and as director of athletics. I know also that their support is critical to the success of all Wisconsin's teams.

This book—which chronicles more than 100 years of Wisconsin sports, athletes, coaches and administrators—is also the story of these dedicated fans without whom the victories never would have been possible.

On, Wisconsin!

Elroy Hirsch
Madison, Wis.

MESSAGE FROM PAT RICHTER

henever someone stops to chronicle the exploits of athletes and athletics, it is, of course, a snapshot in time. Athletics are constantly changing, and athletes and their teams seemingly get better and better.

The University of Wisconsin-Madison has had a long, rich and glorious history, filled with outstanding teams and numerous championships. The individual athletes who have performed admirably on behalf of their team and themselves are the centerpiece of our legacy. They, together with their dedicated coaches and the thousands of support staff that have assisted them in their efforts to achieve their potential, both academically and athletically, are the tradition of excellence in Wisconsin athletics.

The more than 100 years of Wisconsin sports history represented on these pages allows us to relive the excitement and enthusiasm of Wisconsin athletics, to feel the emotion and pageantry of competition and to appreciate the outstanding fans throughout the world who support their beloved Badgers.

Pat Richter
Director of Athletics

SPONSORS

A special thank you to the following sponsors,
without whose support this book would not be possible:

Mendota Gridiron Club

Wisconsin Alumni Association

Suby Von Haden and Associates

Wisconsin Physicians Service

MacNeil & Purnell

Madison Gas and Electric

Gordon Flesch Company

A WORLD-CLASS UNIVERSITY

The University of Wisconsin-Madison, one of the nation's leading institutions of higher education, is dedicated to the support of academic freedom.

Founded in 1848, the university enrolled 17 students in its first class on Feb. 5, 1849. Today, it ranks as the nation's seventh largest university with 39,826 students. It is one of the nation's most productive institutions of higher learning and the student body is one of the most diverse in the country, with students coming from every state. UW-Madison also ranks third in the nation in foreign student enrollment.

More than 4,546 courses and 12,762 sections are offered in UW-Madison's 12 schools and colleges. Majors are available in 150 undergraduate, 182 master's and 125 doctoral and professional degree programs.

Award-winning research spanning the academic disciplines has earned UW-Madison a place among the world's elite institutions. Wisconsin has ranked among the top 10 universities in the United States in every scholarly reputational study since 1910.

One survey ranked 49 different undergraduate programs at UW-Madison among the top 10 in the nation. Among those were sociology, business, German, chemical engineering, geography, ecology, genetics, statistics, molecular biology and biochemistry, French, Spanish, political science, industrial engineering, computer science, chemistry, mathematics and history.

UW-Madison faculty or alumni have been awarded 13 Nobel Prizes and 21 Pulitzer Prizes. There are 44 faculty members who are winners of Presidential Young Investigator awards, nine winners of the National Medal of Science and four Searles scholars. Forty-six professors are members of the National Academy of Sciences, 14 are members of the National Academy of Engineering, three are in the National Academy of Education and 48 are fellows in the American Physical Society.

UW-Madison, one of the nation's first land-grant colleges, established a tradition of research in agriculture and the life sciences. The founders of the university developed the "Wisconsin idea" as making "the beneficent influence of the university available to every home in the state."

The largest institution in the University of Wisconsin system, UW-Madison has the only public law and medical schools as well as the only school of veterinary medicine.

Schools and Colleges

College of Agriculture and Life Sciences

School of Business

School of Education

College of Engineering

School of Family Resources and Consumer Sciences

College of Letters and Science

School of Nursing

School of Pharmacy

Graduate School

School of Veterinary Medicine

Law School

Medical School

UNIVERSITY OF WISCONSIN-MADISON FACTS

Location: Madison, Wisconsin
Founded: 1848
Affiliation or support: State
Calendar: Semester
Enrollment: 39,826
Chancellor: David Ward

Enrollment: 40,740
- **Undergraduates:** 28,270
- **Freshmen:** 5,789
- **Sophomores:** 6,395
- **Juniors:** 7,238
- **Seniors:** 8,848
- **Graduate students:** 8,620
- **Professional students:** 2,164
- **Special students:** 1,704
- **Men:** 19,649
- **Women:** 21,091
- **Wisconsin residents:** 25,907

Costs per year: $11,538
- **Fees and tuition:** $2,880
- **Room and board:** $3,738
- **Books and supplies:** $660
- **Miscellaneous:** $1,890

Living alumni: 322,270
- **Residing in Wisconsin:** 128,537
- **Residing in Illinois:** 25,176
- **Residing in California:** 21,212

Employees: 18,437
- **Faculty:** 2,124
- **Academic staff:** 5,796
- **Classified staff:** 4,945

Area (acres)
- **Main campus:** 933
- **Arboretum:** 1,262
- **Experimental farms and branch stations:** 6,100
- **Off-campus properties:** 2,354

Libraries: 45
- **Volumes in campus libraries:** 5.5 million

UW Hospital and Clinics
- **Beds:** 500
- **Inpatient admissions annually:** 16,000

Academic programs
- **Majors:** 143
- **Master's:** 153
- **Doctoral:** 115
- **Courses, total number offered:** 4,566
- **Sections:** 13,197
- **Classroom space (square-feet):** 431,000
- **Research laboratory space (square-feet):** 2.6 million

Information technology
- **Percent of students owning computers:** 77%
- **General-access computers on campus:** 1,100

Funding
- **Budget:** $1,406,440,162
- **State support:** $366,749,233
- **Percent of budget from state support:** 26.1%
- **Percent of overall UW System budget:** 48.2%
- **Funding for research and development:** $514,502,926

National rankings
- **Research and development expenditures:** 4th
- **Number of volumes, campus libraries:** 14th
- **Voluntary support:** 6th
- **Among public universities:** 1st
- **Number of doctorates granted:** 2nd
- **Number of Peace Corps volunteers produced:** 2nd
- **Undergraduate programs:** 2nd
- **Undergraduate and graduate programs:** 4th
- **Academic programs**
- **Programs ranked in NRC top 10:** 16 of 39
- **Programs ranked in NRC top 25:** 35 of 39
- **Graduate programs in *U.S. News* top 10:** 8

Source: University of Wisconsin-Madison, April, 2000

THE HISTORY OF UW ATHLETICS

The University of Wisconsin Athletic Association was formed in February 1892, by the union of the baseball, football and tennis associations and the University Boat Club.

Its stated objective was to advance the athletic interests of the University of Wisconsin in all lines. All students of the university could become members of the association upon payment of one dollar.

President of the UW Athletic Association for the first year of its existence was E.H. Ahara, a member of both the football and baseball associations, Harvey Clark and Knox Kinney of the baseball association were vice president and secretary, respectively, and G.L. Hunner was treasurer.

In 1895, the UW Athletic Association was headed by John R. Richards as president and the board of directors included a member of the board of regents, an alumnus, three faculty members and 10 undergraduates.

The Women's Athletic Association was founded in 1907. During this year the society was called the "Girls' Athletic Association." Miss Grace Hobbins was the first president of the organization.

In 1908, the name was changed to the Women's Athletics Association and it was reorganized as a secret honorary association with elective membership. Ten honors could be won, three of which entitled the member to a pin, and five honors to a "W" award.

In 1913, the society was again organized on a new basis and, instead of the secret, exclusive organization of the past, W.A.A. became broader and much more inclusive. Its stated purpose was to promote interest in athletics and sports of all kinds, not only among the girls who were "especially adapted for such work," but also among those who had little experience in athletics before they came to the university.

The record shows that the chairman of the physical education department was also in charge of intercollegiate athletics following the dismissal of the graduate manager set-up in the early 1900s.

THE HISTORY OF UW ATHLETICS-CONT.

Thomas E. Jones, who had come to Wisconsin in 1912 as coach of the school's track and cross country teams, received his professorship in 1916 and upon the resignation of Professor George Wolf Ehler, became acting athletic director, serving until George Little came to Madison from Michigan in 1925.

Wisconsin Athletic Directors

1916-24

Professor Thomas E. Jones

1925-32

George Little

1933-35

Dr. Walter E. Meanwell

1936-50

Harry Stuhldreher

1950-55

Guy Sundt

1955-69

Ivan Williamson

1969-87

Elroy Hirsch

1987-89

A.L. "Ade" Sponberg

1989-Present

Pat Richter

THE BIRTH OF UW WOMEN'S ATHLETICS

Women's athletics at the University of Wisconsin actually dates back to 1889 when Clara Ballard introduced women's physical education to the UW. Other early references to women's athletics include Coach Andrew O'Dea consenting to coach a women's crew in 1895 and the beginning of women's basketball in 1897.

In 1917, Women's Recreation Associations were nationally organized by the UW's Blanche Trilling, and Badger yearbooks from that period show women's teams receiving honor letters and wearing athletic sweaters.

Sponsored by the physical education department, Wisconsin's WRA was run by a coalition of students and faculty. The WRA lasted until the 1960s when the growth of women's sports program required more control and consistency.

It wasn't until 1967, that the UW saw an increased interest and growth in the competitive sports programs for women. Facilities, equipment and office space were made available, limited use of fleet cars and a half-time position for the sports coordinator/WRA advisor were funded and some release time was allocated for sports advisors.

In 1967, Kit Saunders was named the administrator of the women's sports program. A club sports program was organized in 1970 through the Intramural Recreation Board with a budget of $2,000. In 1972-73, this was raised to $8,000 and to $18,000 for 1973-74. During this time, the cost and time commitment of women's athletics was getting to be too much for the physical education department. The passage of Title IX of the Educational Amendments Act of 1972, which applied to discrimination on the basis of sex, became the single most important factor in the gains of women's sports.

In July of 1972, UW Chancellor Edwin Young appointed a committee to study women's athletics. With no progress being made on the issue, on April 3, 1973, a complaint against the UW was filed with the HEW Office of Civil Rights in violation of Title IX.

By April 19, 1973, a new committee had been formed and by May, that committee had made recommendations that women be allowed to use all physical recreation facilities on the UW campus and that the division provide for the administration of women's competitive sports.

THE BIRTH OF UW WOMEN'S ATHLETICS-CONT.

During December of that year, a proposal to combine men's and women's athletic programs was put forth. This proposal included appointing a women's athletics director, the hiring of separate coaches, and providing salaries, uniforms, equipment and practice times.

A task force was formed to study this proposal and by May, 1974, the UW Athletic Board voted to add an 11-sport women's intercollegiate athletic program under the Athletic Department. The 11 sports were: badminton, basketball, fencing, field hockey, golf, gymnastics, rowing, swimming and diving, tennis, track and field, and volleyball.

Kit Saunders-Nordeen was named the first Women's Athletics Director as women became an official part of the UW Athletic Department on July 1, 1974.

Wisconsin Women's Athletics Administrators

1974-1983

Kit Saunders-Nordeen

1983-89

Paula Bonner

Associate Athletic Director

1989-90

Kit Saunders-Nordeen

Associate Athletic Director

1990-Present

Cheryl Marra

Associate Athletic Director

1870s

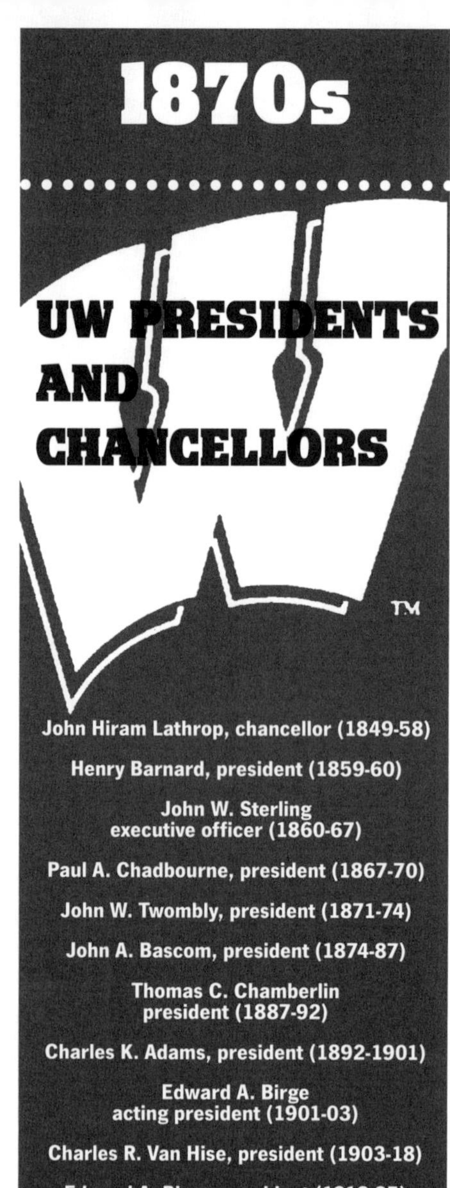

John Hiram Lathrop, chancellor (1849-58)

Henry Barnard, president (1859-60)

John W. Sterling
executive officer (1860-67)

Paul A. Chadbourne, president (1867-70)

John W. Twombly, president (1871-74)

John A. Bascom, president (1874-87)

Thomas C. Chamberlin
president (1887-92)

Charles K. Adams, president (1892-1901)

Edward A. Birge
acting president (1901-03)

Charles R. Van Hise, president (1903-18)

Edward A. Birge, president (1918-25)

Glenn Frank, president (1925-37)

George C. Sellery
acting president (1937)

Clarence A. Dykstra, president (1937-45)

Edwin Broun Fred, president (1945-58)

Conrad A. Elvehjem, president (1958-62)

Fred Harvey Harrington
president* (1962-70)

Robben Fleming, chancellor (1964-67)

William Sewell, chancellor (1967-68)

Bryant Kearl, acting chancellor (1968)

Edwin Young, chancellor (1968-77)

Glenn S. Pound
acting chancellor (1977)

Irving Shain, chancellor (1977-86)

Bernard Cohen
acting chancellor (1987)

Donna E. Shalala, chancellor (1988-93)

David Ward, chancellor (1993- Present)

*administrative structure changed in 1964

Athletic teams begin to develop at the UW

As the University of Wisconsin approached the 25th anniversary of its founding, fledgling sports teams began to develop on the campus. Baseball and rowing were, according to all reliable records, the first and dominant teams throughout the 1870s.

Baseball seems to have been the first intercollegiate sport at Wisconsin, with its beginnings traced back to the spring of 1870 when some of the diamond enthusiasts on campus banded together to form a club known as the Mendotas.

By the middle of the decade, rowing began to develop and by 1878 rowing had become part of intramural competition. But Wisconsin alumnus C.B. Bradish noted in a 1912 letter that his father told him that "he rowed on the first crew Wisconsin ever had" in 1874.

The first recorded baseball game took place on April 30, 1870, with the Mendotas outscoring the Capital City Club 53-18. Lack of a suitable playing field delayed the organization of the 1871 team but before the school term closed a game was arranged with Albion, which promptly defeated the Mendotas 26-24 to avenge their loss of 1870.

No games were played in 1872 or 1875 but a pair of games was played in both 1873 and 1874. The Mendotas split games in '73, losing to Albion but beating Beloit, while in 1874 Milton College swept them. A single game was played in each of the 1876 and 1877 seasons, with Wisconsin winning the former and losing the latter.

A baseball association was finally formed in 1877, with P.V. Larson elected president. No games were played in 1878 and in 1879 the university club split a series with Beloit.

Wisconsin Time Line

1870: The U.S. Weather Bureau was established.

1873: Representatives of Columbia, Princeton, Rutgers and Yale universities drew up the first rules governing intercollegiate football games.

1875: Aristides won the first Kentucky Derby.

1876: Alexander Graham Bell received a patent for the telephone.

1877: Alexander Graham Bell demonstrated the telephone with a hookup between Boston and Salem, Massachusetts.

1878: The first daily college newspaper, the Yale News, began publication in New Haven, Connecticut.

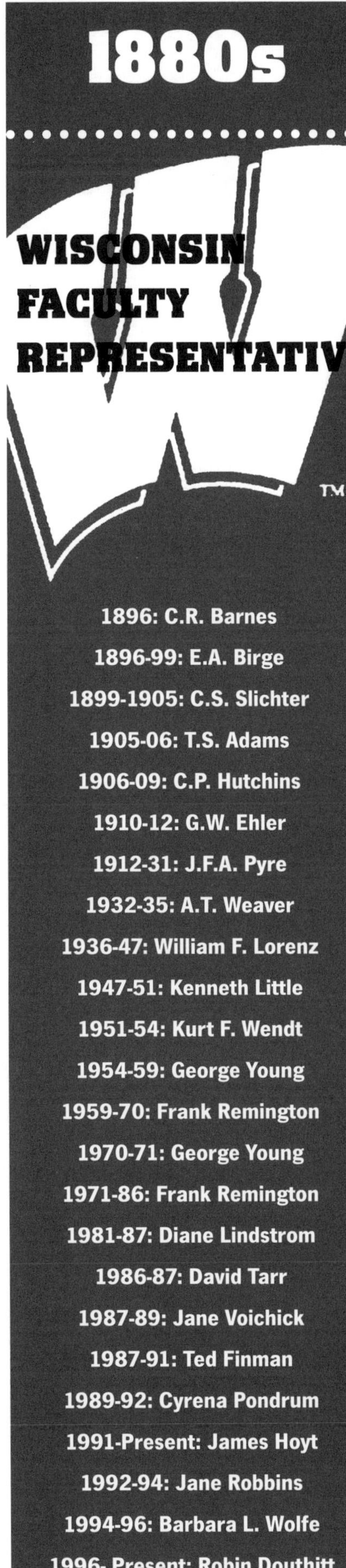

1880s
WISCONSIN FACULTY REPRESENTATIVES
TM
1896: C.R. Barnes
1896-99: E.A. Birge
1899-1905: C.S. Slichter
1905-06: T.S. Adams
1906-09: C.P. Hutchins
1910-12: G.W. Ehler
1912-31: J.F.A. Pyre
1932-35: A.T. Weaver
1936-47: William F. Lorenz
1947-51: Kenneth Little
1951-54: Kurt F. Wendt
1954-59: George Young
1959-70: Frank Remington
1970-71: George Young
1971-86: Frank Remington
1981-87: Diane Lindstrom
1986-87: David Tarr
1987-89: Jane Voichick
1987-91: Ted Finman
1989-92: Cyrena Pondrum
1991-Present: James Hoyt
1992-94: Jane Robbins
1994-96: Barbara L. Wolfe
1996- Present: Robin Douthitt

Sports teams grow, become better organized

Sports continued to flourish at Wisconsin in the 1880s, although lack of coaches, lack of rules and lack of suitable playing sites often contributed to controversy.

Football debuted in 1889, but baseball and crew were the dominant athletic activities on campus. No baseball games were played in 1880 but Chicago, Racine and Northwestern jointly formed the Western Intercollegiate Baseball League, which prodded Wisconsin supporters into some action.

In 1881, another athletic association was formed on the Wisconsin campus and student members planned to get possession of the pasture between State Street and the lake to turn it into a campus suitable for baseball and other sports. However, the fairgrounds at Camp Randall were secured instead and the Wisconsin nine defeated Beloit. In 1882, Wisconsin and Ann Arbor (Michigan) formed a league and played twice, with Michigan winning 20-8 and 16-6.

In 1883, Wisconsin sent a representative to the Western Intercollegiate Baseball Meeting and gained membership for the 1883 season. Two losses to Northwestern eliminated Wisconsin from championship consideration. By 1884, Wisconsin was the champion, winning five of six games, and in 1885, the Badgers repeated with key road wins over Racine and Northwestern.

Crew continued to grow in popularity on the campus with the founding of the Madison Boat Club in 1886. Its sponsors—six professors—were united in their belief that "the natural opportunities for boating at the University are unrivaled by those at any other college in the country."

Football's debut was inauspicious, to say the least. Under Coach Alvin Kletsch—the first "official" coach in UW history—Wisconsin played two games in 1889 and scored nary a point, losing to the Calumet Club 27-0 in Milwaukee and at Beloit 4-0.

Wisconsin Time Line

1880: Thomas Edison received a patent for his electric incandescent light

1881: The first U.S tennis championships were played in Newport, RI

1882: The first hydroelectric power plant in the United States was opened in Appleton, WI

1885: Mark Twain's "Adventures of Huckleberry Finn" was published

1887: The first game of softball, invented by George W. Hancock, was played in Chicago's Farragut Boat Club

1888: The National Geographic Society was incorporated in Washington, D.C.

1889: Paris' Eiffel Tower was opened to the public

1890-96

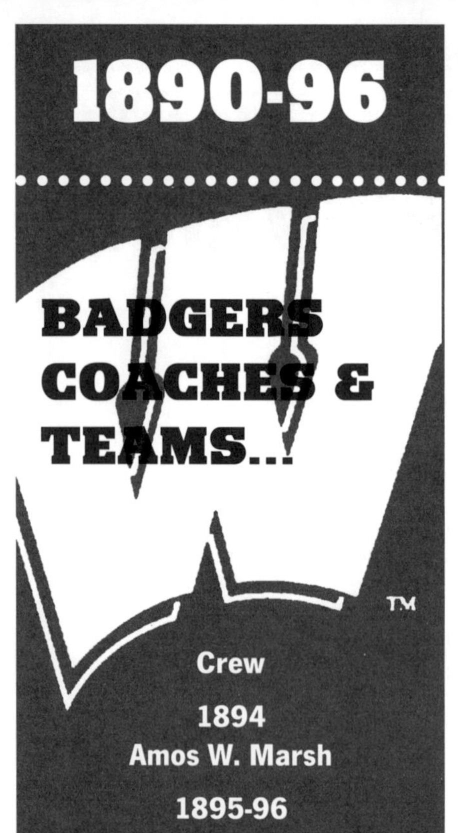

Crew

1894
Amos W. Marsh

1895-96
Andrew O'Dea

Football

1890
Ted Mestre

1891
Herb Alward

1892
Frank Crawford

1893
Parke Davis

1894-95
H.O. Stickney

Track and Field

1893
R.G. Booth

1894
M.J. Gillen

1895
W.B. Overson

1896
Charles Craigie

Football, track teams develop, succeed

While baseball and crew continued to flourish at Wisconsin in the early-to-mid 1890s, football and track teams were formed and quickly found success.

The baseball Badgers again won a title in 1890 when they posted a 5-1 record. By 1891, the first University of Wisconsin athletic association was organized by the merger of the baseball, football and tennis associations along with the University Boat Club. The UW baseball team swept through the league in 1891, winning all its games. The 1893 club finished 12-3 with Michigan, Illinois and Chicago now among its opponents. The 1894 team went 10-4 and counted among its wins an 11-9 bottom-of-the-ninth-inning victory over one of Michigan's truly great teams.

Track and field began to develop in 1893 with the formation of the Western Intercollegiate Track and Field Association. It included Chicago, Michigan, Northwestern and Wisconsin. The Wolverines outscored the Badgers 52-45 to win the first meet. Wisconsin was second in both 1894 and 1895. James Maybury, the first real sprinter of note at Wisconsin, was third in the 100-yard dash and second in the 220. Maybury won the 100 in 10 seconds and the 220 in 22.4 seconds in the 1896 meet won by Wisconsin with 46 points.

In 1892, Wisconsin rowers beat Chicago in a race at Oconomowoc's Lac LaBelle. By 1894, they had a coach, Amos W. Marsh, who had captained the crew at Cornell. Under his guidance, the rowers defeated the Delaware Boat Club and narrowly lost to the Minnesota Boat Club. Andrew O'Dea took over as coach in 1895 and split again with Delaware and Minnesota, but by 1896 the Badgers had defeated Yale and Minnesota for the first time.

Wisconsin had six football coaches in the 1890s, with Ted Mestre gaining credit for the first win in 1890, a 106-0 shellacking of Whitewater Normal to open a 1-3 season. New coaches followed annually as did winning records each season from 1891-1895.

Wisconsin Time Line

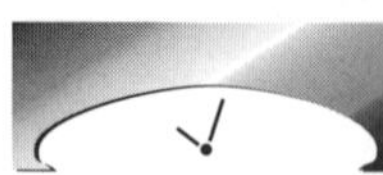

1890: New York World Reporter Nellie Bly completed a trip around the world in 72 hours, 6 days, 11 minutes, beating the fictional 80-day trip of Jules Vernesí Phileas Fogg.

1891: Wisconsin recorded its first football victory, a 106-0 victory over UW-Whitewater.

1892: James J. Corbett knocked out John L. Sullivan in the 21st round to win the world heavyweight crown in New Orleans.

1895: President James Smart of Purdue called a meeting of seven midwestern universities to consider regulation and control of intercollegiate athletics.

Wisconsin won its first Big Ten outdoor track championship under Coach Charles Craigie.

WISCONSIN HEADLINER

J.F.A. (Sunny) Pyre
Football

A fiery spirit and reckless abandon characterized J.F.A. (Sunny) Pyre, who may have been Wisconsin's first real sports hero. Although he played in the days of "beef trust" football and never weighed more than 175 lbs., and often less, Pyre played right tackle for the Wisconsin football teams of 1891 and 1894-96. Press accounts of the day said he was "lightning fast" across the line and knew "how to use his hands and magnificently muscled arms as few linemen did." He also rowed on varsity crew teams of 1893 and 1894. During those latter three football seasons, Pyre was also an instructor in English at the UW, carrying a full teaching load as well as working on his doctorate in English. Pyre's best season was probably his last, 1896, which was also Phil King's first year at Wisconsin. That team went unbeaten until a tie with Northwestern and a loss to the Carlisle Indians. As a professor after his playing days, Pyre remained connected with sports as a member of succeeding athletic committees and boards. He served from 1912-1931 as the UW faculty representative to the Big Ten Conference.

Charles Kendall Adams
President
University of Wisconsin

A strong proponent of athletics and advocate of the formation of a midwestern athletic conference was Charles Kendall Adams, Wisconsin's president from 1892-1901. In the 1895 and 1896 meetings at which the Big Ten was formed, Adams was emotionally involved and eager to get the Conference established. Adams attended Wisconsin games and cheered on the teams, going so far as to help encourage unmotivated students to go out for teams. He also acquired Camp Randall for the UW as a playing field. Born in Vermont in 1835, Adams moved to Iowa with his family as a young man and enrolled at Michigan in 1857, graduating in 1861. He remained in Ann Arbor as a graduate student and then became a history professor before becoming president at Cornell, where he remained for seven years until accepting the post at Wisconsin. Ill health forced his resignation from the presidency in 1901 and he died a year later.

Wisconsin vs. Minnesota

Wisconsin's (and the nation's) longest continuous football rivalry, with Minnesota, didn't start too well for the Badgers but by the turn of the 20th century the UW had evened its budding series with the Gophers. Going into the 1998 season and the teams' 108th game, the UW trailed 57-42-8.

The first 10 games:

1890: Minnesota 63, Wisconsin 0

1891: Minnesota 26, Wisconsin 12

1892: Minnesota 32, Wisconsin 4

1893: Minnesota 40, Wisconsin 0

1894: Wisconsin 6, Minnesota 0

1895: Minnesota 14, Wisconsin 10

1896: Wisconsin 6, Minnesota 0

1897: Wisconsin 39, Minnesota 0

1898: Wisconsin 29, Minnesota 0

1899: Wisconsin 19, Minnesota 0

Badgers among charter members of Western Conference

President Charles Kendall Adams of Wisconsin joined presidents from Chicago, Illinois, Michigan, Minnesota, Northwestern and Purdue in a meeting at Chicago on Jan. 11, 1895, adopted 12 rules for a Midwestern athletic conference. That conference officially became the Intercollegiate Conference of Faculty Representatives and would later become known as the Western Conference and, eventually, as is the case today, as the Big Ten.

The first of the Conference rules, which strengthened the notion of faculty control of athletics, said that "Each college and university which has not already done so shall appoint a committee on college athletics which shall take general supervision of all athletic matters ... and which shall have all responsibility of enforcing the college or university rules regarding athletics and all intercollegiate sports. Other rules mandated that college athletes be full-time, bona fide students, forbade professionals from playing college sports, prohibited pay for play and mandated that games be played at sites under college control.

1896-97

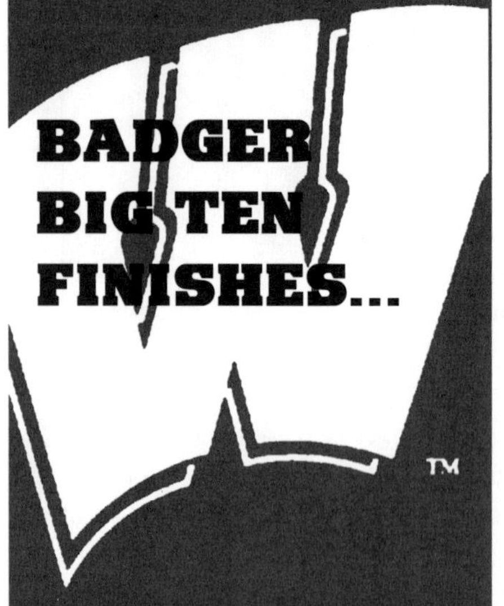

Football: 1st
coached by Phil King

Baseball: 3rd
coached by Phil King

Outdoor Track: 1st
coached by E.W. Moulton

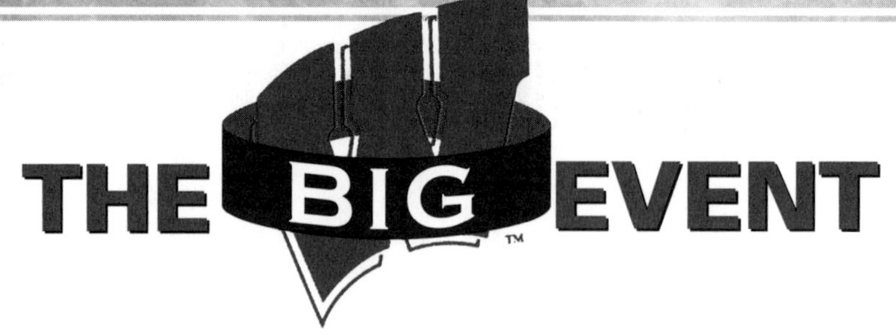

Wisconsin wins first Big Ten football title

Wisconsin won the Western Conference's first football championship soon after the formation of the Conference, which would soon become popularly known as the "Big Ten."

After opening the season with seven wins, Coach Phil King's team was tied 6-6 by Northwestern and then lost to the Carlisle Indians. Despite that late-season slump, the Badgers claimed the first league title with a 2-0-1 record and a 7-1-1 overall mark. The season-ending loss to Carlisle was the first night and indoor game in UW history played at the Chicago Coliseum.

Defense was the key to the Badgers' success, as six of their wins were shutouts.

Wisconsin's record:	Big Ten, overall records:
UW 34, Lake Forest 0	1-0
UW 18, Madison High School 0	2-0
UW 50, Rush Medical 0	3-0
UW 54, Grinnell 6	4-0
UW 6, Beloit 0	5-0
UW 24, Chicago 0	1-0, 6-0
UW 6, Minnesota 0	2-0, 7-0
UW 6, Northwestern 6	2-0-1, 7-0-1
Carlisle Indians 18, UW 8	2-0-1, 7-1-1

Wisconsin Time Line

1896: The first modern Olympic Games were held in Athens.

The "Intercollegiate Conference of Faculty Representatives," to become known as the Big Ten, was formed, with Wisconsin as one of seven charter members along with Chicago, Illinois, Michigan, Minnesota, Northwestern and Purdue.

Wisconsin claimed first outright Big Ten football title with a 7-1-1 record for Coach Phil King.

1897: The famous "Yes, Virginia, there is a Santa Claus" editorial appeared in the New York Sun.

1897-98

Football: 1st
coached by Phil King

Outdoor Track: 1st
coached by James Temple and Charles Craigie

Badgers unbeaten in Big Ten, win second straight football title

Coach Phil King guided the Badgers to their second straight Big Ten football championship on the foot of Australian Pat O'Dea, the famed "Kangaroo Kicker," who kicked 14 field goals to lead the team. Key victories in Wisconsin's 9-1 season were the wins over Minnesota, Chicago and Northwestern that gave Wisconsin a 3-0-0 Big Ten record—the first of only four times that the UW would be undefeated and untied in Conference play.

The '98 team would also post a 9-1 record, losing only to Chicago 6-0 to finish third in the Big Ten with a 2-1 slate.

Wisconsin's 1897 season:

UW 30, Lake Forest 0
UW 8, Madison High School 0*
UW 28, Rush Medical 0
UW 20, Platteville Normal 0
UW 29, Madison High School 0
UW 39, Minnesota 0
UW 11, Beloit 0
UW 25, Chicago 8
UW Alumni 6, UW 0
UW 22, Northwestern 0

**called at halftime because of rain*

Wisconsin Time Line

1897: The Big Ten voted to require a year's residence after changing institutions

Coach Phil King's football team outscores its opponents 210-14 en route to a 9-1-1 campaign and second straight Big Ten crown

1898: The U.S. battleship Maine was blown up in Havana harbor, killing 260 crewmen

The Presidents' Committee devised and printed a set of football rules for Conference teams

WISCONSIN HEADLINER

Edward R. Cochems
Football

Edward Cochems starred at both end and halfback during four stellar seasons with the Badgers' fledgling football program around the turn of the century. The Sturgeon Bay native competed in football, track and baseball, but it was on the gridiron that he excelled for Wisconsin teams that posted a 35-4-1 mark during his playing career. Cochems played at end for his first two seasons but then switched to the backfield. He scored four touchdowns in a 1900 win over Notre Dame and three TDs in 1901 against Chicago–including a 100-yard kickoff return. Cochems moved into the coaching ranks immediately after graduation, heading the North Dakota State program in 1902 and 1903. He served as an assistant at Wisconsin in 1904, moved to Clemson as head coach in 1905 and then to St. Louis University in 1906, where he became known as the "father" of the forward pass. Cochems was inducted into the Madison Sports Hall of Fame in 1968 and into the UW Athletic Hall of Fame in 1994.

WISCONSIN HEADLINER

Andrew O'Dea
Rowing Coach

Andrew O'Dea, though sometimes overshadowed in the newspaper spotlight of the era by the exploits of his younger brother Pat, Wisconsin's famed "Kangaroo Kicker," was a stellar athlete and coach in his own right. He came to the United States in the early 1890s from his native Australia, where he had worked with livestock on his father's Melbourne farm. He first went to Minneapolis, where he coached the Lurlines, an amateur rowing club in the Twin Cities. By 1895, O'Dea had come to Madison, where he soon assumed a role as one of Wisconsin's great athletes, excelling in rowing and football. The latter sport, though new to him, was not difficult for him to pick up as he had played rugby in his native land. Andrew's brother Pat came to the U.S. in 1895 and became one of Wisconsin's all-time great athletes, but it might be fair to speculate whether the younger brother would have come to Madison without the older already being there.

WISCONSIN HEADLINER

Pat O'Dea
Football

Patrick John O'Dea, the fabled "Kangaroo Kicker" who came to Madison from his native Australia, was one of Wiscon-sin's first athletic heroes. O'Dea played fullback on Wisconsin's 1896-99 football teams, excelling as a drop kicker on field goals. He once made four in one game and 14 in the entire 1897 season. O'Dea made a 65-yard dropkick field goal in an 1898 game in a snowstorm at Northwestern. His first play as a Badger was an 85-yard punt against Lake Forest in 1896, and he unleashed a 110-yard punt against Minnesota the next year. He topped his senior year with a 100-yard touchdown run against Beloit in 1899. Following his playing days, O'Dea coached at Notre Dame and Missouri. He later settled in California under an assumed name. His return to campus in 1934, 35 years after his last game, was a highlight of the Badgers' 7-3 Homecoming victory over Illinois. A member of the Wisconsin State Hall of Fame, O'Dea was inducted as a charter member of the UW Athletic Hall of Fame in 1991.

The List

Big Ten members

Seven universities comprised the original "Intercollegiate Conference of Faculty Representatives." Now, more than a century later, the Big Ten has 11 members, with six of the original seven still members.

Here are years of membership:

University of Chicago	1896-1946
University of Illinois	1896-present
Indiana University	1899-present
University of Iowa	1899-present
University of Michigan	1896-1908, 1917-present
Michigan State University	1949-present
University of Minnesota	1896-present
Northwestern University	1896-present
Ohio State University	1912-present
Penn State University	1990-present
Purdue University	1896-present
University of Wisconsin	1896-present

1898-99

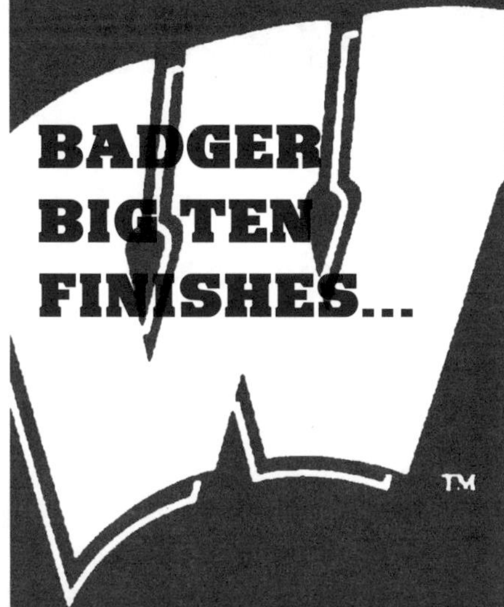

Football: 3rd
coached by Phil King

Baseball: 5th
coached by Bertrand Husting

Outdoor Track: 4th
coached by John Moakley

UW becomes first "Western" school to be recognized in sports

Many of the established eastern schools looked down on Wisconsin and other midwestern colleges as somehow lacking both in academics and athletics. In fact, the Wisconsin rowers who competed against their eastern brethren were known, probably somewhat derisively, as "Haymakers." The Badger rowing teams of the turn of the century went a long way toward dispelling myths of eastern supremacy in 1899 and 1900.

The UW crews finished second in the famed Poughkeepsie Regatta, at that time the principal collegiate race in the nation and one that was long dominated by eastern schools. That gave Wisconsin credibility and was a warning to the older, established colleges that athletic powers were growing in America's heartland.

Wisconsin Time Line

1898: Wisconsin finished 0-3 in its first basketball season.

1899: George F. Grant received a patent for a golf tee.

Indiana and Iowa were admitted to the Big Ten.

Wisconsin recorded its first basketball win, 25-15 over Wayland Academy.

1899-1900

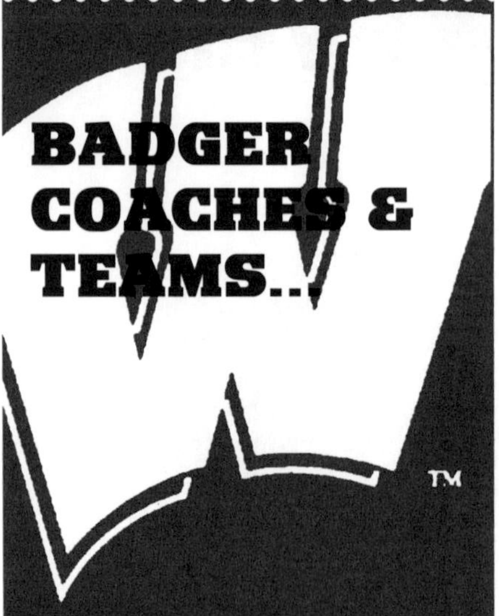

Football: 2nd
coached by Phil King

Baseball: 2nd
coached by Phil King

Outdoor Track: 4th
coached by Charles Kilpatrick

Pat O'Dea kicks 62-yard field goal

Pat O'Dea, "The Kangaroo Kicker," routinely did the unbelievable on the football field, but perhaps no more so than in 1899.

Against Minnesota, the Badger safety fielded a punt and, while angling to his left to avoid Minnesota tacklers, got off a right-footed drop-kick that was at least 60 yards away from the goal posts as far as yardage on the field indicated.

The angle really made it more like 65. It sailed cleanly over the crossbars as the longest successful drop-kick in football history. Minnesota end Gil Dobie, who would become a great coach at Cornell and Washington, later called it the greatest play he'd ever seen.

Spectacular as that play was, O'Dea may have topped himself on Nov. 11 of that same season when the Badgers played Illinois at Milwaukee. After a Bill Juneau fair catch following an Illinois punt, O'Dea nailed a place-kick cleanly from 60 yards out.

Actually, his kick really was a good 80 yards because it cleared not only the Illinois goal but also the baseball bleachers behind it and the high fence behind them and landed in the street outside the park.

Wisconsin Time Line

1900: The first auto show in the U.S. opened in New York's Madison Square Garden.

The Conference approved legislation by which any member may object to new legislation within 30 days after such legislation is introduced. This became known as the "White Resolution."

Miler G.R. Keachie and long jumper F.W. Schule are Wisconsin's first Big Ten track and field champions.

1900-01

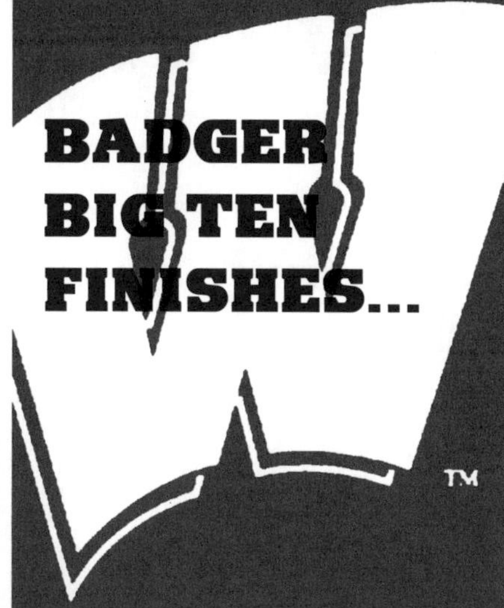

Football: 3rd (tie)
coached by Phil King

Baseball: 4th
coached by Phil King

Outdoor Track: 2nd
coached by Charles Kilpatrick

Badgers second in inaugural Big Ten track championship

Wisconsin finished second to Michigan in the first official Big Ten outdoor track and field championships on June 1, 1901, at Marshall Field in Chicago.

Coach Charles Kilpatrick's squad scored 28 points, 10 behind Michigan, but comfortably ahead of Chicago (17) and Beloit and Minnesota (each with 14) in the nine-team field. The UW had two individual champions, G.R. Keachie in the mile run with a time of 4:34.4 and F.W. Schule in the long jump with a leap of 22'4 4/5". Schule was the Badgers' high scorer, also taking third in the 120-yard high hurdles and third in the 220-yard low hurdles.

Other Wisconsin scorers were George Poage, third in the 440; J.F. Hahn, second in the mile; Edgar McEachron and W. Smith, second and third in the two mile; Meyers, second in the high jump; H. Webster, second in the discus throw; and the mile relay team, which took second.

Wisconsin Time Line

1901: An oil strike in Beaumont, Texas, marked the start of the great Texas oil boom.

The first Big Ten outdoor track meet was held at Chicago.

Wisconsin's football team went 9-0 for Badgers' first undefeated season and the Badger basketball team finished 7-3 for its first winning season.

1901-02

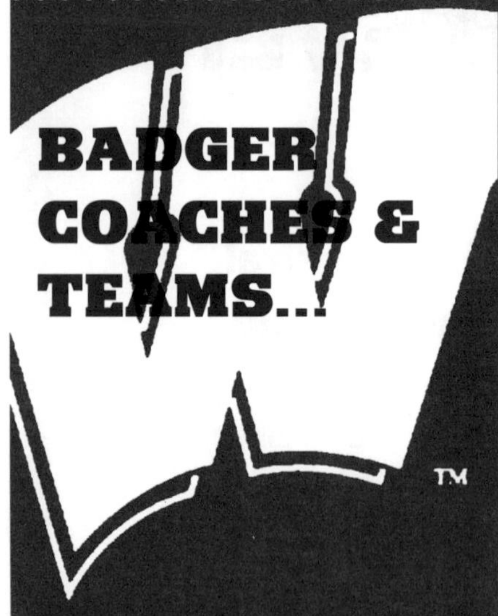

Football: 1st (tie)
coached by Phil King

Baseball: 1st
coached by Oscar Bandelin

Gymnastics: 1st
coached by J.C. Elsom

Outdoor Track: 3rd
coached by Charles Kilpatrick

Wisconsin hosts, wins first Big Ten gymnastics meet

Although the Big Ten didn't officially sponsor a gymnastics champion until 1926, Wisconsin hosted, and won, the first meet of Conference members in 1902.

The meet was also open to teams outside the Big Ten. Wisconsin would go on to win seven of the first 15 titles in the sport. Ironically, the UW never again won a Big Ten gymnastics team title after the sport became part of the Conference's championship slate.

Wisconsin discontinued gymnastics in 1991.

Wisconsin Time Line

1902: The Badgers lost 6-0 to Michigan in football, breaking the UW's 17-game winning streak.

Michigan beat Stanford 49-0 in the first Rose Bowl game.

WISCONSIN HEADLINER

Art Curtis
Football

Four-time letterwinner Art Curtis, according to accounts of the day, rated only superlatives as the right tackle on turn-of-the-century Wisconsin football teams. From his arrival on the field as a freshman in 1898, he had a position won. He never was a second-team player nor did he ever miss a minute of action. He served as captain of Coach Phil King's 1901 team that went 9-0 to become the UW's first undefeated team. That squad outscored the opposition 317-5, defeated every opponent by at least three touchdowns and recorded eight shutouts to share the Big Ten title. Curtis, who was not a big man and never played at more than 178 pounds, was one of the fastest linemen of his day and was the first tackle in the "West" to range widely on the defense. Curtis also starred as a slick fielding first baseman on three UW baseball teams. Following graduation, he coached a year at Kansas, then returned to guide the Badgers to an 11-6-1 mark in the 1903 and 1904 seasons before resigning to complete medical studies. Curtis later became a department head in Northwestern University's school of medicine.

Christian Steinmetz, Sr.
Basketball

The "father" of Wisconsin basketball, Milwaukee native Christian Steinmetz starred on Badger teams of 1902-05. In 1904-05, he set a single season scoring record of 462 points for the 18-game schedule, only one of which was played at home. That team played a nine-game tour of the eastern United States, news reports of which helped popularize the game back home in Madison. Steinmetz had a single-game high of 50 points in the opening game of his senior season against Company G, Sparta. He had a record 20 field goals against Beloit College and 26 free throws against the Two Rivers Athletic Club. A member of the Wisconsin State Hall of Fame and the National Basketball Hall of Fame, Steinmetz was one of 35 charter inductees into the UW Athletic Hall of Fame in 1991.

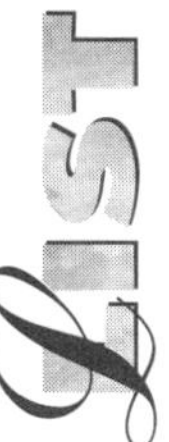

The List

Largest football victory margins (pre-modern era)

Margin	Opponent	Year	Score
106	Whitewater Normal	1890	106-0
87	Beloit	1903	87-0
85	Marquette	1915	85-0
82	Drake	1904	82-0
82	Lawrence	1915	82-0
76	Dixon (Ill.)	1898	76-0
64	Upper Iowa	1900	64-0
62	Hyde Park (Ill.)	1901	62-0
60	Lawrence	1899	58-0
58	Lawrence	1899	58-0
58	Notre Dame	1904	58-0
57	Arkansas	1912	64-7

NICKNAME

So you want to be a Badger

Not surprisingly, UW sports teams' nickname came from the state of Wisconsin, which had been dubbed the "Badger state," not because of animals but an association with lead miners in Southwestern Wisconsin in the 1820s. Prospectors came to the state looking for minerals and without shelter in the winter had to "live like Badgers" in tunnels burrowed into the hillside.

1902-03

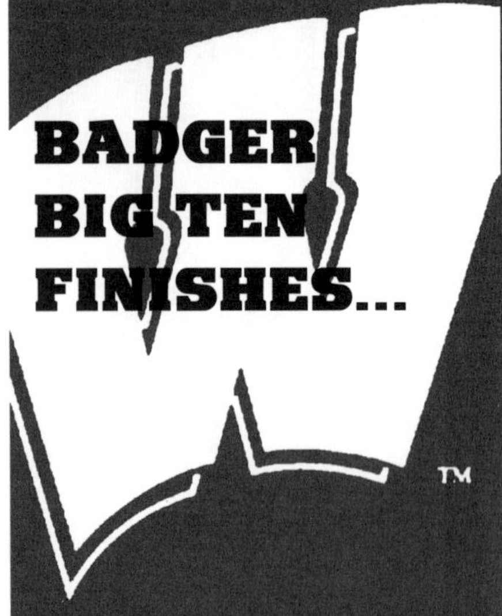

Football: 6th
coached by Phil King

Baseball: 4th
coached by Oscar Bandelin

Outdoor Track: 3rd
coached by Charles Kilpatrick

Wisconsin holds "Point-A-Minute" Michigan to six

Football Coach Phil King's 1902 Badgers finished 6-3 overall, 1-3 in the Big Ten for sixth place, but it was one of those Big Ten losses that made Wisconsin's season memorable.

Michigan had already won games by scores such as 68-0, 119-0, 60-0, 23-0 and 86-0, so little was expected of the Badgers against the grid power. But in a game played before a huge crowd of 18,000 at Chicago, Wisconsin held Coach Fielding Yost's famed "Point-a-Minute" team to just six points, losing 6-0.

It was the closest anyone had come to Michigan in two seasons.

Wisconsin Time Line

1903: The United States and Panama signed a treaty granting the U.S. rights to build the Panama Canal.

First-year coach Emmett Angell saw his Badger cagers rout Sparta's Company C 75-10 as Christian Steinmetz scored 50 points.

1903-04

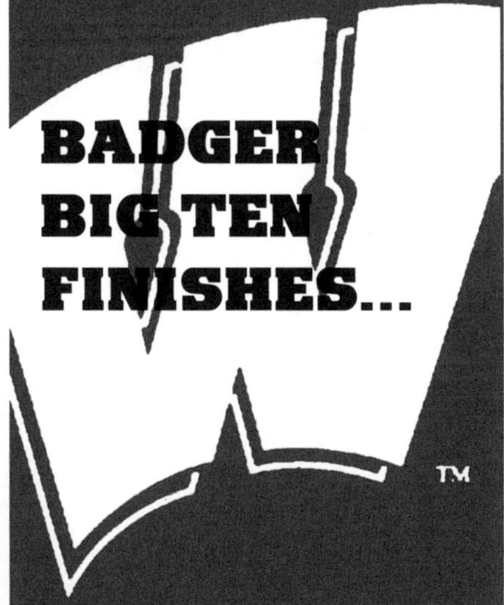

Football: 8th (tie)
coached by Art Curtis

Baseball: 2nd
coached by Bemis Pierce

Gymnastics: 1st
coached by J.C. Elsom

Outdoor Track: 3rd
coached by Charles Kilpatrick

Wisconsin wins Big Ten gymnastics

The Badgers won their third Big Ten gymnastics title in four years in 1904, winning at home as they had in their two previous triumphs since the meet's inception in 1902.

In those formative days of the Big Ten Conference, gymnastics had joined the "Big Three" of baseball, football and outdoor track as the league's championship events. Coached by J.C. Elsom, who also coached the UW basketball team, the gymnasts scored 40 points to win the meet.

Wisconsin went on to win Big Ten gymnastics championships in 1908, 1913, 1915, 1916 and 1923. After that, the Badgers never again won a league crown in the sport. Wisconsin dropped gymnastics after the 1991 season.

Wisconsin Time Line

1904: The first Olympic Games to be held in the U.S. opened in St. Louis.

The Big Ten ruled that for a student to be eligible for athletic competition, he must have completed a full semester's work in residence; it was termed a radical departure in college athletics.

Wisconsin made its first basketball road trip and comes home 2-6 after games in New Jersey, New York, Pennsylvania and Ohio.

1904-05

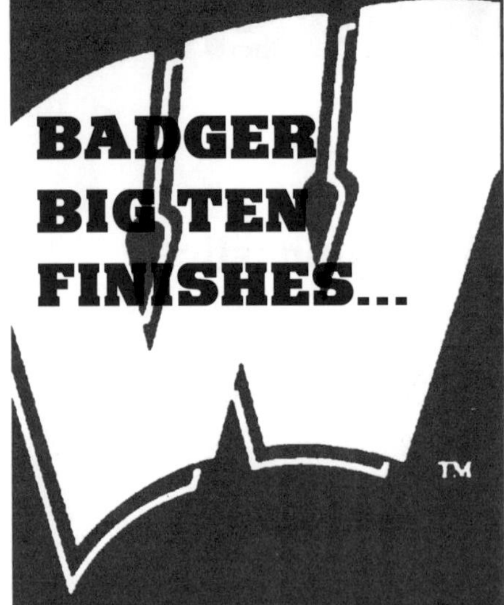

Football: 7th (tie)
coached by Art Curtis

Baseball: 3rd (tie)
coached by Bemis Pierce

Gymnastics: 1st
coached by J.C. Elsom

Outdoor Track: 5th (tie)
coached by James Temple

Chris Steinmetz becomes first basketball all-American

Chris Steinmetz, generally regarded as the player who put Wisconsin basketball on the map, became the Badgers' first all-American in 1905. The Milwaukee native—a high scorer in an era when low scores were common—was also named the Helms Foundation player of the year after a season in which he had his single game high 50 points against Company G, Sparta. Called the "father" of UW basketball, Steinmetz was instrumental in establishing the Wisconsin program.

In 1905, as a senior, Steinmetz led the Badgers to a berth in the national championship game, where they lost to Columbia. One of his teammates that year was Bob Zuppke, who would go on to no little fame as the 28-year football coach at Illinois. Steinmetz's career statistics showed 462 points in a season, including 233 free throws (one player could then shoot all a team's free throws).

Steinmetz was the first Badger named to the National Basketball Hall of Fame and also was a charter inductee into the UW Athletic Hall of Fame.

Wisconsin Time Line

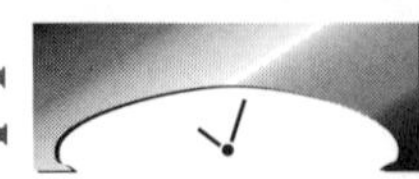

1905: Actor Henry Fonda was born in Grand Island, Nebraska.

The Intercollegiate Conference of Faculty Representatives was incorporated in Illinois; it eventually became popularly known as the Big Ten.

1905-06

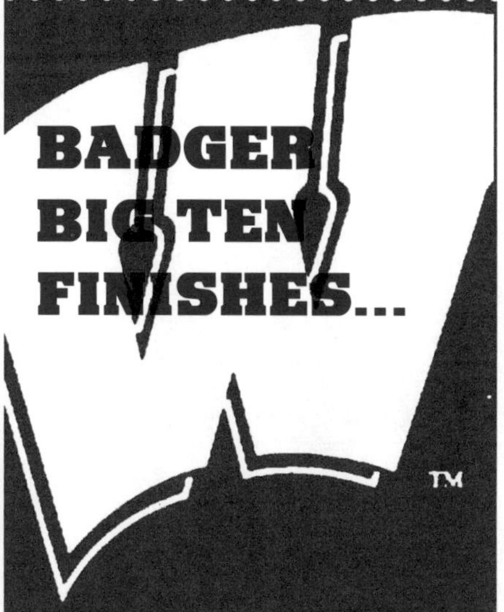

Football: 5th (tie)
coached by Phil King

Cross Country: 3rd
(no coach)

Basketball: 2nd
coached by Emmett Angell

Outdoor Track: 4th
coached by George Downer
and Emmett Angell

Coach Angell leads UW to second in Big Ten as player Angell tops all scorers

Wisconsin's Emmett Angell showed versatility the likes of which has never again been seen in the Big Ten—or perhaps anywhere in the nation—when as player-coach he led the Badgers to a runner-up finish in the inaugural season of Big Ten Conference basketball.

Angell, a student of the game as well as a teacher of it, scored 96 points for a 6.9 average in 14 games to pace Wisconsin to a 12-2 record. The Badgers' 6-2 Big Ten mark was good for second behind Minnesota.

Angell served as coach from the 1904-05 through 1907-08 seasons, compiling a 43-15 mark for a .741 winning percentage, best in Wisconsin history. His last two teams tied for Big Ten titles.

WISCONSIN TIME LINE

1906: The federal penitentiary in Leavenworth, Kansas was completed.

The "Angell Conference"—named after Michigan president A.A. Angell—set far-sighted rules and regulations for the Big Ten.

The Badgers finished 5-0 and won the Big Ten football championship.

1906-07

Football: 1st (tie)
coached by C.P. Hutchins

Cross Country: 2nd
(no coach)

Basketball: 1st (tie)
coached by Emmett Angell

Baseball: 6th
coached by C.P. Hutchins

Gymnastics: 2nd
coached by Emmett Angell

Outdoor Track: 3rd
coached by Emmett Angell

THE BIG EVENT

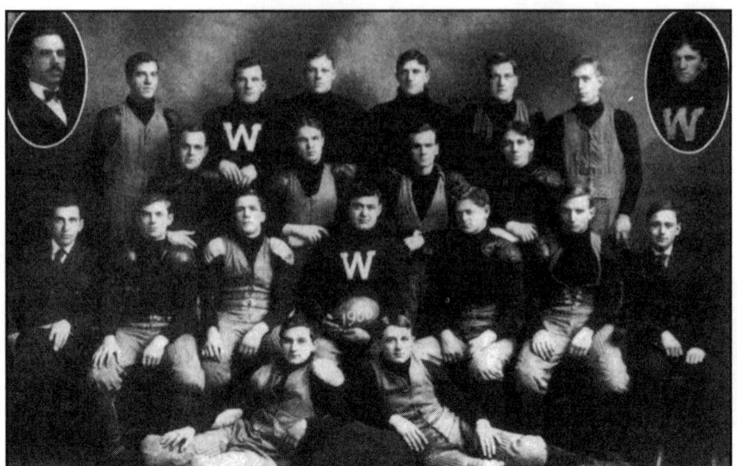

UW shares football title in shortened season

Wisconsin shared a notable Big Ten first in 1906 when its football team went unbeaten over a limited schedule to claim a share of the Conference title with Michigan and Minnesota. Each claimed a share based on its undefeated Big Ten season—Wisconsin at 3-0, Minnesota at 2-0 and Michigan at 1-0. It marked the only time in Big Ten history that three teams were perfect in Conference play.

Wisconsin didn't play traditional powers Michigan, Minnesota or Chicago enroute to its perfect 5-0 mark; a short-lived faculty reform movement had limited the number of games the team could play. Nonetheless, Coach C.P. Hutchins' team, paced by all-league center Ewald Stiehm, notched victories over Iowa, Illinois and Purdue by a combined 63-15 score.

Wisconsin Time Line

1907: The Big Ten raised the limit on football games per season from five to seven.

Oklahoma became the 46th state in the Union.

WISCONSIN HEADLINER

J.C. Elsom
Basketball Coach

J.C. Elsom was one of those coaching pioneers who set the stage for generations of Big Ten coaches to follow. As coach of fledgling UW basketball teams in the years just prior to Conference basketball competition, Elsom was at the forefront of what would become a golden era of basketball excellence in Madison. Building on the tradition established by Elsom's teams, Wisconsin (coached by Walter Meanwell) won 12 Big Ten hoop titles between 1906 and 1929. Elsom, who also served as a professor of physical therapy from 1894-1936, compiled a 25-14 record in six seasons. His first team went 0-3 in 1899 but he never again had a losing record and, in fact, Wisconsin teams would post winning marks until 1918. His best squad was his last one, which posted an 11-4 mark. Elsom died in 1949.

Bringing home the bacon

One of the first trophies of any kind in college football was the "Slab of Bacon" trophy which served as the prize in the Wisconsin-Minnesota football series. According to the Wisconsin football media guide, the trophy was apparently presented to the winning school in any given year by a sorority from the losing school. The trophy was discontinued in the 1940s and was discovered in an athletic department storage room in 1994. It's now in the football office at Wisconsin. "We took home the bacon," said current UW Coach Barry Alvarez, "and kept it."

Wisconsin's longest football winning streaks

Number	First win	Broken by
17	Notre Dame 1900	Michigan 1902
9	Lawrence 1912	Purdue 1913
8	Iowa 1894	Illinois 1895
8	Lake Forest 1897	UW Alumni 1897
8	Minnesota 1920	Michigan 1921
8	Purdue 1951	Ohio State 1952
7	Lake Forest 1896	Northwestern 1896
7	Northwestern 1961	Ohio State 1962

Badgers held out of "big" games

College football was under the gun, figuratively, soon after the turn of the century. The Big Ten had been founded on the principle of faculty control and, in 1906, it was the Wisconsin faculty that asserted itself. Upset by the "proselytizing" and "subsidizing" of athletes, the faculty voted to abolish football. Protests followed and the decision was reversed, to a degree. The UW team was limited to a five-game schedule and prevented from playing its major rivals—Minnesota, Michigan and Chicago. As those were the only games that made any sort of money, revenue fell to $3,400 from $35,000 the previous season. But Wisconsin did have a perfect 5-0 mark and shared the Big Ten title with two of the teams—Michigan and Minnesota—which it was not allowed to play. The faculty relented and allowed the traditional rivals back on the schedule, one at a time.

1907-08

Football: 2nd
coached by
C.P. Hutchins

Cross Country: 2nd
(no coach)

Basketball: 1st (tie)
coached by Emmett Angell

Baseball: 4th
coached by
Tom Barry

Gymnastics: 1st
coached by
J.C. Elsom

Outdoor Track: 2nd
coached by
Emmett Angell

Badgers are Big Ten gymnastics champs again

Led by all-around champion Felix Zeidelhack, Wisconsin claimed its fourth Big Ten gymnastics championship in six tries in the meet at Madison.

Coach J.C. Elsom's team easily outdistanced runner-up Chicago, which had 10 points, as well as Minnesota (7) and Nebraska (5).

Zeidelhack won his second straight all-around title. He also won three other events: the rings, the parallel bars and the horizontal bar, the latter two for the second straight season.

WISCONSIN TIME LINE

1908: The first Boy Scout troops were organized by Sir Robert Baden-Powell in England.

Michigan withdrew from the Conference to protest "retroactive provisions" of certain Conference enactments.

WISCONSIN HEADLINER

John Messmer
Football, Track and Field, Baseball

Milwaukee native John Messmer was a three-sport star for Badger football, track and baseball teams of the first decade of the 20th century. The East Side High School product won nine major "W" awards in the three sports, but achieved his greatest success in football. Captain of the 1907 Wisconsin team, Messmer was a first-team all-Big Ten pick and a second-team Walter Camp all-American at guard in 1908. Messmer also won the discus throw in the Big Ten outdoor track meets of 1907 and 1908 and was a member of the UW baseball team that toured Japan in 1909. He was president of the athletic board in 1908 as a student member. Inducted into the Wisconsin State Athletic Hall of Fame in 1959, Messmer was named to the UW Athletic Hall in 1993.

WISCONSIN HEADLINER

Felix Zeidelhack
Gymnastics

Felix Zeidelhack dominated events at the 1908 Big Ten gymnastics championship, winning the all-around title for the second straight season. He also won the horizontal bars and parallel bars to lead Wisconsin to its fourth team title.

Zeidelhack had won the same events, plus the pommel horse, in pacing the Badgers to the 1907 championship.

WISCONSIN HEADLINER

Harlan Bethune "Biddy" Rogers
Football, Basketball and Baseball

His play in all three sports was characterized by "consistency with coolness in emergencies," say accounts of the time of Harlan Bethune "Biddy" Rogers. The Portage, Wis., native starred in football, basketball and baseball for the Badger teams at the end of the 20th century's first decade, winning nine letters. A three-year regular at left end, Rogers recovered the kick for the winning touchdown in Wisconsin's 6-5 win over Iowa in 1907. A basketball forward, "Biddy" captained the 1908 team that tied for the Big Ten title. He was a centerfielder on the Badger nine that ended his collegiate career with an exhibition trip to Japan in 1909. The Harlan B. Rogers Scholarship has been established in his memory. A member of the Wisconsin State Hall of Fame, Rogers was one of 35 members in the initial class inducted into the UW Athletic Hall of Fame in 1991.

Wisconsin's record at Homecoming

Against	UW record
Chicago	4-2-1
Illinois	6-4
Indiana	7-2
Iowa	8-4
Michigan	0-2
Michigan State	1-4
Minnesota	2-6-2
Northwestern	8-8
Ohio State	1-4
Pennsylvania	1-0
Purdue	4-4-2
San Diego State	1-0
Toledo	1-0
Western Michigan	1-0

1908-09

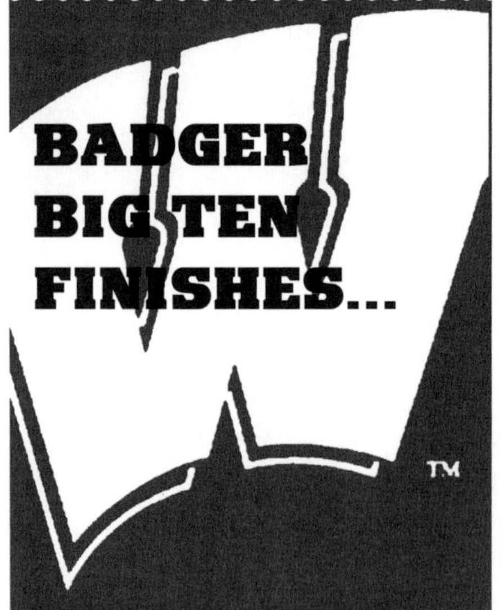

Football: 3rd
coached by
J.A. Barry

Cross Country: 3rd
(no coach)

Basketball: 3rd
coached by
Haskell Noyes

Baseball: 5th
coached by
Tom Barry

Outdoor Track: 4th
coached by
E.W. Moulton

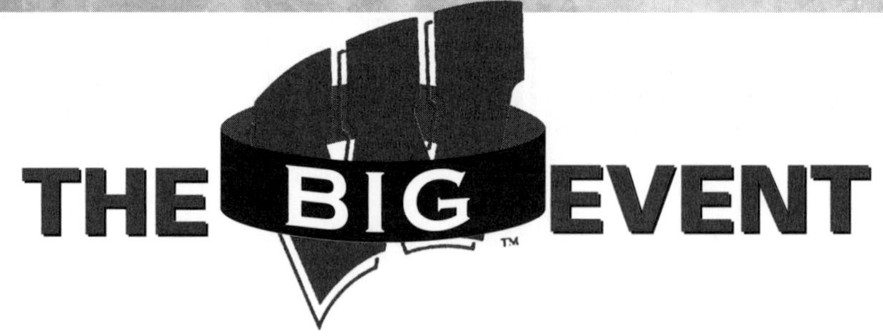

Wisconsin third in first cross country championship

Wisconsin, which today has won more Big Ten cross country team and individual titles than any other school, finished third behind Nebraska and Purdue in the first official Conference meet.

Nebraska (non-Conference teams were then allowed to compete) scored 41 points to upend Purdue while the Badgers—without the benefit of a coach—were third with 59 points.

Top finisher for Wisconsin over the five-mile course at Chicago was William Hover in third place. Hover would take second the next time around although the UW would finish fifth in the team standings.

Wisconsin Time Line

1909: Orville Wright set a record by staying aloft in an airplane for 72 minutes, 40 seconds, over Virginia.

Conference members took an active part in the new National Collegiate Athletic Association.

1909-10

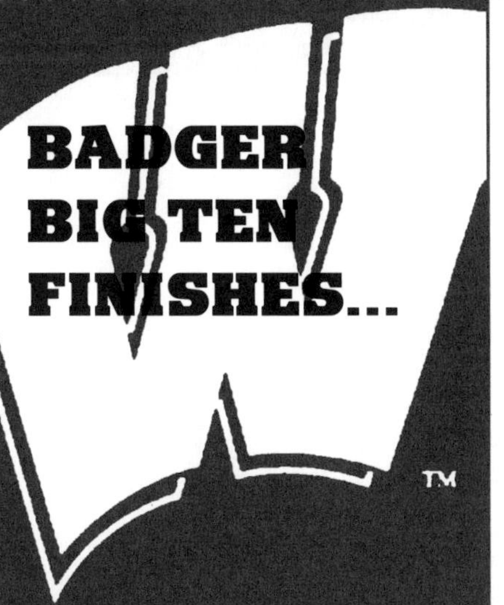

Football: 4th
coached by
J.A. Barry

Cross Country: 5th
coached by
J.C. Elsom

Basketball: 3rd
coached by
Haskell Noyes

Baseball: 5th
coached by
Tom Barry

Outdoor Track: 6th
coached by
Charles Hutchins &
James Lathrop

Beck writes "On, Wisconsin"

A Wisconsin student who was forced to drop out of school for a year used that time to forge a tradition. Carl Beck, who had enrolled at the UW in 1908, withdrew from school to work in Chicago and earn money to further his education. There he met William T. Purdy, who knew music and had started to write music for a song to be entered in a University of Minnesota contest. But Beck suggested that they do a song for Wisconsin, so Purdy wrote the music and Beck the words to provide one of the most famous college songs.

Introduced at a pre-game rally before the Wisconsin-Minnesota game in the fall of 1909, it was instantly a hit with students and townspeople. Beck returned to Madison in 1911, was graduated and became one of the founders of the Wisconsin Alumni Club of New York.

Over the years, it grew in popularity but the need for words which would fit occasions other than football had long been recognized. The original words included a reference to "run the ball clear 'round Chicago." In 1955, Beck composed some new, "all-purpose" lyrics for the famous song, noting in a letter that "These new words are to meet numerous requests for words for possible use on occasions other than football. Instead of stringing out a lot of words, brevity, as in the original, is their aim, having swing and action in keeping with the music and title."

The new lyrics, as written in 1955:

On, Wisconsin! On, Wisconsin!
Stand up, Badgers, sing!

"Forward" is our driving spirit
Loyal voices ring.

On, Wisconsin! On, Wisconsin!
Raise her glowing flame!

Stand, Fellows, let us now
Salute her name!

Wisconsin Time Line

1910: A cork-center baseball was used in the World Series.

The first Big Ten Conference tennis championship was held at Chicago.

Clarence Cleveland (2 mile) and L.W. Johnson (high jump) become Wisconsin's first Big Ten indoor track champions.

1910-11

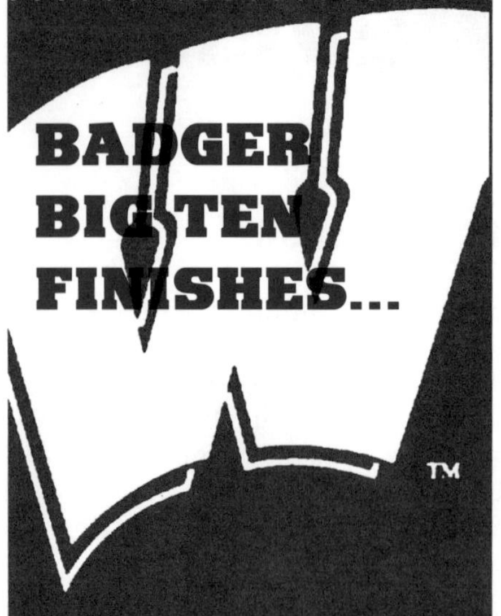

Football: 5th
coached by J.A. Barry

Cross Country: 1st
coached by Charles Wilson

Basketball: 5th
coached by Haskell Noyes

Indoor Track: 4th (tie)
coached by Charles Wilson

Baseball: 6th
coached by Tom Barry

Gymnastics: 3rd
coached by H.D. MacChesney

Outdoor Track: 5th
coached by Charles Wilson

Wisconsin wins first cross country title

There was a home course advantage of sorts for Coach Charles Wilson's 1910 UW cross country team. The Badgers, running in Madison, scored a low 33 points to win their first Big Ten team title.

Irvin Dohman, who covered the 4.75-mile route in 26:21, became Wisconsin's second individual champ. Wisconsin would go on to win three of the next four Big Ten meets and eight more between that first title and 1927.

It was the start of a streak that by 1997 had seen the Badgers win 33 Conference crowns.

Wisconsin Time Line

1911: The first Indianapolis 500-mile race was won by Ray Harroun.

The first Conference indoor track and swimming championships were held.

1911-12

Football: 3rd
coached by J.R. Richards

Cross Country: 2nd
coached by Charles Wilson

Basketball: 1st
coached by Walter Meanwell

Indoor Track: 2nd
coached by Charles Wilson

Swimming: 3rd
coached by Chaunce Hyatt

Baseball: 1st
coached by Gordon Lewis

Outdoor Track: 5th
coached by Charles Wilson

Badgers share basketball crown with Purdue

Wisconsin won its second Big Ten basketball title in 1911-12, sharing the Conference championship with Purdue. The Badgers had previously tied with Minnesota and Chicago for the new Con-ference's second basketball title in 1906-07. Leading Coach Walter Meanwell's team was Otto Stangel, who scored a Big Ten record 177 points.

Wisconsin Time Line

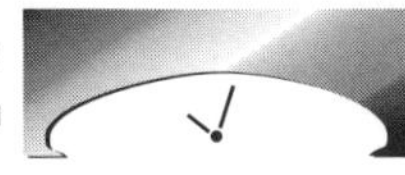

1911: Led by Jim Thorpe, the United States won the most medals in the Olympic Games in Stockholm.

Ohio State University was admitted to membership in the Big Ten.

The Badgers' last unbeaten football team (7-0) won its fifth Big Ten title for rookie coach Bill Juneau.

WISCONSIN HEADLINER

Otto Stangel
Basketball

Otto Stangel led the Big Ten in scoring with 177 points in the Badgers' Conference championship season of 1911-12, a mark that would stand as the league record for eight seasons. Stangel, a native of Two Rivers, Wis., scored 13 field goals in a 38-12 Wisconsin win over Iowa that year. The team was one of Wisconsin's best and was named national champion for 1912 by the Helms Athletic Foundation. Stangel was inducted into the UW Athletic Hall of Fame in 1995.

LEADING THE WAY

Walter Meanwell
Basketball Coach
Athletic Director

Dr. Walter E. "Doc" Meanwell presided over a golden era in Badger basketball, compiling a 246-99-1 record and winning eight Big Ten titles in 20 years as the Badgers' head coach. A native of Leeds, England, who came to the United States in 1885 at 3 years of age, Meanwell received his medical degree from Maryland in 1909. He joined the UW in 1911 as director of gymnasium and wrestling coach. He became basketball coach with the 1911-12 season and posted a 44-1 mark en route to three straight Big Ten titles as well as the 1915-16 crown before leaving for the same post at Missouri, where he coached the Tigers to two titles in three seasons. Meanwell returned to Madison for the 1920-21 campaign and guided the Badgers to the conference title, which his teams also won in 1923, 1924 and 1929. Meanwell served as Wisconsin's athletic director from 1933-35. A member of the National Basketball Hall of Fame, the Wisconsin State Hall of Fame and the Madison Pen and Mike Club-Bowman Sports Foundation Hall of Fame, Meanwell was a charter inductee into the UW Athletic Hall of Fame in 1991.

Winningest UW Football Coaches
*through 1997 season

Coach (Years)	Career Victories
Phil King (1896-1902, 1905)	65
Milt Bruhn (1956-66)	52
Barry Alvarez (1990-Present)	49
Dave McClain (1978-85)	46
Harry Stuhldreher (1936-48)	45
Ivy Williamson (1949-55)	41
John Jardine (1970-77)	37
J.R. Richards (1911, 1917, 1919-22)	29
Glenn Thistlewaite (1927-31)	26
William Juneau ((1912-15)	18

Badgers win first baseball title

Playing an unbalanced Big Ten schedule, Wisconsin—under first-year coach Gordon "Slim" Lewis—won its first Conference baseball championship in 1912, going 6-1 for an .857 winning percentage. It was enough to edge two-time defending champion Illinois, which had a 10-1 mark and .833 winning percentage.

1912-13

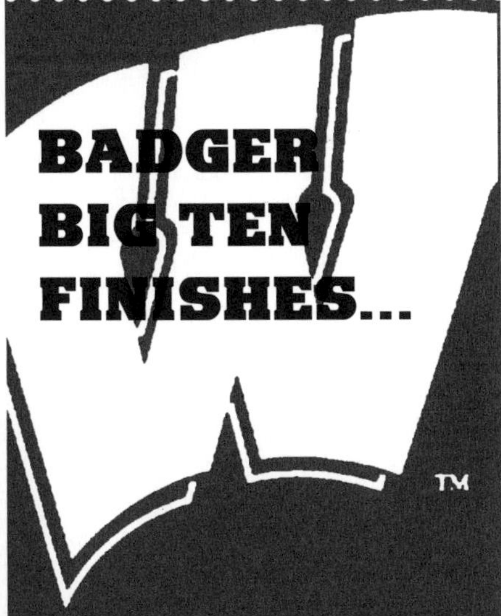

Football: 1st
coached by William Juneau

Cross Country: 1st
coached by Clarence Cleveland

Basketball: 1st
coached by Walter Meanwell

Indoor Track: 2nd
coached by Thomas Jones

Swimming: 2nd
coached by Chauncey Hyatt

Wrestling: 6th
coached by E.B. Nolte

Baseball: 7th
coached by William Juneau

Gymnastics: 1st
coached by H.D. MacChesney

Outdoor Track: 2nd
coached by Thomas Jones

Wisconsin becomes a football power

Wisconsin became a football power in 1912 as Coach Bill Juneau's team won all seven of its games en route to the Badgers' fifth Big Ten championship. Wisconsin scored 246 points and allowed only 29 while in conference play it outscored its five opponents by a combined 169-22.

So domineering was Wisconsin that *Chicago Tribune* sports editor Walter Eckersall picked nine Badgers on his all-Western team, including Joe Hoeffel and Hod Ofstie at ends; Robert "Butts" Butler and Ed Samp at tackles; Ed Gelein and "Tubby" Keeler at guards; Eddie Gillette at quarterback; John Van Riper at halfback; and Al Tandberg at fullback. Butler and Keeler were named all-Americans.

Following Wisconsin's season-ending 28-10 victory at Iowa, there was agitation for the Badgers to meet Harvard for the national championship; the 9-0 Crimson had won the Big Three title and had impressive wins over Yale and Princeton. But John Wilce, 1909 UW captain and the school's graduate manager, said that talk about matching teams for the national title was just that and there would be no such game. Wilce said that such a post-season game was contrary to Western Conference regulations and that, furthermore, the Wisconsin faculty would never approve.

Game scores:
Wisconsin 13, Lawrence 0
Wisconsin 56, Northwestern 0
Wisconsin 41, Purdue 0
Wisconsin 30, Chicago 12
Wisconsin 64, Arkansas 7
Wisconsin 14, Minnesota 0
Wisconsin 28, Iowa 10

Wisconsin Time Line

1913: The first crossword puzzle was published in the Sunday supplement of the *New York World.*

The Big Ten prohibited post-season basketball games.

Tom Jones guided the Badgers to seconds in both the Big Ten indoor and outdoor track meets in the first of his 36 seasons at the helm.

WISCONSIN HEADLINER

Robert Parker "Butts" Butler Football

Robert "Butts" Butler was an all-American tackle on the Badgers' 1912 football team that was undefeated and won the Big Ten championship. In the 1912 season finale against Minnesota, Butler and his 10 teammates played the entire game. He was Wisconsin's first consensus all-American and was named to Walter Camp's first team as a junior and second team as a senior. A native of Glen Ridge, N.J., Butler was a three-time "W" award-winner on Wisconsin teams that posted a 15-4-2 mark over his playing career. Twice an all-Big Ten selection, Butler played professionally for the Canton Bulldogs—with the legendary Jim Thorpe as a teammate—following his graduation in 1914. He was named to the National Football Foundation Hall of Fame in 1972 and was inducted into the UW Athletic Hall of Fame in 1992.

LEADING THE WAY

William J. Juneau Football Coach

William Juneau compiled an 18-8-3 record in four seasons as Wisconsin football coach from 1912-15, including an undefeated campaign in 1912. The Badgers won their fourth Big Ten title and at 7-0 were the last UW team to post a perfect record. Led by consensus all-America (and future UW Athletic Hall of Famer) Robert "Butts" Butler, the Badgers placed a school-record nine players *Chicago Tribune* sports editor Walter Eckersall's all-Western team. Juneau enrolled at Wisconsin in 1899 and won major "W" awards in football the next four years, starring at halfback and end. He also won letters in track in 1900 and 1901, competing in the pole vault, hammer throw and 440-yard dash. He was third in the pole vault in the 1900 Western Intercollegiate meet at Chicago. Juneau also coached at Colorado College, South Dakota State and Marquette before coming to Wisconsin and after his UW stint coached at Texas and Kentucky. Juneau died in 1949 at age 70 in Milwaukee.

Wisconsin's Men's Conference Medal of Honor winners

In 1914, the Big Ten Conference endowed a Medal of Honor to be awarded at each member institution to a student in the graduating class who demonstrated proficiency in scholarship and athletics.

1915
Martin Thomas Kennedy

1916
William Dow Harvey

1917
Meade Burke

1918
Ebert Edward Simpson, Jr.

1919
Charles H. Carpenter

Four Badgers among all-Big Ten cagers

Legendary Wisconsin basketball coach Walter "Doc" Meanwell had the kind of team in the 1912-13 season that most coaches only dream about. Four of his players—Gene Van Gent, Allan Johnson, Carl Harper and John Van Riper—were named to the all-Big Ten first team. It was a season to remember for the Badgers, who won the second of three straight Big Ten championships in a golden era of UW basketball. They were unbeaten through 14 games—11 in the Big Ten—until losing 23-10 at Chicago in the season finale. Their closest game prior to that was a 16-15 win at Illinois.

1913-14

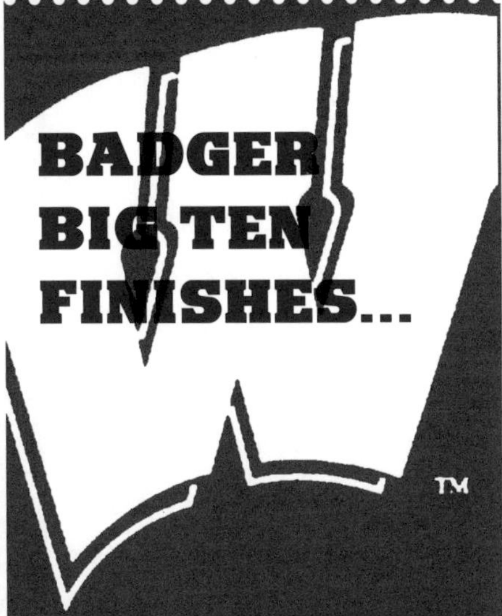

Football: 6th (tie)
coached by William Juneau

Cross Country: 1st
coached by Thomas Jones

Basketball: 1st
coached by Walter Meanwell

Indoor Track: 2nd
coached by Thomas Jones

Swimming: 4th
coached by Harry Hindman

Wrestling: 2nd
coached by Fred Schlatter

Baseball: 3rd
coached by Gordon Lewis

Gymnastics: 2nd
coached by H.D. MacChesney

Outdoor Track: 4th
coached by Thomas Jones

Badgers are national basketball champs

For the second time in three seasons, Wisconsin celebrated national and Big Ten basketball championships. Under Coach Walter "Doc" Meanwell, the UW rattled off 15 wins without a loss to claim best-in-the-nation honors. Its 12-0 Big Ten mark also gave Wisconsin its first undisputed Conference crown. Noteworthy was the only shutout in Big Ten basketball history: The Badgers blanked Parsons 50-0 on Jan. 6, 1914, at home.

Wisconsin's record season:

Wisconsin 48, Knox 15*
Wisconsin 45, Beloit 15*
Wisconsin 50, Parsons 0*
Wisconsin 26, Illinois 25
Wisconsin 57, Indiana 15
Wisconsin 28, Minnesota 7*
Wisconsin 16, Chicago 14
Wisconsin 38, Northwestern 9*
Wisconsin 25, Purdue 20 (OT)*
Wisconsin 33, Northwestern 26
Wisconsin 29, Illinois 16*
Wisconsin 46, Indiana 24*
Wisconsin 27, Minnesota 9
Wisconsin 25, Chicago 18*
Wisconsin 27, Purdue 13

*Home games

Wisconsin Time Line

1914: Britain declared war on Germany and the United States declared its neutrality in World War I.

The Conference Board of Directors put aside $2,000 for the endowment of the ICAA Medal (Medal of Honor).

WISCONSIN HEADLINER

Ray Keeler
Football

Three-time letterwinner Ray Keeler was a consensus all-American lineman for the Wisconsin football team of 1913, which posted a 3-3-1 mark for second-year Coach William Juneau. Keeler, nicknamed "Tubby" in "recognition" of his 185-lb. frame, earned all-American recognition in his junior season from the International News Service. Keeler also won three major "W" awards in track and field. He was captain of the 1914 football team and also served on the athletic board in 1914 and 1915. Keeler went on to coach the Wisconsin-LaCrosse football team to a 45-24-15

A basketball blanking— one for the record books

It was a basketball game for the ages, at least in the minds of Wisconsin fans. Everyone knew that the Badgers could score and, after all, they had only lost one game in the two prior seasons. And Coach Walter Meanwell's Badgers had racked up a lot of points (for the day) in beating Knox 48-15 and Beloit 45-15 to start their season. But a shut-out, still the only one in Big Ten annals, was unexpected to say the least. Nonetheless, it was in the books as one of those games to be remembered: Wisconsin 50, Parsons 0, on Jan. 6, 1914, at Madison.

Wahl jumps to Big Ten victories

High jumper Robert Wahl became Wisconsin's first three-time Big Ten track and field champion in 1914, winning the high jump at 6' 1/2" in the Conference indoor meet at Evanston. The Badgers finished second to Illinois for the third straight season. Wahl had won the high jump at 5'10" in 1912 and had tied for the crown in the event at 5'11 1/2" in the 1913 meet. He also took the high jump titles at the Big Ten outdoor championships in 1913 and 1914.

The Badgers' first Big Ten championships

Sport	1st UW title	1st year championship held
Baseball	1901-02	1895-96
Basketball	1906-07	1905-06
Cross Country	1910-11	1908-09
Fencing	1954-55	1925-26
Football	1896-97	1896-97
Golf	1956-67	1919-20
Gymnastics	1901-02	1901-02
Hockey	1971-72	1958-59
Soccer	1995-96	1991-92
Swimming	none	1910-11
Tennis	none	1909-10
Outdoor Track	1914-15	1900-01
Indoor Track	1926-27	1910-11
Wrestling	none	1911-12

1914-15

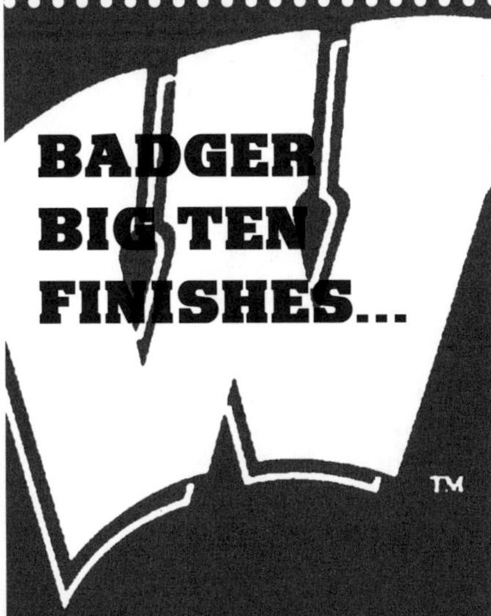

Football: 4th (tie)
coached by William Juneau

Cross Country: 5th
coached by Thomas Jones

Basketball: 3rd
coached by Walter Meanwell

Indoor Track: 4th
coached by Thomas Jones

Swimming: 4th
coached by Harry Hindman

Wrestling: 4th
coached by Fred Schlatter

Baseball: 2nd
coached by Gordon Lewis

Gymnastics: 1st
coached by H.D. MacChesney

Outdoor Track: 1st
coached by Thomas Jones

Wisconsin takes Big Ten track title by one point

Wisconsin won its first Big Ten outdoor track and field championship under the tutelage of Coach Tom Jones as the Badgers edged Chicago 38-37 on June 5, 1915, at Champaign, Illinois. It was the first of five one-point decisions in the annals of Big Ten outdoor track. Wisconsin had three champions, all in the field events.

Arlie Mucks, Sr., claimed titles in the shot put (46'3") and discus throw (137'7") while Phil Stiles won the long jump at 23'9" Mucks also added a third in the hammer throw as the Badgers made every point count, scoring in 10 of the 15 events.

It was the first of 20 Big Ten championships that Jones-coached teams would win over the next three decades.

Wisconsin Time Line

1915: The U.S. House of Representatives rejected a proposal to give women the right to vote.

Coach H.D. MacChesney's Wisconsin gymnasts won their sixth Big Ten title.

1915-16

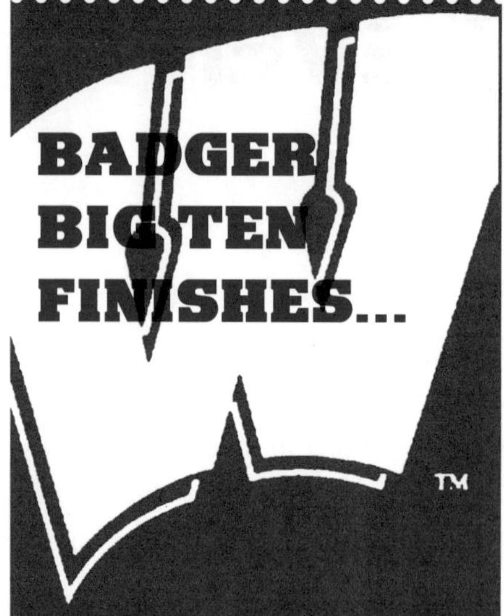

Football: 6th
coached by William Juneau

Cross Country: 1st
coached by Fred G. Lee

Basketball: 1st
coached by Walter Meanwell

Indoor Track: 2nd
coached by Thomas Jones

Swimming: 4th
coached by Harry Hindman

Wrestling: 6th
coached by Art Knott

Baseball: 6th (tie)
coached by Gordon Lewis

Gymnastics: 1st
coached by H.D. MacChesney

Outdoor Track: 1st
coached by Thomas Jones

Badgers win national basketball crown again

None of the great Wisconsin basketball teams of the first decade and one-half of the 20th century may have been as dominating as the Badgers of 1915-16. Coach Walter Meanwell's team posted a 20-1 overall mark and went 11-1 in the Big Ten to coast to the league title.

Undefeated in 10 home games, the Badgers were named the Helms Athletic Foundation national champions, the third UW (and Meanwell-coached) team to be so honored. The 1915-16 Wisconsin five was also the first Big Ten team to win 20 games in a season, a feat that would not be duplicated until 1940 .

Leading the Badgers were all-American (and two-time all-Big Ten) performer George Levis along with his running mates, William Chandler, Mel Haas, Paul Meyers and Harold Olsen. Illinois handed Wisconsin its only loss by a 27-20 count at Champaign to break the Badgers' 12-game winning streak.

Wisconsin Time Line

1916: The Supreme Court ruled that the federal income tax was constitutional.

Wisconsin won four Big Ten championships: cross country, basketball, gymnastics and outdoor track.

WISCONSIN HEADLINER

Howard "Cub" Buck
Football

Called the finest lineman he had ever played with by pro football teammate Jim Thorpe, Howard "Cub" Buck played tackle on Wisconsin's 11-8-2 football teams of 1913-15. Buck, an Eau Claire native, captained the 1915 squad, earning all-Big Ten and all-American honors that season. He is a member of Wisconsin's all-time football team. He played professionally with the Canton Bulldogs from 1915-19 and with the Green Bay Packers from 1921-25, with assistant coaching stops at Wisconsin and Carleton College sandwiched between his pro football stints. Buck later became head coach at Lawrence College (1824-25) and Miami of Florida (1926-28). A member of the Wisconsin State Hall of Fame (1956) and the Green Bay Packers Hall of Fame (1977), Buck was a charter inductee of the UW Athletic Hall of Fame in 1991.

WISCONSIN HEADLINER

George Levis
Basketball

All-American forward George Levis was one of the mainstays of the 1916 Wisconsin basketball team that compiled a 20-1 mark enroute to the Big Ten championship. Levis, a Madison native, earned all-Conference honors at forward in both 1915 and 1916; he gained all-America status in 1916 after scoring 109 points in 12 Big Ten games in that era of low scores. Levis also was a third baseman for the Badgers' baseball squad. Levis later coached basketball at Indiana for two seasons in the early 1920s, compiling a 25-16 record. He later played a prominent role in developing basketball's glass backboards for his family's firm, Illinois Glass Company. Levis was one of 35 charter inductees into the UW Athletic Hall of Fame in 1991.

Wisconsin's Big Ten fencing champions

Since Al Stirns won the Big Ten foil title in 1915, 24 Badgers won 33 fencing championships until 1986 when the Big Ten discontinued fencing Wisconsin dropped the sport after the 1991 season.

Foil
Al Stirns (1915), Edward Hampe (1941), Jack Heiden (1955), Jerry Bodnar (1958), Richard Green (1959), Bruce Taubman (1967-68), Neal Cohen (1970, 1972), Harry Chiu (1973), Bob Tourdot (1975), Dean Rose (1978-79), Michael Pedersen (1985)

Epee
Bob Serles (1953), Paul Mortonson (1955), Pat Laper (1967), Steve Vandenberg (1977-78), Mike Glennon (1980), Tim Gillham (1983-84-85)

Sabre
Art Kaftan (1935-36), Fred Kaftan (1937-38), Ron LeMieux (1959), Tom Giaimo (1971), Dave DeWahl (1976), Joe Kroeten (1981-82), Mark Draeger (1984)

Badger teams win four Big Ten titles

Paced by the national champion basketball team, 1915-16 marked one of the great years in Wisconsin sports history, with four Wisconsin teams claiming Big Ten championships. Coach Walter Meanwell's cagers posted a 20-1 overall record and 11-1 Big Ten mark to earn not only the Big Ten crown but also recognition by the Helms Athletic Foundation as national champions. Not to be outdone, the Badger gymnasts, under Coach H.D. MacChesney, won the Conference title. Coach Tom Jones' track and field squad garnered four individual titles and the mile relay crown in the Big Ten outdoor track meet at Evanston to take a 49-35 win over Illinois. And the UW cross country team, coached by Fred Lee and led by Arlie Schardt's third-place finish, scored a low 38 points to win the Big Ten.

1916-17

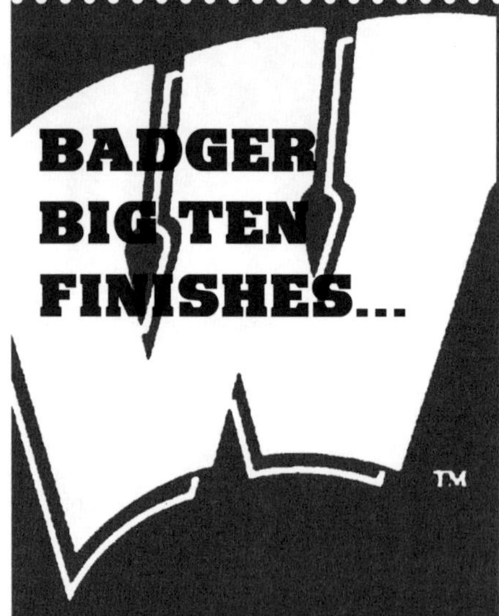

Football: 6th (tie)
coached by Paul Withington

Cross Country: 6th
coached by Irvin A. White

Basketball: 4th
coached by Walter Meanwell

Swimming: 4th
coached by Harry Hindman

Badgers post mildly successful season in all sports

Wisconsin had mixed success during the 1916-17 campaign.

The football Badgers won their first four games—all at home—under one-year Coach Paul Withington against lightly regarded foes. However, the UW was 0-2-1 in its last three games against Big ten opposition, losing 14-13 to Ohio State and 54-0 to Chicago before playing Illinois to a scoreless tie.

Coach Walter Meanwell's national basketball champions "slipped," barely, to 15-3 and a 9-3 fourth-place finish in the Big Ten. However, three players, guards Paul Meyers and Harold Olsen and center Bill Chandler, were all-Conference picks, the latter two for the second consecutive season.

The Badgers placed seventh in Big Ten cross country. In track and field, Wisconsin was third in the Conference indoor meet, with sprinter Carman Smith and miler Arlie Schardt winning their specialties, but didn't compete in the outdoor meet.

The Badgers were fourth of four in the Big Ten swimming and diving championships.

Wisconsin Time Line

1917: Rev. Edward Flanagan founded Boys Town near Omaha.

Michigan resumed its membership in the Big Ten.

Only four Wisconsin teams competed in Big Ten championship play, with the football and cross country teams each sixth in the Conference and the basketball and swimming teams fourth.

1917-18

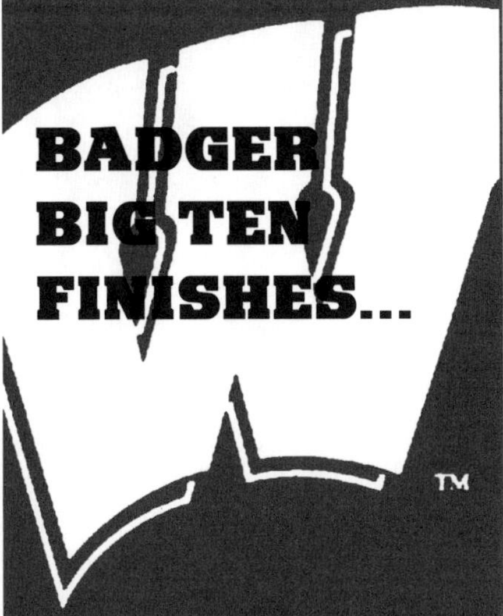

Football: 3rd (tie)
coached by J.R. Richards

Cross Country: 3rd
coached by Thomas E. Jones

Basketball: 1st
coached by Guy Lowman

Indoor Track: 3rd
coached by Thomas Jones

Swimming: 3rd
coached by Harry Hindman

Baseball: 6th (tie)
coached by Guy Lowman

Outdoor Track: 5th
coached by Thomas Jones

Lowman guides Badgers to Big Ten cage crown

Guy Lowman didn't miss a beat when he took over Wisconsin's basketball coaching reins for the 1917-18 season with Walter Meanwell's departure for military service. The UW chalked up a 14-3 mark overall, with its 9-3 Big Ten slate good enough to give Wisconsin its seventh Big Ten title.

The Badgers, acclaimed as national champions for three of the previous six seasons by the Helms Athletic Foundation, had dropped to an uncharacteristic fourth in the Big Ten standings in 1916-17, albeit with 15-3 overall and 9-3 Big Ten records. But Lowman, who would coach the UW for three seasons until Meanwell's return, got the Badgers off to a quick start with five straight wins to open the campaign.

After a loss at Northwestern, a four-game win skein followed before a 23-21 loss at Chicago. The Badgers recouped and won five in a row again before falling 19-11 to Minnesota in the season finale.

WISCONSIN TIME LINE

1918: Units of the U.S. 1st Division, in the first American offensive of World War I, captured the area around Cantigny, France, from the Germans.

The Conference tendered to the War Department "its services in carrying on athletic activities in and among its members."

Guy Lowman's Badgers won their sixth Big Ten basketball championship in 12 years.

WISCONSIN HEADLINER

Arlie Mucks, Sr.
Football, Track and Field

"Great" is a word that can't be tossed around lighly, but in the case of Arlie Mucks, Sr., it hardly does the man justice. A football all-American, an Olympic silver medalist as a teenager, Mucks boasted an athletic resume that wasn't far removed from that of Jim Thorpe. The Oshkosh native was an all-Big Ten and all-America guard for the Badgers in 1914, but he had already made his mark. As a teen in 1912, he won the silver medal in the discus in the Stockholm Olympics. Prior to that, he had played tackle on his three-time state champion high school football team. Unbeaten in the shot put and discus as a collegian, Mucks won national titles in the shot and discus three consecutive years, the only man ever to do so. He won U.S. Olympic trials in the shot in 1916, 1920 and 1924 and was Penn Relays shot and discus champ in 1916. Mucks served as a Big Ten football official after his playing career ended. He was named to Wisconsin's all-time football team in 1969, to the Wisconsin State Hall of Fame and, in 1991, as a charter member of the UW Athletic Hall of Fame.

WISCONSIN HEADLINER

Arthur C. Nielsen, Sr.
Tennis

Even 80 years after his graduation, Arthur C. Nielsen, Sr., remains one of the great tennis players in Wisconsin history. Nielsen captained the UW tennis teams of 1914-15 through 1917-18. He teamed with Edwin Hammen to win the Big Ten doubles title in 1918. Nielsen later teamed with his son, Arthur, Jr., to win two national titles in father-son doubles competition. He also won the national U.S. hard court title in father-daughter competition. Nielsen was elected to the National Lawn Tennis Hall of Fame in 1971. A 1918 graduate in electrical engineering, Nielsen founded and spent 50 years with A.C. Nielsen Co., the largest firm in marketing and television audience research. His contribution also made possible the 1968 construction on the UW campus of a tennis stadium named for him. Nielsen received an honorary doctorate from Wisconsin in 1974. He was named to the UW Athletic Hall of Fame in 1992.

LEADING THE WAY

Tom Jones
Track and Cross Country Coach

If any name is synonymous with Wisconsin track and field, it's that of Tom Jones, a coach whose stellar teams from 1913-48 defined the UW's great tradition in track and cross country. And although he had great success, Jones believed more in the amateur spirit and development of men than in victories. Nonetheless, victories were numerous. Jones coached 20 Big Ten championship teams and the 1948 Olympic team. Seven of his teams finished among the top 10 in the NCAA championships, with the Chuck Fenske-led team of 1938 topping that group with a fourth-place national collegiate finish. He guided 137 athletes to Big Ten titles and five to NCAA crowns. Named to halls of fame by the Helms Foundation, the Wisconsin State hall, the Madison Pen and Mike Club-Bowman Foundation and the Drake Relays coaches hall, Jones was inducted as a charter member of the UW Athletic Hall of Fame in 1991. He died in 1969 at age 91.

Camp Randall Stadium opens

Wisconsin's famed Camp Randall Stadium is the oldest football stadium in the Big Ten. Now seating 76,027, the stadium sits on a site used variously as a training site for Union soldiers during the Civil War, as a prison for Confederate troops and as a state fair grounds. When the Wisconsin state legislature donated the land to the University, veterans groups prevailed upon the school to call it Camp Randall rather than Randall Field so as to honor veterans buried in a nearby cemetery. Originally seating 10,000, the facility was built for $15,000 and has been expanded nearly a dozen times since then. Wisconsin beat Minnesota 10-7 in its opening game there for the 1917 Homecoming celebration.

1918-19

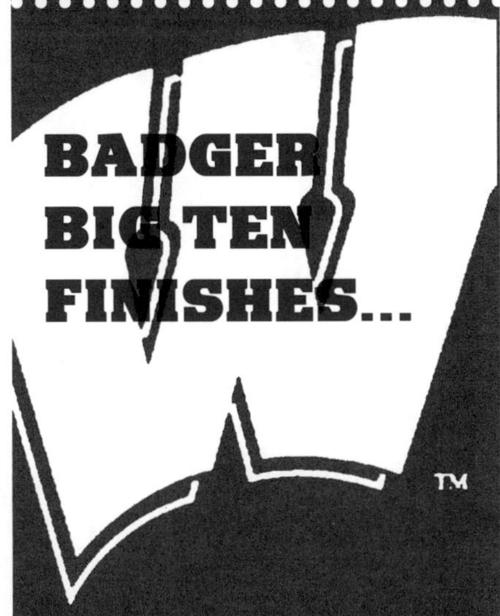

Football: 7th
coached by Guy Lowman

Cross Country: 1st
coached by
George T. Bresnahan

Basketball: 10th
coached by Guy Lowman

Indoor Track: 8th
coached by Thomas Jones

Swimming: 4th
coached by Harry Hindman

Baseball: 7th
coached by Maury Kent

Outdoor Track: 9th (tie)
coached by Thomas Jones

Doughboys come home from war

The "war to end all wars" didn't put a stop to intercollegiate athletics, but it certainly slowed things down a bit and teams were admittedly sub-par. The Big Ten Conference had suspended its activities as a "controlling body" and had tendered to the War Department "its services in carrying on athletic activities in and among its members."

With the return of young men from the European theater of operations, college coaches could again turn their attention to sports rather than war. Illinois, which won the 1919 Conference football title via a last-minute upset of Ohio State, lost 14-10 to the Badgers.

Wisconsin center Charles Carpenter earned all-American honors. In basketball, Wisconsin fell from its national championship heights of a year earlier and ended 5-11 overall and 3-9 in the Big Ten for its first last-place finish.

Wisconsin Time Line

1919: A federal amendment to give women the right to vote was passed by the U.S. House of Representatives.

Wisconsin, coached by George Bresnahan, won the "unofficial" Big Ten cross country title with a low 24 points as Bernardo Elsom became the Badgers' fifth individual champion in 27:13 for the five-mile course. No official meet was held because of World War.

1919-20

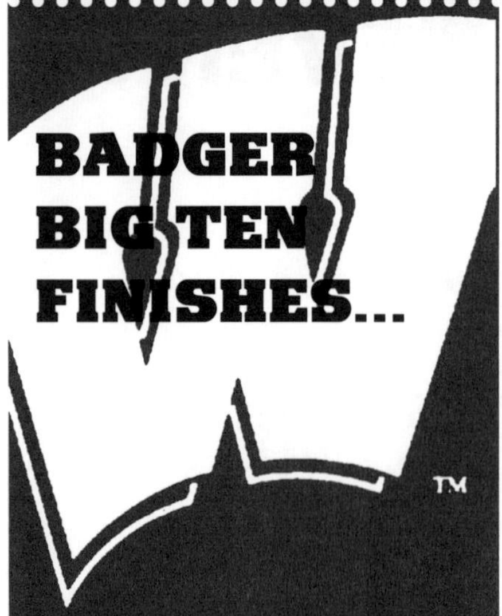

Football: 4th
coached by J.R. Richards

Cross Country: 2nd
coached by
George T. Bresnahan

Basketball: 5th
coached by Guy Lowman

Indoor Track: 3rd
coached by Thomas Jones

Swimming: 3rd
coached by Joe Steinauer

Baseball: 7th
coached by Maury Kent

Golf: 7th
(no coach)

Outdoor Track: 3rd
coached by Thomas Jones

Badgers 5-2 in football for 4th in Big Ten

In his first year of his third stint as Badger football coach, John Richards returned from World War I to guide Wisconsin to a 5-2 season in 1919. The UW shut out its first two opponents, Ripon (37-0) and Marquette (13-0), and beat Big Ten rivals Northwestern (10-6) and Illinois (14-10) before dropping its next two.

Minnesota beat the Badgers 19-7 and Ohio State squeaked by the UW 3-0. Wisconsin rebounded to beat Chicago 10-3 in its last game. Two-time all-American center Charles Carpenter, the first UW all-American at his position, captained the 1919 team.

Wisconsin Time Line

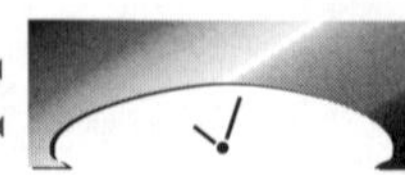

1920: New York-to-San Francisco air mail service was inaugurated.

The first Big Ten golf tournament was held at Olympia Fields Country Club in suburban Chicago.

Lloyd Wilder won the pole vault to become Wisconsin's first NCAA track and field champion.

1920-21

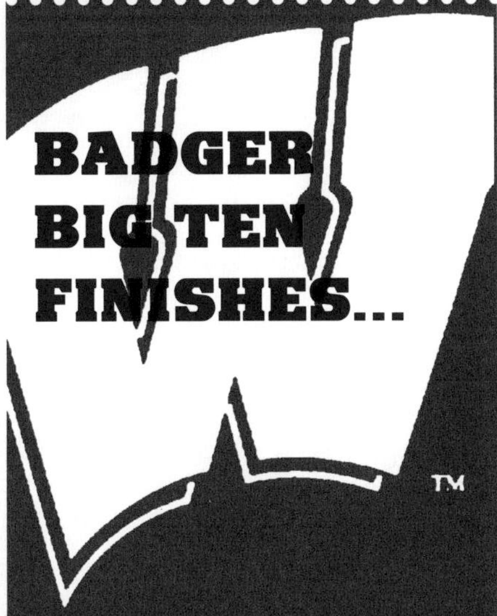

Football: 2nd
coached by J.R. Richards

Cross Country: 5th
coached by
George T. Bresnahan

Basketball: 1st (tie)
coached by Walter Meanwell

Indoor Track: 3rd
coached by Thomas Jones

Swimming: 5th
coached by Joe Steinauer

Wrestling: 2nd
coached by George Hitchcock

Baseball: 3rd
coached by Guy Lowman

Outdoor Track: 3rd
coached by Thomas Jones
(5th, NCAA)

Badgers return to top of Big Ten basketball

After two years away from the top of the Big Ten basketball standings, the Badgers made a triumphant return to Conference supremacy in the 1920-21 season. Wisconsin had slipped to 10th and fifth place finishes in the Big Ten in the two intervening years.

Coach Walter Meanwell, back after a three-year hiatus because of World War I, took over from Guy Lowman and guided the UW to a 13-4 overall record. The Badgers' 8-4 Big Ten mark was good for a tie for the championship.

Wisconsin split its first eight conference games but snared a share of its eighth Big Ten title with a road win over Ohio State and home victories over Chicago, Minnesota and the Buckeyes.

WISCONSIN TIME LINE

1921: Iowa became the first state to impose a cigarette tax.

Official action against post-season football games was taken by the Conference.

Ice hockey officially became a sport at Wisconsin, with the first game a 4-1 loss to the Milwaukee Athletic Club.

WISCONSIN HEADLINER

Frank L. Weston
Football,
Basketball

Frank Weston was a two-time all-Big Ten end for Badger football teams of 1917, 1919 and 1920 and was a second-team Walter Camp All-American in 1921. The Mason City, Iowa, native captained that 1920 Wisconsin team, which posted a 6-1 mark. He also earned a "W" award in basketball in 1919 and 1920. Weston went on to an illustrious career, receiving his medical degree from Rush Medical College. He served as president of the Wisconsin Medical Alumni Association for 1964-65 and received the outstanding alumnus award from the Wisconsin Alumni Association in 1956. He also was a member of the Wisconsin Athletic Board from 1948-63. Weston was inducted into the Madison Sports Hall of Fame in 1965 and into the UW Athletic Hall of Fame in 1994.

WISCONSIN HEADLINER

Paul Meyers &
Charles Carpenter
Football

End Paul Meyers and center Charles Carpenter each earned all-America football honors in 1916 and again in 1919. Meyers, an all-Big Ten choice those same years who played for three different coaches, received first-team all-America honors from Walter Eckersall for his senior season. Eckersall had named him third-team all-America in 1916. Carpenter, the Wisconsin recipient of the Big Ten Medal of Honor in 1919, also made Eckersall's third and first team all-America units in the same years as Meyers. The first all-American center at Wisconsin, Carpenter was captain of the 1919 team. A Madison native, he later served as president of the UW Athletic Board.

WISCONSIN HEADLINER

George Bunge
Football

George Bunge was a two-time all-American in 1920 and 1921 for Coach J.R. Richards, Wisconsin football teams. Bunge, a center, was a first-team all- America choice in 1920 by Consolidated Press. He earned third-team all-America honors on 1921 from Charles Parker and International News Service. The Badgers posted a three-year mark of 16-4-1, including a runner-up finish in the Big Ten in 1920, during Bunge's career.

WISCONSIN HEADLINER

Ralph Scott
Football

Ralph Scott, a 210-lber., starred at tackle for the Badgers' 6-1 team of 1920, which finished second in the Big Ten under coach J.R. Richards. Scott was an all-Conference pick as well as a first-team all-American selection on the Walter Camp Team. Scott was noted for his blocking ability on offense and also played tackle on defense.

WISCONSIN HEADLINER

Rollie Williams
Football, Basketball, Baseball

Rollie Williams, an Edgerton, Wisconsin, native who excelled in football, basketball and baseball in high school, continued to shine at Madison. He earned nine letters for the Badgers and was an all-Big Ten choice as a football halfback in 1922 and a basketball guard for the 1922-23 season. His 75-yard run from scrimmage helped the Badgers defeat Minnesota in the 1921 Homecoming game. He played on Big Ten basketball championship teams as a sophomore and senior and in the spring was an outfielder for the Badger nine. Following his graduation, Williams served as head basketball coach at Millikin University for a season before heading to Iowa for a five-year stint as assistant football and basketball coach. He became head basketball coach at Iowa in 1929 and served through the 1941-42 season and also for the 1950-51 campaign, guiding Hawkeye teams to a 147-139 record. Williams also served as an assistant director of athletics. A member of the Wisconsin State Hall of Fame, Williams was a charter member of the UW Athletic Hall of Fame in 1991.

LEADING THE WAY

John R. Richards
Football Coach

John R. Richards was one of Wisconsin's greatest athletes and coaches. The Lake Geneva native starred on early Badger teams in the last decade of the 19th century, playing end for the Badgers in 1892 and fullback from 1893-96. He also earned five track letters as a hurdler and another in crew. Richards had three different terms as Wisconsin's football coach, guiding the team a 5-1-1 mark in 1911 and third in the Big Ten (2-1-1). He coached football at Ohio State in 1912 and then returned to Madison in 1917, where his team went 4-2-1. He left for World War I service and then returned again in 1919 four a four-year stint. His best squad was the 1920 unit that went 6-1 and finished second in the Big Ten. Among the many UW stars he coached were Guy Sundt, "Red" Weston, Chuck Carpenter, George Bunge and "Rowdy" Elliott. After leaving Wisconsin, Richards became a partner in a California investment firm. He died at age 72 in 1947.

Badgers in the College Football Hall of Fame

Pat Richter
two-time all-American receiver
(elected in 1996)

Pat Harder
all-America fullback
(elected in 1993)

Marty Below
all-America tackle
(elected in 1988)

Alan Ameche
two-time all-America,
Heisman Trophy winner
(elected in 1975)

Robert Butler
all-America tackle
(elected in 1972)

Pat O,Dea
two-time all-America kicker & fullback
(elected in 1962)

Dave Shreiner
two-time all-America end
(elected in 1955)

Wilder wins first NCAA pole vault title

Lloyd Wilder was Wisconsin's—and the Big Ten's—first NCAA pole vault champion in the inaugural NCAA outdoor track and field championships at Chicago. Wilder, who lettered only that season for Coach Tom Jones, shared the vault title at 12'0" with Longino Welch of Georgia Tech, Eldon Jenne of Washington State and Truman Gardner of Yale. The Badgers finished fifth in the meet with 9 points as Illinois won the first NCAA team championship. Wilder remains the only Badger to win an NCAA vault crown and is one of only three men—javelin thrower Bob Ray and high jumper Pat Matzdorf are the others—to win a field event in the NCAA outdoor meet.

1921-22

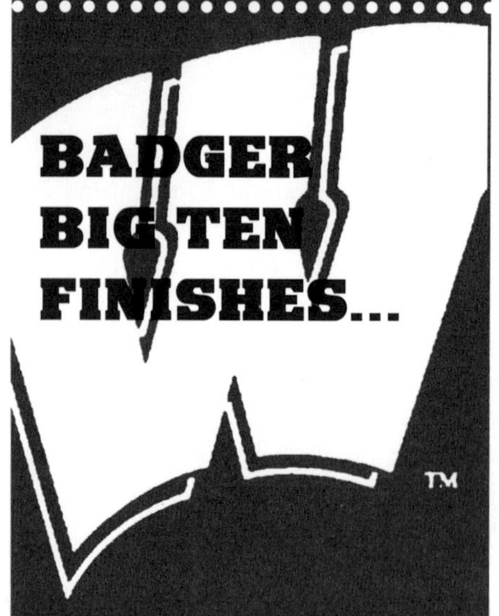

Football: 4th
coached by J.R. Richards

Cross Country: 3rd
coached by Meade Burke

Basketball: 2nd (tie)
coached by Walter Meanwell

Indoor Track: 2nd
coached by Thomas Jones

Swimming: 2nd
coached by Joe Steinauer

Wrestling: 5th
coached by George Hitchcock

Baseball: 3rd
coached by Guy Lowman

Golf: 3rd
(no coach)

Gymnastics: 2nd
coached by Fred Schlatter

Outdoor Track: 6th
coached by Thomas Jones

UW gridders go 5-1-1, fourth in the Big Ten

Wisconsin started well but finished not so well in the 1921 Big Ten football season. Coach J.R. Richards' team only allowed 13 points in its seven games, but 10 of them came in the final two games of the season.

The Badgers won their first five convincingly, blanking Lawrence 28-0 in the opener before allowing South Dakota State three points in a 28-3 win. Shutouts of Big Ten opponents Northwestern (27-0), Illinois (20-0) and Minnesota (35-0) followed.

But Michigan and Wisconsin tied at 7-7 in the penultimate game before the Badgers lost a 3-0 heartbreaker to Chicago in the season finale.

Four UW players earned all-America honors, with center George Bunge a third-team choice of International News Service; back Alvah Elliott a second-team pick by Walter Eckersall; tackle R.H. Brumm a second unit Consolidated Press selection; and tackle Jimmy Brader a third-team choice by Football World.

WISCONSIN TIME LINE

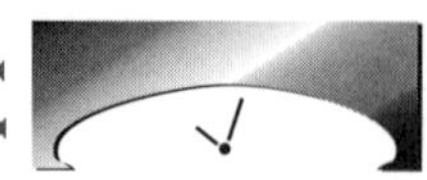

1922: The Lincoln Memorial in Washington was dedicated.

The Big Ten established the office of Commissioner of Athletics and elected Maj. John L. Griffith to the post.

1922-23

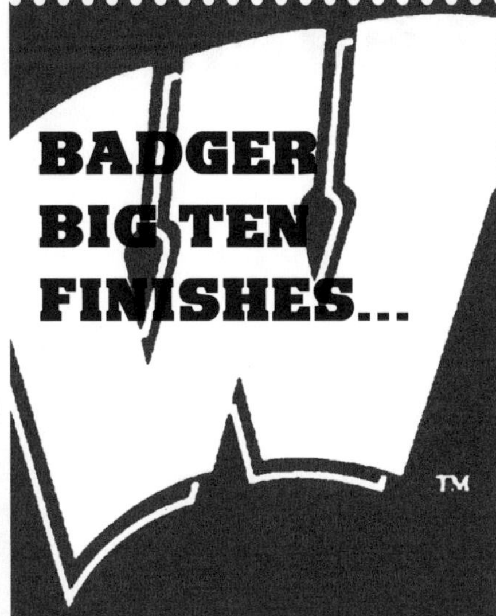

Football: 4th
coached by J.R. Richards

Cross Country: 2nd
coached by Meade Burke

Basketball: 1st (tie)
coached by Walter Meanwell

Indoor Track: 8th
coached by Thomas Jones

Swimming: 3rd
coached by Joe Steinauer

Baseball: 4th
coached by Guy Lowman

Golf: 3rd
(no coach)

Gymnastics: 1st
coached by Frank Leitz

Outdoor Track: 3rd
coached by Thomas Jones

Wisconsin wins its last gymnastics title

The Badgers scored 1,114 points to win the 1923 Big Ten gymnastics championship under the direction of one-year coach Frank Leitz. It was Wisconsin's eighth and last title in the sport.

No other records exist from that year's meet in Big Ten or Wisconsin archives. When Wisconsin dropped the sport almost 70 years later, the Badgers showed an all-time list of 21 individual event champions and five all-around winners to go with their eight team titles.

Wisconsin Time Line

1923: The tomb of King Tut was opened by archeologists in Egypt's Valley of the Kings.

The Big Ten raised the limit on football games from seven to eight.

1923-24

Football: 7th
coached by Jack Ryan

Cross Country: 3rd
coached by Meade Burke

Basketball: 1st (tie)
coached by Walter Meanwell

Indoor Track: 8th
coached by Thomas Jones

Swimming: 5th
coached by Joe Steinauer

Baseball: 3rd
coached by Guy Lowman

Golf: 4th
(no coach)

Gymnastics: 4th
coached by Fred Schlatter

Outdoor Track: 5th
coached by Thomas Jones

Badgers lose 6-3 to Michigan in wild game

Leading mighty Michigan 3-0 before 20,000 fans at Camp Randall Field, Wisconsin was on the verge of salvaging its 1923 football season. Coach Jack Ryan's first Wisconsin football team had opened the 1923 season in fine fashion, winning three straight games. But a scoreless tie with Minnesota and a 10-0 loss at Illinois had put the Badgers on downward spiral.

What some called "the biggest robbery ever pulled off in Madison" changed everything and gave the Wolverines a 6-3 win and share of the Big Ten title. Wisconsin had punted and Michigan quarterback and safety Tod Rockwell had returned the ball about 20 yards before being tackled by two Badgers near the sidelines at midfield.

Rockwell remained on the ground for several seconds before he got up and walked nonchalantly out of a group of players who had gathered. He then sprinted madly for the end zone, with all watching stupefied.

The official judgment, from referee Walter Eckersall, was that he had not blown his whistle to stop the play and that Colonel Mumma, the field judge, had ruled that forward progress had not been stopped. The touchdown was upheld while Ryan, the Wisconsin bench and the UW fans went into a "mass seizure," as accounts described it.

Eckersall needed an escort of Wisconsin players to leave the field safely and over the following days, in his other role as the *Chicago Tribune*'s football writer, defended his decision again and again.

Wisconsin Time Line

1924: Congress granted citizenship to all American Indians.

The UW basketball team tied for the Big Ten championship with an 8-4 mark. Coach Walter Meanwell's Badgers were 11-5 overall, with the rare tie a triple-overtime 25-25 deadlock at home against DePauw.

WISCONSIN HEADLINER

Martin P. "Marty" Below
Football

No less an authority than Red Grange said that Marty Below "was the greatest lineman I ever played against." It was high praise indeed for the Oshkosh native, who had been a football and basketball star and captain at Oshkosh High School. He served with the U.S. Marine Corps in World War I and then enrolled at Oshkosh State Teachers College, where he played on championship football and basketball teams. Below transferred to Wisconsin in 1922 and promptly became a first-team all-Big Ten pick in 1922 and 1923 on Badger teams that went 7-5-2. In 1923, Below captained the Badgers and earned all-America honors as a lineman. He was named to the National Football Foundation Hall of Fame in 1988 and to the UW Athletic Hall of Fame in 1992.

LEADING THE WAY

Guy Lowman
Baseball, Basketball and Football Coach

It was only fitting that a three-sport winner in college should have become a three-sport coach. That was Guy Lowman's unique resume at Wisconsin, where he served variously as coach of the baseball, basketball and football teams as well as director of the professional course in physical education from 1917-43. Lowman, a native of Griswold, Iowa, attended Iowa State Teachers, Drake University and the Springfield (Mass.) School of Physical Education. Prior to his arrival in Madison in 1917, Lowman made basketball, baseball and football coaching stops from 1906 at Warrensburg (Missouri) Normal, Missouri, Alabama and Indiana. He coached the UW football team to a 3-3 season in 1918; the Badger basketball teams of 1918-20, winning the Big Ten title in 1920; and Wisconsin baseball teams in 1918 and again from 1921-32, capturing the Conference championship in 1930. Lowman directed the department of physical education for 26 years until his death in Madison at age 66 in 1943. The varsity baseball field on Walnut Avenue near Lake Mendota was named in his honor in 1952.

LEADING THE WAY

Edward H. Templin
Wrestling

Ed Templin was one of Wisconsin's first wrestling stars, winning major "W" awards in 1921, 1922 and 1923. The Baraboo native wrestled as a middleweight for the Badgers, placing second in the 1922 Big Ten meet at 158 lbs. and also taking runner-up honors in 1923 at 175 lbs. He served as the Badgers' team captain as a senior. Templin was inducted into the UW Athletic Hall of Fame in 1995.

Gage become first "SID"

Les Gage became the first sports information director, commonly called the "SID," at Wisconsin in 1923 and served six years as publicist for Badger teams. Gage, along with contemporaries Mike Tobin of Illinois, Jim Hassleman of Michigan State, Eric Wilson at Iowa and Walter Paulison at Northwestern, was one of the pioneers in a profession that has become an integral element of intercollegiate athletics.

1924-25

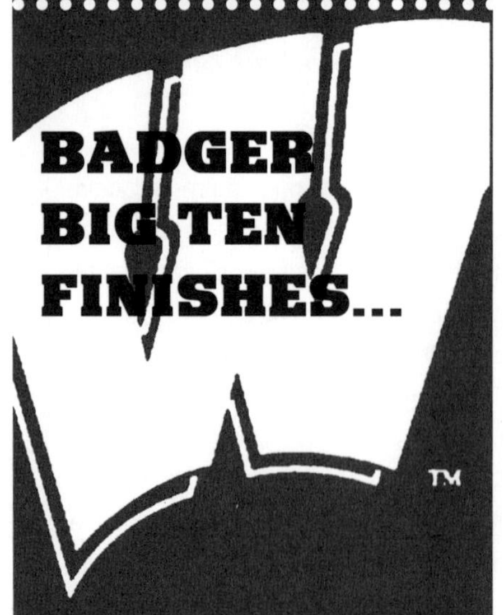

Football: 10th
coached by Jack Ryan

Cross Country: 1st
coached by Meade Burke

Basketball: 9th
coached by Walter Meanwell

Indoor Track: 2nd
coached by Thomas Jones

Swimming: 2nd
coached by Joe Steinauer

Wrestling: 3rd
coached by George Hitchcock

Baseball: 8th
coached by Guy Lowman

Golf: 5th
(no coach)

Outdoor Track: 2nd
coached by Thomas Jones

First Midwest football broadcast: Wisconsin vs. Michigan

It was a year of firsts for Big Ten football, and Wisconsin played a prominent role in one of them. The Badgers lost 21-0 at Michigan in the first college football game broadcast in the Midwest. WWJ Radio's Ty Tyson and Doc Holland called the action at Michigan Stadium.

In that same year, the *Chicago Tribune* began presenting its "Silver Football" award to the football player voted the Big Ten's most valuable player by coaches and media. Red Grange of Illinois was the first winner. It's an award still given today.

Wisconsin Time Line

1925: Tennessee biology teacher John Scopes was arrested for teaching the theory of evolution in violation of a state statute.

It was a year of contrast for the Badgers, with three of the "major" sports, football, baseball and basketball, finishing 10th, eighth and ninth, respectively, in the Big Ten. The other big sport, track, was second both indoors and outdoors while cross country (second), swimming (second) and wrestling (third) upheld UW honor.

1925-26

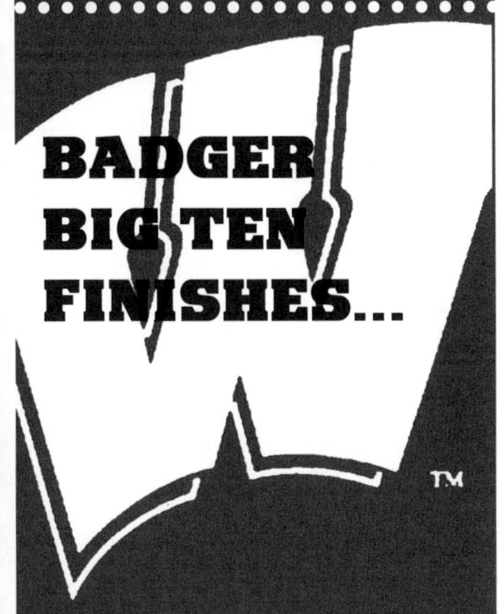

Football: 2nd (tie)
coached by George Little

Cross Country: 1st
coached by Meade Burke

Basketball: 8th (tie)
coached by Walter Meanwell

Indoor Track: 3rd
coached by Thomas Jones

Swimming: 3rd
coached by Joe Steinauer

Wrestling: 3rd
coached by George Hitchcock

Baseball: 2nd
coached by Guy Lowman

Golf: 5th
coached by Joe Steinauer

Outdoor Track: 5th
coached by Thomas Jones

Badgers win Big Ten cross country title

Led by Victor Chapman, Wisconsin won its second straight Big Ten cross country championship at Ann Arbor, Michigan. It was the Badgers' seventh Conference title. Chapman covered the five-mile course in 26:12 to become the UW's seventh individual champion.

Coach Tom Jones's team scored 39 points to Ohio State's 75 and Illinois's 78. Chapman was awarded the Bill Goldie Trophy as Wisconsin's most valuable runner.

Wisconsin Time Line

1926: The National Broadcasting Company made its debut as a radio network of 24 stations.

The first Big Ten championships in fencing, gymnastics and wrestling were held at Purdue.

Wisconsin played its first international game in ice hockey, losing 7-0 to the University of Manitoba.

WISCONSIN HEADLINER

Charles McGinnis
Track and Field

Charles McGinnis, who enrolled at Wisconsin out of Kansas City, Missouri, won six Big Ten titles during his three-year Badger career. McGinnis claimed the Conference high jump title at 6'2" as a sophomore and then in 1926 earned all-American honors in the event, placing sixth in the NCAA meet. The next two seasons would be his best, however, as McGinnis won the 60-yard high hurdles (7.6 seconds), the high jump (6'5") and the pole vault (12'9") as Wisconsin won its first Big Ten indoor track title in 1927. Outdoors, it was more of the same as McGinnis captured wins in the 120-yard high hurdles (15.2 seconds) and in the pole vault (13'3"). He capped his career with a bronze medal in the 1928 Olympics in Paris by clearing 12'11" in the pole vault. McGinnis was inducted into the UW Athletic Hall of Fame in 1993.

LEADING THE WAY

George E. Little
Football Coach
Athletic Director

In seven years as director of athletics at Wisconsin, George E. Little proved a doer and a builder. In 1925, Little took over a UW football team that had won only one of 12 Big Ten games over the three previous seasons and transformed Wisconsin into a winner. Only a loss to Michigan and tie with Minnesota marred the '25 season, when the Badgers finished 6-1-1 and ended second in the Big Ten. Little's two teams were 11-3-2. After the '26 season Little devoted full-time to his director's duties and began upgrading Wisconsin's facilities.The Wisconsin Fieldhouse was built during his tenure. Additional thousands of seats were added to Camp Randall Stadium. Practice fields for various sports were developed and intramurals became an important part of the UW's physical activity program. Little left Wisconsin in 1932 to become athletic director at Rutgers. He was later named to the National College Football Hall of Fame.

Wisconsin's Men's Conference Medal of Honor winners

1920
Anthony G. Zulfer

1921
Allan C. Davey

1922
George Bunge

1923
Gustave K. Tebell

1924
Harold J. Bentson

1925
Lloyd Vallely

1926
Stephen H. Pulaski

1927
Jefferson DeMent Burrus

1928
Louis Behr

1929
Theodore A. Thelander

Badgers, Hawks in "Snow Bowl"

The modern-era "Ice Bowl" game in Green Bay between the Packers and Dallas Cowboys in 1967, was pre-dated by Wisconsin and Iowa in 1925 in a "snow bowl" of sorts in Madison. The Badgers won the early November game, 6-0, but the most interesting statistic was the 34 fumbles, 18 in the first quarter alone. The teams had an excuse: blowing snow obliterated the sidelines and every yardline marker.

1926-27

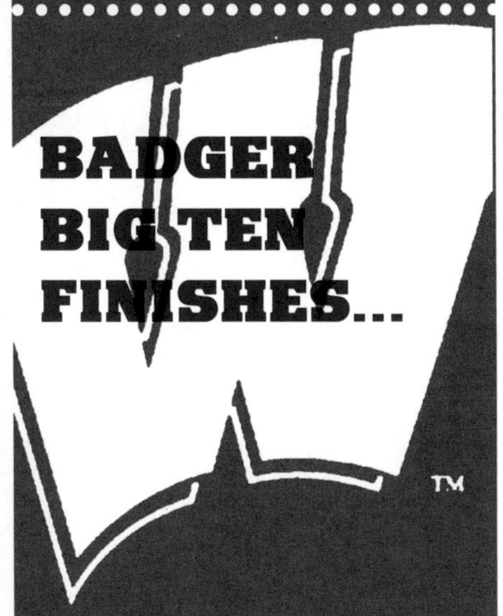

Football: 5th
coached by George Little

Cross Country: 1st
coached by Thomas Jones

Basketball: 4th (tie)
coached by Walter Meanwell

Indoor Track: 1st
coached by Thomas Jones

Swimming: 4th
coached by Joe Steinauer

Baseball: 7th
coached by Guy Lowman

Golf: 5th
coached by George Levis

Gymnastics: 2nd
coached by Arpad Masley

Outdoor Track: 3rd
coached by Thomas Jones

Wisconsin wins harrier crown again

Coach Tom Jones's Badger harriers won the third in a string of four straight Big Ten Conference cross country championships in 1926.

Running at Minneapolis, Wisconsin scored 34 points to easily outdistance Ohio State (63) and Iowa (65). Defending champion Victor Chapman of Wisconsin lost his title to Iowa's Jock Hunn, but his fourth-place effort still paced the Badgers to their eighth overall Conference triumph.

Wisconsin Time Line

1927: Charles Lindbergh reached Paris in his monoplane, the Spirit of St. Louis, completing the first solo trans-Atlantic flight.

The Conference ruled that athletes should not engage in athletic writing nor use their names for commercial advertising.

WISCONSIN HEADLINER

Rolland Barnum
Football, Basketball, Baseball

Rolland Barnum, a native of Evansville, Wisconsin, was a nine-time letterwinner for the Badgers in football, basketball and baseball from 1924-27. A fullback and punter in football and a catcher and outfielder in baseball, Barnum most distinguished himself in basketball. He was an all-Big Ten choice at guard in 1926 and captained the 1926-27 Badger cagers. Following college, he played basketball as one of the original Oshkosh All-Stars and also played semi-pro baseball with the Madison Blues. He officiated both Big Ten basketball and football, the latter for 21 years, during which Barnum officiated the 1958 College All-Star Game and the 1952 Rose Bowl. A member of the Madison Pen and Mike Club-Bowman Sports Foundation Hall of Fame, Barnum was named a charter member of the UW Athletic Hall of Fame in 1991.

McGinnis a winner on track and in field

Charles McGinnis became the first Wisconsin track and field athlete to win Big Ten Conference championships in the same meet on both the track and in the field. McGinnis won the 60-yard high hurdles in 7.6 seconds in the indoor meet at Evanston and also claimed titles in the high jump (6'5") and pole vault (12'9"), leading Tom Jones's team to the championship. McGinnis just about repeated the feat in the outdoor championships in Madison, with the Badgers finishing third in the team battle. He won the 120-yard high hurdles in 15.2 and tied for the pole vault title at 13'3". The UW accomplishment would not be equaled until 1994 when freshman Reggie Torian won the 55-meter high hurdles and the long jump in the Conference indoor meet at Ann Arbor.

Wisconsin swimming coaches

In the 87-year history of men's swimming at Wisconsin, only seven men have served as coach. Two—Joe Steinauer and Jack Pettinger—coached Badger swimmers for 56 seasons.

They are:

1911-13
Chauncey Hyatt

1913-19
Harry Hindman

1919-51
Joe Steinauer

1951-69
John Hickman

1969-93
Jack Pettinger

1993-94
John Davey

1994-present
Nick Hansen

Kratz wins NCAA swimming title

Winston Kratz became Wisconsin's first NCAA swimming champion in 1927, winning the 200-yard breaststroke in 2:46.3 in the third national collegiate swim meet. He also was named the Badgers' first swimming all-American. Kratz also won the now-discontinued event in 2:43.3 in the Big Ten meet that year for Coach Joe Steinauer's team, which placed a distant fourth. Kratz is a member of the Wisconsin swimming program's Hall of Fame. Fred Westphal, who won the 50-freestyle in 1959, is the only other Badger male to have won an NCAA swim title.

1927-28

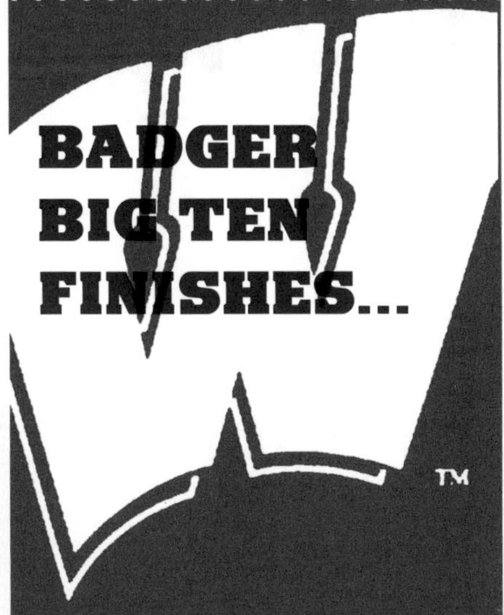

Football: 9th (tie)
coached by
Glenn Thistlethwaite

Cross Country: 1st
coached by Thomas Jones

Basketball: 3rd (tie)
coached by Walter Meanwell

Indoor Track: 3rd (tie)
coached by Thomas Jones

Wrestling: 2nd
coached by George Hitchcock,
(5th, NCAA)

Baseball: 3rd
coached by Guy Lowman

Gymnastics: 2nd
coached by Arpad Masley

Outdoor Track: 6th
coached by Thomas Jones

UW wins in Big Ten cross country

It truly was a golden era for Wisconsin cross country teams. Coach Tom Jones's Badgers pulled off the "four-peat" in 1927, scoring 51 points in the Big Ten meet at Ann Arbor for their fourth consecutive Conference victory.

John Zola, who ran 24:57 for the five-mile course, became Wisconsin's eighth individual Conference titlist. It was the tightest of the UW's four victories from 1924-27; Illinois was close behind with 57 points.

Wisconsin Time Line

1928: The first respirator, or iron lung, was used at a Boston hospital.

Construction began on the Wisconsin Field House.

Wisconsin was 10-7-2 in hockey, its only 10-win season of the pre-modern era.

1928-29

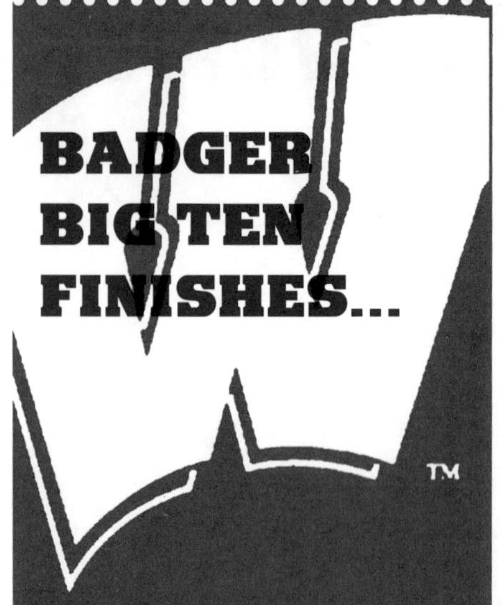

Football: 2nd
coached by
Glenn Thistlethwaite

Cross Country: 4th
coached by Thomas Jones

Basketball: 1st (tie)
coached by Walter Meanwell

Indoor Track: 3rd
coached by Thomas Jones

Swimming: 4th
coached by Joe Steinauer

Wrestling: 4th
coached by George Hitchcock

Baseball: 3rd
coached by Guy Lowman

Golf: 5th
coached by George Levis

Gymnastics: 3rd
coached by Arpad Masley

Outdoor Track: 7th
coached by Thomas Jones

Badgers post first 10-win season in ice hockey

Coach John Farquhar's Badger hockey team recorded its first 10-win season, going 11-7-2 despite a season-ending four-game winless string. It marked a sharp turnaround from the UW's initial season in 1921-22, when the Badgers were 0-8, and from the next six seasons, when the UW only had one winning campaign.

Wisconsin opened the season with a 1-1 tie against Houghton School of Mines (to become future WCHA rival Michigan Tech) and then rattled off five straight wins over the Marquette (Michigan) Owls, the Wausau Hockey Club, the Chicago Athletic Assn. and the North Dakota Aggies (twice).

The Badgers didn't fare as well against Big Ten and Western Intercollegiate Hockey League (WIHL) foes Michigan and Minnesota. The UW was 1-2-1 against the Wolverines and 1-3 against the Gophers. Farquhar had a 21-20-7 record in his three seasons as coach.

WISCONSIN TIME LINE

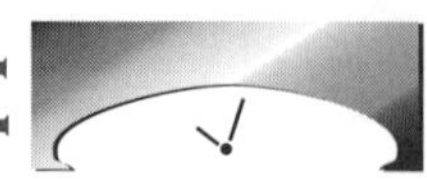

1929: Pluto was discovered by astronomer Clyde Tombaugh as he worked in the Lowell Observatory in Flagstaff, Arizona.

The University of Iowa was suspended from Conference membership due to infractions of an athletic nature.

WISCONSIN HEADLINER

Lloyd Larson
Football, Baseball

A later generation may have known Lloyd Larson as "Mr. Wisconsin," the long-time sports editor of the *Milwaukee Sentinel*, where he spent 50 years chronicling pro and college sports and five times was named Wisconsin "Sports Writer of the Year." But his time as a Badger came well before his induction into the UW Athletic Hall of Fame in 1993. Larson enrolled at the UW out of Milwaukee South Division High School, where he was an all-city quarterback. He won "W" awards in football in 1924 and 1925 and in baseball in 1925, 1926 and 1927, captaining the latter team. Larson also became a Big Ten football and basketball official and officiated the 1951 Rose Bowl game. Always an active participant in things related to the UW, Larson served as president of the National W Club (1959) and was named that group's "Man of the Year" in 1974. He also served as 1962-63 president of the Wisconsin Alumni Association, from which he received the Distinguished Service award in 1967.

LEADING THE WAY

Glenn Thistlewaite
Football Coach

One of Wisconsin's top coaches in the 1920s was football coach Glenn Thistlewaite. His .611 winning percentage in his five seasons as Badger mentor still ranks him eighth on the all-time UW list. His five seasons in Madison produced a 26-16-3 record, including a 7-1-1 mark and runner-up finish in the Big Ten (3-1-1) in 1928. All-Americans he coached at Wisconsin included tackle Rube Wagner, tackle Milo Lubratovich and guard Greg Kabat. Thistlewaite came to Madison after five years at Northwestern (23-16-1), where he guided the Wildcats to two Big Ten titles. Prior to that, he had spent nine years at Oak Park (Illinois) High School, where he compiled a 78-9 record. Thistlewaite was a 1908 graduate of Earlham (Indiana) College, where he captained the football team, played baseball and competed in track. He began his coaching career with a one-year stint at Illinois College before returning to Earlham, where his teams went 22-7-1 in four seasons before Thistlewaite left for Oak Park.

UW Football All-Americans
(first team)

1912
Robert Butler
1913
Ray Keeler
1914
Arlie Mucks
1915
Howard Buck
1919
Charles Carpenter
Paul Meyers
1920
George Bunge
Ralph Scott
Frank Weston
1921
George Bunge
1923
Marty Below
1930
Milo Lubratovich
1938
Howard Weiss
1941
Dave Schreiner
1942
Marlin Harder
Dave Schreiner
1944
Earl Girard
1950
Ed Withers
1951
Harold Faverty
Pat O'Donahue
1952
Dave Suminski
Don Voss
1953-54
Alan Ameche
1959
Dan Lamphear
1961-62
Pat Richter
1975
Dennis Lick
1979
Ray Snell
1981
Tim Krumrie
1984
Richard Johnson
1987
Paul Gruber
1991
Troy Vincent
1994
Cory Raymer
1996
Tarek Saleh

Sprachen ze English?

Multilingualism is not something generally associated with football, but there was a new twist to the announcing in the season-ending Wisconsin-Minnesota game on November 24, 1928, in Madison. The UW announcer called the game in five languages—Norwegian, Swedish, German, Yiddish and Chinese—and, presumably, English. A 19-19 tie with Purdue and a 6-0 loss to the Gophers were the only blemishes on Wisconsin's 7-1-1 season. In any language, the loss was still a loss.

1929-30

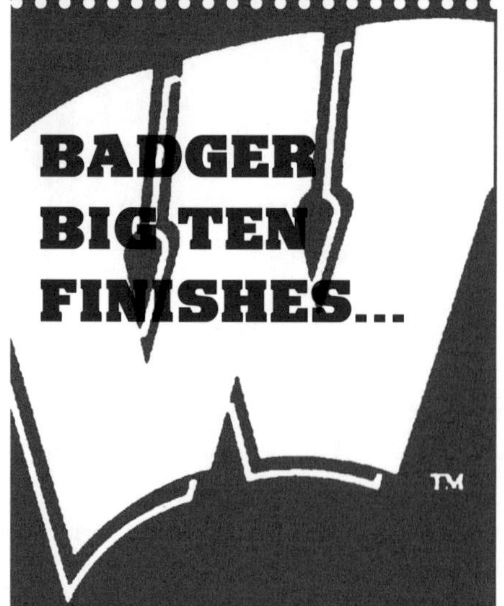

BADGER BIG TEN FINISHES...

Football: 10th
coached by
Glenn Thistlethwaite

Cross Country: 2nd
coached by Thomas Jones

Basketball: 2nd
coached by Walter Meanwell

Indoor Track: 1st
coached by Thomas Jones

Swimming: 5th
coached by Joe Steinauer

Baseball: 1st
coached by Guy Lowman

Golf: 5th
coached by George Levis

Outdoor Track: 3rd
coached by Thomas Jones

Badger nine wins Big Ten title; trackmen take indoor crown

The stock market had crashed in October, 1929, but Wisconsin fortunes in two sports rose in 1930. Coach Guy Lowman's Badgers won their first Big Ten baseball championship in 18 years in 1930, posting a 9-1 Big Ten mark to edge Illinois by a game.

It was the third title ever for the UW. Pacing the UW were Moe Winer, the shortstop and team captain, and pitchers Nello Pacetti and Art Sommerfield.

In track, another Tom Jones-coached team won its second Conference indoor track championship in four seasons, scoring 21 points in the meet at Minneapolis to hold off Illinois (18) and Indiana (17).

Three Badgers won their events: Bill Henke in the 440-yard dash in 51.1; Sammy Behr in the shot put with a throw of 46'1"; and Ted Shaw in the high jump with a leap of 6'1".

Wisconsin Time Line

1930: American novelist Sinclair Lewis won the Nobel prize in literature.

Iowa resumed its membership in the Conference.

The Wisconsin Field House was dedicated on December 18 as the Badger cagers defeat Penn 25-12.

WISCONSIN HEADLINER

John F. (Bobby) Poser Baseball, Basketball

Bobby Poser was a two-sport star for Wisconsin in the early 1930s, earning "W" awards in baseball (1930-31) and basketball (1931-33). The Columbus, Wisconsin, native earned both bachelor's and medical degrees from Wisconsin. As a pitcher and outfielder on the 1930 Big Ten Championship team, Poser hit .391 to lead the team in hitting en route to all-Conference honors. He captained the basketball team as a senior in 1932-33. Following graduation, he coached the 1935 and 1936 Wisconsin baseball team and also pitched for the Chicago White Sox and the St. Louis Browns. In 1933, while playing for Des Moines, Poser had nine RBIs to set a single game Western Minor League record. He also served as president of the National "W" Club in 1957-58. Poser was inducted into the UW Athletics Hall of Fame in 1996.

Behr throws to three titles

Sammy Behr claimed a place among Wisconsin's great shot putters with his performances in 1929, 1930 and 1931, becoming the first UW weightman to win three Big Ten titles in the event. Not even the legendary Arlie Mucks, Sr., a two-time Olympian in the discus, won three shot titles. Behr claimed his first win indoors in '29, putting the shot 45'7 1/2", followed in 1930 with a 46'1" throw and then ended his indoor career with a 48'9" heave in '31. He also won outdoor titles in Big Ten meets in 1929 and 1930. Not until Jeff Braun won four Conference shot titles from 1976-79 would a Badger match the feat.

Track and Field Olympians

1904 Emil Breikreutz, 800 meters
George Poage, 400-meter hurdles
Frank Waller, 400 meters

1912 Arlie Mucks, Sr., discus

1916 Arlie Mucks, Sr., discus

1920 Arlie Schardt, 3,000-meter relay

1928 Charles McGinnis, pole vault

1948 Don Gehrmann, 1500 meters
Tom Jones, coach
Lloyd LaBeach, 100 & 200

1964 Charles "Rut" Walter, coach

1972 Mike Manley, steeplechase

1980 Steve Lacy, 1500 meters

1984 Steve Lacy, 1500 meters
Cindy Bremser, 1500 meters

1992 Suzy Favor Hamilton, 1500 meters

1996 Suzy Favor Hamilton, 800 meters
Kathy Butler, 5,000 meters
Maxwell Seales, 4x400 relay

All were on the United States team except LaBeach (Panama), Butler (Canada) and Seales (St. Lucia).

Wisconsin's Fencing Coaches

1911
Dr. Walter E. Meanwell

1912-17
H.D. MacChesney

1920-26
Fred Schlatter

1927-51
Arpad L. Masley

1952-72
Archie Simonson

1973-90
Tony Gillham

1990-91
Jerzy Radz

1930-31

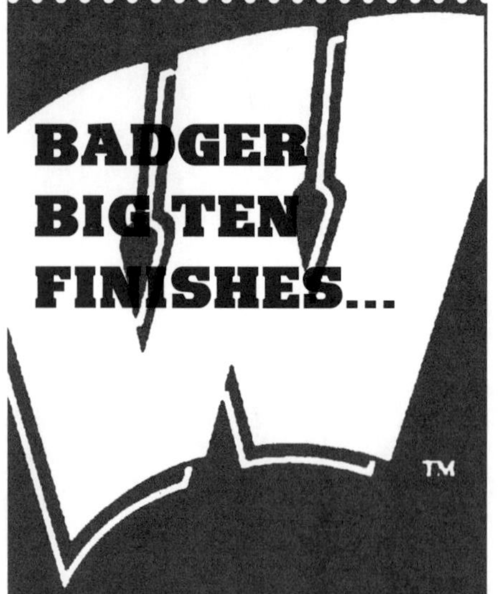

Football: 4th (tie)
coached by
Glenn Thistlethwaite

Cross Country: 2nd
coached by Thomas Jones

Basketball: 7th (tie)
coached by Walter Meanwell

Indoor Track: 4th
coached by Thomas Jones

Baseball: 5th (tie)
coached by Guy Lowman

Golf: 5th
coached by George Levis

Gymnastics: 2nd
coached by Arpad Masley

Outdoor Track: 1st
coached by Thomas Jones,
(6th, NCAA)

UW Field House opens

Discussions of replacing the antiquated Red Gym on Langdon Street began several years before the UW Field House actually opened in 1930. It was not, however, until athletics director George Little, who came to Wisconsin from the University of Michigan in 1925, made upgrading the UW's athletic facilities a top priority that discussions became reality.

By 1927, Little, who served for two years as the Badger football coach, produced a detailed master plan for the general renewal of several facilities, including what would become the UW Field House.

Critics, who felt the proposed facility's seating capacity in excess of 8,000 was far too large, tabbed the project "Little's Folly." Nonetheless, state architect Arthur Peabody, along with Paul Cret of the Laird and Cret firm,moved forward with their design, which reflected the strong influences of Lathrop Hall, another UW project created by Laird and Cret with Peabody's assistance some 20 years earlier.

Groundbreaking for the project, located at the open end of the Camp Randall horseshoe, took place on September 26, 1929, and the official building dedication occurred a little more than a year later when the Badger basketball team defeated Pennsylvania 25-12 on December 18, 1930, in front of a sellout crowd of 8,600.

The Field House, one of the last buildings constructed before the stock market crash of 1929, cost $453,756, with $51,000 to be repaid by the Division of Intercollegiate Athletics through revenues and private gifts over the following 10 years. The UW had established a facility that was comparable in merit to any of its kind in the country.

Wisconsin Time Line

1931: "The Star Spangled Banner" became the national anthem.

Coach Glen Thistlewaite's Wisconsin football team posted a 6-2-1 record, winning all six of its games at home, four by shutouts, but tied Ohio State and lost to Purdue and Northwestern on the road.

1931-32

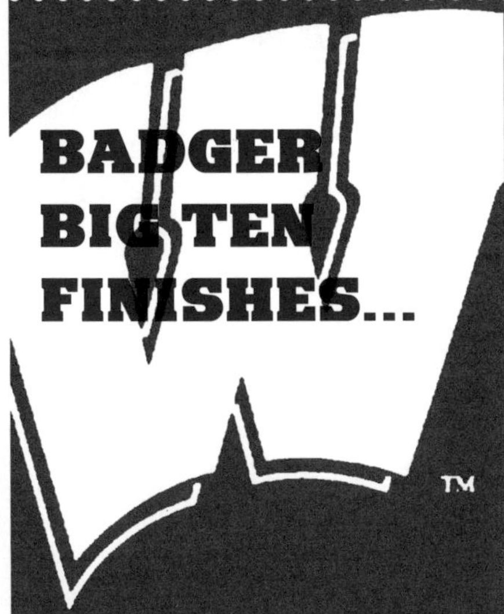

Football: 6th
coached by
Glenn Thistlethwaite

Cross Country: 2nd
coached by Thomas Jones

Basketball: 8th (tie)
coached by Walter Meanwell

Indoor Track: 5th
coached by Thomas Jones

Baseball: 3rd (tie)
coached by Guy Lowman

Golf: 7th
coached by Joe Steinauer

Outdoor Track: 7th
coached by Thomas Jones

Badgers struggle through so-so seasons

No Badger teams won Big Ten championships during the 1931-32 campaign. Wisconsin finished 5-4-1, 3-3 in the Conference, in football coach Glenn Thistlewaite's last year at the reins while Tom Jones's harriers placed second to Indiana, which was in the middle of a six-year championship run.

The Badger cagers didn't fare any better, chalking up an 8-10 overall mark and 3-9 Big Ten eighth-place finish. The UW golfers finished seventh in the Conference tourney while the baseball Badgers tied for third in the Big Ten with a 6-4 slate.

In the 1932 track meets, Wisconsin finished fifth indoors and dropped to seventh in the Big Ten after winning the Conference the previous season. High jumper Robert Murphy was the Badgers' sole indoor champ while teammate Ted Shaw claimed the outdoor high jump crown for the UW's only win.

Wisconsin Time Line

1932: The Summer Olympics opened in Los Angeles.

Art Thomsen took over as Wisconsin hockey coach and led the team until the 1935 season.

1932-33

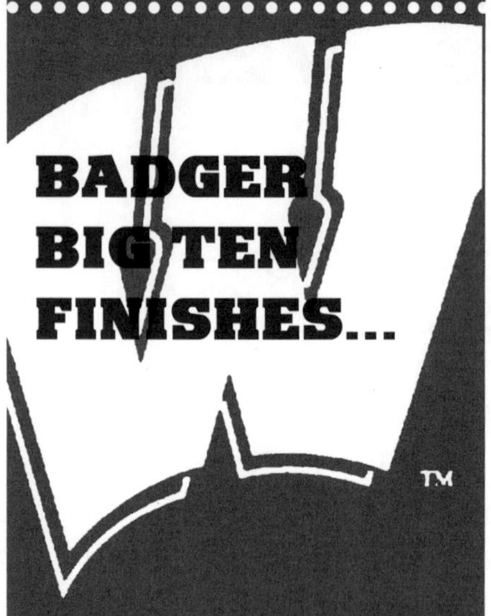

Football: 3rd
coached by Clarence Spears

Cross Country: 5th
coached by Thomas Jones

Basketball: 8th
coached by Walter Meanwell

Indoor Track: 6th (tie)
coached by Thomas Jones

Swimming: 7th
coached by Joe Steinauer

Baseball: 7th
coached by Irv Uteritz

Golf: 5th
coached by Joe Steinauer

Outdoor Track: 8th
coached by Thomas Jones

Wisconsin begins boxing program

Over the course of its 28-year history, the NCAA boxing scene was dominated by Wisconsin, with a 134-28-18 overall dual mark, eight NCAA team titles and 38 individual championships.

Two men deserve most of the credit for this splendid record. They were George F. Downer, athletic publicity director at the UW until his death in 1941, and John J. Walsh, a Madison attorney, who coached the team for 23 years.

Downer is known as the "father" of intercollegiate boxing at Wisconsin. He was the first to see the possibilities of boxing as a successful intercollegiate sport at the UW and he turned his vision into reality by organizing the first university team in 1933.

Downer's first team fought its first match with St. Thomas College of St. Paul, Minn. in Madison on March 21, 1933. Walsh was the St. Thomas coach and one of the members of that team that battled the Badgers to a 4-4 draw. The impression Walsh made on Downer that day was such that, through the latter's efforts, Walsh was hired as Wisconsin's coach in 1934.

The George F. Downer Award became the most coveted honor a Wisconsin boxer could attain. It was presented to the boxer coming closest, in the coach's estimation, to Downer's ideals of a champion, including scholarship, sportsmanship, boxing ability and competitive spirit.

Wisconsin Time Line

1933: The first motion picture drive-in opened in Camden, New Jersey.

Because of the Great Depression, hockey is dropped as an intercollegiate sport, but the Badgers continued to play until 1935.

WISCONSIN HEADLINER

Walter F. (Mickey) McGuire
Football

Walter F. (Mickey) McGuire lettered for Wisconsin football teams of the early 1930s that posted a 17-7-3 record from 1930-32, including third place in the Big Ten and a 6-1-1 overall mark in 1932, McGuire's senior season. The Honolulu native, who had a stellar prep career at Honolulu High School, led the 1932 Badgers with 36 points and scored all three Wisconsin touchdowns in the UW's 20-13 win over Minnesota. He was also named the Big Ten's most valuable player and was the top punter in the Conference with a 43.0 average. After graduation, McGuire went on to a noteworthy career in business, athletics and government. For 30 years, he was managing director of the Hula Bowl and past president and director of Honolulu Stadium. McGuire also served as managing director of the 1979 NFL Pro Bowl Game. He served five terms in the Territorial House of Representatives and was a special assistant to the president of United Airlines. He was inducted into the UW Athletics Hall of Fame in 1996.

WISCONSIN HEADLINER

Milo Lubratovich
Football

Three-time letterwinner Milo Lubratrovich starred at tackle for the Badgers in 1930, earning all-America honors two years after he broke his leg as a sophomore in a game against Alabama. By his senior season, Lubratovich had rebounded nicely. He had become a consensus all-America end and played in the annual East-West Game. He received all-America mention from 10 different authorities, including the Newspaper Enterprise Association, United Press and Hearst. Lubratovich played professional baseball in the Brooklyn Dodger organization from 1931-35.

WISCONSIN HEADLINER

Gregory Kabat
Football, Track and Field

Gregory Kabat was an all-Big Ten lineman for Wisconsin football teams that compiled a 17-7-3 record from 1930-32. He also served as the Badgers' captain in his senior season. The Milwaukee native earned major "W" awards three times in football and twice in track. He won the discus throw at the 1931 Big Ten outdoor track and field championships with a throw of 150'10 1/2" and also earned all-America honors that year in the event. Kabat was inducted into the UW Athletic Hall of Fame in 1995.

WISCONSIN HEADLINER

Ted Shaw
Track and Field

Two-time Big Ten high jump champion Ted Shaw was a mainstay of Coach Tom Jones Wisconsin track teams of the early 1930s. The native of River Forest, Illinois, who prepped at Elgin Academy where he starred in football and track, held the national high school record in his specialty during his junior and senior years. As a UW sophomore in 1930, Shaw set a national record of 6'6 3/16". A three-time "W" award-winner, he was the Wisconsin track captain in 1932 and later that year competed in the U.S. Olympic trials in Los Angeles.

1933-34

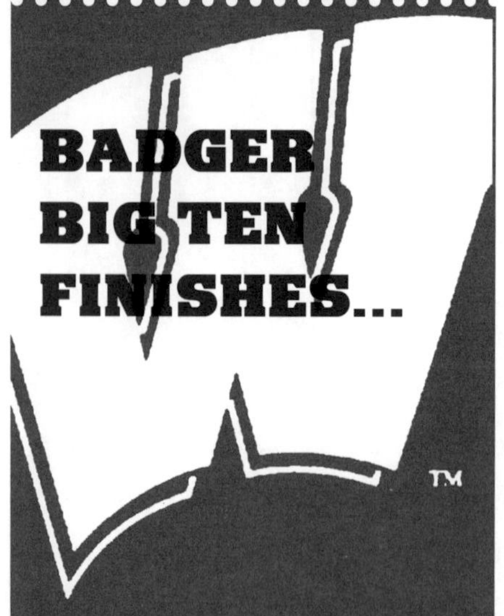

Football: 8th (tie)
coached by Clarence Spears

Cross Country: 2nd
coached by Thomas Jones

Basketball: 2nd (tie)
coached by Walter Meanwell

Indoor Track: 9th
coached by Thomas Jones

Baseball: 3rd (tie)
coached by Irv Uteritz

Golf: 9th
coached by Joe Steinauer

Tennis: 6th (tie)
coached by Arpad Masley

Outdoor Track: 5th (tie)
coached by Thomas Jones

Badgers rebound to second in Big Ten basketball

After three straight second division finishes in the Big Ten, Wisconsin's 1933-34 basketball team posted a 14-6 overall record and 8-4 Big Ten mark, good for second in the Conference. The season marked the end of Walter Meanwell's basketball coaching career at the UW, a tenure that had begun with the 1911-12 season and been continuous save for his three-year absence during World War I.

The Badgers, who had ended the 1932-33 campaign with nine losses in its final 10 games, did an about-face to start the next campaign. Wisconsin won its first five games in December, slumped with losses at Marquette, Illinois and Iowa right after the first of the year, but then won seven of its last eight.

That finish set the table for the Badgers' return to the top of the Big Ten the following season as co-champs under Meanwell's successor, Harold "Bud" Foster. Rolf Poser paced the Badgers, earning the first of his two all-Big Ten mentions.

WISCONSIN TIME LINE

1934: Elzire Dionne gave birth to quintuplets in a farmhouse near Callander, Ontario.

Harold "Bud" Foster took over as men's basketball coach.

Wisconsin placed ninth in the Big Ten indoor track meet, its worst finish to date under Coach Tom Jones, but the Badgers rebounded to take fifth outdoors.

1934-35

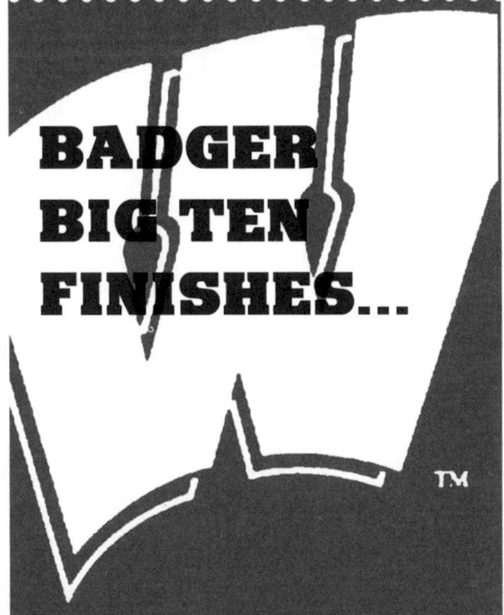

Football: 5th (tie)
coached by Clarence Spears

Cross Country: 1st (tie)
coached by Thomas Jones

Basketball: 1st (tie)
coached by Harold Foster

Indoor Track: 3rd
coached by Thomas Jones

Swimming: 7th
coached by Joe Steinauer

Wrestling: 8th
coached by Paul Gerling

Baseball: 6th
coached by Robert Poser

Golf: 4th
coached by Joe Steinauer

Tennis: 8th
coached by Arpad Masley

Outdoor Track: 3rd
coached by Thomas Jones

Men's basketball shares Big Ten title

Wisconsin's 1934-35 men's basketball team was long on experienced players—in fact, the entire team returned from the previous season's squad—but short on experienced coaching. In fact, it was to be Bud Foster's first season guiding the Badgers, for whom he was an all-American in 1930.

With veterans such as Rolf "Chub" Poser, Gilly McDonald, Nick DeMark, Ed Stege, Bob Knake, Pete Preboski and Ray Hamann, Wisconsin was met with high expectations as the season began.

After losing a practice game to the school's freshman squad, the Badgers began the season with four straight wins before dropping back-to-back outings against Marquette and Pittsburgh. A win over Michigan State (not yet a Big Ten member) concluded the non-conference portion of the season.

The Conference campaign began with a 19-18 loss to Purdue. Wisconsin rebounded, however, with a stellar defensive effort in a 12-9 win over then-Conference favorite Northwestern. Two more wins followed before the Wildcats got their revenge with a 36-31 victory over the Badgers. That loss left Wisconsin with a 3-2 mark in league play.

Wisconsin, however, went on to win six of its final seven games, including a 37-27 overtime thriller over Indiana at the UW Field House. The Badgers finished the season tied with Illinois and Purdue for the Big Ten title. Poser and McDonald were named all-Big Ten.

Wisconsin Time Line

1935: The first automatic parking meters were installed in Oklahoma City.

The Big Ten adopted regulations governing broadcasting rights to home games.

The Badgers won the Big Ten basketball title with a 15-5 record under new head coach "Bud" Foster.

1935-36

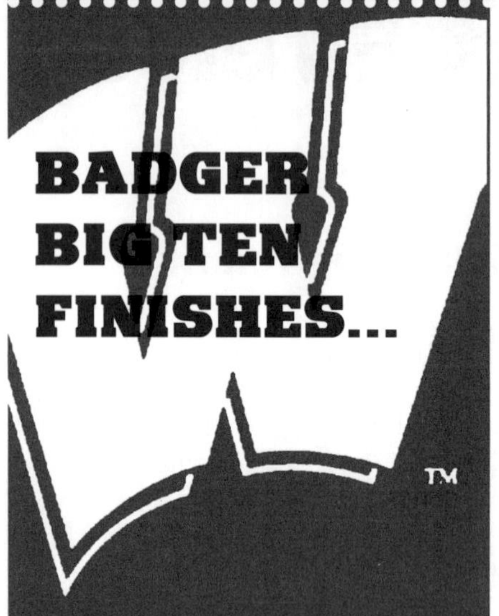

Football: 9th (tie)
coached by Clarence Spears

Cross Country: 3rd
coached by Thomas Jones

Basketball: 8th
coached by Harold Foster

Indoor Track: 2nd
coached by Thomas Jones

Baseball: 7th
coached by Robert Poser

Golf: 5th
coached by Joe Steinauer

Tennis: 4th
coached by William Kaeser

Outdoor Track: 4th
coached by Thomas Jones, (6th, NCAA)

Harry Stuhldreher hired as football coach

After four seasons under Clarence Spears during which Wisconsin football fortunes had declined from a 6-1-1 mark to a 1-7 ninth-place Conference finish, Harry Stuhldreher was hired to resuscitate the UW program starting with the 1935 season.

As one of Notre Dame's famed "Four Horsemen," Stuhldreher had a name that resonated gridiron glory. In 13 years at the Badger helm, he never won a Big Ten title, but he restored some respect to the Wisconsin program. His best team, the 1942 unit, had an 8-1-1 record and finished second in the Conference at 4-1.

Three other Stuhldreher-coached teams posted winning records and his 45 career victories are fifth highest in Wisconsin football annals. Three of his players at Wisconsin—end Dave Schreiner (1941-42), fullback Marlin "Pat" Harder (1942) and quarterback Earl "Jug" Girard (1944)—earned first-team all-American honors.

Wisconsin Time Line

1936: Jesse Owens won four gold medals in the Olympic Games in Berlin.

The Conference voted to accept a resolution by the University of Wisconsin that its faculty considers itself in control of athletic affairs.

Chuck Fenske won the NCAA 1500-meter run in the NCAA track meet, beginning a legacy of Badger excellence in the 1500 and mile.

WISCONSIN HEADLINER

John Gerlach
Baseball

"Good field, good hit." That was John Gerlach, who starred at shortstop for Wisconsin baseball teams of the late 1930s. The Shullsburg, Wisconsin, native won three "W" awards in 1936, 1937 and 1938 and served as captain of the Badger nine his junior and senior seasons. His errorless play at shortstop was a key to the team's success; the Badgers were 44-27 in his three varsity years, with third-place Big Ten finishes in the latter two seasons. But Gerlach's hitting was no less remarkable as he batted .415 in 1936 and .320 in 1938. Gerlach saw action in the major leagues with the Chicago White Sox in 1938 and 1939. He served as a major with a pilot-troop carrier command group in World War II. Gerlach was named to the Madison Sports Hall of Fame in 1972 and inducted into the UW Athletic Hall of Fame in 1994.

WISCONSIN HEADLINER

Rolf "Chub" Poser
Basketball, Baseball

Two-time all-Big Ten guard Rolf Poser enrolled at the Madison campus out of Columbus, Wisconsin, in 1932 and eventually earned three major "W" awards each in basketball and baseball. Nicknamed "Chub," he served as captain of the 1933-34 cagers who placed second in the Big Ten. He was also captain and leading scorer on the 1934-35 unit that tied for the Big Ten title. Poser was named all-Conference for his junior and senior seasons and also was an All-Western pick at guard in 1934-35. He was the 1935 Wisconsin recipient of the Big Ten Medal of Honor for proficiency in scholarship and athletics. Poser was inducted into the UW Athletic Hall of Fame in 1993.

WISCONSIN HEADLINER

Edward "Eddie" Jankowski
Football

Edward "Eddie" Jankowski was a standout fullback and linebacker on three Wisconsin teams of the mid-1930s. The Milwaukee native, out of Riverside High School, was the Badgers' MVP in 1935-36. He played in the East-West Shrine Game of 1936 and in the 1937 College All-Star Game. A first-round selection of the Green Bay Packers in the 1937 National Football League draft, Jankowski went on to a stellar professional career and eventually was named to the Packers' Hall of Fame. He was inducted into the UW Athletic Hall of Fame in 1992.

WISCONSIN HEADLINER

Robert Fadner
Boxing

Wisconsin boxer Bob Fadner made history with his NCAA title in 1936. The 125-lber. was the first winner in that particular weight class in the 1936 championship tournament at Charlottesville, Virginia. More important, however, is his place in Wisconsin boxing annals as the first of an NCAA-record 38 men who would win national collegiate finals bouts for the Badgers. Since the NCAA discontinued the sport after the 1960 championships, Wisconsin's hold on that record is secure.

1936-37

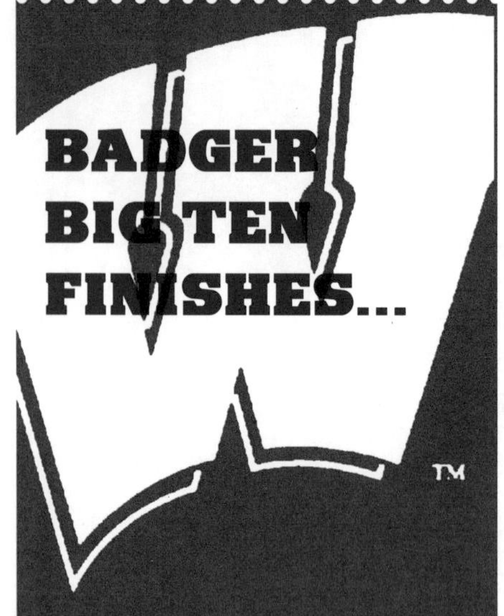

Football: 8th (tie)
coached by Harry Stuhldreher

Cross Country: 1st (tie)
coached by Thomas Jones

Basketball: 8th (tie)
coached by Harold Foster

Indoor Track: 3rd
coached by Thomas Jones

Swimming: 8th
coached by Joe Steinauer

Baseball: 3rd (tie)
coached by Lowell Douglas

Golf: 4th
coached by Joe Steinauer

Tennis: 4th (tie)
coached by William Kaeser

Outdoor Track: 5th
coached by Thomas Jones,
(10th, NCAA)

Fenske wins NCAA mile run championship

Chuck Fenske, Wisconsin's "Monarch of the Mile," lived up to that nickname as he became the school's first NCAA champion on the track in 1937. He won the mile run in 4:13.9 in the national collegiate meet at Berkeley, California.

It was the second NCAA individual track and field title for the UW since the meet's inception in 1921; pole vaulter Lloyd Wilder tied for the victory in that first-ever meet. Fenske was a three-time Big Ten mile champion and at one time held world records in the 1,000-yard run (2:09.3) and three-quarter mile run (2:59.7).

Wisconsin Time Line

1937: The Golden Gate Bridge across San Francisco Bay was opened.

Pole vaulter Al Haller successfully defended his Big Ten indoor and outdoor champion ships and became the Badgers' only four-time Conference pole vault champ.

1937-38

Football: 4th (tie)
coached by Harry Stuhldreher

Cross Country: 2nd
coached by Thomas Jones

Basketball: 7th
coached by Harold Foster

Indoor Track: 2nd
coached by Thomas Jones

Swimming: 7th
coached by Joe Steinauer

Wrestling: 4th
coached by George Martin

Baseball: 3rd (tie)
coached by Lowell Douglas

Golf: 6th
coached by Joe Steinauer

Tennis: 7th
coached by Roy Black

Outdoor Track: 2nd
coached by Thomas Jones,
(4th, NCAA)

Badgers place third in Big Ten indoor and outdoor track meets

Four champions in both the indoor and outdoor Big Ten track and field championships propelled the Badgers to second-place finishes behind Michigan. Only once before (1927) had Wisconsin had as many as four champs and only in 1913 had the Badgers won five events.

Earning Conference titles in the indoor meet at Chicago were Chuck Fenske, a double winner in the 880-yard run (1:55.4) and mile (4:11.1); Walter Mehl in the two-mile run at 9:18.3; and pole vaulter Milt Padway at 13'4". Michigan won the meet with 32 1/3 points followed by Coach Tom Jones's Badgers (26) and Iowa (20 1/3).

Outdoors, four champions were again the order of the day for Wisconsin in the meet at Columbus, Ohio. The same foursome reprised their indoor victories, with Fenske at 1:52.9 in the 880 and 4:10.9 in the mile; Mehl at 9:10.4 in the two mile; and Padway at 13'8" in tying for the pole vault crown. Wisconsin's 37 points placed it well behind Michigan's 61 but were enough to edge Ohio State (31).

Wisconsin Time Line

1938: Cincinnati Reds left-hander Johnny Vander Meer became the only major leaguer to pitch successive no-hit, no-run games.

The Big Ten affirmed a ruling that the football season end the last Thursday before Thanksgiving Day.

WISCONSIN HEADLINER

Charles H. Fenske
Track and Field,
Cross Country

Wisconsin had its own "king," at least in track and field, prior to World War II. Chuck Fenske, known as the "Monarch of the Mile," was three-time Big Ten mile champion from 1936-38 and the NCAA outdoor titlist in the event in 1937. He also held world records in the 1000-yard run (2:09.3) and the three-quarter mile run (2:59.7). Fenske also set an indoor mile record of 4:07.4 in the famed Wanamaker Mile. He captain the Badgers' cross country and track teams in 1937-38, his senior season, and won the Big Ten Conference Medal of Honor that year. Fenske was named "Miler of the Year" in 1940 after he went unbeaten in eight prestigious races against the best runners in the world. Named to halls of fame at the Drake Relays, the State of Wisconsin and the Pen and Mike Club-Bowman Sports Foundation, Fenske was a charter member of the UW Athletic Hall of Fame in 1991.

WISCONSIN HEADLINER

Howard Weiss
Football

A three-sport star in high school at Fort Atkinson in football, basketball and golf, fullback Howard Weiss earned all-Big Ten and all-America recognition in 1938 as well as Big Ten MVP honors. To top it off, he also was class president and twice the Badgers' most valuable player. An outstanding runner, effective and effective blocker, Weiss played linebacker on defense. To this day, his 40-yard run at Northwestern in 1938 ranks as one of the greatest in Badger annals. He played in the East West Shrine Game in 1938 and the College All-Star Game in 1939. Picked by the Detroit Lions in the 1939 NFL draft, Weiss played two seasons in the professional ranks. He was one of 35 charter members named to the UW Athletic Hall of Fame in 1991.

Wisconsin's Men's Conference Medal of Honor winners

1930
Donald W. Mieklejohn

1931
Louis E. Oberdeck

1932
Harvey H. Schneider

1933
Nello Anthony Pacetti

1934
Robert A. Schiller

1935
Rolf Falk Poser

1936
Howard Thurston Heun

1937
Leonard L. Lovshin

1938
Charles H. Fenske

1939
Walter I. Bietila

Badgers post best NCAA track finish

Wisonsin placed fourth in the NCAA outdoor track and field championships, its best finish ever under Coach Tom Jones and a standing that would not be equaled until 59 years later. Leading the Badgers were champion Walter Mehl (5,000-meter run) and all-Americans Milt Padway (second, pole vault) and Chuck Fenske (fourth, 800 meters, and third, 1,500 meters).

1938-39

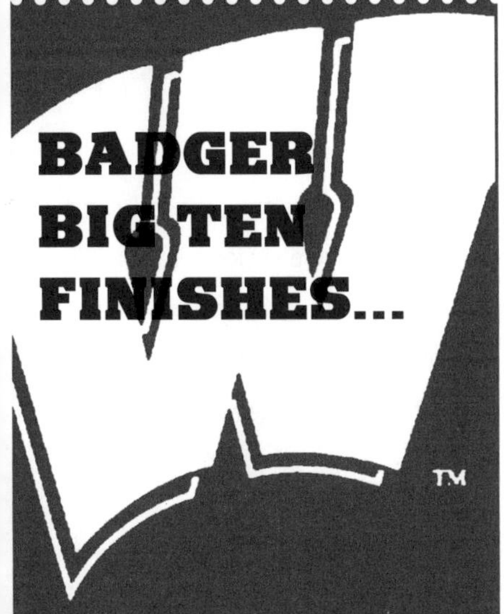

Football: 6th
coached by Harry Stuhldreher

Cross Country: 2nd
coached by Thomas Jones

Basketball: 7th
coached by Harold Foster

Indoor Track: 2nd
coached by Thomas Jones

Swimming: 5th
coached by Joe Steinauer

Baseball: 6th (tie)
coached by Lowell Douglas

Golf: 9th
coached by Joe Steinauer

Tennis: 7th
coached by Roy Black

Outdoor Track: 2nd
coached by Thomas Jones,
(5th, NCAA)

Boxers win Wisconsin's first NCAA team title

Just six years after Wisconsin established a varsity boxing program, it had its first national collegiate championship in the sport. It marked also the first official NCAA title won by any Wisconsin team.

The Badgers of Coach John Walsh had been building momentum toward a team title. They had gone unbeaten and untied in 1935, but the first NCAA championships were not held until 1937 at the University of California at Davis. After another unbeaten and untied season in 1938, but no NCAA title, the third boxing tournament in 1939 proved the magic one for Walsh and his team. The Badgers were ready, winning four championships.

Gene Rankin at 135 lbs., Omar Crocker at 145, Woodrow Swancutt at 155 and Truman Torgerson at 175 all won titles, giving the Badgers 25 points and the team championship. Rankin would go on to become a three-time champ while Swancutt would successfully defend his title in 1940.

WISCONSIN TIME LINE

1939: Lou Gehrig called himself "the luckiest man on the face of the Earth" in his farewell speech at Yankee Stadium.

William R. Reed was hired to establish the Big Ten Service Bureau as the "Modern Era" of Conference competition began.

WISCONSIN HEADLINER

Woodrow P. "Woodie" Swancutt Boxing

The "Fightin'est Fighter" in the 1938 All-University Tournament, Woodrow P. "Woodie" Swancutt was a two-time NCAA champion for the great Badger boxing teams of the late 1930s and early 1940s. Born in 1915 in Edgar, Wisconsin, Swancutt prepped at both Stevens Point and LaCrosse high schools before enrolling at the UW. He won the 1939 national collegiate 155-lb. title as the Badgers won the team championship. Swancutt successfully defended his title in 1940 but enlisted in the Air Force in 1941, passing up his final year of eligibility when due to enter medical school. He was inducted into the UW Athletic Hall of Fame in 1992.

Var-sity! Var-sity!

The traditional arm-waving at the end of the song, "Varsity," came from the University of Pennsylvania, where students waved their caps after losing a game. In 1934, UW band leader Ray Dvorak instructed students to salute UW President Glenn Frank after each game. It led to one of the most famous college alma maters.

The words:

Var-sity! Var-sity!
U-rah-rah! Wisconsin!
Praise to thee we sing
Praise to thee our Alma Mater
U-rah-rah, Wisconsin!
Our Team is RED HOT!

Wrestling coaches' records

Coach (Seasons)	Years	Record
E.R. Finley (1911-12)	2	0-0-2
E.B. Nolte (1913)	1	1-0-0
Fred Schlatter (1914-15)	2	3-0-1
Art Knott (1916-17)	2	1-5-0
Joe Steinauer (1919-20)	2	2-2-0
George Hitchcock (1921-33)	13	28-37-1
Paul Gerling (1934-35)	2	1-14-0
George Martin (1936-42, 46-70)	32	181-166-12
John Roberts (1943)	1	4-2-0
Frank Jordan (1944-45)	2	1-5-1
Duane Kleven (1971-82)	12	132-46-5
Russ Hellickson (1983-86)	4	70-22-1
Andy Rein (1987-93)	7	69-35-3
Barry Davis (1994-Present)	5	40-45-3

Badgers make first West Coast trip

Wisconsin's football team made its first trip to the West Coast in 1938, bringing national recognition to Harry Stuhldreher's third team. The Badgers, ranked 15th nationally after winning four of their first six games, defeated UCLA 14-7. The UW ended its season 5-3 after losing 21-0 at home to Minnesota in the season finale. Pacing the Badgers was first-team all-American halfback Howard Weiss, the Big Ten's most valuable player.

1939-40

Football: 9th (tie)
coached by Harry Stuhldreher

Cross Country: 1st
coached by Thomas Jones

Basketball: 9th
coached by Harold Foster

Indoor Track: 3rd
coached by Thomas Jones

Wrestling: 7th
coached by George Martin

Baseball: 6th
coached by Art Mansfield

Golf: 6th
coached by Joe Steinauer

Tennis: 7th
coached by Roy Black

Outdoor Track: 3rd
coached by Thomas Jones

Badgers win Big Ten cross country

Wisconsin won the 1939 Big Ten cross country championship, its first since its four straight victories from 1924-27. Indiana had won six consecutive crowns from 1928-32 and in 1938. No meets were held from 1933-37. Wisconsin scored a low 28 points to upend the defending champion Hoosiers at Chicago.

Walter Mehl, who went on to win the NCAA title later that fall, won his only Big Ten harrier race in 20:34.7 over the four-mile course. The Badgers' 28-point score, almost 60 years later, still stands eighth on the Conference's list of all-time lowest winning scores.

Wisconsin Time Line

1940: The United States began its first peacetime draft lottery.

The Big Ten voted to permit nine football games per season, six Conference games to be required and at least two at each home institution.

Wisconsin won its only NCAA basketball championship as John Kotz is named tournament MVP.

WISCONSIN HEADLINER

Walter J. "Wally" Mehl
Cross Country, Track

That Walter J. "Wally" Mehl's name is legendary in track annals at Wisconsin, where many great milers have run over the decades, shows just how good this Wauwatosa native was. He competed for the Badgers from 1935-39, winning the 1939 NCAA and Big Ten cross country titles his senior season after taking second in both as a junior. He won the NCAA two-mile run in 1938 after taking indoor and outdoor Conference crowns in that event, but it was in the mile that Mehl really made his name. He won the Big Ten indoor and outdoor mile titles in 1939 and then, following his graduation, started winning miles with abandon. Mehl was the National AAU indoor champ in 1940 and then took its metric equivalent outdoors. He also won the Penn Relays special mile that year and took the win in the famed Wanamaker Mile in 1941. He later earned a Ph.D. in education from Wisconsin. A member of the Drake Relays Hall of Fame, Mehl was inducted into the UW Athletic Hall of Fame in 1992.

WISCONSIN HEADLINER

Omar Crocker
Boxing

Omar Crocker was called "the greatest of all the boxing representatives we ever had" by no less than legendary Badger boxing coach John Walsh. Crocker, a native of Norcross, Minnesota, came to Wisconsin in the late 1930s and proceeded to post a three-year collegiate mark of 22-1-1. He won the 1939 NCAA title at 145 lbs. and lost the 1940 national collegiate title at the same weight on a judge's error. He was the Contender's Tournament champion in 1936 at 135 lbs. Crocker also won all-university titles from 1938-40, the first at 135 lbs. and the latter two at 145 lbs. He won "W" awards in 1938, 1939 and 1940 and was inducted as a charter member of the UW Athletic Hall of Fame in 1991.

The List

First-round NFL & AFL draft choices from Wisconsin

1937 Ed Jankowski, Green Bay Packers

1941 George Paskvan, Green Bay Packers

1944 Pat Harder, Chicago Cardinals

1945 Elroy Hirsch, Cleveland Rams

1947 Don Kindt, Chicago Bears

1948 Earl Girard, Green Bay Packers

1955 Alan Ameche, Baltimore Colts

1960 Dale Hackbart, Minnesota (AFL); Jim Heinke, Dallas Texans (AFL); Bob Nelson, Dallas Texans (AFL); Jerry Stalcup, Minnesota (AFL); Bob Zeman, Los Angeles Chargers (AFL)

1963 Pat Richter, Denver Broncos (AFL)

1976 Dennis Lick, Chicago Bears

1980 Ray Snell, Tampa Bay Buccaneers

1985 Richard Johnson, Houston Oilers; Al Toon, New York Jets; Darryl Sims, Pittsburgh Steelers

1988 Paul Gruber, Tampa Bay Buccaneers

1992 Troy Vincent, Miami Dolphins

The List

Camp Randall coaching records

Thirteen of Wisconsin's 17 football coaches have posted winning records at Camp Randall.

Football Coach (years)	**Record**
William Juneau (1913-15)	9-4-1
Paul Withington (1916)	4-0-1
J.R. Richards (1917, 1920-22)	15-4-2
Guy Lowman (1918)	2-2
Jack Ryan (1923-24)	4-3-3
George Little (1925-26)	8-2
Glenn Thistlewaite (1927-31)	20-7-1
Clarence Spears (1932-35)	11-7
Harry Stuhldreher (1936-48)	29-31-4
Ivy Williamson (1949-55)	25-7-2
Milt Bruhn (1956-66)	33-20-4
John Coatta (1967-69)	3-13-1
John Jardine (1970-77)	27-19-2
Dave McClain (1978-85)	29-21-1
Jim Hilles (1986)	2-4
Don Morton (1987-89)	6-13
Barry Alvarez (1990-97)	29-17-3

1940-41

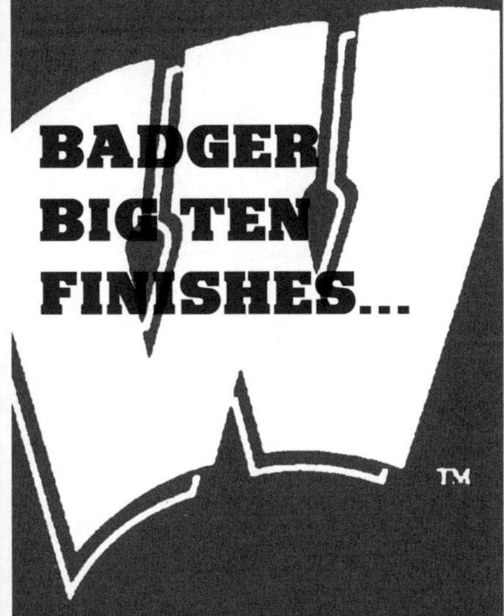

Football: 4th (tie)
coached by Harry Stuhldreher

Cross Country: 4th
coached by Thomas Jones

Basketball: 1st
coached by Harold Foster,
(1st, NCAA)

Indoor Track: 5th (tie)
coached by Thomas Jones

Swimming: 9th
coached by Joe Steinauer

Wrestling: 6th
coached by George Martin,
(tie for 5th, NCAA)

Baseball: 6th
coached by Art Mansfield

Golf: 5th
coached by Joe Steinauer

Tennis: 5th
coached by Carl Sanger

Outdoor Track: 5th
coached by Thomas Jones

Badgers win 1941 NCAA basketball title

Wisconsin won its first and only NCAA basketball championship, defeating Washington State 39-34. Coach Harold "Bud" Foster's team ended the season with 15 straight wins, including three in the NCAA tournament, to finish with a 20-3 record.

Leading the Badgers in the title game at Kansas City, Missouri, were Gene Englund with 13 points and tournament MVP John Kotz with 12. The Badgers trailed the Cougars 10-8 and 12-9 early in the game but a pair of baskets by Kotz gave Wisconsin a lead; the Badgers never again trailed and jumped to a six-point lead at 30-24 after WSU had tied the game.

Wisconsin's run to the title began in the NCAA East Regional at the UW Field House when it downed Dartmouth 51-50 in a game in which the lead changed hands five times. Englund and Kotz scored 18 and 15 points, respectively, to lead the UW.

In the regional title game, also at the Field House, the Badgers avenged a 36-34 home loss to Pittsburgh with a 36-30 victory. Although Pitt had a 23-18 lead early in the second period, an Englund basket and four points from Kotz put the Badgers up 24-23, a lead they never relinquished enroute to the NCAA championship game. Englund ended with 11 points and Kotz with 10.

Wisconsin Time Line

1941: The United States entered World War II one day after the Japanese bombing of Pearl Harbor.

The Conference permitted service teams to schedule a limited number of football and basketball games with Big Ten teams.

John Kotz was picked as the Big Ten's most valuable basketball player, marking the second straight season a Badger is so honored.

WISCONSIN HEADLINER

John Kotz
Basketball

Two-time all-American John Kotz was one of the stars in an era of Badger basketball excellence. The Rhinelander native, who had an outstanding prep career at Wisconsin Valley and led his team to the 1939 state title, continued his stellar play under Coach Bud Foster at Wisconsin. Only a sophomore when the Badgers won the 1941 NCAA basketball title, Kotz was named outstanding player in the championship game following a season in which he was named all-Big Ten. In 1942, Kotz led the Big Ten in scoring with a record 242 points over a 15-game schedule. He set a single game mark with 31 points against Iowa. His 841 point career total was then a UW record. Kotz was named a charter member of the UW Athletic Hall of Fame in 1991.

WISCONSIN HEADLINER

Gene Englund
Basketball

Kenosha native Gene Englund, the Big Ten's most valuable basketball player in 1941, led Bud Foster's Badgers to the conference title and the UW's only NCAA championship in the sport. Englund was named all-Big Ten and all-American at center after a season that saw him finish second in the Big Ten scoring race with a then-Wisconsin record 162 point (for conference games). He scored a career-high 27 points against Purdue that year enroute to a Badger single season scoring record of 304 points; in fact, he led Wisconsin in scoring in 15 of the team's 23 games that championship season. Englund scored 42 points in the three NCAA tournament games, including 18 in Wisconsin's 51-50 first-round victory over Dartmouth. Englund was a charter inductee into the UW Athletic Hall of Fame in 1991.

WISCONSIN HEADLINER

George Paskvan
Football; Track and Field

Fullback George Paskvan was a two-time all-Conference choice in 1939 and 1949 and both times was the Badgers' most valuable player. The LaGrange, Illinois native led the UW in rushing in 1939 with 459 yards and in scoring the following year with 30 points. His career rushing total was 1,029 yards. He was named to the second team Associated Press all-American team in 1939 and the United Press third team that season. Drafted by the Green Bay Packers in the first round of the 1941 NFL draft, Paskvan also played in the College All-Star game. He also won the shot-put in the 1941 Big Ten indoor track championships. Paskvan received the Harlan N. Rogers Scholarship awarded to the outstanding student-athlete in the study of the U. S. Constitution. Paskvan was inducted into the UW Athletic Hall of Fame in 1993.

LEADING THE WAY

Harold E. "Bud" Foster
Basketball

Twenty-five year basketball coach Harold E. "Bud" Foster remains a legend in the state as the only coach to guide a team to the NCAA championship. Foster's magic season came in 1940-41 as the Badgers won the Big Ten crown and then took the three-game NCAA tournament. But his playing and coaching careers were more than that one season. He was an all-Big Ten center in 1929 and 1930 for UW and then earned all-America honors in 1930. He also played professionally with the Oshkosh All-Stars. Foster became Wisconsin's freshman coach in 1933 and head coach the following season, where he remained for 25 years, leading Wisconsin to conference titles in 1935 and 1947 as well. His career mark was 265-267. He was a president of the basketball coaches association and also was named to numerous halls of fame, including Helms, the National Basketball Hall, the Wisconsin Sate Athletic Hall and the Madison Pen and Mike Bowman Sports Foundation Hall. Foster was a charter inductee into the UW Athletic Hall of Fame in 1991.

1941-42

Football: 5th
coached by Harry Stuhldreher

Cross Country: 5th
coached by Thomas Jones

Basketball: 2nd (tie)
coached by Harold Foster

Indoor Track: 5th
coached by Thomas Jones

Swimming: 8th
coached by Joe Steinauer

Wrestling: 6th
coached by George Martin

Baseball: 3rd
coached by Art Mansfield

Golf: 6th
coached by Joe Steinauer

Tennis: 8th
coached by Carl Sanger

Outdoor Track: 5th
coached by Thomas Jones

Badgers win another NCAA boxing crown

By the early 1940s, intercollegiate boxing was well into its golden era at Wisconsin. The 1942 Badgers won their second NCAA title and posted their fifth season without a loss or a tie. In the NCAA championships, four UW boxers again won titles for Coach John Walsh.

Gene Rankin won his third 135-lb. crown while Warren Jollymore (145), Cliff Lutz (155) and George Makris (175) also won their championship bouts. The Badgers would again win in 1943, with their five individual winners a mark that another Wisconsin team would equal in 1956.

Winning in '43 were Lutz at 145 lbs., Don Miller at 155, Myron Miller at 165, Makris at 175 and John Verdayne at heavyweight. The Wisconsin boxing teams of 1940-44 ran up a string of 24 consecutive victories and routinely drew large crowds for their matches at the Wisconsin Fieldhouse. Attendance records were set each of the six times Wisconsin hosted the tournament.

Wisconsin Time Line

1942: Glenn Miller's orchestra recorded its hit song "(I've Got a Gal in) Kalamazoo" at Victor Studios in Hollywood.

Certain rules were waived by the Big Ten because of war-time conditions, including inter-freshman team competition.

Wisconsin is named mythical national football champion by the Helms Foundation after its 8-1-1 season.

WISCONSIN HEADLINER

David N. Schreiner
Football

Twice an all-American, Lancaster, Wisconsin, native David N. Schreiner has been called by some one of the finest ends to ever play the game. His No. 80 has been retired by Wisconsin. An all-Big Ten and all-American choice in 1941 and 1942, Schreiner caught three touchdown passes in the second period of a 1942 game against Marquette as the Badgers won 35-7. He was the team's leading pass receiver in 1942 with 18 catches for 386 yards and five touchdowns. He was named both the Big Ten's and Wisconsin's most valuable player. Selected in the second round of the National Football League draft by the Detroit Lions, Schreiner also played in the 1943 East West Shrine Game. A member of the all-time Wisconsin football team and the Wisconsin State Hall of Fame, Shreiner was named to the charter class of the UW Athletic Hall of Fame in 1991. He died in service to his country in Okinawa in 1945. The David N. Schreiner Memorial Scholarship has been established in his memory.

WISCONSIN HEADLINER

Gene Rankin
Boxing

Gene Rankin remains the only boxer in NCAA history to win three NCAA championships in the same weight class, taking national collegiate titles for the Badgers at 135 pounds in 1939, 1941 and 1942. The '39 and '42 squads—the latter captained by Rankin—won NCAA team titles as well. Rankin, who was born in 1916 in Duluth, Minnesota, graduated from Superior Central High School. He won the 1937 National Diamond Belt title in 1937 in Boston before enrolling at Wisconsin to box under the soon-to-be-legendary John Walsh. Rankin's trademarks in the ring were his speed and finesse. He later saw service in the U.S. Navy during World War II. Rankin was inducted into the UW Athletic Hall of Fame in 1992.

WISCONSIN HEADLINER

John Roberts
Football; Wrestling

From his high school days at Valley High School in West Des Moines through his wrestling and football careers at Wisconsin, John Roberts excelled. A two-time Iowa state wrestling champ as a prep and a football all-stater, Roberts continued his winning ways in Madison. He earned "W" awards in both football and wrestling and was a member of the 1942 UW football team that went 8-1-1 en route to a third-place Big Ten finish and No. 3 national ranking. But it was in wrestling that Roberts made his mark, winning Big Ten titles in the 165-lb. weight class in 1941 and at 175 pounds a year later. He also was NCAA runner-up in 1941. Following graduation, Roberts coached the 1943 UW wrestling team and then embarked on a long career in high school athletics. He coached football at Stevens Point High School from 1946-51 and then at UW-Stevens Point from 1952-56. Roberts then served as executive director of the Wisconsin Interscholastic Athletic Association from 1957-85. He was inducted into the UW Athletic Hall of Fame in 1994.

LEADING THE WAY

Elroy "Crazylegs" Hirsch
Football, Director of Athletics

Elroy Hirsch was a triple-threat halfback for the 1942 Badgers, carried his talents to Michigan and then became one of the great wide receivers in National Football League history. He became the UW's athletic director in 1969 and over the next 18 years presided over an era of growth, change and success in Wisconsin sports. In 1942, he paced the Badgers to the brink of a national championship as they finished 8-1-1, second in the Big Ten and ranked third nationally. His No. 40 was retired by Wisconsin. He was the MVP in the 1946 College All-Star game and then went on to professional stardom with the Chicago Rockets of the old All-American Conference and later with the Los Angeles Rams. In 1951, he set a pro record of 1,495 yards on 66 receptions and 17 touchdown passes as the Rams won the NFL title. Hirsch was a charter member of the UW Athletics Hall of Fame and a member of the NFL All-Time All-Star team. But it's as an administrator that many alumni of the past 30 years remember him and as a tireless promoter of all things Wisconsin.

1942-43

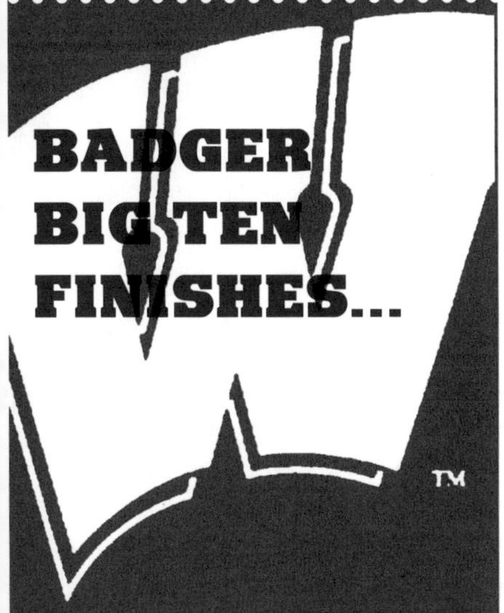

Football: 2nd
coached by Harry Stuhldreher

Cross Country: 5th
coached by Thomas Jones

Basketball: 4th (tie)
coached by Harold Foster

Indoor Track: 2nd
coached by Thomas Jones

Swimming: 7th
coached by Joe Steinauer

Wrestling: 9th
coached by John Roberts

Baseball: 2nd
coached by Art Mansfield

Golf: 6th
coached by Joe Steinauer

Tennis: 3rd
coached by Carl Sanger

Outdoor Track: 5th
coached by Thomas Jones

Badgers second in Big Ten football, ranked third nationally

Wisconsin's 1942 football team, coached by Harry Stuhldreher and featuring standouts Elroy "Crazylegs" Hirsch and Dave Schreiner, put together one of the best seasons in school history and was named mythical national champion by the Helms Foundation. The Badgers compiled an 8-1-1 overall record and No. 3 national ranking by the Associated Press.

Wisconsin started the season 6-0-1, the only blemish being a 7-7 tie with Notre Dame in the second game of the year. It was in that game that Hirsch earned his nickname when a local writer, commenting on a 60-yard touchdown run, said, "his crazy legs were gyrating."

Also included in the seven-game unbeaten string was the UW's first-ever win over a No. 1-ranked opponent. The Badgers toppled Coach Paul Brown's Ohio State Buckeyes 17-7 in the UW's homecoming game on October 31.

The following week, however, Wisconsin (after moving up to No. 2 in the Associated Press rankings) was upset 6-0 before a homecoming crowd at Iowa. That loss kept the Badgers from the Big Ten title and possibly the national championship. The UW concluded the season with victories over Northwestern and Minnesota to finish second in the Conference race.

Schreiner, an end, was named the Big Ten MVP and earned consensus first-team all-American acclaim. Fullback Marlin "Pat" Harder, along with Hirsch, also earned all-America mention.

Wisconsin Time Line

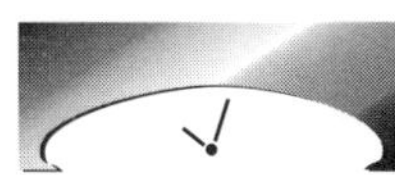

1943: American bombers staged the first air raid on Germany in World War II.

The Conference allowed freshmen to play on varsity teams for the duration of the war.

End Dave Schreiner and fullback Marlin "Pat" Harder become the first pair of Badgers since 1920 to earn all-America honors in the same season. Schreiner, honored for the second time, was the UW's first two-time All-American while Harder led the Big Ten in scoring.

WISCONSIN HEADLINER

Marlin "Pat" Harder
Football

One of the all-time Wisconsin football greats is Marlin "Pat" Harder, who starred on nationally ranked Badger teams as well for two National Football League champions. A Milwaukee native out of Washington High School, Harder led the Big Ten in rushing (590 yards) and scoring (58 points) as a sophomore in 1941. He was an all-American and all-Conference fullback on the Badgers' 1942 unit that was second in the Big Ten and ranked third nationally. In the 1943 College All-Star game, Harder was named MVP after scoring on a 37-yard pass play and a 33-yard run in the collegians' 27-7 win over the Washington Redskins. He played professionally with the Chicago Cardinals and Detroit Lions, leading the NFL in scoring in 1947 and 1948 and tying for scoring honors in 1949. Harder became an NFL official following his playing career. A member of the Wisconsin State Athletic Hall of Fame, Harder was a charter inductee into the UW Athletics Hall of Fame in 1991.

WISCONSIN HEADLINER

Frederick W. Negus
Football, Baseball

Fred Negus, a first-team all-Big Ten center for Wisconsin football teams in 1942 and 1946, also earned similar honors for Michigan in 1943. Like many servicemen during World War II, Negus attended Michigan for a year in conjunction with the Marine Corps' V-12 program; he also ran on the Wolverines' Big Ten title-winning mile relay team in 1944. The Martins Ferry, Ohio native starred immediately at Wisconsin and was named a member of the Associated Press sophomore All-American team in 1942. Following his service time, Negus returned to Madison and again earned all-Conference honors at center as well as the Badgers' MVP award. He was a member of the 1947 College All-Stars who defeated the Chicago Bears. After receiving his B.S. degree from Wisconsin, Negus played professionally with the Chicago Rockets of the All-America Football Conference from 1947-49 and with the NFL's Bears in 1950. He tied as AAFC record with a 97-yard fumble return for a touchdown in 1948. Recipient of the Fort Atkinson (WI) Chamber of Commerce Small Business Person Award in 1997, Negus was inducted into the UW Athletic Hall of Fame in 1998.

LEADING THE WAY

Harry Stuhldreher
Football Coach
Director of Athletics

All-American quarterback Harry Stuhldreher contributed to intercollegiate athletics as head football coach and director of athletics in his 15-year tenure at Wisconsin. A member of the famed Notre Dame "Four Horsemen", the native of Massillon, Ohio, earned all-American honors in 1923 and 1924 for the Fighting Irish. He then compiled a 65-25-10 record as head coach at Villanova before coming to Madison in 1936. As head football coach at the UW for 13 years, his record of 45-62-6 was not a winning one, but his philosophy as athletic director of "Athletics for All" was a winner as his leadership produced well-rounded development of all sports and facilities. His 1942 Badger team was second in the Big Ten (8-1-1) and ranked third nationally. He also coached the College All-Stars to a 27-7 win over the NFL champion Washington Redskins in 1943. He received the A.A. Stagg Award in 1965 for his contributions to college football. A member of the National Football Foundation Hall of Fame, Stuhldreher was inducted into the UW Athletic Hall of Fame in 1994.

Five Badgers win NCAA boxing titles

Winning its second straight NCAA boxing title—and third ever—to conclude the 1942-43 season was impressive enough for Wisconsin's dominant boxing team, but even more noteworthy than that were the individual achievements that made that championship possible. Five Badgers won NCAA crowns, a first in the sport's history and a record that would not be matched until another Wisconsin quintet turned the trick in 1956. Winning in 1943 for Coach John Walsh's team were Cliff Lutz at 145 lbs., Don Miller at 155, Myron Miller at 165, George Makris at 175 and John Verdayne at heavyweight. They were the second NCAA wins for Lutz and Makris.

1943-44

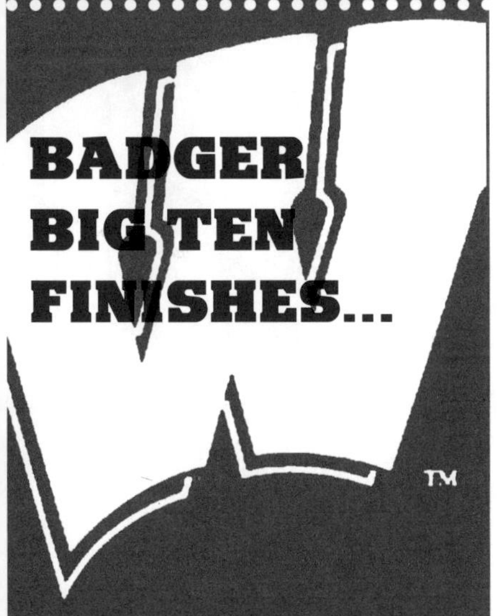

Football: 8th
coached by Harry Stuhldreher

Cross Country: 5th
coached by Thomas Jones

Basketball: 2nd (tie)
coached by Harold Foster

Indoor Track: 8th
coached by Thomas Jones

Swimming: 6th
coached by Joe Steinauer

Wrestling: 3rd
coached by Frank Jordan

Baseball: 7th
coached by Art Mansfield

Golf: 5th
coached by Joe Steinauer

Tennis: 6th
coached by Harold A. Taylor

Outdoor Track: 8th
coached by Thomas Jones

Athletes at war

The war that fathers of athletes of the 1940s had fought in a little more than a generation earlier unfortunately wasn't the last one that would affect American life and intercollegiate athletics.

The Big Ten and its member schools tried their best to maintain a semblance of normalcy in their programs but finally acknowledged the haphazardness of applying rules in a time of war.

Initially, the Conference removed eligibility restrictions on freshmen and then waived all eligibility rules for students in the military attending member institutions. Finally, all eligibility rules were discarded, save those requiring a student-athlete's regular enrollment and maintenance of amateur status.

One of the most famous Badgers of them all, Elroy "Crazylegs" Hirsch, would compete, and star, at Michigan between playing stints at Wisconsin because of wartime service. Another Badger star, NCAA champion boxer Cliff Lutz, would have his collegiate career split because of military service.

Most sports were affected in some way. No Big Ten gymnastics or fencing championships were held from 1943-46 and the league's golf tournament was shortened to 36 holes in 1944 and 1945.

Wisconsin Time Line

1944: D-Day: Allied forces began the invasion of Europe.

The University of Chicago announced its withdrawal from scheduling athletic championships for 1944-45.

Big Ten Commissioner John L. Griffith died.

WISCONSIN HEADLINER

Cliff Lutz
Boxing

One of only two three-time NCAA boxing champions in an era dominated by Wisconsin boxers, Cliff Lutz won his first national collegiate title in 1942 and his third five years later because of World War II. The Badgers, under legendary coach John Walsh, won the NCAA crown each of those three seasons. Lutz won at 155 pounds in 1942, dropped a class to 145 lbs. and won again in 1943 and then again in 1947 at the lighter weight. The Appleton native was the "Fightin'est Fighter" in the All-University Tournament in 1941 and 1942. Lutz was inducted into the UW Athletic Hall of Fame in 1993.

LEADING THE WAY

Arthur W. Mansfield
Football, Baseball;
Baseball Coach

The name of Arthur W. "Dynie" Mansfield is another that's synonymous with Wisconsin. The Cleveland, Ohio, native enrolled at the UW in 1925 and spent nearly all of the next 45 years on the Madison campus. A versatile athlete, Mansfield won major "W" awards in 1926 and 1928 and baseball letters from 1927-29. He was also the all-university heavyweight boxing champion in 1928 and 1929. He played baseball in the New York Giants organization and semi-pro football with the Madison Blues in the early 1930s before joining the Wisconsin physical education faculty in 1936. In 1940, Mansfield became the Badgers' baseball coach, a post he would hold through 1970, compiling a 441-339 record and Big Ten titles in 1946 and 1950. Mansfield also coached Wisconsin's 1947 and 1948 150-lb. football teams. Mansfield was a member of the 1956 U.S. Olympic baseball committee and was elected in 1970 to the American Association of Baseball Coaches Hall of Fame. He was inducted into the UW Athletic Hall of Fame in 1998.

UW baseball's .400 hitters

These Badgers hit .400 in Big Ten play:

1940-Bob Smith, .441
1942-John Kasper, .431
1944-Merlin Brinker, .455
1945-Jim Ackeret, .429
1949-Bob Shea, .410
1952-Harvey Kuenn, .444*
1963-64-Rick Reichardt, .471*
1965-Joe Romary, .400
1968-Geoff Baillie, .400
1970-Mike Johnson, .415
1973-Lee Bauman, .400
1973-Tom Shipley, .446
1974-Steve Bennett, .458
1975-Lee Bauman, .457
1975-Duane Gustavson, .408
1977-John Hnath, .409
1977-Randy Johnson, .406
1982-Joe Scime, .404
1983-Joe Scime, .426
1983-Mike Verkuilen, .419
1985-Joe Armentrout, .464

* led Big Ten

Wisconsin's NCAA boxing champions

1936: Robert Fadner, 125 lbs.
1939: Gene Rankin, 135 lbs.
1939: Omar Crocker, 145 lbs.
1939: Woodrow Swancutt, 155 lbs.
1939: Truman Torgerson, 175 lbs.
1940: Woodrow Swancutt, 155 lbs.
1940: Nick Lee, Hwt.
1941: Gene Rankin, 135 lbs.
1942: Gene Rankin, 135 lbs.
1942: Warren Jollymore, 145 lbs.
1942: Cliff Lutz, 155 lbs.
1942: George Makris, 175 lbs.
1943: Cliff Lutz, 145 lbs.
1943: Don Miller, 155 lbs.
1943: Myron Miller, 165 lbs.
1943: George Makris, 175 lbs.
1943: Verdayne John, Hwt.
1947: Cliff Lutz, 145 lbs.
1947: John Lendenski, 165 lbs.
1948: Donald Dickinson, 148 lbs.
1948: Steve Gremban, 148 lbs.
1948: Calvin Vernon, 176 lbs.
1948: Vito Parisi, Hwt.
1951: Dick Murphy, 155 lbs.
1951: Bob Ranck, Hwt.
1952: Bob Morgan, 147 lbs.
1952: Bob Ranck, Hwt.
1953: Pat Sreenan, 147 lbs.
1953: Ray Zale, 178 lbs.
1954: Bob Meath, 156 lbs.
1956: Dean Plemmons, 112 lbs.
1956: Dick Bartman, 139 lbs.
1956: Vince Ferguson, 156 lbs.
1956: Orville Pitts, 178 lbs.
1956: Truman Sturdevant, Hwt.
1959: Charles Mohr, 165 lbs.
1960: Brown McGhee, 132 lbs.
1960: Jerry Turner, 156 lbs

1944-45

Football: 7th
coached by Harry Stuhldreher

Cross Country: 1st
coached by Thomas Jones

Basketball: 6th (tie)
coached by Harold Foster

Indoor Track: 8th
coached by Thomas Jones

Swimming: 8th
coached by Joe Steinauer

Wrestling: 9th
coached by Frank Jordan

Baseball: 2nd
coached by Art Mansfield

Golf: 6th
coached by Joe Steinauer

Tennis: 5th (tie)
coached by Harold A. Taylor

Outdoor Track: 6th
coached by Thomas Jones

Big Ten cross country title goes to Wisconsin

Wisconsin hadn't won a Big Ten cross country championship in five years, almost unconscionably long given the UW tradition in the sport. But the 1944 meet at Chicago ended a three-year string of fifth-place finishes as the Badgers scored 44 points to Indiana's 52.

Bill Lawson claimed the individual win in 21:16 for the four-mile course. He was Wisconsin's 10th Big Ten champion and Coach Tom Jones's first winner since Walter Mehl led the UW to the '39 team title.

Wisconsin would go on to win the next two Big Ten meets and begin a run of six titles in seven years, with the top UW runner each of those years placing first, second or third.

Wisconsin Time Line

1945: President Franklin D. Roosevelt died; less than a month later, the war in Europe ended

Big Ten Conference faculty approved Kenneth L. (Tug) Wilson, Northwestern's Athletic Director, as commissioner

Wisconsin boxers lose their first match in the Field House to an Iowa Pre-Flight team, snapping a 57-match winning streak for the Badgers.

1945-46

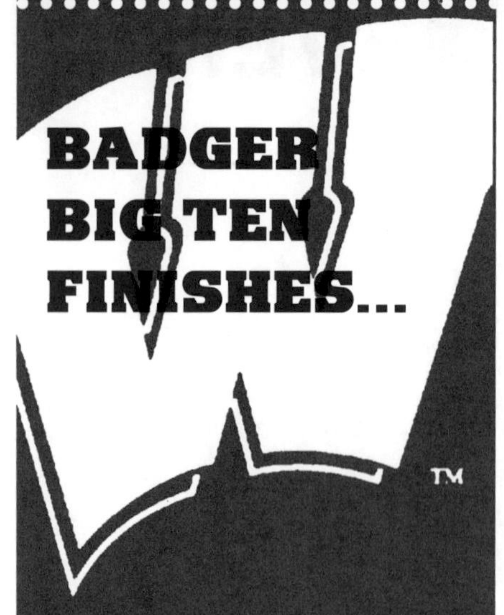

Football: 6th
coached by Harry Stuhldreher

Cross Country: 1st
coached by Thomas Jones

Basketball: 9th
coached by Harold Foster

Indoor Track: 3rd
coached by Thomas Jones

Swimming: 8th
coached by Joe Steinauer

Wrestling: 10th
coached by George Martin

Baseball: 1st
coached by Art Mansfield

Golf: 7th
coached by Joe Steinauer

Tennis: 8th
coached by Carl Sanger

Outdoor Track: 8th
coached by Thomas Jones, (5th, NCAA)

Badgers first in Big Ten baseball

Wisconsin returned to the top of the Big Ten baseball standings in 1946, posting a 9-2 record to take the title by 1-1/2 games over defending champion Michigan.

It was the UW's first Conference baseball championship since 1930. Coach Dynie Mansfield's team had set the stage for its climb to the top with an 8-4 campaign in 1945.

Four-time letterwinner Gene Jaroch, the Badgers' most valuable player, became the first pitcher in Big Ten history to win six games in a season.

Wisconsin Time Line

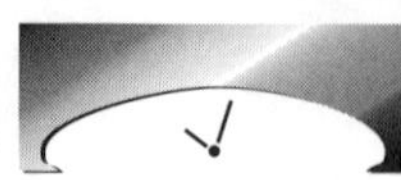

1946: The United States defeated Australia 5-0 in the Davis Cup, the worst defeat ever for a defending champion.

The University of Chicago formally withdrew from the Big Ten.

The Big Ten championship Badgers took third place in the NCAA basketball East Regional in New York.

1946-47

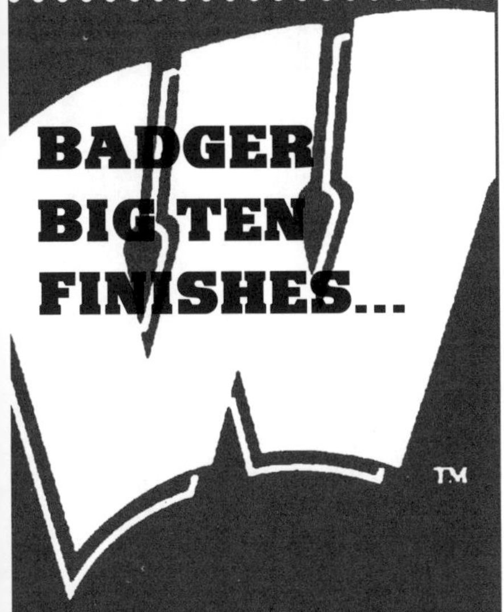

Football: 8th
coached by Harry Stuhldreher

Cross Country: 1st (tie)
coached by Thomas Jones

Basketball: 1st
coached by Harold Foster

Indoor Track: 4th
coached by Thomas Jones

Swimming: 7th
coached by Joe Steinauer

Wrestling: 7th
coached by George Martin

Baseball: 4th
coached by Art Mansfield

Golf: 7th
coached by Joe Steinauer

Tennis: 4th
coached by Carl Sanger

Outdoor Track: 4th
coached by Thomas Jones

Badger cagers climb from cellar to Big Ten title

Just a year earlier they were cellar-dwellars. Coach Bud Foster's Wisconsin men's basketball team went from a last-place finish in 1946 (4-17 overall, 1-11 in league play) to a 15-5 overall regular-season record and 9-3 Conference slate that was good for the 1947 Big Ten title and an invitation to the 1947 NCAA Tournament.

The Conference crown was Wisconsin's first since 1941 when Foster guided the Badgers to their first and only NCAA title. Paced by forward Bob Cook, the team's leading scorer, and guard Glen Selbo, the team and Big Ten MVP, Wisconsin remained in first place all season and led the league in scoring with 677 points behind 248 field goals and a then-Big Ten standard 181 free throws. Wisconsin also led the league in field goal percentage at 29.8 percent.

Cook scored 70 field goals and 47 free throws, while shooting 34.7 percent from the field. Cook and guards Walt Lautenbach, the team captain, and Selbo were first-team all-Big Ten selections.

The Badgers lost their first game in the NCAA East Regional in New York City, 70-56, to City College of New York before defeating Navy 50-49 in the consolation game.

Among the games the Badgers played in 1947 was a 54-42 win over Northwestern at Chicago Stadium on February 15. The crowd of 19,165 for that contest was the largest for the Badgers in a Big Ten game.

Wisconsin Time Line

1947: Auto pioneer Henry Ford died at age 83 in Dearborn, Michigan.

Wisconsin, Illinois, Michigan and Ohio State began 150-pound, intercollegiate football competition

Tom Jones's cross country team won its 15th Big Ten championship, and third straight, as freshman sensation Don Gehrmann took second in the four-mile race at Chicago.

WISCONSIN HEADLINER

Thomas C. Bennett
Football, Track and Field

Six-time letterwinner Tom Bennett starred for Wisconsin's football teams as a receiver and for Badger track squads as a pole vaulter. The Green Bay (West High School) native won "W" awards in football in 1946, 1947 and 1948 and track letters from 1947-49. He was the Badgers' top pass receiver on the '46 and '47 teams and also punted. He won four Big Ten titles in the pole vault from 1947-49 and in both his sophomore and senior seasons tied for the vault title at the Drake Relays. Bennett earned all-America honors in his specialty in 1949 with a second-place effort in the NCAA meet and was also voted "Senior Athlete of the Year" by student "W" Club members. Holder of bachelor's and master's degrees from the UW, Bennett then served as assistant track coach from 1951-69 and as varsity golf coach from 1970-77. In 1963, he authored "The Twentieth Century Track." The 1969-70 state games director for Wisconsin Special Olympics, Bennett was named "Mr. Olympics" in 1972 by Madison service clubs. Bennett was inducted into the UW Athletic Hall of Fame in 1998.

WISCONSIN HEADLINER

Robert "Bobby" Cook
Basketball, Baseball

Bobby Cook was a high-scoring forward and two-time all-Big ten selection for four Wisconsin basketball teams during and just after World War II. Cook, a native of Harvard, Illinois, just south of the state line, led the Big Ten in scoring in 1947, totaling 187 points in 12 games, after finishing fourth and sixth in Conference scoring the previous two seasons. He was the top scorer on the 1947 Badger five that won the Big Ten title and took third in the NCAA Eastern Regional. His 847 points in three seasons were then the most in UW history. Cook, who drained 8 of 11 field goal attempts in a 1948 game against Northwestern for a Big Ten record, was the Badgers' MVP in both 1946 and 1948. A standout third baseman,Cook starred on Wisconsin's 1946 Big Ten co-champions and earned major "W" awards three times in each of his sports. He later played professionally with the She-boygan Redskins. Cook was named to the UW Athletic Hall of Fame in 1992.

WISCONSIN HEADLINER

Glen Selbo
Basketball

Glen Selbo is one of only four Wisconsin basketball layers to win the Silver Basketball Award, presented by the Chicago Tribune to the Big Ten's top basketball player. Selbo, who lettered from 1944-47, led Coach Harold "Bud" Foster's team to a 16-6 overall record and the Big Ten title at 9-3. In the NCAA tournament—in Wisconsin's first appearance since its 1941 championship season—the Badgers lost 70-56 to City College of New York in the regional in New York City. The UW defeated Navy 50-49 in the third-place game. Selbo was named to the all-Big Ten team, of course, and was joined on that honor squad by teammates Bob Cook and Walt Lautenbach.

UW wins its fourth NCAA boxing championship

Wisconsin scored 24 points to earn its fourth NCAA boxing championship in 1947. Leading Coach John Walsh's Badgers, and hardly missing a beat since his return from World War II service, was Cliff Lutz, who won his third title and his second at 145 lbs., following his initial win in 1942 at 155 lbs. Also claiming an individual championship for the Badgers was John Lendenski at 165 lbs.

1947-48

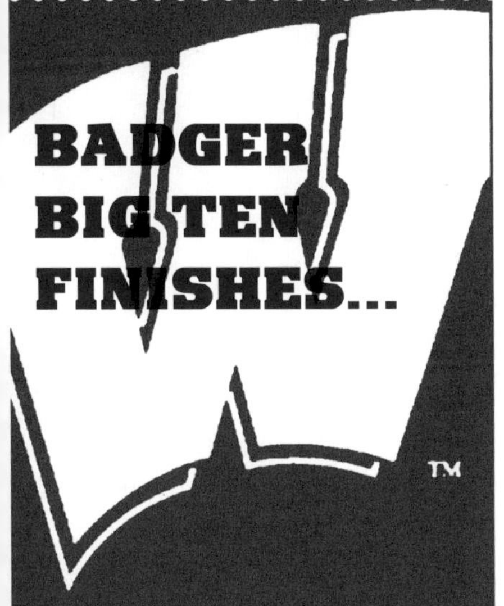

Football: 2nd
coached by Harry Stuhldreher

Cross Country: 2nd
coached by Thomas Jones

Basketball: 3rd (tie)
coached by Harold Foster

Indoor Track: 6th
coached by Thomas Jones

Swimming: 7th
coached by Joe Steinauer

Wrestling: 7th
coached by George Martin

Baseball: 5th (tie)
coached by Art Mansfield

Golf: 8th
coached by Joe Steinauer

Gymnastics: 4th
coached by Dean Mory

Tennis: 3rd
coached by Al Hildebrandt

Outdoor Track: 6th
coached by Thomas Jones

Boxers win again ... their fifth NCAA title

It never got boring, but it certainly became almost routine. Wisconsin again racked up back-to-back NCAA boxing titles, following its 24-point victory in the 1947 tournament with a 45-point win, scoring its most points to date, in the 1948 national collegiate bouts.

Four Badgers won individual crowns: Donald Dickinson (148 lbs.), Steve Gremban (156), Calvin Vernon (176) and Vito Parisi (heavyweight). The season also marked the continuation of another lengthy winning streak by Wisconsin.

The boxers of 1946-49 went undefeated in 27 straight matches before being stopped by Minnesota, 4 to 3, in the 1950 season opener. Wisconsin also had a home unbeaten streak of 72 wins and 2 ties that lasted until 1950, when Michigan State ended that string.

Wisconsin Time Line

1948: "Kukla, Fran and Ollie" and the rest of the Kuklapolitan players premiered, live, on NBC-TV.

The first Big Ten Records Book was published

Don Rehlfeldt took 37 shots as the Badgers trounced Iowa 70-47 in basketball; it's still a UW single-game record

More than 15,000 people boxing fans jammed the Field House to see the Badgers battle Washington State

WISCONSIN HEADLINER

Don Gehrmann
Track and Field,
Cross Country

One of the legendary names in one of Wisconsin's most successful sports is Don Gehrmann, a Milwaukee (Pulaski High School) product who dominated the American middle distance scene from 1947-51. Gehrmann won 39 consecutive major mile races from the 1948 Olympic Games to March 3, 1951. He was a four-time Big Ten outdoor mile champion from 1947-50 and the NCAA mile champ in 1948, 1949 and 1950. Three times he won the outstanding performer award at the Drake Relays and twice he won Big Ten individual cross country titles while the Badgers won team championships overland from 1948-50. Gehrmann is in various halls of fame, including the state of Wisconsin, Drake Relays, Madison Pen and Mike-Bowman Sports Foundation. He was a charter inductee into the UW Athletic Hall of Fame in 1991.

WISCONSIN HEADLINER

Eugene A. Jaroch
Baseball

Gene Jaroch was a mainstay on the mound for Wisconsin baseball teams from 1944-47. Jaroch, a native of Chicago (Wells High School), earned four major "W" awards. He was a strikeout specialist, striking out 52 batters in 46 1/3 innings in the Badgers' 1946 Big Ten championship season. He set a Conference record with 16 K's in a 7-0 win over Chicago that year. His six wins (against no losses) set a Conference mark and accounted for two-thirds of the UW's Big Ten victories. For his career, Jaroch struck out 156 batters in 138 2/3 innings in Big Ten play. He posted a career mark of 18-13 but was especially tough on Conference foes, against whom he was 15-4. Jaroch earned a B.S. degree in physical education. He was inducted into the UW Athletic Hall of Fame in 1998.

WISCONSIN HEADLINER

Earl Girard
Football

Earl "Jug" Girard played two seasons at Wisconsin, 1944 and 1947, and earned first-team all-America honors from Look magazine as a 17-year-old freshman in his first season. Regarded as a triple-threat quarterback, Girard was equally skilled at running, passing and punting. Drafted after his freshman year, he returned to school for the '47 season and scored two touchdowns off 158 yards in punt returns against Iowa. He's still the only Wisconsin player to return two punts for touchdowns in a game and his return yardage still stands as a game record. Girard, who also played baseball, was drafted in the first round of the NFL draft by the Green Bay Packers. He also spent some time in the Cleveland Indians' farm system.

LEADING THE WAY

John Walsh
Boxing Coach

Boxing at Wisconsin was THE sport under Coach John Walsh. The Minneapolis native, who as a youth was one of the great boxers in the Twin Cities, coached and boxed at St. Thomas College, which fought the Badgers to a 4-4 tie in 1933. Encouraged the next year by Wisconsin officials to enroll in the UW Law School while coaching boxing, Walsh stayed for 23 years. He guided the Badgers to eight NCAA team titles, most in any sport in UW history. Nine of Walsh's Wisconsin teams were unbeaten and 29 boxers won 35 NCAA championships under his tutelage. His great dedication to boxing and his unique methods of developing young boxers earned him the position of co-coach of the 1948 U.S. Olympic team. He ended his Wisconsin coaching career in 1956, having compiled a 116-22-1 mark. A member of the Madison Pen and Mike Club-Bowman Sports Foundation Hall of Fame, Walsh was a charter member of the UW Athletic Hall of Fame in 1991.

1948-49

Football: 9th
coached by Harry Stuhldreher

Cross Country: 1st
coached by Guy Sundt

Basketball: 7th
coached by Harold Foster

Indoor Track: 1st (tie)
coached by Guy Sundt

Swimming: 8th
coached by Joe Steinauer

Wrestling: 8th
coached by George Martin

Baseball: 8th (tie)
coached by Art Mansfield

Golf: 9th
coached by Joe Steinauer

Gymnastics: 4th
coached by Dean Mory

Tennis: 3rd
coached by Al Hildebrandt

Outdoor Track: 3rd
coached by Guy Sundt,
(tie for 7th, NCAA)

Badgers win indoor track title for new coach Guy Sundt

Guy Sundt's debut as Wisconsin's track coach and successor to 36-year veteran Tom Jones was an auspicious one. The Badgers claimed their first indoor title since 1930, scoring 38 points at Champaign, Illinois, to share the top spot with defending champ Ohio State.

Distance star Don Gehrmann paced Wisconsin, winning the 880-yard run in 1:53.1 and the mile in 4:16.1. Also winning individual championships for the UW were two-miler Jim Urquhart at 9:25.7 and pole vaulter Tom Bennett with a 14'0" clearance.

The mile relay quartet of Dick Whipple, Mel Goldin, Gehrmann and Bob Mansfield was also victorious in 3:18.6. Gehrmann (mile), Urquhart (two mile) and Bennett (pole vault) repeated their indoor wins outdoors as the Badgers took third in the spring meet.

Wisconsin Time Line

1949: "South Pacific" opened on Broadway.

Michigan State College was admitted to membership in the Conference.

Don Rehlfeldt became Wisconsin's last basketball all-American to date and was picked second in the NBA draft.

WISCONSIN HEADLINER

Robert "Red" Wilson
Football, Baseball

Three-time Wisconsin football MVP Robert "Red" Wilson was the Big Ten's most valuable player in 1949. The former all-state grid star and state discus champ out of Milwaukee, Wisconsin, started on offense as an end and defense as a linebacker for Ivy Williamson's first Wisconsin team in 1949. He had been a center on offense for his first three Badger seasons starting in 1946, winning the first of his three UW MVP honors in 1947. He was later named to Wisconsin's all-time football team. A top catcher for the Badger baseball squad from 1947-50 and MVP in 1948, Wilson hit .342 that year and .426 in 1949. The 1950 Badgers shared the Big Ten title and placed fourth in the NCAA tournament as Wilson was named Wisconsin's Big Ten Medal of Honor recipient. He later went on to a professional career with the Chicago White Sox, Detroit Tigers and Cleveland Indians. A member of the Wisconsin State Hall of Fame and the Madison Pen and Mike Club-Bowman Sports Foundation Hall of Fame, Wilson was a charter inductee of the UW Athletic Hall of Fame in 1991.

LEADING THE WAY

Art Lentz
Sports Information Director

Art Lentz served as sports information director at Wisconsin for 10 years, winning numerous national sports publicity awards during his tenure, including recognition by the Helms Athletic Foundation in 1956. Lentz, a Milwaukee native who was a graduate of the University of Iowa, worked for the *Des Moines Register* and *Tribune* for two years before coming to the (Madison) *Capital Times* in 1933. He became assistant sports editor in 1943, did football, basketball and track play-by-play on radio and left the Capital Times in 1946 to become the Badgers' SID. Lentz left Wisconsin in 1956 to become publicity director for the U.S. Olympic Committee and handled press duties at the 1956 Olympics in Melbourne, Australia. He became the USOC's assistant executive director in 1959 and executive director in 1965, a post he held until 1973. He died at 65 in 1973 in New York City.

Wisconsin's Men's Conference Medal of Honor winners

1940
Ralph H. Moeller

1941
Kenneth E. Boxby

1942
Burleigh E. Jacobs

1943
Frederick R. Rehm

1944
Edward M. Dzirbik

1945
Ken Chandler

1946
Jerry Thompson

1947
Exner Menzel

1948
Carlyle Fay, Jr.

1949
Donald R. Peterson

Stuhldreher, Jones depart

There were more than a few good moments in the careers of Harry Stuhldreher and Tom Jones. Stuhldreher, the 13-year football coach at Wisconsin, called it quits after the 1948 season. Stuhldreher's 45 wins at Wisconsin are fifth in Badger annals. Veteran track mentor Jones, a fixture in Madison since 1913, also bid adieu. In his 36 years, Jones coached 20 Big Ten championship teams as well as the 1948 U.S. Olympic team.

1949-50

Football: 4th
coached by Ivy Williamson

Cross Country: 1st
coached by Guy Sundt

Basketball: 2nd
coached by Harold Foster

Indoor Track: 5th
coached by Guy Sundt

Swimming: 7th
coached by Joe Steinauer

Wrestling: 6th
coached by George Martin

Baseball: 1st (tie)
coached by Art Mansfield

Golf: 9th
coached by Joe Steinauer

Tennis: 4th
coached by Al Hildebrandt

Outdoor Track: 4th
coached by Guy Sundt

UW beats Michigan twice, shares baseball title

Wisconsin took top honors in Big Ten baseball for the second time in five years in 1950, chalking up a 9-3 mark that was good enough for a share of the title with Michigan. The Badgers handed the Wolverines two of their three losses.

Pacing Coach Dynie Mansfield's nine was one of the Conference's top batteries in pitcher Thornton Kipper and Bob Wilson. The latter was regarded for some 20 years afterward as one of the finest catchers in Big Ten history and once scored six runs and had seven RBIs in a 1949 slugfest against Western Michigan.

Also critical to the Badgers' success were slugging outfielders Paul Furseth and Bruce Elliott, each of whom hit .333 for the season. It was the last Big Ten baseball pennant that Wisconsin would win and the Badgers' only NCAA appearance.

Wisconsin Time Line

1950: The comic strip "Peanuts," created by Charles Schulz, was first published in nine newspapers.

The Big Ten increased the football traveling squad limit from 36 to 40 players.

Don Gehrmann won his third straight 1500-meter run title in the NCAA track and field championships.

WISCONSIN HEADLINER

Don Rehfeldt
Basketball

Two-time all-Big Ten center Don Rehfeldt was a mainstay of Badger basketball teams in the post-World War II years. Rehfeldt, a Chicago native who enjoyed a great prep career at Amundsen High School, originally enrolled at Wisconsin in 1944, but was called into the service. He returned in early 1947 to join the Badgers' Big Ten championship team of that season. It was in 1949 and 1950 that Rehlfeldt starred, leading the Big Ten in scoring with 229 points in 1949 and 265 in 1950 over the 12-game schedules; only five other players ever scored 200 or more points in a 12-game Conference season. He was named most valuable player in the Big Ten for 1950 and twice was named Wisconsin's MVP. Rehfeldt scored 35 points against Northwestern in 1950, a Wisconsin mark that held up for 15 years. He was picked by the Baltimore Bullets in 1950 as the second choice in the NBA draft. A member of the Illinois Basketball Coaches Hall of Fame, Rehfeldt was named a charter member of the UW Athletic Hall of Fame in 1991.

WISCONSIN HEADLINER

Edward "Eddie" Withers
Football

Edward "Eddie" Withers earned all-American honors for the Badgers as a star defensive halfback on the 1950 Badger football team. Prior to enrolling at Wisconsin, Withers starred as an all-city linebacker and as a basketball center for Madison Central High School. In pacing the Badgers to a 14-0 win at Iowa in 1950, Withers interecepted three passes for 103 yards off returns of 30, 34 and 39 yards, the first for a touchdown. During his playing career, Wisconsin posted an 18-7-2 mark from 1949-51. Withers, who had eight career interceptions for 200 return yards, also earned all-Big Ten honors as a defensive back in 1951 and was drafted by the Green Bay Packers. He received a degree in physical education from Wisconsin in 1952. Forty years later, he was inducted into the UW Athletic Hall of Fame.

Wisconsin sports facilities

Camp Randall Stadium
(football)

Camp Randall Memorial Sports Center (The Shell)
(track)

Kohl Center
(basketball, ice hockey)

Wisconsin Field House
(wrestling, volleyball)

McClain Athletic Facility
(football & soccer practice)

Nielsen Tennis Stadium
(tennis)

Dan McClimon Memorial Track
(track and field, soccer)

Natatorium
(swimming, diving)

Southeast Recreational Facility (SERF)
(swimming)

Lake Mendota
(rowing)

University Ridge Golf Course
(golf)

Goodman Softball Complex
(softball)

Rehlfeldt the first first-rounder

Don Rehlfeldt—Wisconsin's last first-team all-American—was picked second overall and thus became the first UW basketball player selected in the first round of the NBA draft. Four other Badgers were chosen in the first round in subsequent years. Al Henry was 12th overall in 1970; Wes Matthews was 14th in 1980; and Michael Finley and Paul Grant were each taken with the 25th pick in 1995 and 1997, respectively.

1950-51

Football: 2nd (tie)
coached by Ivy Williamson

Cross Country: 1st
coached by Riley Best

Basketball: 4th (tie)
coached by Harold Foster

Indoor Track: 6th (tie)
coached by Riley Best

Swimming: 9th
coached by Joe Steinauer

Wrestling: 6th
coached by George Martin

Baseball: 5th
coached by Art Mansfield

Golf: 3rd
coached by Joe Steinauer

Tennis: 7th
coached by Al Hildebrandt

Outdoor Track: 8th
coached by Riley Best

Badgers win Conference cross country

Wisconsin's 1950 Big Ten cross country championship, another in the Badgers' proud tradition, would be noteworthy, although no one would know it at the time.

Under first-year coach Riley Best, who had succeeded the legendary Tom Jones, the Badgers scored 56 points to hold off Big Ten newcomer and national power Michigan State, which had 61.

Walter Deike, a year away from winning his first individual title, placed third. But the win—the UW's 18th Big Ten triumph—would be Wisconsin's last in the sport until 1977.

Wisconsin Time Line

1951: Coast-to-coast dial telephone service began.

The Big Ten renewed its Rose Bowl agreement with the Pacific Coast Conference for a three-year period.

Wisconsin's "Hard Rocks" football team led the nation in total defense en route to a 7-1-1 season.

WISCONSIN HEADLINER

Albert (Ab) Nicholas
Basketball

High-scoring guard Albert (Ab) Nicholas starred on Badger teams of the early 1950s, twice earning first-team all-Big Ten honors and in 1952 gaining second-team all-American recognition from *Look* magazine. Nicholas had come to Wisconsin from Rockford, Illinois, where he was a second-team Illinois all-stater in 1948. Twice the Badgers' most valuable player, Nicholas scored 982 points in 66 varsity games, making him at that time the highest-scoring guard in UW basketball history. Nicholas was the 1951-52 Harlan B. Rogers scholarship recipient for 1951-52 and was named the 1952 "W" Club "Athlete of the Year." He's a past president and member of the board of directors of the National "W" Club and served on the UW System Board of Regents from 1987-94. President of the Milwaukee-based Nicholas Company, he was a major donor to the new Kohl Center, a pavilion which bears his name. Nicholas was inducted into the UW Athletic Hall of Fame in 1994.

WISCONSIN HEADLINER

Pat O'Donahue
Football

Pat O'Donahue starred at defensive end on Wisconsin's "Hard Rocks" football teams from 1949-51. The Eau Claire native came to Madison out of St. Patrick's High School, where he earned all-state honors in both football and basketball as a senior in 1947-48. O'Donahue's senior season at the UW was a stellar one. An all-Big Ten pick, he also was a first-team all-America selection of the Football Writers Association, the Associated Press and the Newspaper Enterprise Association. O'Donahue played in the 1951 Blue-Gray Game and was a member of the 1952 College All-Stars. He played professionally with the San Francisco 49ers (1952) and the Green Bay Packers (1955). O'Donahue was inducted into the UW Athletic Hall of Fame in 1993.

LEADING THE WAY

Guy Sundt
Football, Cross Country and Track Coach
Athletic Director

Guy Sundt's 35 years at Wisconsin took him from his days as an eight-time "W" award winner in football, track and basketball through coaching stints in five sports and finally to the director's chair. Sundt enrolled at Madison out of nearby Stoughton and made his mark as football team captain and a first-team all-Big Ten pick in 1921. He also was an outdoor track all-American in the long jump. After graduating, Sundt coached football, basketball and track at Ripon College from 1922-24 before returning to Wisconsin, where he served as freshman basketball coach (1924-29), freshman baseball coach (1925-26), assistant football, track and cross country coach (1924-48) and as assistant athletic directory (1936-50). Sundt became head track and cross country coach in 1948 and guided the Badgers to Big Ten cross country title in '48 and '49 and to a co-championship in the 1949 Conference indoor track meet. He then served as Wisconsin's athletic director from 1950-55. Sundt was inducted into the UW Athletic Hall of Fame in 1993.

Men's Basketball Honors

Naismith Hall of Fame

Dr. Walter Meanwell (inducted in 1959)
Harold Olsen (1959)
Chris Steinmetz Sr. (1959)
Harold "Bud" Foster (1964)

All-America (first team)

Chris Steinmetz Sr. (1905)
George Levis (1916)
Harold "Bud" Foster (1930)
Gene Englund (1941)
John Kotz (1942)
Don Rehlfeldt (1950)

Big Ten MVP

Gene Englund (1941)
John Kotz (1942)
Glen Selbo (1947)
Don Rehlfeldt (1950)

1951-52

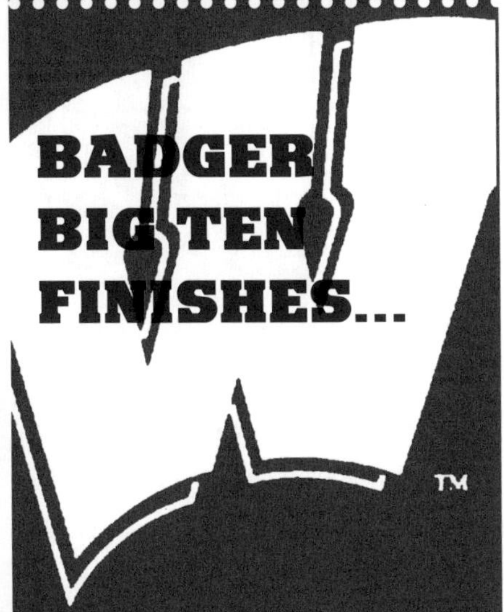

Football: 2nd
coached by Ivy Williamson

Cross Country: 2nd
coached by Riley Best

Basketball: 7th
coached by Harold Foster

Indoor Track: 6th
coached by Riley Best

Swimming: 7th
coached by John Hickman

Wrestling: 5th (tie)
coached by George Martin

Baseball: 3rd
coached by Art Mansfield

Golf: 3rd
coached by John Jamieson

Tennis: 8th
coached by Carl Sanger

Outdoor Track: 9th
coached by Riley Best

Boxers win another NCAA title

Wisconsin's boxers had never gone longer than four years between national collegiate titles and they weren't about to rewrite a successful script in 1952.

Coach John Walsh's team, last a winner in 1948, got back on top with 27 points. It was the UW's sixth championship since 1939 and re-established Wisconsin as the premier collegiate boxing power.

Two men won championship bouts, Bob Morgan in the 147 lb. class and Bob Ranck in the heavyweight division, his second straight NCAA win there.

Wisconsin Time Line

1952: NBC's "Today" show premiered with Dave Garroway as the host.

The Conference approved an 18-game round-robin basketball schedule.

Wisconsin was selected as the Big Ten's representative in the 1953 Rose Bowl after tying Purdue for the Conference title.

WISCONSIN HEADLINER

Harvey Kuenn
Baseball

Milwaukeean Harvey Kuenn came full circle in his athletic career from his days as a football, basketball and baseball star at Milwaukee Lutheran High School to his American League pennant-winning stint in 1982 as manager of the Milwaukee Brewers. In between, there was stardom at Wisconsin and a long professional baseball career. Kuenn won major "W" awards at Wisconsin in 1951-52 in basketball and in both the 1951 and 1952 seasons, in baseball. He earned all-Big Ten and all-American honors at shortstop in 1952, his junior season, while captaining the Badgers and leading them to third place in the Conference. Kuenn led the Big Ten with 63 at bats, 28 hits, 16 runs, 6 doubles, 5 triples and 16 RBIs. His single season average of .436 was the third best ever by a Wisconsin ballplayer. His career batting average of .382 was second best in Badger history. Kuenn signed with the Detroit Tigers after his junior year and also played with Cleveland, San Francisco, Philadelphia and the Chicago Cubs. A member of the Wisconsin State Hall of Fame, Kuenn was a charter inductee of the UW Athletic Hall of Fame.

WISCONSIN HEADLINER

Harold Faverty
Football

Harold (Hal) Faverty, an end and linebacker, was a four-time "W" award winner in football over a seven-season span. He earned first-team all-America honors in 1951 from the International News Service. Faverty played for the Badgers in 1945, 1948, 1950 and 1951, with service in the military interrupting his schooling and playing career. As a 25-year-old senior, he was one of the most experienced players on the 1951 Wisconsin team that went 7-1-1 under Coach Ivy Williamson. Faverty, who played on both sides of the ball, was integral to the Badgers as a linebacker on the famed "Hard Rocks" defense, which allowed a school record low 5.9 points per game. He also played in the 1952 College All-Star game in Chicago.

WISCONSIN HEADLINER

Walter Dieke
Track and Cross Country

Walter Dieke starred for Wisconsin cross country and track teams from 1948-52. Dieke led the Badgers to the 1950 Big Ten championship with a third place finish in the Conference meet and that year also earned all-American honors. He captained the 1951 squad and won the Big Ten individual title. His senior track season in 1952, however, was his best. Dieke became Wisconsin's first NCAA long distance champion, winning the NCAA 10,000-meter run in 32:25.1 in the meet at Berkeley, Cal. He's a member of Wisconsin's track and field "Hall of Honor."

Koepcke is Big Ten golf medalist

Doug Koepcke became the first of Wisconsin's four Big Ten golf champions in 1952. Koepcke had rounds of 73, 74, 79 and 80 en route to his winning 306 total in the 72-hole tournament at Champaign. Coach John Jamieson's first Wisconsin team finished third behind Michigan and Purdue.

1952-53

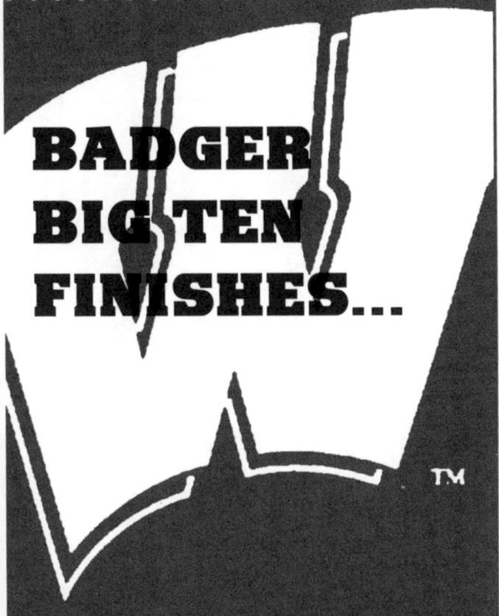

Football: 1st
coached by Ivy Williamson

Cross Country: 4th
coached by Riley Best

Basketball: 5th
coached by Harold Foster

Indoor Track: 10th
coached by Riley Best

Swimming: 7th
coached by John Hickman

Wrestling: 9th
coached by George Martin

Baseball: 6th
coached by Art Mansfield

Golf: 5th
coached by John Jamieson

Tennis: 8th
coached by Carl Sanger

Outdoor Track: 9th
coached by Riley Best

Wisconsin wins first Big Ten football title in 40 years, goes to Rose Bowl

Wisconsin's 1952 football team earned the first bowl bid in the school's history after winning its first Big Ten title since 1912. Paced by four all-Big Ten selections, back Alan Ameche, tackle Dave Suminski, guard Bob Kennedy and guard George O'Brien, the Badgers posted a 6-3-1 record and made the UW's first Rose Bowl appearance on New Year's Day in 1953.

Coming off a 7-1-1 season in 1951 and a runner-up Big Ten finish, the Badgers were ready for a great season. Ranked seventh in the pre-season polls, Wisconsin stopped Marquette 42-19 in the season opener. And after a 20-6 win over second-ranked Illinois in the next game, fourth-year Coach Ivy Williamson's Badgers were even ranked first nationally—the only time that's happened in Wisconsin history.

Losses to Ohio State and eighth-ranked non-conference foe UCLA were sandwiched around a 42-13 win over Iowa. A non-league win over Rice and victories over Northwestern (24-20) and Indiana (37-14) kept the Badgers in the Big Ten lead and even a 21-21 tie with Minnesota didn't hurt the UW cause. After losing 7-0 to USC in Pasadena, Wisconsin ended the season ranked 10th by United Press International and 11th by the Associated Press.

Wisconsin Time Line

1953: President Harry Truman announced that the U.S. had developed a hydrogen bomb.

The Conference reduced football traveling squads to 38 and adopted a 14-game Conference basketball schedule for 1954-55.

Badgers beat top-ranked Illinois 34-7 in football at Camp Randall.

WISCONSIN HEADLINER

Dave Suminski
Football

Dave Suminski, a three-year standout for Wisconsin in the early 1950s, made his debut as a defensive tackle in 1952 a great one. Suminski had started the two previous seasons on the Badgers, offensive line. On defense, he earned all-Big Ten and all-American honors on a Wisconsin team that would win the Conference with a 4-1-1 mark and go on to play in the 1953 Rose Bowl. It was the UW's first bowl appearance. In that game, a 7-0 loss to USC, the Badger defense held the vaunted Trojan offense to just 48 yards rushing. Suminski was selected by the Washington Redskins in the 1953 National Football League draft and later played with the Chicago Cardinals and the Hamilton Tiger Cats of the Canadian Football League.

WISCONSIN HEADLINER

Don Voss
Football

Despite playing only two seasons before a knee injury in the 1953 Rose Bowl ended his career, Don Voss was one of the top ends in Wisconsin history. In his first season, 1951, Voss was named to the Associated Press freshman all-America team and was a member of Wisconsin's "Hard Rocks," the best defensive unit in the nation. A year later he helped guide Coach Ivy Williamson's Big Ten champion Badgers to their first-ever bowl game. He was the youngest member of Look magazine's 1952 all-America team.

LEADING THE WAY

Ivan (Ivy) Williamson
Football Coach
Athletic Director

Ivy Williamson is a name that is synonymous with Wisconsin football excellence as he presided over one of the most successful eras in Badger gridiron history and led the UW to its first Rose Bowl. As a player, Williamson earned all-Big Ten honors at Michigan in 1932, when he captained the Wolverines. He also played on Michigan's 1930 and 1931 teams and lettered in basketball at Ann Arbor in his junior and senior seasons. Following assistant coaching stints at Yale sandwiched around service in World War II, Williamson compiled a 13-5 record in two years at Lafayette College before coming to Madison in 1949. In seven years as head man at Wisconsin, Williamson posted a 41-19-4 mark, 29-13-4 in the Big Ten, and led the 1952 Badgers to the Conference title and 1953 Rose Bowl berth. He also served as chairman of the NCAA Football Rules Committee. Williamson became director of athletics in 1955 and led Wisconsin until his death in 1969. A member of the Wisconsin State Hall of Fame, Williamson was one of the charter inductees into the UW Athletic Hall of Fame in 1991.

Badgers in the bowls

1953 Rose Bowl
USC 7, Wisconsin 0

1960 Rose Bowl
Washington 44, Wisconsin 8

1963 Rose Bowl
USC 42, Wisconsin 37

1981 Garden State Bowl
Tennessee 28, Wisconsin 21

1982 Independence Bowl
Wisconsin 14, Kansas State 3

1984 Hall of Fame Bowl
Kentucky 20, Wisconsin 19

1994 Rose Bowl
Wisconsin 21, UCLA 16

1995 Hall of Fame Bowl
Wisconsin 34, Duke 20

1996 Copper Bowl
Wisconsin 38, Utah 10

1998 Outback Bowl
Georgia 33, Wisconsin 6

1953-54

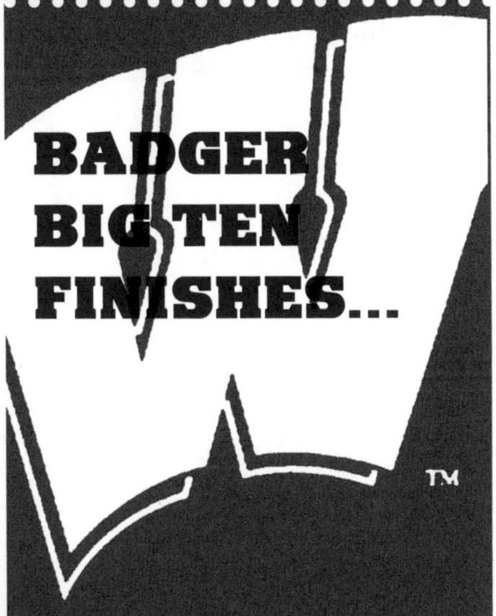

Football: 3rd
coached by Ivy Williamson

Cross Country: 3rd
coached by Riley Best

Basketball: 5th (tie)
coached by Harld Foster

Indoor Track: 9th
coached by Riley Best

Swimming: 5th
coached by John Hickman

Wrestling: 5th
coached by George Martin

Baseball: 2nd
coached by Art Mansfield

Golf: 10th
coached by John Jamieson

Tennis: 7th
coached by Carl Sanger

Outdoor Track: 10th
coached by Riley Best

Boxers take seventh NCAA crown

It took only 19 points and the Badgers had just one championship, but it was enough to give Wisconsin and Coach John Walsh their seventh NCAA boxing title in 1954. Bob Meath claimed the Badgers' lone individual win in the 156 lb. weight class.

Wisconsin Time Line

1954: The world's first atomic submarine, the USS Nautilus, was launched in Groton, CT.

Big Ten directors adopted a procedure for selection of the Rose Bowl representative.

Wisconsin's Alan Ameche won the Heisman Trophy.

1954-55

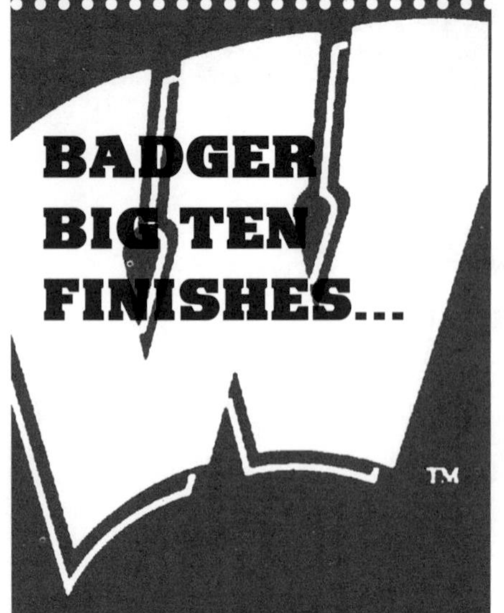

Football: 2nd
coached by Ivy Williamson

Cross Country: 6th
coached by Riley Best

Basketball: 6th (tie)
coached by Harold Foster

Indoor Track: 5th
coached by Riley Best

Swimming: 6th
coached by John Hickman

Wrestling: 4th
coached by George Martin

Baseball: 7th
coached by Art Mansfield

Golf: 3rd
coached by John Jamieson

Tennis: 5th
coached by Carl Sanger

Outdoor Track: 8th
coached by Riley Best

Ameche wins Heisman Trophy

Fullback Alan "The Horse" Ameche in 1954 became the only Badger to ever win the Heisman Trophy—emblematic of college football's best player. The Kenosha native won the trophy after rushing for 641 yards and nine touchdowns.

In the voting by sports writers throughout the nation, Ameche totaled 1,068 points to outdistance Oklahoma linebacker-center Kent Burris (838) and Ohio State halfback Howard "Hopalong" Cassady (810). Ameche, who was sixth in the 1953 voting, dominated in 1954, receiving 214 first-place votes and a majority of votes cast in the east and midwest.

Ameche made first-team all-America squads as picked by the Football Writers Association, *Look* magazine, Newspaper Enterprise Association, Paramount News, All-Academic, *Athletic Publications*, *Catholic Weekly* and UNICO (National Italian Association).

Besides Ameche, five other Badgers have finished among the top 10 in balloting for the Heisman. They are Howard Weiss, sixth in 1938; Dave Schreiner, 10th in 1942; Dale Hackbart, seventh in 1959; Pat Richter, sixth in 1962; and Ron Vander Kelen, ninth in 1962.

Wisconsin Time Line

1955: The new Air Force Academy was dedicated at Lowry Air Force Base in Colorado.

The Conference approved the pending NCAA TV plan and voted to pool and share equally all proceeds.

Wisconsin won the last of its eight NCAA boxing titles in the tournament held at the Wisconsin Field House.

WISCONSIN HEADLINER

Alan Ameche
Football

Alan "The Horse" Ameche remains the only Wisconsin football player to have won the Heisman Trophy. Three times an all-Big Ten selection and twice an all-American as a fullback, the Kenosha native was the Conference's most valuable player in 1954. He set a Rose Bowl record of 133 yards on 28 carries in the 1953 game for Ivy Williamson's Big Ten champion Badgers. Ameche was selected by the Baltimore Colts in the first round of the 1955 NFL draft and ran 79 yards for a touchdown against the Chicago Bears on the first play of his pro football career. A member of the National Football Foundation Hall of Fame, Ameche also had his number 35 retired by Wisconsin. He was named a charter member of the UW Athletic Hall of Fame in 1991.

WISCONSIN HEADLINER

Richard W. Cable
Basketball

Dick Cable was one of the Badgers' top basketball performers in the early 1950s, earning major "W" awards from 1952-55. He was a second-team all-Big Ten pick as a senior and earned honorable mention all-Conference status in his first two seasons. The 1955 team captain and most valuable player, Cable scored had a career best 31 points against Tulane and later equaled that performance against Notre Dame. He set a Badger single-game assist mark with 11 against California in 1952. Cable led the Badgers in scoring in 1953-54 and 1954-55, setting a UW record for field goal accuracy (.436) in his junior campaign. He was the Badgers' career scoring leader when he graduated and still is 12th on the all-time list. Cable was the Badgers' Big Ten Medal of Honor recipient as a senior. Drafted by the NBA's Milwaukee Hawks in the second round, Cable chose to pursue a business career. He served as a volunteer fund-raiser for the Kohl Center project from 1995-98. Cable was inducted into the UW Athletic Hall of Fame in 1998.

LEADING THE WAY

George Martin
Wrestling Coach

George Martin, an NCAA wrestling champion who as a coach stayed in superb condition, guided Wisconsin wrestling fortunes from 1935 until 1970. Wrestling was at a low ebb when he came to Wisconsin but in his first season the UW won more dual matches than in the five previous years combined. Although Martin's UW teams never won a Big Ten championship, the Badgers were competitive and featured such top wrestlers as John Roberts, Clarence Self, Larry Lederman, Rick Heinzelman, Mike Gluck and future Badger coach Russ Hellickson. An Iowa native, Martin twice won the Big Six 165-lb. championship for Iowa State. He won the NCAA title at that weight in 1933 and the national AA 175-lb. title in 1934. He captained Iowa State to the 1933 NCAA crown and qualified for the 1936 Olympics, but was disqualified for the Olympic berth when he accepted the Wisconsin coaching position. Martin was inducted into the Helms Hall Wrestling Hall of Fame in 1969. He drowned at age 59 in 1970 while on a canoeing trip in Ontario.

Alan Ameche's Heisman Trophy-winning season

Game	Attempts	Yards	TD
Marquette	18	107	1
Michigan State	17	127	1
Rice	21	90	2
Purdue	18	73	1
Ohio State	16	42	0
Iowa	26	117	1
Northwestern	17	59	1
Illinois	0	0	0
Minnesota	13	26	2

1955-56

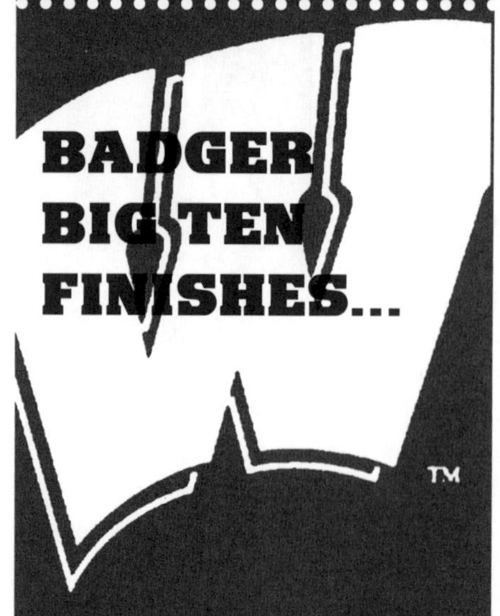

Football: 6th
coached by Ivy Williamson

Cross Country: 6th
coached by Riley Best

Basketball: 8th (tie)
coached by Harold Foster

Indoor Track: 7th
coached by Riley Best

Swimming: 9th
coached by John Hickman

Wrestling: 7th
coached by George Martin

Baseball: 3rd
coached by Art Mansfield

Golf: 4th
coached by John Jamieson

Tennis: 9th
coached by Carl Sanger

Outdoor Track: 9th
coached by Riley Best

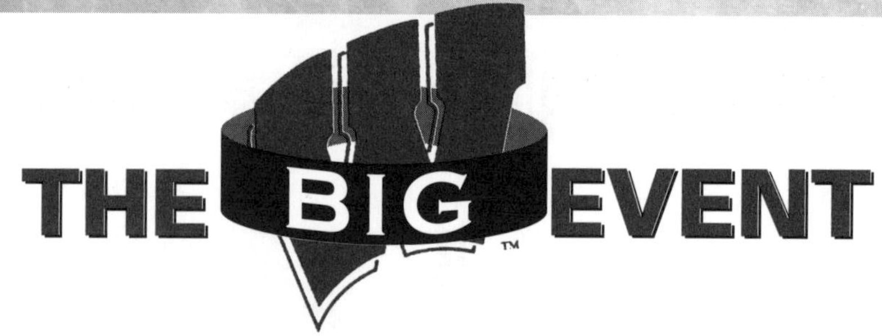

Boxers win last boxing title

The 1956 NCAA boxing championships marked the end of an era in the collegiate sport. Wisconsin won its eighth and last boxing title as legendary Coach John Walsh neared the end of his coaching career.

The Badgers' 47 points were the most a Wisconsin team had ever scored in the NCAA tournament. And the five individual crowns won by Badger boxers had only been equaled by the Wisconsin team of 1943, another NCAA title-winning unit.

Taking their championship bouts were Dean Plemmons at 112 lbs., Dick Bartman at 139, Vince Ferguson at 156, Orville Pitts at 178 and Truman Sturdevant at heavyweight. All were first-time champions.

Wisconsin Time Line

1956: Don Larsen of the New York Yankees became the first pitcher to throw a perfect game in the World Series, beating the Brooklyn Dodgers 2-0.

The Council of Ten extended Big Ten Commissioner Tug Wilson's contract for a five-year term.

1956-57

Football: 9th
coached by Milt Bruhn

Basketball: 9th
coached by Harold Foster

Indoor Track: 8th
coached by Riley Best

Swimming: 6th
coached by John Hickman

Wrestling: 8th
coached by George Martin

Baseball: 9th
coached by Art Mansfield

Golf: 1st
coached by John Jamieson

Tennis: 9th
coached by Carl Sanger

Outdoor Track: 10th
coached by Riley Best

Wisconsin wins Big Ten golf, fencing tournaments

Wisconsin emerged with two Big Ten championships during the 1956-57 season.

Coach Archie Simonson's Badgers earned their second fencing title in three years and got the better of fencing power Illinois in doing so. Epee champ Paul Mortensen and his teammate in the same weapon, Chuck Barnum, paced the Badgers along with Frank Tyrell, a scorer in sabre, and Gerry Bedner and Paul Lamba, who scored in foil.

John Jamieson's golfers captured the '57 Conference golf championship at Iowa City. The Badgers totaled 1,512 strokes for the 72-hole tourney, eight strokes ahead of Iowa.

Leading Wisconsin were Roger Rubendall, who carded a 291 (74-76-71-70) to finish third, and Dave Forbes, who came in fourth at 299 off rounds of 79, 76, 70 and 74. It was Rubendall's third consecutive top five finish.

Wisconsin Time Line

1957: Althea Gibson was the women's clay court singles championship, making her the first black player to win a major U.S. tennis crown.

The Conference created a Financial Aids Service to make determinations of financial aid.

1957-58

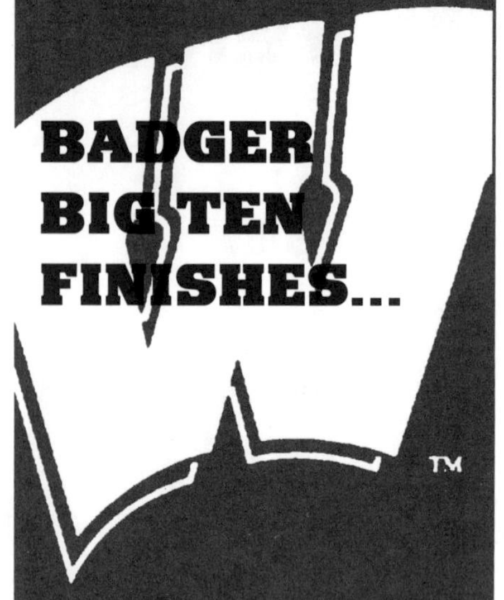

Football: 4th (tie)
coached by Milt Bruhn

Basketball: 10th
coached by Harold Foster

Indoor Track 9th
coached by Riley Best

Swimming: 7th
coached by John Hickman

Wrestling: 9th
coached by George Martin

Baseball: 5th
coached by Art Mansfield

Golf: 8th
coached by John Jamieson

Tennis: 8th
coached by Carl Sanger

Outdoor Track: 9th
coached by Riley Best

Badger teams generally struggle in transition year

The 1957-58 season was a transition year of sorts for many of Wisconsin's teams, with little success. Second-year Coach Milt Bruhn's football squad tied for fourth in the Big Ten. The Badgers won their first three, dropped their middle three to Iowa, Ohio State and Michigan State and then rebounded to score wins over Northwestern, Illinois and Minnesota in a 6-3 campaign.

Coach Bud Foster's next-to-last basketball team, despite having two honorable mention all-Big Ten picks in most valuable player Walt Holt (15.4 points per game) and Bob Litzow (14.7), suffered through an 8-14 season. The Badgers started out 8-6 but lost their final eight to finish last in the Conference.

It was the end of an era in boxing at Wisconsin as retiring coach John Walsh's last team placed fourth in the NCAA meet. Archie Simonson's fencers were 10-4 in dual meets and placed second in the Big Ten, the best finish by a Wisconsin team this year.

Gerald Bodner won the foil title and also placed fifth in the NCAA meet, leading the UW to eighth place nationally.

Dynie Mansfield's baseball team was 17-12 overall and finished fifth in the Big Ten at 8-7. Leading the Badgers was first-team all-American centerfielder Ron Nieman, who hit .327.

Wisconsin's track teams placed ninth in the indoor and outdoor championships.

Wisconsin Time Line

1958: America's first successful Earth satellite, Explorer I, was launched from Cape Canaveral, Florida.

The Conference approved a 10-game football schedule effective in 1965.

1958-59

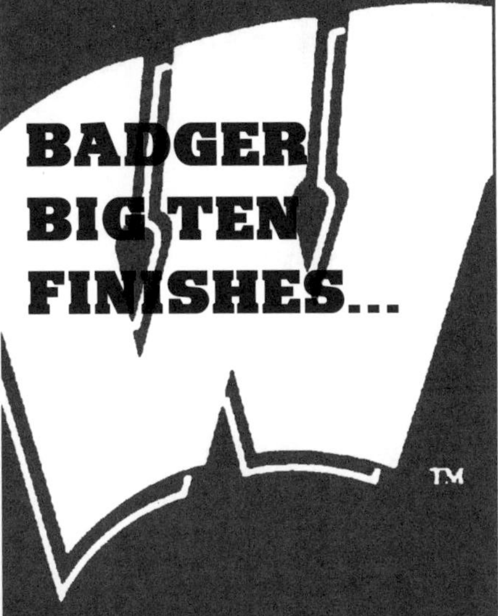

Football: 2nd
coached by Milt Bruhn

Basketball: 10th
coached by Harold Foster

Indoor Track: 5th
coached by Riley Best

Swimming: 7th
coached by John Hickman

Wrestling: 6th
coached by George Martin

Baseball: 2nd (tie)
coached by Art Mansfield

Golf: 6th
coached by John Jamieson

Tennis: 9th
coached by Carl Sanger

Outdoor Track: 9th
coached by Riley Best

Westphal wins NCAA 50-freestyle

Fred Westphal became Wisconsin's second—and last, to date—national collegiate champion in swimming in 1959, winning the 50-yard freestyle in the 1959 championships at Cornell. His time, 22.3 seconds, equaled the fifth-best mark ever posted by a winner in the event.

In the qualifying heats, Westphal set NCAA and American records of 21.9 seconds. The Janesville native was a three-time swimming all-American for the Badger teams in the late 1950s, three times placing among the top five in national collegiate meets.

As a high school star, he won an individual state title and led Janesville to the 1955 WIAA state swimming championship. At Wisconsin, he compiled a 28-9 dual meet record swimming 50, 60 and 100-yard freestyle events in collegiate competition while serving as Badger captain in 1958 and co-captain in 1959.

As a sophomore in 1957, Westphal won the 50 free at the Big Ten meet and went on to place second in the NCAA. He was runner-up in the Conference in that event as a junior and senior and also took second in the NCAA in his second year of eligibility. Westphal was a charter member inductee in the UW Athletic Hall of Fame in 1991.

Wisconsin Time Line

1959: Alaska and Hawaii were admitted to the Union as the 49th and 50th states.

The Big Ten revised its summer competition rule to permit limited basketball play.

Wisconsin won its second Rose Bowl berth after rallying to beat Minnesota 11-7.

1959-60

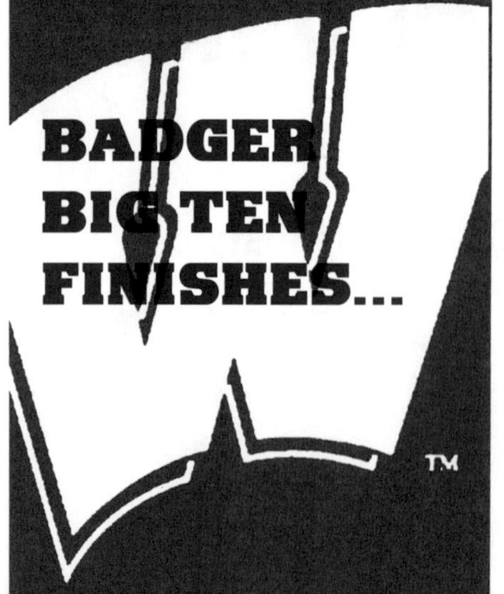

Football: 1st
coached by Milt Bruhn

Basketball: 9th
coached by John Erickson

Indoor Track: 10th
coached by Riley Best

Swimming: 8th
coached by John Hickman

Wrestling: 10th
coached by George Martin

Baseball: 3rd
coached by Art Mansfield

Golf: 6th
coached by John Jamieson

Tennis: 7th
coached by Carl Sanger

Outdoor Track: 10th
coached by Riley Best

Wisconsin wins Big Ten football title

Wisconsin won its first undisputed Big Ten football championship since 1912 with a come-from-behind 11-7 win at Minnesota to clinch the title. It also gave Coach Milt Bruhn's team a return to the Rose Bowl seven years after the Badgers had played in Pasadena for the first time.

Defensive end Dan Lanphear rebounded from an injury-plagued junior season to earn all-America honors for Wisconsin. His fumble recovery and blocked punt for a safety were critical plays in the Badgers' 12-3 win over Ohio State. Also starring for the UW were all-Conference quarterback Dale Hackbart and all-league guard Jerry Stalcup.

Despite losing 44-8 to Washington in the 1960 Rose Bowl, the Badgers finished the season ranked sixth by both the Associated Press and United Press International.

The 1959 season:

Wisconsin 16, Stanford 14*
Wisconsin 44, Marquette 6*
Purdue 21, Wisconsin 0
Wisconsin 25, Iowa 16*
Wisconsin 12, Ohio State 3*
Wisconsin 19, Michigan 10
Wisconsin 24, Northwestern 19
Illinois 9, Wisconsin 6*
Wisconsin 11, Minnesota 7
Washington 44, Wisconsin 8

*Designates home game

Wisconsin Time Line

1960: Sen. John F. Kennedy (D-Mass.) announced his bid for the Democratic presential nomination.

Junior college graduates were made immediately eligible upon enrollment in a Conference university.

WISCONSIN HEADLINER

Dale L. Hackbart
Baseball, Basketball, Football

Madison native Dale Hackbart earned six major "W" awards in three sports, and went on to a distinguished 14-year professional football career with Green Bay, Washington, Minnesota, St. Louis and Denver. He also played for the Vikings in the 1970 Super Bowl against Kansas City. Hackbart, who prepped at Madison East High School, quarterbacked Wisconsin's 1957-59 football teams and was selected by Green Bay in the third round of the 1960 National Football League draft. As a senior, he was an all-Big Ten pick after leading the Conference in total offense with 686 yards. Hackbart scored 134 points in this career off 21 touchdowns and eight extra points. He was a forward on the 1959 Badger basketball squad and as a two-year outfielder for the UW baseball team, he posted a career .290 batting average; he also played in the Pittsburgh Pirates' minor league system. Hackbart was named to the Madison Pen and Mike Club-Bowman Sports Hall of Fame in 1983 and to the UW Athletics Hall of Fame in 1996.

WISCONSIN HEADLINER

Dan Lanphear
Football

Dan Lanphear earned all-America honors as a defensive end for Wisconsin in 1959, atoning for a injury-plagued junior season. The Madison native was accorded first-team all-America honors by *The Associated Press, United Press, News Enterprise Association, The Sporting News*, the American Football Coaches Association and *Look* magazine. His best game may have been the Badgers' 12-3 win over Ohio State in 1959. Lanphear recovered a fumble, blocked a punt for a safety and knocked two OSU running backs out of the game with strong hits. Lanphear played defensive end for the American Football League's Houston Oilers and was a member of their AFL championship teams of 1960 and 1961.

LEADING THE WAY

Milt Bruhn
Football Coach

Milt Bruhn remains the only UW football coach to lead the Badgers to a pair of Big Ten titles in the 20th century, with his 1959 and 1962 teams having accomplished that feat and played in the 1960 and 1963 Rose Bowl games. Bruhn, who in 11 seasons posted a 52-45-6 mark, had three of his squads—1958 (8th), 1959 (6th) and 1960 (2nd)—ranked among the top 10 in final national polls. Those three teams' combined 20-6-1 regular season mark stands as the best for any three-year span since the turn of the century. Bruhn came to Wisconsin from Lafayette College in 1949 with Ivy Williamson after coaching stops at Amherst, Minnesota, Colgate, and Franklin and Marshall. A Minnesota native, Bruhn played guard on Minnesota's undefeated 1934 and 1935 national title teams and was a catcher on the Gophers' 1835 Big Ten champion baseball team. He was a charter member of the UW Athletic Hall of Fame in 1991.

Two UW winners in NCAA boxing championship

It was more a Wisconsin ending than a beginning as a glorious era of Badger sports ended tragically in the final NCAA boxing championships. Under new coach Vern Woodward, who had succeeded John Walsh after the 1958 season, the Badgers finished sixth in the 1959 NCAA tourney and second in 1960. Charles Mohr had claimed the 165 lb. title in '59 and Brown McGhee (132 lbs.) and Jerry Turner (156 lbs.) were the final Wisconsin boxing champions. The sport was discontinued after Mohr died of an injury suffered in the 1960 NCAA championship in a 165 lb. bout with Stu Bartell of San Diego State.

1960-61

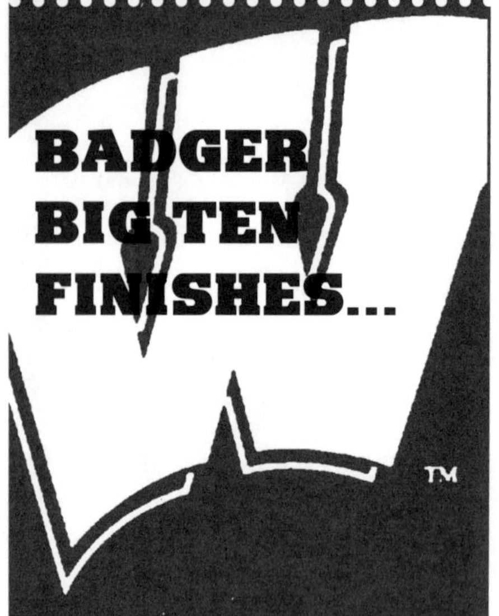

Football: 9th
coached by Milt Bruhn

Cross Country: 4th
coached by Tom Bennett

Basketball: 8th
coached by John Erickson

Indoor Track: 9th
coached by Charles Walter

Swimming: 8th
coached by John Hickman

Wrestling: 9th
coached by George Martin

Baseball: 6th
coached by Art Mansfield

Golf: 9th
coached by John Jamieson

Tennis: 8th
coached by Carl Sanger

Outdoor Track: 10th
coached by Charles Walter

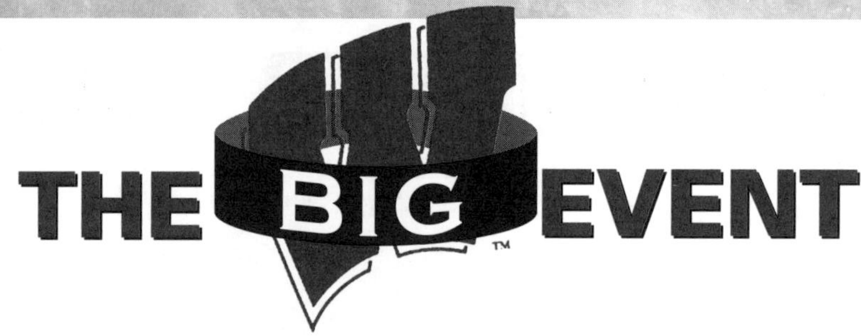

Unheralded Miller stars at quarterback

Ron Miller, who wasn't even on the 1960 Badger football roster, let alone the depth chart, was the surprise of the 1960 season. The junior walk-on became the Big Ten's top passer, completing 72 of 144 attempts and leading the Conference in total offense with 966 yards, only 15 of which were by rushing.

For the season, Miller had 1,395 yards, all except 44 in the air, and eight touchdowns. He had 200-yard-plus games in 1960 against Marquette (224 yards on 9 of 19) and Purdue (223 yards on 12 of 23). Milt Bruhn's Badgers, still a year away from a winning record and two years away from their next Rose Bowl, weren't as effective as their quarterback.

The UW finished 3-6, dropping five of its last six games. Miller again was the Badgers' starter in 1961, passing for 11 touchdowns and 1,487 yards off 104 completions in 198 attempts. But no story could have been greater than his in 1960, when he walked on to Badger football stardom.

Wisconsin Time Line

1961: Two U.S. helicopter companies arrived in Saigon, the first direct support for South Vietnam's battle against communist guerillas.

Kenneth L. (Tug) Wilson retired as commissioner and was succeeded by Bill Reed.

Wisconsin defeated top-ranked Ohio State 86-67 in basketball at the Field House, ending the Buckeyes' 47-game winning streak.

1961-62

Football: 5th
coached by Milt Bruhn

Cross Country: 4th
coached by Charles Walter

Basketball: 2nd
coached by John Erickson

Indoor Track: 1st
coached by Charles Walter

Swimming: 9th
coached by John Hickman

Wrestling: 4th
coached by George Martin,
(6th, NCAA)

Baseball: 4th
coached by Art Mansfield

Golf: 5th
coached by John Jamieson

Tennis: 7th
coached by Carl Sanger

Outdoor Track: 2nd
coached by Charles Walter

Hockey returns after 28-year absence

Wisconsin played its first intercollegiate hockey game in 1922, but the program was disbanded 12 years later and did not return to the Madison campus until 1962, thanks to the work of several individuals.

UW Athletics Director Ivan Williamson had become a fan of a local youth hockey team called the Madison Hawks, who were coached by John Riley. Williamson enjoyed the Hawks' games and had visions of returning the game to the UW.

Fenton Kelsey, a successful local businessman interested in promoting and developing the sport in Madison, was instrumental in hastening hockey's return to the area by building Hartmeyer Ice Arena with the hope that the facility would speed up the return of the game on campus and bolster interest locally.

With a first-rate arena now in place, and Williamson's full commitment to the sport, the University's Athletic Board approved hockey's return in March, 1962. Williamson hired Riley as the coach and the program played a number of scrimmages and games against teams of all kinds.

That first year—1962-63—Williamson and Riley laid the foundation for what became Wisconsin's first modern era hockey season in 1963-64.

Wisconsin's first game, played in front of 695 curious fans, resulted in a 13-6 loss to St. Mary's College of Winona, Minn. The Badgers fell behind 12-0 before Tom French scored Wisconsin's first modern-era goal on a penalty shot.

WISCONSIN TIME LINE

1962: Astronaut John Glenn became the first American to orbit the Earth.

Conference offices were moved to the Sheraton-Chicago Hotel.

Second-ranked Badgers made their second Rose Bowl appearance in three years, with their rally falling short in a 42-37 loss to USC.

1962-63

Football: 1st
coached by Milt Bruhn

Cross Country: 3rd
coached by Charles Walter

Basketball: 6th
coached by John Erickson

Indoor Track: 3rd
coached by Charles Walter

Swimming: 7th
coached by John Hickman

Wrestling: 5th
coached by George Martin

Baseball: 5th
coached by Art Mansfield

Golf: 2nd
coached by John Jamieson

Tennis: 8th
coached by David G. Clark

Outdoor Track: 2nd
coached by Charles Walter

Badgers lose most exciting Rose Bowl after Winning Big Ten title

The '62 Wisconsin football team rolled to an 8-1 record, including a win over top-ranked Northwestern on November 10, and the school's second Big Ten title in four years. The Badgers finished the campaign with a consensus No. 2 national ranking after a thrilling meeting with top-ranked USC in the Rose Bowl.

Wisconsin's 23-point fourth quarter explosion wasn't quite enough as it dropped a season-ending 42-37 Rose Bowl encounter to Southern Cal. The Trojans had claimed a 42-14 lead on the first play of the fourth quarter before the huge Badger comeback.

USC raced to a 21-7 halftime lead and extended it on the first play of the third stanza, before Ron VanderKelen led one of the biggest charges in bowl history.

VanderKelen reached paydirt on a 17-yard scamper to reduce the margin to 28-14. USC responded with a pair of TD passes by Pete Beathard and the Trojans led 42-14.

Lou Holland (13-yard run) and Gary Kroner (4-yard reception) tallied for the Badgers within three minutes. A bad center snap on a punt resulted in a UW safety. After the free kick, VanderKelen hit three straight passes, including a 19-yard score to Pat Richter for the final 42-37 margin.

VanderKelen, the game MVP, set both Wisconsin and Rose Bowl records with 401 yards passing. Richter caught 11 of those aerials for 163 yards. The 79 total points was a Rose Bowl record that stood for 28 years.

Wisconsin Time Line

1963: President John F. Kennedy was assassinated in Dallas.

Conference participation in the "Inter-Conference Letter of Intent" plan was approved.

Wisconsin lost 13-6 to St. Mary's (Minnesota) in the first ice hockey game of the modern era; a week later, the Badgers defeated Macalaster 3-2 for their first win.

WISCONSIN HEADLINER

Roger Everhart
Golf

Roger Everhart became Wisconsin's third Big Ten golf champion in 1963. He carded a 292 over the 72-hole course in Madison off rounds of 73, 73, 68 and 78. But his heroics weren't enough to give Coach John Jamieson's Badgers their second team title. Minnesota scored 1,523 to the UW's 1,524.

LEADING THE WAY

Pat Richter
Football, Basketball, Baseball
Director of Athletics

Pat Richter was the last of Wisconsin's nine-letter winners, earning "W" awards in football, basketball and baseball from 1960-63. Richter had the magic touch, particularly in football and baseball. Twice an all-Big Ten and all-American end, the Madison (East High School) product led the Conference in pass receiving in 1961 and 1962 and as the Badgers' punter led the Conference as a senior. He caught scoring passes in eight straight games in 1962 and set Rose Bowl records with 11 catches for 163 yards in 1963. In baseball, Richter was almost as awesome, three times earning all-Big Ten first- or second-team honors as an outfielder. He hit safely twice in each of 10 straight games in 1962. The UW's Big Ten Conference Medal of Honor winner in 1963, Richter was a first-round draft choice of the Washington Redskins and played professionally for eight seasons. He was an NCAA Silver Anniversary Top Six Award recipient in 1988. Richter was named the UW's athletic director in 1989.

LEADING THE WAY

Bill Aspinwall
Athletic Business Manager

Bill Aspinwall's career at Wisconsin spanned 46 years over six decades. To say that the Hurley, Wis., native knew Wisconsin's coaches well would be an understatement. He served six athletic directors, seven football coaches, six each in baseball, wrestling and track, three in swimming and fencing, four in golf, seven each in boxing and hockey, nine in crew and 11 in tennis. A 1928 UW accounting graduate, Aspinwall had begun working in the athletic department as a student in 1926 and upon graduation became its first full-time accountant. He succeeded George Levis as business manager in 1932 and added the ticket manager's duties 10 years later upon Harry Schwenker's death. The jobs were split in 1956 and Aspinwall reverted to his role as business manager until his retirement in June, 1972. He was the 40-year secretary of the athletic board and was a charter member of the College Athletic Business Managers Association, serving as its president in 1957 and later as its permanent secretary-treasurer. Aspinwall was named CABMA's "Business Manager of the Year" in 1970. He died at age 76 in January, 1983, in Madison.

BUCKY BADGER

From Benny to Regbad to Bucky

Badgers have been recognized for years as the UW mascot. The version currently known as Bucky, sporting a cardinal and white letter sweater, was first drawn in 1940 by artist Art Evans. He went by names like Benny, Buddy, Bernie, Bobby and Bouncey.

Sports publicist Art Lentz had the idea of bringing the Badger to life. Unfortunately, the first live Badger mascot was too difficult to control and once escaped handlers at a game. In the interest of fan and player safety, he was retired to the Madison Zoo. The Badger Yearbook replaced the live Badger with a small raccoon named "Regbad" (badger spelled backwards) and called it a "badger in a raccoon coat."

In 1949, Connie Conrad, a student in the art department, was commissioned to mold a papier-mâché badger head. Bill Sagal, a gymnast and cheerleader, wore the outfit at a homecoming game. A contest was held to name the mascot, with the winning entry, Buckingham U. Badger, or Bucky, apparently coming from song lyrics which urged the football team to "buck right through the line."

Bucky has survived and prospered, weathering even a 1973 attempt by the state attorney general to replace him with a "lovable and productive" cow, "Henrietta Holstein."

1963-64

Football: 5th
coached by Milt Bruhn

Cross Country: 2nd
coached by Charles Walter

Basketball: 10th
coached by John Erickson

Indoor Track: 2nd
coached by Charles Walter

Swimming: 6th
coached by John Hickman

Wrestling: 5th (tie)
coached by George Martin

Baseball: 4th (tie)
coached by Art Mansfield

Golf: 5th
coached by John Jamieson

Gymnastics: 4th
coached by George Bauer

Tennis: 5th
coached by John Powless

Outdoor Track: 1st
coached by Charles Walter

Badgers win outdoor track title

It took Coach Charles "Rut" Walter only four years to bring Wisconsin back to the top of the Big Ten outdoor track standings. In his first return to Evanston since leaving Northwestern in 1960 to become Wisconsin's coach, Walter guided the 1964 Badgers to the Conference title, the UW's fourth ever. It was Wisconsin's first Big Ten outdoor crown since a Tom Jones-coached team won in 1931, also in Evanston.

The Badgers scored 64 points to beat Michigan by 12 points. The UW scored in 13 of the 15 events and had four individual champions: Barry Ackerman in the long jump (23'11"), Don Henrickson in the discus (166'4"), Mike Manley in the mile (4:12.0) and Gene Dix in the 120-yard high hurdles (14.5). The win climaxed a great turnaround for Wisconsin under Walter.

His first team, in 1961, finished last in the Big Ten as had two of the four teams prior to his arrival, but by 1962 the Badgers had won the indoor crown and climbed to second outdoors. They repeated that runner-up outdoor finish in '63. Wisconsin finished the season with a string of 17 consecutive victories in indoor and outdoor dual and triangular meets.

Wisconsin Time Line

1964: Cassius Clay (later to become Muhammad Ali) defeated Sonny Liston to become world heavyweight boxing champion.

Big Ten sports information directors established the Robert C. Woodworth Award to honor the long-time Purdue SID, who had died, and to be presented to members of the press, radio or TV who had made meritorious contributions to the Big Ten.

Ken Barnes scored a then-school-record 42 points as the Badgers lost 92-73 to Indiana at the Field House.

WISCONSIN HEADLINER

Rick Reichardt
Baseball, Football

Rick Reichardt was one of Wisconsin's greatest two-sport stars, excelling in both football and basketball in the early 1960s. The Stevens Point native earned all-America honors in 1964, finishing second in national batting statistics with a .443 average on 47 hits in 106 at-bats. With a .472 average in Big Ten play, he repeated as Conference batting champion, becoming only the second player since 1939 to repeat as the league's top hitter. He also led the Badgers in home runs and stolen bases. Reichardt had hitting streaks of 15 games (from the '63 season) and 17 games. In football, the Badgers also counted on him. He was also the Big Ten's leading pass receiver in 1963, with 26 receptions for 383 yards and one touchdown. His TD came on a 50-yard pass play from quarterback Hal Brandt for a 17-14 UW victory. Reichardt signed a baseball contract with the Los Angeles Angels after his junior season.

LEADING THE WAY

Oscar C. Damman
National "W" Club

Oscar C. Damman has been a familiar name to Wisconsin athletes for more than three generations. A 1931 UW graduate, the Madison native has enjoyed a 60-year-plus association with the university, serving since 1958 as National "W" Club coordinator. Damman began his university service in 1936 at the Wisconsin Union, where he held a variety of positions, including Theater Ticket Sales Manager, for the next 14 years. From 1950-55, Damman managed student loans and supervised non-federal gift accounts. He became Athletic Ticket Sales Manager in 1956 and two years later was named by athletic director Ivan Williamson as the department's coordinator to the National "W" Club. He was named assistant to the athletic director in 1964 and served in various administrative roles until his 1991 retirement from the Division of Intercollegiate Athletics. Damman received the "Know Your Madisonian" Distinguished Person Award in 1965 and was National "W" Club "Man of the Year" for 1986. Damman was inducted into the UW Athletics Hall of Fame in 1996.

LEADING THE WAY

Archie Simonson
Fencing Coach

Archie Simonson spent 22 seasons as Wisconsin's fencing coach, compiling a 195-121 record (.617 winning percentage) against national and Midwest competition. Succeeding the "father" of Wisconsin fencing, Arpad Masley, in 1951, Simonson guided the Badgers to Big Ten championships in 1955, 1957 and 1959. Twelve of his fencers won Conference titles, with foilists Bruce Taubman (1967-68) and Neal Cohen (1970, 1972) repeat winners. And 13 Badger fencers earned all-America honors under his tutelage. Rick Baumann and Dick Odders earned back-to-back-to-back-to-back all-America honors in epee from 1966-69.

Paul Bunyan Axe symbolizes rivalry

The Paul Bunyan Axe is not as old as the story of the mythical giant of lumber camps in the Midwest, but it's only appropriate that it's the primary symbol of the Wisconsin-Minnesota football rivalry, the longest running in the nation. Each year the winner of game between the UW and UM—heading into its 90th straight contest and 106th in the last 107 seasons—is presented with the axe, complete with scores inscribed on the handle. The tradition began after a 16-0 Badger loss to the Gophers in 1948 when the National "W" Club presented Minnesota an axe "wielded by Bunyan" and another tradition was born.

1964-65

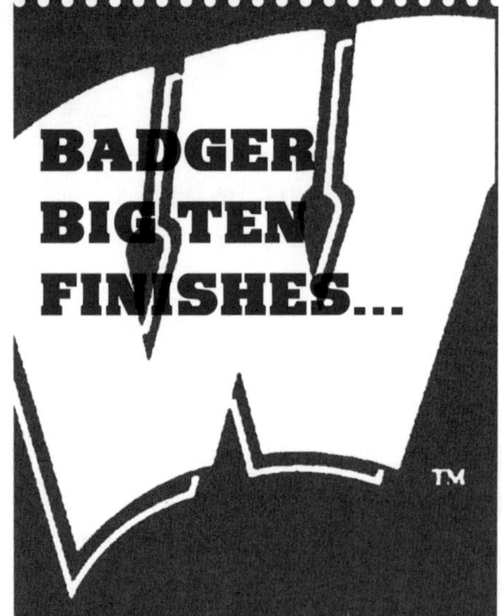

Football: 7th (tie)
coached by Milt Bruhn

Cross Country: 3rd
coached by Tom Bennett

Basketball: 8th
coached by John Erickson

Indoor Track: 1st
coached by Charles Walter

Swimming: 6th
coached by John Hickman

Wrestling: 9th
coached by George Martin,
(tie for 10th in NCAA)

Baseball: 9th
coached by Art Mansfield

Golf: 4th
coached by John Jamieson

Tennis: 8th
coached by John Powless

Gymnastics: 4th
coached by George Bauer

Outdoor Track: 3rd
coached by Charles Walter

Wisconsin wins Big Ten indoor track title

Wisconsin's track fortunes continued on the upswing in 1965, with the UW winning its second Big Ten indoor track championship in three seasons. Coach Charles "Rut" Walter's Badgers scored 46 points in the meet at Champaign, Illinois, to hold off Michigan State by a half-point in what remains the tightest margin between the first- and second-place teams in Big Ten indoor track history.

Wisconsin had three individual champions: Ken Latigo-Olal in the 880-yard run (1:53.3); Gerry Beatty in the 70-yard high hurdles (8.5 seconds); and Bill Holden, who cleared 6'6" to win the high jump. A couple weeks later, Wisconsin finished in a 25th place tie in the inaugural NCAA indoor championships at Cobo Arena in Detroit. Holden was third in the high jump and Al Montalbano fourth in the 600-yard run to become Wisconsin's first indoor track all-Americans.

Wisconsin Time Line

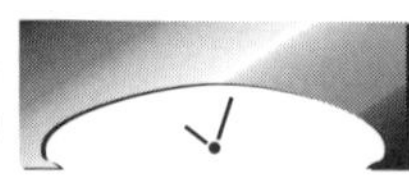

1965: President Lyndon Johnson signed the Voting Rights Act into law.

The Conference provided team championship trophies in football, basketball, baseball and hockey.

Wisconsin beat Minnesota 5-4 in overtime for its first win against as Western Collegiate Hockey Association team after 13 straight losses; six weeks later, Bob Johnson was named head coach.

1965-66

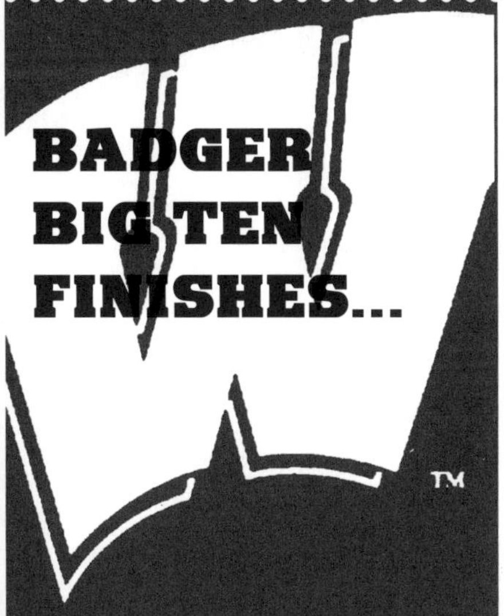

Football: 7th (tie)
coached by Milt Bruhn

Cross Country: 4th
coached by Charles Walter

Basketball: 7th
coached by John Erickson

Indoor Track: 2nd
coached by Charles Walter

Swimming: 5th
coached by John Hickman

Wrestling: 4th
coached by George Martin

Baseball: 7th
coached by Art Mansfield

Golf: 3rd
coached by John Jamieson

Tennis: 5th
coached by John Powless

Outdoor Track: 5th
coached by Charles Walter

Coatta, Johnson take over football, hockey duties

Coaching change was the order of the day at Wisconsin in 1965, with high profile football and hockey programs undergoing changes in leadership.

Veteran football coach Milt Bruhn resigned and John Coatta, a former Badger who had lettered in 1949, 1950 and 1951 for Ivy Williamson-coached teams that went 18-7-2, was hired.

In his 11 years as Wisconsin's head man, Bruhn compiled a 52-45-6 mark, second only to turn-of-the-century coach Phil King on the all-time UW victory list. He guided the Badgers to Rose Bowl appearances in 1960 and 1963 and posted six winning seasons.

Coatta, in three seasons, couldn't find the winning touch. His first team was 0-9-1 and tied for ninth in the Big Ten followed by a winless campaign and last place finish in 1968. Though his 1969 team improved to 3-7 overall and 3-4 in the Big Ten for a fifth-place tie, he was replaced by John Jardine.

In hockey, Wisconsin's reborn varsity program was on the verge of becoming nationally prominent. On April 1, 1966, Bob Johnson was hired as head coach following John Riley's retirement.

Johnson resigned June 1, 1982, after 15 years as head coach with a 267-175-23 record. His Badgers won three NCAA titles, made seven national tournament appearances and attracted the largest crowds in the nation.

WISCONSIN TIME LINE

1966: The National and American football leagues announced that they would merge in 1970.

The Conference authorized freshman competition in sports other than football for a two-year trial period.

The Badgers mounted the greatest comeback in the school's basketball history, coming from a 22-point deficit to beat Ohio State 82-81 in overtime.

1966-67

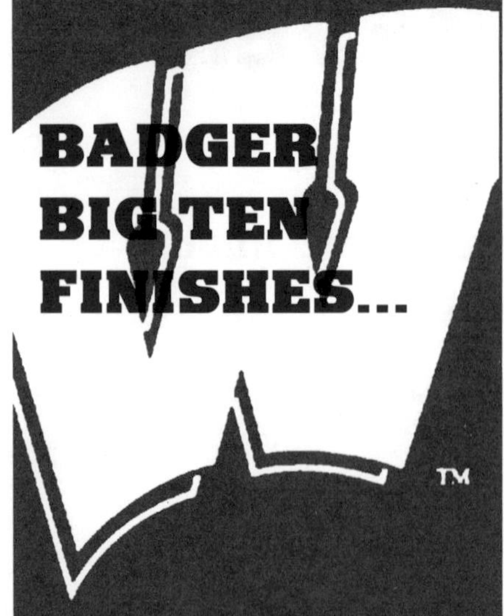

Football: 7th
coached by Milt Bruhn

Cross Country: 3rd
coached by Charles Walter

Basketball: 4th, coached by John Erickson

Indoor Track: 1st
coached by Charles Walter, (5th-tie, NCAA)

Swimming: 5th
coached by John Hickman

Wrestling: 6th
coached by George Martin

Baseball: 4th
coached by Art Mansfield

Golf: 9th
coached by John Jamieson

Gymnastics: 6th
coached by George Bauer

Tennis: 5th
coached by John Powless

Outdoor Track: 4th
coached by Charles Walter

Wisconsin wins first of five straight Big Ten track crowns

Coach Charles "Rut" Walter and assistants Bob Brennan and Tom Bennett had established a Big Ten track juggernaut at Wisconsin by the mid-1960s. The Badgers reclaimed the indoor Big Ten title in 1967 after relinquishing the honors to Michigan State the year earlier. Wisconsin would not lose an indoor championship until 1972.

Ironically, the front and back ends of the five-year win skein would take place in Madison. In 1967, the Badgers piled up 56 points at home to edge the Spartans by 3 points for the title, Coach Charles "Rut" Walter's third indoor win (and fourth overall) since coming to Wisconsin from Northwestern in 1960. Badgers winners in that 1967 meet were Ray Arrington in the 880-yard run (1:51.8) and Mike Butler in both the 70-yard high hurdles (8.2 seconds) and low hurdles (7.6 seconds).

Both would become all-time UW track greats, with Arrington that year winning the first of his three straight Big Ten and NCAA indoor 880 titles and Butler due to win five more indoor hurdles championships. Brennan succeeded Walter after the 1969 season and in his two years as Badger coach guided teams to firsts indoors and seconds outdoors.

Wisconsin Time Line

1967: Dr. Christian Barnard and a team of surgeons performed the first human heart transplant in Cape Town, South Africa.

The Conference liberalized the recruiting regulation, including an increase to two home visitations.

Wisconsin set a single-game men's basketball scoring team record with a 120-82 win over Southern Methodist.

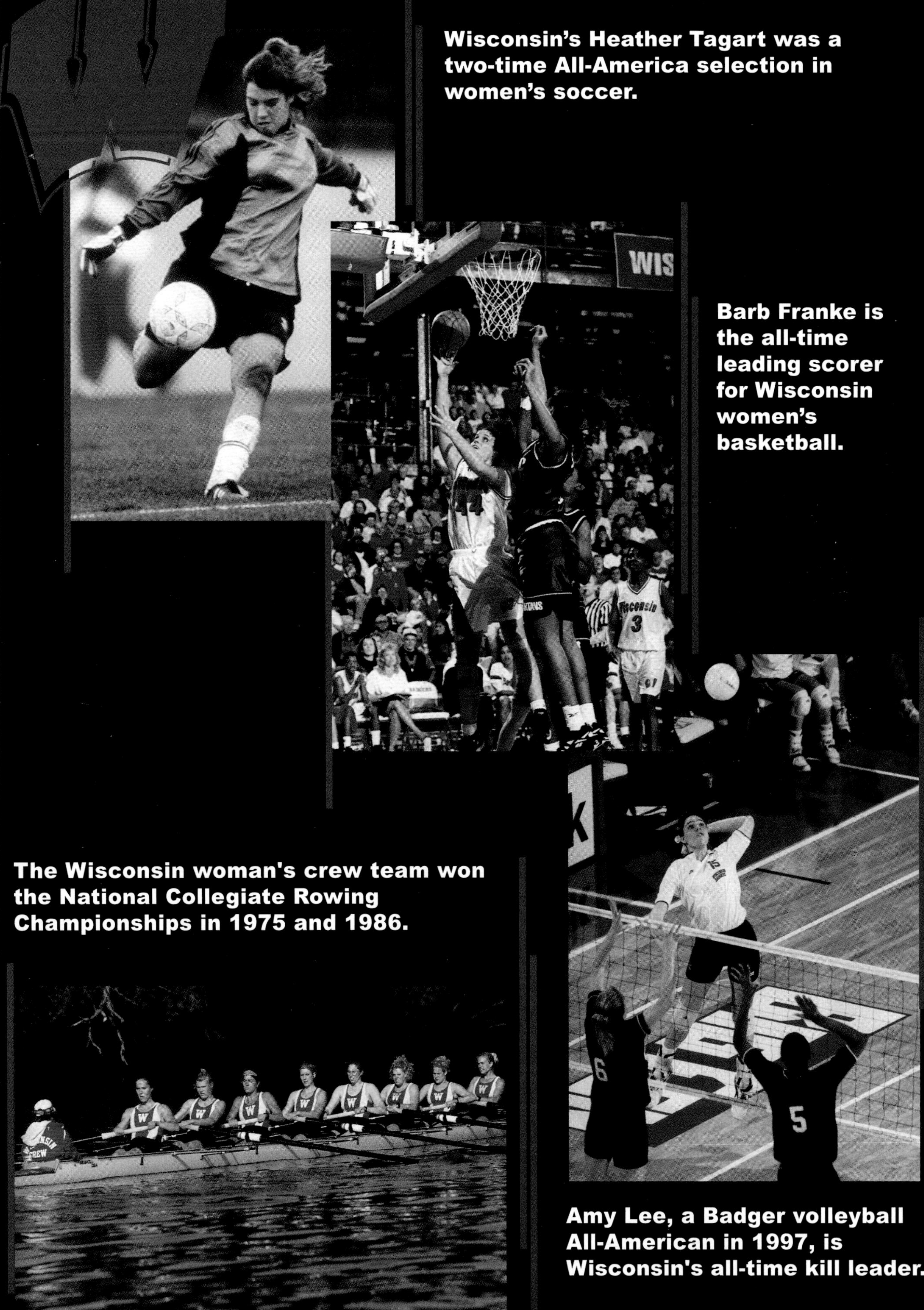

Wisconsin's Heather Tagart was a two-time All-America selection in women's soccer.

Barb Franke is the all-time leading scorer for Wisconsin women's basketball.

The Wisconsin woman's crew team won the National Collegiate Rowing Championships in 1975 and 1986.

Amy Lee, a Badger volleyball All-American in 1997, is Wisconsin's all-time kill leader.

Athletic Director Pat Richter and Head Coach Barry Alvarez celebrate Wisconsin's Rose Bowl victory

The University of Wisconsin's Kohl Center made its debut on January 17, 1998, when a capacity crowd of 17,142 saw the Badgers beat Northwestern.

Wisconsin's four-time All-America swimmer Gina Panighetti is the Big Ten's conference record holder in the 100 fly and 200 fly.

Wisconsin hurdler Reggie Torian was a five-time All-American when he graduated in 1997. His time of :13.03 at the USA Track & Field Outdoor Championships on June 21, 1998, set a world record in the 110-meter high hurdles event.

1967-68

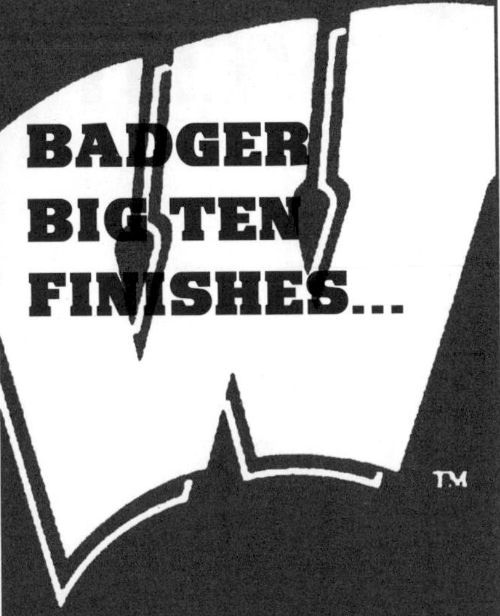

Football: 9th (tie)
coached by John Coatta

Cross Country: 5th
coached by Charles Walter

Basketball: 5th
coached by John Erickson

Indoor Track: 1st
coached by Charles Walter

Swimming: 4th
coached by John Hickman

Wrestling: 6th
coached by George Martin

Baseball: 3rd
coached by Art Mansfield

Golf: 9th
coached by John Jamieson

Gymnastics: 5th (tie)
coached by George Bauer

Tennis: 7th
coached by John Powless

Outdoor Track: 3rd
coached by Charles Walter

Badgers win 20 hockey games for first time

It took only three seasons for Wisconsin hockey coach Bob Johnson to guide the Badgers to their first 20-victory season. Wisconsin's 21-10 record would begin a string of six straight 20-plus win seasons.

In fact, since that breakthrough season, only four UW teams have failed to win 20. The UW's previous season high was the 16-win total posted in 1966-67 but the '68 campaign showed the college hockey world that Wisconsin hockey had not only come of age but was on the rise.

Only in 1973-74 and 1979-80 would a team coached by "Badger Bob" fail to win 20 games. The Badgers were led by two-time UW scoring leader Bert DeHate, who scored 15 hat tricks from 1967-69, including 12 in the '67-68 season, and is one of only three UW players to have scored five goals in a game. With 108 career goals, DeHate is second only to Mark Johnson (125 goals) on the all-time UW goal-scoring list.

Wisconsin Time Line

1968: Civil rights leader Martin Luther King, Jr., was assassinated in Memphis.

Herman F. Rohrig became the Big Ten's first full-time supervisor of Conference football and basketball officials.

Wisconsin joined the Western Collegiate Hockey Association, joining Big Ten rivals Michigan, MSU and Minnesota.

1968-69

Football: 10th
coached by John Coatta

Cross Country: 3rd
coached by Robert Brennan

Basketball: 8th (tie)
coached by John Powless

Indoor Track: 1st
coached by Charles Walter

Swimming: 5th
coached by John Hickman

Wrestling: 6th
coached by George Martin

Baseball: 5th (tie)
coached by Art Mansfield

Golf: 9th
coached by John Jamieson

Gymnastics: 5th
coached by George Bauer

Tennis: 7th
coached by John Desmond

Outdoor Track: 1st
coached by Charles Walter

Badgers sweep track titles for retiring coach

The best gift Wisconsin could come up with for retiring track coach Charles "Rut" Walter was something every coach likes: a winner. In fact, the Badgers doubled that pleasure for the veteran coach in 1969, winning the Big Ten indoor and outdoor titles. The Badgers had come close before Walter, taking a first in one meet and a second in the other in the same year, but it was the first time they had pulled off the indoor-outdoor double.

Led by veterans Ray Arrington and Mike Butler, Wisconsin won its third straight indoor title, scoring 65 points at Champaign to easily outpace runner-up Indiana (42). Arrington, who would win his third straight NCAA indoor championship in the 1,000-yard run two weeks later, was a double winner in the 880-yard run and in the mile.

The Badgers' third individual win came from Mike Butler, whose 70-yard high hurdles victory was his third straight. In the outdoor affair at West Lafayette, Indiana, the Badgers' 80 points was more than enough to replicate their indoor victory over Indiana (64). Nine individual titlists, a UW record, carried Wisconsin to its first outdoor championship in five years.

Winners included Arrington in the 880 and mile; Mark Winzenreid in the 660; Dean Martell in the three-mile run; Fred Lands in the steeplechase; Butler in the 120-yard high hurdles; Pat Murphy in the intermediate hurdles; Tom Thies in the pole vault; and Mike Bond in the triple jump. The mile relay team of Dick Hewlett, Larry Floyd, Winzenreid and Mark Kartman capped the Wisconsin triumph with a win in the meet's last event. Assistant Coach Bob Brennan succeeded Walter and guided the UW to Conference indoor titles in his two years at the helm.

WISCONSIN TIME LINE

1969: Apollo 11 astronauts Neil Armstrong and Edwin ìBuzzî Aldrin became the first men to set foot on the moon.

The Conference authorized freshman competition in sports other than football and basketball effective with the 1969-70 academic year.

Senior Ray Arrington won the third of his three straight NCAA indoor 1,000-yard run titles for the Badger track team.

WISCONSIN HEADLINER

Ray Arrington
Track, Cross Country

Ray Arrington epitomized the excellence of the middle distance runner on stellar Wisconsin track teams of the late 1960s. The smooth-striding native of Clairton, Pennsylvania, won eight Big Ten Conference titles in the 880 and mile during his three years of varsity competition from 1967-69. But it was in the recently-established NCAA indoor championships at Detroit's Cobo Arena that Arrington really made his mark. He won three consecutive NCAA titles and all-American honors at 1000 yards from 1967-69, setting an NCAA record of 2:07.8 in his first NCAA meet effort. In 1969, Arrington set Big Ten indoor marks in both the 880 (1:49.9) and mile (4:02.2). He captained the Wisconsin team that won indoor and outdoor titles his senior season and was named Wisconsin Athlete of the Year for both 1967 and 1969. Arrington was inducted into the UW Athletic Hall of Fame in 1993.

WISCONSIN HEADLINER

Joe Franklin
Basketball

A unanimous first-team all-Big Ten selection in 1968 who set a UW career scoring record, Joe Franklin was a fifth-round draft choice of the Milwaukee Bucks in that year's NBA draft. Franklin, a Madison native who prepped at Central High School, scored 1,215 points in three seasons from 1965-68. He averaged 22.7 points per game as a senior and had a career rebounding average of 11.9 per game, including a single-game high of 27 vs. Purdue. Franklin scored 30 or more points a game on seven occasions. He was team captain for 1967-68 and the Badgers' MVP for both his junior and senior seasons. Franklin was inducted into the UW Athletic Hall of Fame in 1997.

WISCONSIN HEADLINER

Russ Hellickson
Wrestling, Football

The name of Stoughton native Russ Hellickson is synonymous with wrestling excellence at Wisconsin, with his career running the gamut from athlete to to head coach. Holder of both a bachelor's and a master's degree from the UW, Hellickson was a three-time "W" award-winner in wrestling and a 1967 football letterman. Holder of 10 national freestyle wrestling titles, Hellickson was a three-time Pan American Games gold-medal winner and a member of the 1976 and 1980 U.S. Olympic teams, winning a silver at 220 lbs. in Montreal in '76 and serving as captain of the Olympic-boycotting U.S. squad of 1980. Inducted into the National Wrestling Hall of Fame in 1989 and a charter member of the Midlands Wrestling Hall of Fame in 1993, Hellickson has served as a TV commentator for wrestling at the Olympics and at the Goodwill Games. After 14 years as the assistant or head coach at his alma mater, Hellickson became Ohio State's head coach in 1987. He was named to the UW Athletic Hall of Fame in 1995.

LEADING THE WAY

Charles "Rut" Walter
Track and Field Coach

Charles "Rut" Walter's life was track and field, and he spent it all at two Big Ten schools, Northwestern and Wisconsin. In 1960, the Badgers lured the 31-year NU coach to Madison, where he coached Wisconsin for 10 seasons and enjoyed his greatest successes. The Kokomo, Indiana, native guided Wisconsin to Big Ten indoor titles in 1962, 1965, 1967, 1968 and 1969 and to Conference outdoor championships in 1964 and 1969. That double win by the Badgers in '69 would stand alone in UW track history for 26 years until equaled by the 1995 team. Walter posted a 50-9 career dual meet mark, 17-3 in triangulars, and coached 57 individual Big Ten champions. Rut was no slouch himself as an undergraduate at Northwestern in the late 1920s, winning Big Ten 440-yard dash titles from 1927-29 and the NCAA crown in 1929. A member of the Drake Relays Hall of Fame, Walter was inducted into the UW Athletic Hall of Fame in 1993.

1969-70

Football: 5th (tie)
coached by John Coatta

Cross Country: 3rd
coached by Robert Brennan

Basketball: 6th (tie)
coached by John Powless

Indoor Track: 1st
coached by Bob Brennan,
(5th-tie, NCAA)

Swimming: 5th
coached by Jack Pettinger

Wrestling: 7th
coached by George Martin

Baseball: 4th
coached by Art Mansfield

Golf: 9th
coached by Tom Bennett

Gymnastics: 7th
coached by George Bauer

Tennis: 8th
coached by John Desmond

Ice Hockey: 4th (WCHA)
coached by Bob Johnson,
(3rd, NCAA)

Outdoor Track: 2nd
coached by Robert Brennan

Alan Thompson runs for 220 yards in debut

Wisconsin's season-opening football game in 1969 against No. 6-ranked Oklahoma was supposed to be a stage on which Sooners' running back and Heisman Trophy-hopeful Steve Owens could showcase his considerable talents. Owens didn't disappoint. But neither did Badger Alan "A-Train" Thompson.

Owens, who went on to win the '69 Heisman, rushed 40 times for 189 yards and scored on four short touchdown plunges to lead the Sooners to a 48-21 victory at Camp Randall Stadium in Madison.

Owens, however, was outgained by Thompson, the Badgers' sophomore fullback making his collegiate debut. Thompson, a native of Dallas, set an all-time Wisconsin record by rushing for 220 yards on 33 carries, breaking the old mark of 200 yards set by Alan "The Horse" Ameche in 1951 against Minnesota.

Only one other back (Jerry Thompson, 37 times vs. Iowa in 1944) in Wisconsin history had carried the ball more times in a game than Alan Thompson did against the Sooners. The "A-Train" scored on touchdown runs of 13 and 14 yards against Oklahoma.

Alan Thompson went on to rush for 907 yards in 1969, a total second only to Ameche's 946-yard season in Wisconsin annals. Thompson also scored nine touchdowns. His performance against the Sooners was the only time during his career that he rushed for 200 yards in a game.

WISCONSIN TIME LINE

1970: Legendary football coach Vince Lombardi died of cancer in Washington.

The Big Ten approved 11 football games in 1971, providing the additional game be with a Conference opponent to assure a minimum of eight Big Ten games.

Clarence Sherrod finished the year with 570 points to become the third Wisconsin basketball player in five years to set a single-season scoring mark.

WISCONSIN HEADLINER

Mark Winzenreid
Track

Five-time all-American Mark Winzenreid was one of the dominant American middle distance runners in the late 1960s and early 1970s for Wisconsin coaches "Rut" Walter and Bob Brennan. The Monroe native won three NCAA titles, including the indoor 880-yard crowns in 1969 and 1971 and the outdoor 800 in his senior season of 1971. He also won five Big Ten titles and was the indoor U.S. Track and Field Federation 880 champ in 1968. Winzenreid represented the United States in international competition numerous times over his career and once held the world indoor record in the 1,000-yard run. He's a member of the Wisconsin track and field "Hall of Honor."

WISCONSIN HEADLINER

Alan Thompson
Football

Alan "A-Train" Thompson electrified Wisconsin fans from 1969-71. He led the Badgers in scoring in 1969 with nine touchdowns and throughout his career was a dependable back for John Coatta's last team and John Jardine's first two.Thompson, a native of Dallas, set an all-time Wisconsin record by rushing for 220 yards on 33 carries, scoring on TD runs of 13 and 14 yards against Oklahoma. Thompson had five more 100-yard-plus rushing games in his career but never again approached the totals of his first game. His career total of 2,005 rushing yards ranks him ninth on the all-time Wisconsin list. The Dallas Cowboys selected Thompson in the 14th round of the 1972 NFL draft.

LEADING THE WAY

Robert "Badger Bob" Johnson, Hockey Coach

As long as hockey is played at Wisconsin, the legacy of Robert "Badger Bob" Johnson will last. The late Wisconsin coach (1966-82) guided the Badger hockey teams to NCAA titles in 1973, 1977 and 1981 before turning his coaching magic to the National Hockey League and winning the 1991 Stanley Cup with the Pittsburgh Penguins. Johnson remains the only coach to ever guide teams to both NCAA and Stanley Cup victories. His record at Wisconsin was 367-125-23 over 15 seasons. A Minneapolis native who played collegiate hockey at North Dakota and Minnesota, Johnson graduated from Minnesota in 1954 and coached at the high school level for seven years before moving to Colorado College as hockey and baseball coach in 1963. Johnson served as executive director of USA Hockey from 1987-90 before returning to the bench with the Penguins. He also coached the 1976 U.S. Olympic team that took fourth in the Olympic Winter Games. His son Mark, a former Badger and NHL star who is now a UW assistant coach, was a 1991 inductee into the UW Athletic Hall of Fame that his father was named to a year later.

Wisconsin's Men's Conference Medal of Honor winners

1960
Dale L. Hackbart

1961
Gerald L. Kulcinski

1962
Thomas M. Hughbanks

1963
Hugh V. (Pat) Richter

1964
William R. Smith

1965
Gary V. Kirk

1966
David N. Fronek

1967
Dennis J. Sweeney

1968
Michael Gluck

1969
Karl Rudat

1970-71

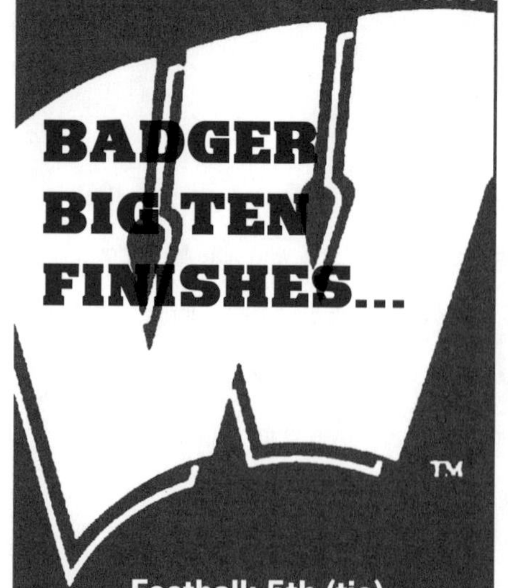

Football: 5th (tie)
coached by John Jardine

Cross Country: 5th
coached by Robert Brennan

Basketball: 7th (tie)
coached by John Powless

Indoor Track: 1st
coached by Robert Brennan, (3rd, NCAA)

Swimming: 6th
coached by Jack Pettinger

Wrestling: 5th
coached by Duane Kleven

Baseball: 6th
coached by Tom Meyer

Golf: 9th
coached by Tom Bennett

Gymnastics: 8th
coached by George Bauer

Tennis: 6th
coached by John Desmond

Ice Hockey: 3rd (WCHA)
coached by Bob Johnson

Outdoor Track: 2nd
coached by Robert Brennan

New coaches change "look" of Wisconsin teams

Five new head coaches changed the look of Wisconsin teams during and after the 1970-71 school year.

Most notably, John Jardine had taken over the football reins from John Coatta for the 1970 season. The veteran prep coach and long-time college assistant guided the Badgers to a 4-5-1 season and with victories in three of the last five games offered hope of better days ahead.

Duane Kleven took over the wrestling program following the drowning death of 32-year veteran coach and hall-of-famer George Martin in a boating accident.

Tom Meyer succeeded another Wisconsin legend, Art "Dynie" Mansfield as baseball coach and took the Badgers to a 9-9 Big Ten season and sixth in the standings.

Following two Big Ten indoor titles and a pair of seconds outdoors, Bob Brennan resigned as track and cross country coach just two years after succeeding Charles "Rut" Walter. Long-time Indiana assistant Bill Perrin was named head track coach while Dan McClimon became the Badgers' head cross country coach.

Wisconsin Time Line

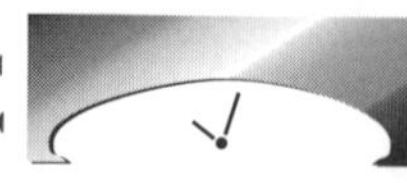

1971: The 26th amendment to the Constitution, lowering the voting age to 18, was ratified.

Commissioner William R. Reed died; Wayne Duke became the Conference's fourth commissioner.

Wisconsin high jumper Pat Matzdorf cleared 7'6 3⁄4" to set a world record in the U.S.-U.S.S.R. meet at Berkeley, California.

1971-72

Football: 6th (tie)
coached by John Jardine

Cross Country: 4th
coached by Dan McClimon

Basketball: 5th (tie)
coached by John Powless

Indoor Track: 3rd
coached by Bill Perrin

Swimming: 5th
coached by Jack Pettinger

Wrestling: 9th
coached by Duane Kleven

Baseball: 6th
coached by Tom Meyer

Golf: 9th
coached by Tom Bennett

Gymnastics: 8th
coached by Raymond Bauer

Tennis: 5th
coached by John Desmond

Ice Hockey: 2nd (WCHA)
coached by Bob Johnson,
(3rd, NCAA)

Outdoor Track: 5th
coached by Bill Perrin

Badgers win Big Ten hockey, take 3rd nationally

Wisconsin got off to a quick start in the 1971-72 hockey season, winning 14 of its first 15 games, including pairs of victories at home against Michigan and Michigan State. Those victories, coupled with a split of the games at Michigan and two more wins at MSU, allowed the Badgers to win the four-team "race" for the Big Ten championship despite losing three of four to Minnesota.

It was a strange year for Coach Bob Johnson's club, which lost three of its last five regular season contests but then rebounded to win the Western Collegiate Hockey Association playoff. The Badgers advanced to the NCAA and lost 4-1 to Boston University in the national semifinals.

The UW defeated Denver 5-2 in the third-place game, setting the stage for its NCAA championship run of the next season. Jeff Rotsch was a first-team all-American on defense for Wisconsin.

Wisconsin Time Line

1972: Eleven Israeli athletes taken captive by Arab guerrillas at the Munich Olympics were killed in an abortive rescue attempt.

Approval was given by the Big Ten for freshman competition in football and basketball in the fall of 1972.

WISCONSIN HEADLINER

Pat Matzdorf
Track and Field

High jumper Pat Matzdorf, one of the last great straddle jumpers, starred for UW track teams in the early 1970s, winning a pair each of Big Ten and NCAA titles. But the Sheboygan native leaped into track and field history in 1971 when he cleared 7'6 1/4" in the U.S.-U.S.S.R. meet in San Francisco to set a world record. Matzdorf won Conference indoor titles in 1970 and 1971, setting a league mark of 7'3" in the latter. He also won NCAA championships indoors (1971, with a meet record 7'2" jump) and outdoors (1970, at 7'1"). Matzdorf twice won Drake Relays high jumped titles and has been named to that prestigious meet's hall of fame. He was named Wisconsin's "Sports Personality" for 1971 and in 1972 received the UW Big Ten Conference medal of honor. Matzdorf was one of 35 charter members inducted into the UW Athletic Hall of Fame in 1991.

LEADING THE WAY

George "Buck" Backus
National "W" Club

Racine native George "Buck" Backus was a fixture with the National "W" Club for more than 20 years, serving as executive director from 1965-83. Backus quietly and soundly built the club into a powerful arm of Wisconsin's athletic program. He first joined it as director of concessions in 1962 and moved into the executive director's role three years later. Thanks to his efforts, monies generated by the club have helped build the athletic ticket office, the club's Kubly and Culver Rooms in Camp Randall Stadium, the football and hockey offices, the Dan McClimon Memorial Track and the Dave McClain indoor practice facility. Backus was honored by the Madison Pen and Mike Club with the Pat O'Dea Award in 1980.

Wisconsin's Men's Big Ten Cross Country Champions

1907
William Bertles

1910
Irvin Dohman

1911
C.R. Cleveland

1912
Irvin White

1918
Bernardo Elsom

1921
George Finkle

1925
Victor Chapman

1926
John Zola

1939
Walter Mehl

1947
Don Gehrmann

1948
Don Gehrmann

1951
Walter Dieke

1972
Glenn Herold

1978
Steve Lacy

1981
Tim Hacker

1983
John Easker

1984
Tim Hacker

1985
Tim Hacker

1991
Donovan Bergstrom

The List

UW Rowing Coaches

Men's

1894-Amos W. Marston
1895-98-Andrew O'Dea
1899-C.C. McConville
1900-06-Andrew O'Dea
1907-10-Edward Ten Eyck
1911-28-Harry "Dad" Vail
1929-34-George "Mike" Vail
1935-40-Ralph Hunn
1941-42-Allen Walz
1943-George Rea
1946-Allen Walz
1947-68-Norm Sonju
1969-96-Randy Jablonic
1996-present-Chris Clark

Women's

1973-79-Jay Mimier
1980-present-Sue Ela

1972-73

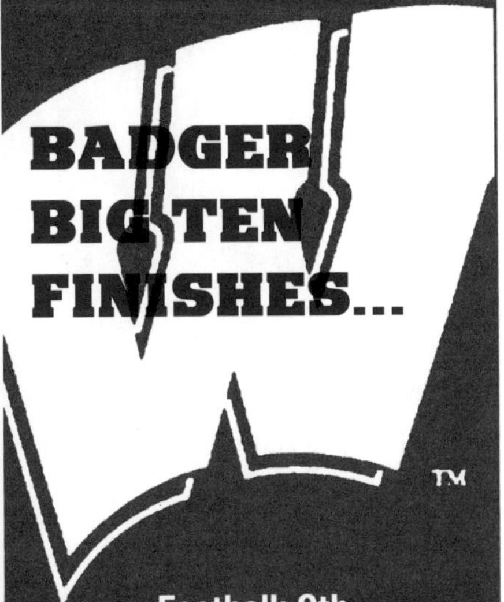

Football: 9th
coached by John Jardine

Cross Country: 3rd
coached by Dan McClimon

Basketball: 9th
coached by John Powless

Indoor Track: 4th
coached by Bill Perrin,
(8th-tie, NCAA)

Swimming: 3rd
coached by Jack Pettinger

Wrestling: 3rd
coached by Duane Kleven

Baseball: 4th (tie)
coached by Tom Meyer

Golf: 9th
coached by Tom Bennett

Gymnastics: 8th
coached by Raymond Bauer

Tennis: 4th (tie)
coached by Denny Schackter

Ice Hockey: 3rd (WCHA)
coached by Bob Johnson,
(1st, NCAA)

Outdoor Track: 6th
coached by Bill Perrin

Wisconsin wins first NCAA hockey title

In the 10th season since the hockey program at Wisconsin was resuscitated, the Badgers reached the promised land, winning their first NCAA championship with a 4-2 win over Denver on March 17, 1973. The win at fabled Boston Garden, on St. Patrick's Day, no less, culminated a 29-9-2 campaign for the Badgers and seventh-year Coach Bob Johnson.

The UW won 11 of its first 12 games, lost two games at Michigan Tech in early February and slumped a bit as the season wound down, but gained momentum in the playoffs. Wisconsin knocked off Minnesota, a 2-1-1 regular season series winner over the Badgers, by 8-6 and 6-4 scores in first round of the Western Collegiate Hockey Association playoffs. The Badgers then edged Notre Dame, 4-4 and 4-3 in a total goals series, to move into the NCAA tourney.

Freshman Dean Talafous was the hero of the NCAA semis against Cornell, scoring with five seconds left in regulation to tie the game 5-5 and force overtime. He then scored again with 33 seconds remaining in the OT to give Wisconsin a 6-5 win. It gave the Badgers momentum for the final, where the UW's pressure defense stopped Denver.

Wisconsin Time Line

1973: The Conference allowed graduate students to compete under certain specific conditions.

Accords ending the Vietnam War were signed in Paris.

Wisconsin's men's cross country team finished fifth in the inaugural NCAA district qualifying meet and advances to the NCAA nationals. The UW has qualified for the national meet every year since, the only university in the nation to do so.

WISCONSIN HEADLINER

Rufus Ferguson
Football

Rufus "Roadrunner" Ferguson still stands seventh on the all-time Badger career rushing list with 2,814 yards, more than a generation after ending his Wisconsin career. The Miami native, who prepped at Killian High School, was a first-team all-Big Ten pick at running back in 1971 and in 1972. The first UW back to exceed 1,000 yards in a season (1,222 in 1971), Ferguson also set a single-season scoring mark that year with 80 points. Ferguson ran for 100 yards or more 12 times in his career, reaching a single-game high of 211 yards against Minnesota in 1971. A standout student as well, Ferguson was a second-team academic All-American in 1971 and a first-team all-academic pick as a senior. He was the MVP of the 1972 North-South Shrine Game. Ferguson was inducted into the UW Athletic Hall of Fame in 1993.

WISCONSIN HEADLINER

D'Lynn Damron
Diving

D'Lynn Damron, one of the pioneering women athletes at Wisconsin, became the UW's first women's national diving

Champion in 1970, winning national one- and three-meter diving events.

The Madison West product went on to win the one-meter crown again in 1973 and earn runner-up honors in the three-meter event that same year. The women's program was not phased in to the Division of Intercollegiate Athletics until 1974 so Damron, like some other UW women's athletes, was forced to compete with little support and minimal publicity. Recognition of her accomplishments and of the role that she played in paving the way for a generation of athletes to follow came in 1992, when she was inducted into the UW Athletic Hall of Fame.

UW's men's basketball coaches

Coach	Seasons	Years	Record
James Elsom	1899-1904	6	25-14
Emmett Angell	1904-08	4	43-15
Haskell Noyes	1908-11	3	26-15
Walter Meanwell	1911-17, 20-34	20	246-99
Guy Lowman	1917-20	3	34-19
Harold "Bud" Foster	1934-59	25	265-267
John Erickson	1959-68	9	100-114
John Powless	1968-76	8	88-108
Bill Cofield	1976-82	6	63-101
Steve Yoder	1982-92	10	128-165
Stu Jackson	1992-94	2	32-25
Stan Van Gundy	1994-95	1	3-14
Dick Bennett	1995-	3	47-44

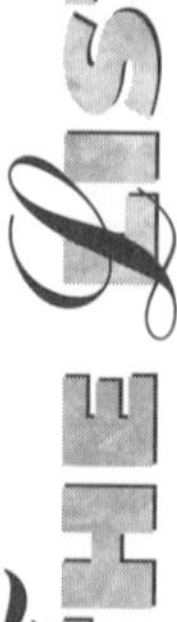

UW's men's basketball 1,000 point scorers

Michael Finley (1991-95)	2,147
Danny Jones (1986-90)	1,854
Claude Gregory (1977-81)	1,745
Rick Olson (1982-86)	1,736
Trent Jackson (1985-89)	1,545
Clarence Sherrod (1968-71)	1,408
Cory Blackwell (1981-84)	1,405
Tracy Webster (1991-94)	1,264
Wes Mathews(1977-80)	1,251
Joe Franklin (1965-68)	1,215
Dale Koehler (1972-76)	1,200
Dick Cable (1951-55)	1,180
Joe Chrnelich (1976-80)	1,171
Don Rehfeldt (1944-45, 1946-50)	1,169
Leon Howard (1970-73)	1,165
Scott Roth (1981-85)	1,156
James Johnson (1966-69)	1,147
Ken Siebel (1960-63)	1,084
Tim Locum (1987-91)	1,077
Larry Petty (1977-81)	1,066
Chuck Nagle (1966-69)	1,064
J.J. Weber (1983-87)	1,021
Willie Simms (1987-91)	1,015

1973-74

MEN'S

Football: 8th
coached by John Jardine

Cross Country: 2nd
coached by Dan McClimon

Basketball: 4th (tie)
coached by John Powless

Indoor Track: 4th
coached by Bill Perrin

Swimming: 2nd
coached by Jack Pettinger

Wrestling: 4th
coached by Duane Kleven

Baseball: 8th
coached by Tom Meyer

Golf: 9th
coached by Tom Bennett

Gymnastics: 8th
coached by Raymond Bauer

Tennis: 6th (tie)
coached by Denny Schackter

Ice Hockey: 5th (WCHA)
coached by Bob Johnson

Outdoor Track: 3rd
coached by Bill Perrin

WOMEN'S

Swimming: 9th
coached by Jack Pettinger

UW cagers' 16 wins most in 12 years

Wisconsin started out like a house afire in the 1973-74 basketball season, winning nine of its first 10 game. The sole loss was a 49-48 overtime heartbreaker on the road to rising national power Marquette. Coach John Powless's squad trounced Northwestern 87-53 in the Big Ten opener at the Wisconsin Fieldhouse, won a non-conference game at Ohio and the lost a 52-51 nail-biter at Indiana, where the Badgers had won only three times in 25 years.

Wins at the Fieldhouse over Illinois and Ohio State gave the UW a 3-1 Big Ten slate but a string of five losses in six games—three of them close and two blowouts—punctured Wisconsin's hopes of contending for the title. An 87-80 home win over Michigan State and road wins at Iowa and Northwestern gave Wisconsin a 16-8 overall mark and 8-6 Big Ten record, good for a fourth-place tie in the Conference.

The wins were the most for Wisconsin since a 17-7 campaign in 1961-62. And until 1997, Powless's 1974 Badgers were the last to post a winning Big Ten season. Three of his players that year earned Big Ten recognition, with Gary Anderson named to the Associated Press all-Big Ten second team, Kim Hughes to United Press International's third unit and Dale Koehler to UPI honorable mention. Hughes was a three-time UW rebounding leader and with twin brother Kerry was featured on the February 9, 1974, cover of *The Sporting News* as "Wisconsin's Twin Terrors."

WISCONSIN TIME LINE

1974: Richard Nixon became the first U.S. president to resign from office.

Charles D. Henry II and John D. Dewey were named assistant commissioners of the Big Ten; Conference offices were moved to Schaumburg, Illinois.

Billy Marek scored five touchdowns and runs for 304 yards as Wisconsin beats Minnesota 49-14.

WISCONSIN HEADLINER

Cindy Bremser
Track and Field

Cindy Bremser was one of the pioneers in women's sports at Wisconsin and the first track and field athlete to make a national impact for Coach Peter Tegen's fledgling women's track program in 1974. In fact, her career is filled with firsts. Bremser, a Mishicot, Wisconsin, native, didn't begin her UW track career until her junior year, a year prior to its becoming a varsity sport. She became UW's first track all-American with her third place finish in the AIAW mile in 1975. Bremser went on to compete on 15 national teams from 1975-88, including the 1984 Olympics in Los Angeles, where she became the first UW female track Olympian, placing fourth in the 3000-meter run. She is the only woman to have won six Drake Relays 1500 meter titles and was inducted into the Drake Relays Hall of Fame in 1985. A 1974 nursing graduate, she added a masters in pediatric nursing in 1985. She was the first woman member of the National "W" Club Board of Directors and was a charter inductee in the UW Athletic Hall of Fame in 1991.

WISCONSIN HEADLINER

Billy Marek
Football

Tailback Billy Marek paced the Badgers in scoring and all-purpose yardage during his last three seasons of varsity competition at Wisconsin, putting together three straight 1,200-yard seasons. The Chicago native had been recruited at Wisconsin along with by Badger mentor (and former Chicago Catholic League coach) John Jardine. The 5'8" Marek had 17 100-yard rushing games in his Wisconsin career and stands first on the all-time UW rushing list, 143 yards ahead of Ron Dayne, prior to the 1998 season. Marek led the nation in scoring in 1974 with 114 points, a 12.7 average. With 278 career points off 46 touchdowns and one PAT, Marek is tied with kicker Todd Gregoire at the top of the UW scoring list. His biggest day came in 1974 against Minnesota, when he scored a Badger record five touchdowns and rushed for 304 yards in a 49-14 UW win. He was named *Sports Illustrated's* national offensive back of the week.

WISCONSIN HEADLINER

Mike Webster
Football

Rhinelander native Mike Webster starred at center for Badger football teams of the early 1970s before starting a 17-year National Football League career. Webster won "W" awards in 1971, 1972 and 1973 and earned all-Big Ten honors the latter two seasons. He was also the Badgers' tri-captain and MVP his senior season before seeing post-season action in the East-West Shrine Game, the Hula Bowl, the Senior Bowl and the College All-Star Game. Selected by the Pittsburgh Steelers in the fifth round of the 1974 NFL draft, Webster played 15 years with them—including four Super Bowl championship teams—before ending his career with the Kansas City Chiefs. Webster was selected to and played in nine all-Pro football games. He was inducted into the UW Athletic Hall of Fame in 1995.

Wisconsin's national collegiate rowing championships in the 1970s

Men's national collegiate titles (all at 2000 meters)

1972—Freshman 8

1973—Varsity 8

1973—Junior Varsity 8

1973—Freshman 8

1974—Varsity 8

1974—Junior Varsity 8

1975—Varsity 8

1975—Varsity 4 w/o Coxswain

1976—Varsity 4 w/o Coxswain

1979—Freshman 8

Women's national collegiate titles (both at 1000 meters)

1975—Varsity 8

1979—Novice 8

1974-75

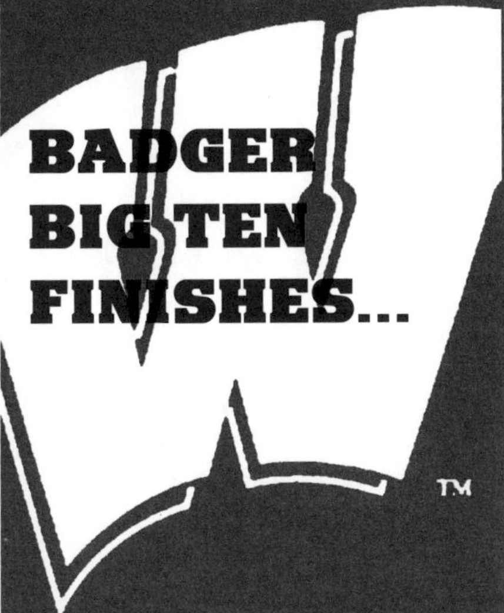

BADGER BIG TEN FINISHES...

MEN'S

Football: 4th
coached by John Jardine

Cross Country: 2nd
coached by Dan McClimon

Basketball: 8th
coached by John Powless

Indoor Track: 3rd
coached by Bill Perrin

Swimming: 2nd
coached by Jack Pettinger

Wrestling: 2nd
coached by Duane Kleven, (6th, NCAA)

Baseball: 5th
coached by Tom Meyer

Golf: 8th
coached by Tom Bennet

Gymnastics: 6th
coached by Raymond Bauer

Tennis: 2nd
coached by Denny Schackter

Ice Hockey: 4th (WCHA)
coached by Bob Johnson

Outdoor Track: 5th
coached by Bill Perrin

WOMEN'S

Swimming: 5th
coached by Roger Ridenour

THE BIG EVENT

Women's athletics debuts at UW

The first year of women's intercollegiate athletics at Wisconsin was highly successful. Despite having a budget of only $118,000, the Badger women's teams won one national championship and competed on the national level in cross country, swimming and diving and track.

Twelve women's sports began practice and competition during the fall of 1974—badminton, basketball, cross country, fencing, field hockey, golf, gymnastics, rowing, swimming and diving, tennis, track and field and volleyball.

In women's rowing, the varsity eight boat won the National Women's Rowing Association national championship. The Badgers covered the 1,000-meter course in 3:07.3, winning by over three seconds over Vesper Rowing Club.

In cross country, Cindy Bremser finished sixth in a national invitational. She also earned all-American honors in track with a third-place finish in the mile. As a team, Wisconsin finished 19th at the Association of Intercollegiate Athletics for Women (AIAW) Championship.

The women's swimming and diving team finished 30th at the AIAW Championship and fifth in the Big Ten meet. Peggy Anderson finished second on the one-meter board and sixth on the three-meter board to earn all-American honors.

Several other teams posted winning records or competed in unofficial Big Ten or regional competition during their initial seasons. The volleyball team was 28-4 and finished fifth in the AIAW regional. Fencing was 10-5 overall and tied for fifth in the Great Lakes Tournament.

The gymnastics team was 20-15, including a fifth-place finish in unofficial Big Ten competition and 10th in the region. The tennis team finished third in the Big Ten while the basketball team finished with an 11-7 mark.

WISCONSIN TIME LINE

1975: Work began on the Alaska oil pipeline.

Big Ten athletic directors voted to use three-man crews in basketball effective with the 1975-76 season.

Wisconsin erased a 22-point deficit for its greatest men's basketball comeback ever in an 82-81 overtime win over Ohio State at the Field House.

LEADING THE WAY

John Jardine
Football Coach

John Jardine served as Wisconsin's football coach from 1970-77 during an era of revitalization of the Badger program. The Chicago native compiled a 25-38-1 record in eight seasons as the UW coach, including a 7-4 mark in 1974, Wisconsin's first winning season since 1963. Starring for that squad were tackle Dennis Lick and tailback Billy Marek, both of whom shared Jardine's Chicago Catholic League roots. Jardine was a coaching prodigy and was actually helping coach at St. George High School in Evanston before he had even graduated. At Purdue, Jardine played both ways at guard and linebacker. A year after graduation, he became head coach at Fenwick High School in Oak Park, Illinois, and posted a 51-6-1 record in five years. He then assisted at Purdue and UCLA before coming to Madison. Jardine remained in Madison and was active in the insurance business and Badger football broadcasts. He died in Madison at age 54 in 1990.

Badgers star on TV

Wisconsin looked good on television in 1974. Coach John Jardine's Badgers played two regional, non-conference foes in televised games for the first time. Playing in Madison, the UW took the measure of two Big Eight opponents, beating fourth-ranked Nebraska 21-20 on September 21 and Missouri 59-20 two weeks later in games broadcast by ABC. Wisconsin, behind running back Billy Marek, finished 7-4 for Jardine's only winning season in Madison.

Marek scores five touchdowns against Gophers

Billy Marek, the Badgers' dependable running back from 1973-75, was never so reliable as on November 23, 1974, at home against Minnesota. No Badger had ever scored five touchdowns in a game before the junior from Chicago turned the trick while running for 304 yards. Coach John Jardine's best Wisconsin team crushed the Gophers 49-14 en route to a 7-4 season. Marek's five touchdowns and 30 points are still Wisconsin single game marks. He led the Badgers in all-purpose yardage in each of his three seasons and ranks second to Terrell Fletcher on the all-time UW list.

First women's basketball season produces good results

The first women's intercollegiate basketball practices were held at the Wisconsin Field House in October, 1974, under the direction of Coach Marilyn Harris. The Badger women played their first home game on January 11, 1975, beating UW-Green Bay 45-38. Wisconsin finished 11-7 overall and 6-2 at home in its first season.

1975-76

BADGER BIG TEN FINISHES...

MEN'S

Football: 6th
coached by John Jardine

Cross Country: 2nd
coached by Dan McClimon

Basketball: 9th
coached by John Powless

Indoor Track: 2nd
coached by Bill Perrin

Swimming: 2nd
coached by Jack Pettinger

Wrestling: 3rd
coached by Duane Kleven, (4th, NCAA)

Baseball: 7th
coached by Tom Meyer

Golf: 9th
coached by Tom Bennett

Gymnastics: 4th
coached by Raymond Bauer

Tennis: 3rd
coached by Denny Schackter

Ice Hockey: 7th (WCHA)
coached by Bill Rothwell

Outdoor Track: 2nd
coached by Bill Perrin

WOMEN'S

Swimming: 5th
coached by Roger Ridenour

Volleyball: 6th
coached by Pat Hielscher

Golf: 8th
coached by Jane Eastham

Outdoor Track: 1st
coached by Peter Tegen

Wrestlers win three NCAA titles

Wisconsin wrestling served notice it was to be taken very seriously as one of the nation's top programs in 1976 when the Badgers had a school-record three national champions and earned their highest finish ever (fourth) at the NCAA Championships in Tucson, Arizona.

The Badgers entered the national meet having finished third at the Big Ten championships after a compiling a 13-3 dual record. Lee Kemp (158) and Gary Sommer (Hwt.) won conference titles. The UW won regular-season duals with Michigan, Michigan State and Oklahoma, with the three losses coming to Iowa, Iowa State and Oklahoma State.

It was in Tucson, however, that Coach Duane Kleven's Badgers showed their depth as a team. Kemp, a native of Chardon, Ohio, was the only undefeated wrestler (39-0) in the nation in '75-76 and went on to defeat Washington's Tom Brown in the NCAA title match. Kemp won two more NCAA crowns at 158 and compiled a 143-6-1 record during his Wisconsin career.

Jack Reinwand, wrestling at 126 pounds, defeated Harold Wiley of UC-Santa Barbara for his national title. Reinwand had finished fourth at the NCAA the year before. Pat Christensen won his '76 NCAA title at 167 pounds with a win over Iowa's Dan Wagemann.

The Badgers finished the tournament with 64 points, just one-half point behind third-place Oklahoma State.

WISCONSIN TIME LINE

1976: The supersonic Concorde jetliner was put into service by England and France.

Athletic directors voted to establish a minimum price of $8 for football tickets, effective in the fall of 1977.

Edwina Qualls took over for what would become a 10-year stint as UW's women's basketball coach.

WISCONSIN HEADLINER

Craig Norwich
Hockey

Two-time all-American defenseman Craig Norwich lettered three times for Badger hockey teams from 1974-77. The Edina, Minnesota, native was the first Badger to twice earn all-America honors. For his career, Norwich scored 42 goals and had 126 assists for 168 points, second to Theran Walsh on the all-time defensemen's point list. Norwich's 42 career goals are still the most by a Badger defenseman. His 18 goals during the Badgers' 1976-77 NCAA championship season rank him in a second-place tie on the all-time list while his 83 points that same season are the most by a defenseman. Norwich was picked by the Montreal Canadiens in the 1975 National Hockey League draft and saw action from 1979-81 with Winnipeg, St. Louis and Colorado.

WISCONSIN HEADLINER

Dennis Lick
Football

Four-time letterwinner (1972-75) Dennis Lick earned consensus all-America honors for Coach John Jardine's Badgers in 1975 despite missing the last three games because of an injury. Lick, a native of Chicago, was one of Wisconsin's most punishing offensive linemen as he blocked for Billy Marek, Wisconsin's all-time leading rusher. Lick also received first-team all-America honors in 1974 from The Sporting News to become Wisconsin's first all-American since Pat Richter in 1962. Lick was selected in the first round of the 1976 National Football League draft by his hometown Bears. He played with Chicago until his retirement in 1981.

Russ Hellickson's most memorable wrestling moment

Former Wisconsin wrestling star (and coach) Russ Hellickson had many great memories from his career as a competitor, including a silver medal in the 1976 Olympic Games. But no single moment in his own career stood out for Hellickson as much as the 1976 NCAA wresltling finals in Tucson. Three Badgers—Jack Reinwand, Lee Kemp and Pat Christenson—won national championships and provided Hellickson his greatest memory. "No feeling generated through my own competition has ever matched the extreme satisfaction and pride I felt," he remembers. "On that Saturday evening I had made no personal sacrifices, yet I achieved a level of emotional elation higher than any other wrestling has ever provided me. It was gratifying to have been able to share probably their most memorable moment and to have felt at least a part of their accomplishment."

Wisconsin's NCAA wrestling champions

1974	Rick Lawinger, 142 lbs.
1976	Jack Reinwand, 126 lbs. Lee Kemp, 158 lbs. Pat Christensen, 167 lbs.
1977	Jim Haines, 118 lbs. Lee Kemp, 158 lbs.
1978	Lee Kemp, 158 lbs. Ron Jeidy, 190 lbs.
1980	Andy Rein, 150 lbs.
1985	Jim Jordan, 134 lbs.
1986	Jim Jordan, 134 lbs.
1989	Dave Lee, 167 lbs.
1991	Matt Demaray, 150 lbs.
1992	Matt Demaray, 150 lbs.
1996	Jeff Walter, Hwt.

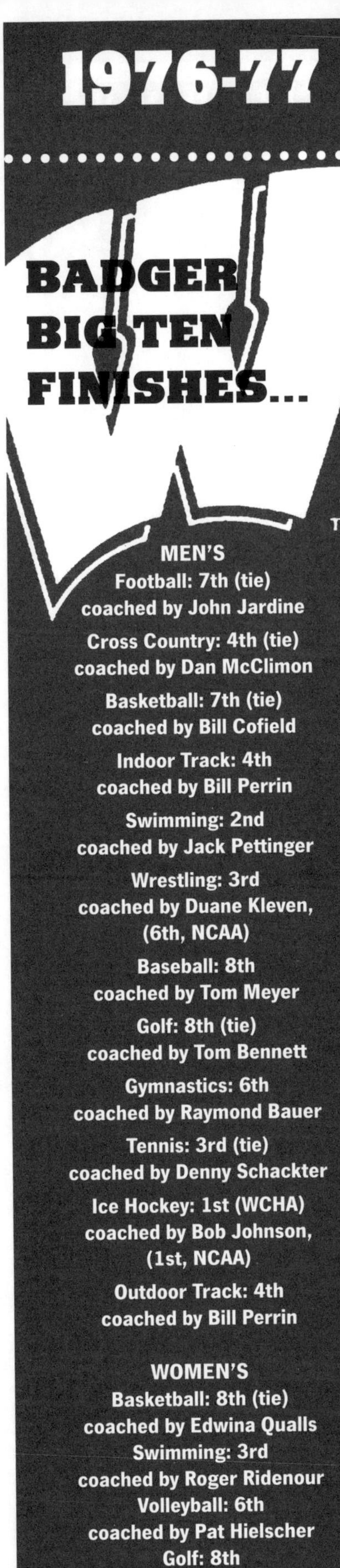

MEN'S
Football: 7th (tie)
coached by John Jardine
Cross Country: 4th (tie)
coached by Dan McClimon
Basketball: 7th (tie)
coached by Bill Cofield
Indoor Track: 4th
coached by Bill Perrin
Swimming: 2nd
coached by Jack Pettinger
Wrestling: 3rd
coached by Duane Kleven,
(6th, NCAA)
Baseball: 8th
coached by Tom Meyer
Golf: 8th (tie)
coached by Tom Bennett
Gymnastics: 6th
coached by Raymond Bauer
Tennis: 3rd (tie)
coached by Denny Schackter
Ice Hockey: 1st (WCHA)
coached by Bob Johnson,
(1st, NCAA)
Outdoor Track: 4th
coached by Bill Perrin

WOMEN'S
Basketball: 8th (tie)
coached by Edwina Qualls
Swimming: 3rd
coached by Roger Ridenour
Volleyball: 6th
coached by Pat Hielscher
Golf: 8th
coached by Jackie Hayes
Outdoor Track: 2nd
coached by Peter Tegen

Badgers take Big Ten, WCHA and NCAA hockey titles

Wisconsin's finest hockey season ever culminated on March 26, 1977, when the Badgers defeated Michigan 6-5 on a Steve Alley goal 23 seconds into overtime for their second NCAA title. It was a bit of delicious irony for Wisconsin, which had lost 7-6 to Michigan at home in its season opener.

Coach Bob Johnson's team finished the season with a 37-7-1 record, a UW record for wins in a season, and became the first team to win Big Ten, Western Collegiate Hockey Association and NCAA championships in the same season. The UW never lost two games in a row and ended the season on a roll, going 22-1-1 in its last 24 contests. And the Badgers' seven losses—to Michigan, Michigan State, Notre Dame, Harvard, Minnesota and Denver and the Spartak Club of Russia in an exhibition game—were all, except Spartak, avenged by UW victories.

In post-season action, Wisconsin swept through the WCHA playoffs, beating Colorado College twice by 3-1 scores and then mowing down Minnesota (9-5, 8-3) and Michigan (4-0, 5-4). It took an overtime goal by Mike Eaves to give the Badgers a 4-3 NCAA semifinal win over New Hampshire and berth in the title game against Michigan. Wisconsin won six of the seven games it played against Michigan, especially the one that really counted.

Honors aplenty came to the Badgers, as well. Johnson was named national coach of the year while his son Mark, a forward who had a UW rookie record 36 goals, was named freshman of the year. Defenseman Craig Norwich, goaltender Julian Baretta and center Mike Eaves were named to the all-American team. Baretta was named NCAA tournament MVP and Norwich and defenseman John Taft were picked for the all-tournament team.

Wisconsin Time Line

1977: Treaties granting eventual control of the Panama Canal to Panama were signed by President Jimmy Carter and Gen. Omar Torrijos Herrera.

Big Ten athletic directors voted that there must be at least six varsity teams in a sport, with the exception of fencing, to hold a Conference championship.

The UW women's basketball team won its first WWIAC state large school championship, beating cross-state rival UW-La Crosse for the first time.

WISCONSIN HEADLINER

Mike Eaves
Hockey

Two-time all-American forward Mike Eaves was a stalwart of four Badger hockey teams. One of them, the 1976-77 unit, won the NCAA title as Eaves earned the first of his all-America honors. Eaves, a native of Kanata, Ontario, became the first Badger to eclipse 200 career points, totaling 267 points—still a school record. He still owns the longest scoring streak in Wisconsin history at 21 straight games, set during the 1977-78 season, and totaled 89 points that season. He was the Western Collegiate Hockey Association's most valuable player as a senior in 1978 and twice was named the Badgers' MVP. The three-time Wisconsin captain shared WCHA scoring honors with teammate Mark Johnson in 1977-78 and was the Wisconsin recipient of the Big Ten Conference Medal of Honor. Eaves went on to a career in the National Hockey League, playing with the Minnesota North Stars from 1978-83 and the Calgary Flames from 1983-86. He's now an assistant coach with the Philadelphia Flyers. He was inducted into the UW Athletic Hall of Fame in 1992.

WISCONSIN HEADLINER

Carie Graves
Crew

Spring Green native Carie Graves is Wisconsin's only three-time Olympian, making the U.S. crew team in 1976, 1980 and 1984. Graves earned a bronze in 1976 a year after leading the UW to its first national championship in crew. She also made the 1980 American team which boycotted the Moscow Olympics but came back four years later in Los Angeles to win the gold as a member of the U.S. eight. Graves, a three-time silver medalist in women's eight at the 1975, 1981 and 1983 world championships, was the first inductee into the UW Women's Athletics Hall of Fame in 1984 and also has been named to the U.S. Rowing Association's Hall of Fame. She was named the U.S. Olympic Committee's Athlete of the Year in 1984 and received the Southland Corporation's "Olympia Award" that year for excellence and achievement. She graduated with an English degree in 1976 and earned a master's in educational administration from Harvard in 1985. She was one of 35 charter inductees into the UW Athletics Hall of Fame in 1991.

THE BUD SONG

When you say Wis-con-sin

The playing of the Bud song is an integral part of any performance by the Wisconsin band. The tune, a spinoff of the song "You've Said It All," a jingle originally written by Steve Karmen for Budweiser beer commercials and copyrighted by Sandlee Publishing Co. in 1970, has become legendary at the UW.

Band director Michael Leckrone said its popularity began at a 1975 hockey game when the crowd wanted a polka and had the beer commercial in the tunes it played. Leckrone told the band that substituting "Wisconsin" for "Budweiser" would work.

It did. And after a come-from-behind football win over Oregon in 1978 during which the song got the crowd revved up and the Badgers scored right after, Leckrone said, "from then on, the band could never play enough 'Bud'."

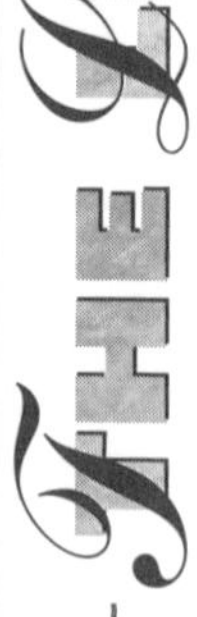

THE LIST

Wisconsin's women's volleyball coaches

Coach	Record	Years
Kay Von Guten	25-4	1974-75
Pat Hielscher	85-42-7	1975-78
Kristi Conklin	89-45-6	1978-81
Niels Pedersen	5-29	1981-82
Russ Carney	38-80	1982-86
Steve Lowe	106-63	1986-91
Margie Fitzpatrick	22-10	1991-92
John Cook	101-65	1992-present

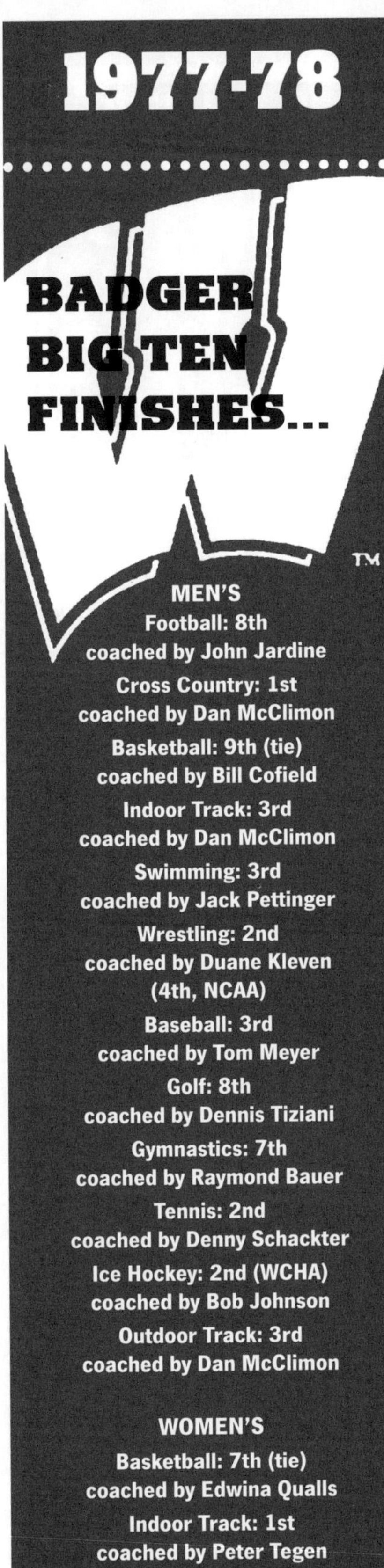

1977-78

BADGER BIG TEN FINISHES...

MEN'S

Football: 8th
coached by John Jardine

Cross Country: 1st
coached by Dan McClimon

Basketball: 9th (tie)
coached by Bill Cofield

Indoor Track: 3rd
coached by Dan McClimon

Swimming: 3rd
coached by Jack Pettinger

Wrestling: 2nd
coached by Duane Kleven
(4th, NCAA)

Baseball: 3rd
coached by Tom Meyer

Golf: 8th
coached by Dennis Tiziani

Gymnastics: 7th
coached by Raymond Bauer

Tennis: 2nd
coached by Denny Schackter

Ice Hockey: 2nd (WCHA)
coached by Bob Johnson

Outdoor Track: 3rd
coached by Dan McClimon

WOMEN'S

Basketball: 7th (tie)
coached by Edwina Qualls

Indoor Track: 1st
coached by Peter Tegen

Swimming: 2nd
coached by Carl Johansson

Volleyball: 2nd
coached by Pat Hielscher

Golf: 7th
coached by Jackie Hayes

Outdoor Track: 1st

Cross country, fencing, hockey take Big Ten titles

Wisconsin, behind Jim Stintzi's second-place finish, won its first Big Ten cross country championship in 27 years in the fall of 1977. Coach Dan McClimon's team scored a low of 52 points to defeat Illinois and Ohio State, which each scored 75 points. Stintzi earned all-America honors as Wisconsin took sixth in the NCAA meet in its highest national finish since 1951. The UW had won 15 Big Ten hill-and-dale titles since the meet's inception in 1910 and had 20 first-division finishes from 1950-76, including three straight runner- up slots from 1973-75 under McClimon. The victory would kick start a remarkable string of 17 Big Ten championships over the next 20 years for the UW harriers.

Coach Bob Johnson's hockey team also took the Big Ten crown, posting an 8-3-1 mark against Conference rivals Michigan, Michigan State and Minnesota. The Badgers, led by Mark Johnson's 48 goal, 86 point season and Mike Eaves's 43 goal, 89 point campaign chalked up a 28-12-3 season en route to the Western Collegiate Hockey Association playoff championship and a fourth-place finish in the NCAA tournament. Eaves, the UW's Big Ten Conference Medal of Honor winner in 1978, was named a first-team all-American for the second straight season while Johnson earned identical honors for the first time.

Coach Tony Gillham's fencers took Wisconsin's third Big Ten championship in the '77-78 campaign. It was the UW's sixth fencing title. Leading the Badgers were Dean Rose and Steve Vandenberg. Rose won the first of his two Big Ten championships in foil while Vandenberg took the second of his two epee titles. Wisconsin successfully defended its championship in 1979 and also won Conference titles in 1982, 1984 and 1985 before fencing was discontinued as a Big Ten-sponsored sport after the 1986 season.

WISCONSIN TIME LINE

1978: Elvis Presley died in Memphis at age 42.

The Conference eliminated the rule requiring, in football, that only Conference opponents be scheduled in November.

The Badgers beat eventual NCAA basketball champion Michigan State 83-81 at the Field House.

WISCONSIN HEADLINER

Mark Johnson
Hockey

Mark Johnson, a two-time UW hockey all-American in the late 1970s for his father, legendary coach "Badger Bob" Johnson, has come full circle to Madison, where as a prep in 1976 he led Madison Memorial High School to the state title. Following an 11-year professional career with five National Hockey League teams, Johnson returned to campus in 1996 as an assistant to Jeff Sauer. Prior to joining the UW staff, Johnson earned coach of the year honors for guiding the Madison Monsters to a winning record and Colonial Hockey League playoff berth in their inaugural season. Johnson still holds UW record for most goals in a career (125) and season (48) and was a member of the UW's 1977 NCAA champs. One of only three Badgers to twice be named a first-team all-American, Johnson was the leading scorer (5 goals, 6 assists) for the 1980 U.S. Olympic hockey team, which stunned the world with its "Miracle on Ice" at Lake Placid. Holder of a degree in kinesiology, Johnson was named a charter member of the UW Athletics Hall of Fame in 1991.

WISCONSIN HEADLINER

Lee Kemp
Wrestling

Lee Kemp, one of the pre-eminent names in Wisconsin wrestling history, did a lot of good things in threes. Kemp, a native of Cardon, Ohio, won three NCAA wrestling titles at 158 lbs. from 1976-78. He also won a like number of Big Ten championships and Midlands Tournament titles over the same span. And three times Kemp parcipated in the East-West College All-Star dual meet. Kemp was undefeated and untied at 39-0-0 in 1975-76 for the Badgers and compiled a career mark of 143-6-1. He was the world freestyle champion in 1978 and then followed that with a spectacular 1979, winning the world freestyle again, the Pan American Games title and the National AAU title. He was awarded the Sun Cup in 1978 as the outstanding amateur wrestler of the year. In 1984, Kemp received the "Olympia Award" from the Southland Corporation for outstanding amateur athletic participation.

LEADING THE WAY

Kit Saunders-Nordeen
Associate Athletic Director
Women's Administrator

A pioneer in the organization and development of women's sports both in Wisconsin and nationally, Kit Saunders Nordeen was named the UW's first athletic director for women in 1974. She guided the transition of women's sports in Madison from the recreational level to intercollegiate status. In 1983, she was named an associate athletic director supervising 22 men's and women's non-revenue sports; she resumed her role as primary women's administrator in 1986 until her retirement in 1989. She earned master's and doctoral degrees from Wisconsin. Nordeen, the first inductee into the UW Women's Athletics Hall of Fame in 1984, was one of the founders of the Wisconsin Women's Intercollegiate Athletic Conference in 1971 and later served as its president. She also was first vice president of the Association of Intercollegiate Athletics for Women from 1979-82 and was inducted into the UW Athletic Hall of Fame in 1998.

LEADING THE WAY

Tamara J. Flarup
Women's Sports
Information Director

One of the leaders for women in the field of sports information, Tam Flarup is in her 20th year as the women's sports information director at Wisconsin. Since becoming women's SID in 1977, Flarup has been instrumental in a number of successful Big Ten and NCAA Championships and has also worked at the last four NCAA Women's Final Fours. As a member of the College Sports Information Directors of America, Flarup has served on a number of committees including chair of the Publicists for Women's Sports. Through CoSIDA, a number of her media guides have been honored with national awards including several "Best in the Nation" honorees. The native of Eagle Grove, Iowa, came to Wisconsin after one year as the first women's SID at the University of Kansas. The 1975 Iowa State graduate earned a double major in journalism and physical education while playing on the women's golf team.

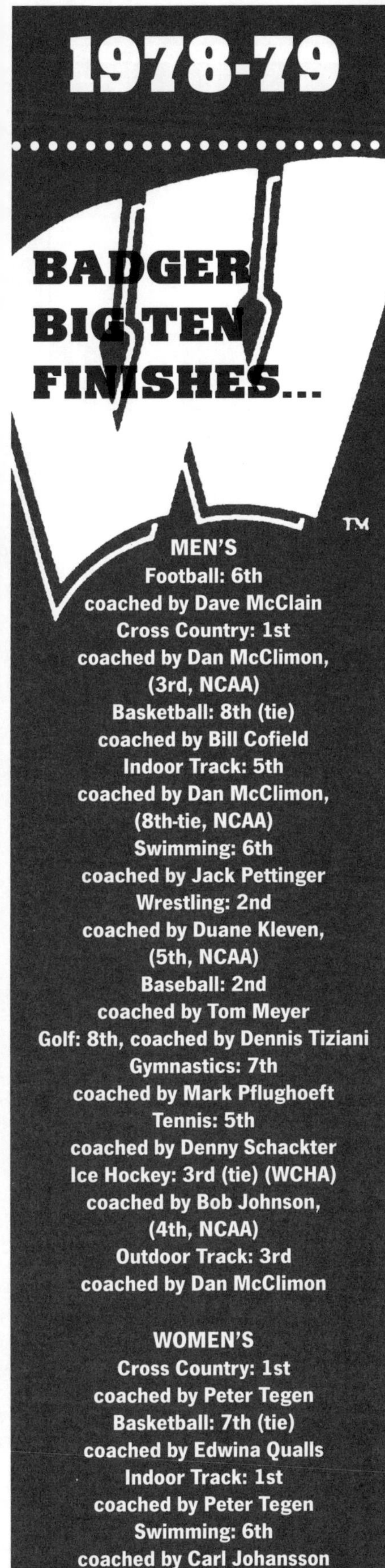

1978-79

BADGER BIG TEN FINISHES...

MEN'S
Football: 6th
coached by Dave McClain
Cross Country: 1st
coached by Dan McClimon,
(3rd, NCAA)
Basketball: 8th (tie)
coached by Bill Cofield
Indoor Track: 5th
coached by Dan McClimon,
(8th-tie, NCAA)
Swimming: 6th
coached by Jack Pettinger
Wrestling: 2nd
coached by Duane Kleven,
(5th, NCAA)
Baseball: 2nd
coached by Tom Meyer
Golf: 8th, coached by Dennis Tiziani
Gymnastics: 7th
coached by Mark Pflughoeft
Tennis: 5th
coached by Denny Schackter
Ice Hockey: 3rd (tie) (WCHA)
coached by Bob Johnson,
(4th, NCAA)
Outdoor Track: 3rd
coached by Dan McClimon

WOMEN'S
Cross Country: 1st
coached by Peter Tegen
Basketball: 7th (tie)
coached by Edwina Qualls
Indoor Track: 1st
coached by Peter Tegen
Swimming: 6th
coached by Carl Johansson
Volleyball: 5th (tie)
coached by Kristi Conklin
Golf: 6th, coached by Jackie Hayes
Outdoor Track: 1st
coached by Peter Tegen

Matthews beats "Magic," Spartans

Coach Bill Cofield's Wisconsin men's basketball team won 12 games in 1978-79—the most at the UW in five years—but none was bigger than the season finale.

Riding a modest three-game winning streak, the Badgers, led by guards Wes Matthews, Arnold Gaines and Dan Hastings, center Larry Petty and forwards Claude Gregory and Joe Chrnelich, played host to a fourth-ranked Michigan State squad that featured the legendary Earvin "Magic" Johnson and all-America forward Greg Kelser in the last game of the regular season for both teams.

Michigan State, which brought a 10-game winning streak of its own to the UW Field House, was as advertised—but the Badgers played a fine first half and led 44-43 at the intermission behind 12 points from Gregory and 11 from Chrnelich. Johnson and Kelser each had 12 points for the Spartans, who shot .548 from the field.

Neither team led by more than four points in the second half until the Badgers took a 78-73 lead with 3:12 remaining. But Michigan State came back and eventually tied it at 81 on a pair of Johnson free throws with 0:03 left.

Matthews put an exclamation point on the tense game with a historic 50-foot buzzer-beater that gave the Badgers a two-point win.

Gregory finished with 25 points and 16 rebounds to pace the Badgers, while Johnson put up 26 points, 13 rebounds and eight assists in his last Big Ten game. MSU went on to win its first NCAA title in the sport.

Wisconsin Time Line

1979: Thousands fled their homes near the Three Mile Island nuclear plant in Pennsylvania when officials warned of the risk of a core meltdown.

Wisconsin connected on 32 of 43 field goal attempts for a single-game men's school record in a 78-54 win over Army.

Mark Johnson closed out his Wisconsin hockey career as the top goal scorer (125) in UW history.

WISCONSIN HEADLINER

Steve Lacy
Track and Cross Country

Two-time Olympian Steve Lacy was the first Wisconsin runner to break 4 minutes in the mile, running 3:59.64 in 1977. A native of nearby McFarland, Wis., "Lace" didn't have far to go when recruited by Coach Dan McClimon. Staying close to home paid off. Lacy won six Big Ten titles, including three consecutive indoor mile crowns. A four-time "W" award winner in both track and cross country, he was also a three-time indoor track all-American and ran the second leg on the Badgers' 1976 NCAA indoor champion two-mile relay unit. Lacy and discus thrower Arlie Mucks, Sr., are the only two-time track and field Olympians from Wisconsin. Lacy earned a spot at 1500 meters on the ill-fated U.S. team that boycotted the 1980 Moscow Olympics. He also competed in Los Angeles in 1984 in the 5,000-meter run. He's a member of the Wisconsin track and field "Hall of Honor."

LEADING THE WAY

Jim Mott
Sports Information Director

Jim Mott has spent a lifetime in Madison. The retired Wisconsin sports information director (1966-90) is knowledgeable on all things Wisconsin. A graduate of Wisconsin, with bachelor's degrees in zoology (1954) and journalism (1956), Mott was assistant sports information director for 12 years before becoming SID. Well-respected by his peers, Mott was named to the College Sports Information Directors Hall of Fame in 1979 and in 1986 received that organ-ization's Arch Ward Award, the highest bestowed by SIDs on one of their own. Mott served on the U.S. Olympic team press liaison staff for the 1980 Olympic Winter Games at Lake Placid, N.Y., handling media relations duties for the gold-medal winning hockey team. No less respected in Madison, Mott is a former president of the Madison Pen & Mike Club and was inducted into the UW Athletic Hall of Fame in 1990. Jim and his wife Dorothy are the parents of three adult sons and still reside in Madison.

McClain wins in debut as football coach

It may not have been pretty, but football Coach Dave McClain's debut at Wisconsin got the Badgers started on a winning note.

The Badgers hosted the University of Richmond to open the '78 gridiron campaign and, despite entering Spider territory only twice all afternoon, registered a 7-6 victory before a crowd of 60,877 at Camp Randall Stadium. The win allowed McClain to become the first Wisconsin football coach to win his debut since Milt Bruhn in 1956.

Richmond's Steve Adams kicked field goals in each of the game's first two periods to give the visitors a 6-0 lead. Wisconsin, however, responded with a school record-tying 80-yard touchdown pass from freshman quarterback John Josten to split end David Charles with 10:13 left in the first half. Steve Veith booted the extra point to conclude the scoring for the day.

Matthews leads nation in punt returns

Ira Matthews had 16 punt returns, three for touchdowns, to lead the nation in 1978. Matthews had return yardage of 270 for an average of 16.9 yards per return, still a UW season record. His longest was a 78-yard return against Minnesota. The four-time letterwinner returned one punt as a freshman but never fell out of double figures after that. He had 15 in 1976 and 13 in 1977. Matthews' career total of 45 still ranks third on the all-time Wisconsin list, as does his yardage total of 443.

1979-80

BADGER BIG TEN FINISHES...

MEN'S

Football: 7th (tie)
coached by Dave McClain

Cross Country: 1st
coached by Dan McClimon

Basketball: 8th
coached by Bill Cofield

Indoor Track: 6th
coached by Dan McClimon

Swimming: 6th
coached by Jack Pettinger

Wrestling: 2nd
coached by Duane Kleven,
(7th, NCAA)

Baseball: 4th
coached by Tom Meyer

Golf: 6th, coached by Dennis Tiziani

Gymnastics: 8th
coached by Mark Pflughoeft

Tennis: 3rd (tie)
coached by Denny Schackter

Ice Hockey: 9th (WCHA)
coached by Bob Johnson

Outdoor Track: 6th
coached by Dan McClimon

WOMEN'S

Cross Country: 1st
coached by Peter Tegen

Basketball: 5th (tie)
coached by Edwina Qualls

Indoor Track: 1st
coached by Peter Tegen

Swimming: 5th
coached by Carl Johansson

Volleyball: 5th (tie)
coached by Kristi Conklin

Golf: 7th, coached by Jackie Hayes

Outdoor Track: 1st
coached by Peter Tegen

UW women claim Big Ten indoor and outdoor track titles

The Wisconsin women's track teams had its most successful season on record in 1979-80, winning unofficial Big Ten indoor and outdoor championships and finishing second in the AIAW Indoor Championship.

The Badgers remained undefeated in Big Ten indoor meets, winning their third title in as many years. Wisconsin scored 128 points to easily outdistance second place Ohio State (79). The UW won seven events and set six Big Ten records.

Wisconsin also continued its dominance at the Big Ten outdoor meet winning its third consecutive title. The Badgers outscored Michigan State, 157-90, and won six events, setting three Big Ten and two UW records.

Wisconsin qualified 16 athletes for the 1980 Association of Intercollegiate Athletics for Women (AIAW) indoor championship and finished second in the team race. Texas-El Paso won the meet with 40 points while the Badgers scored 25 points behind national champion Pat Johnson, who won the long jump on her last attempt of the meet, leaping 20'10". Suzie Houston also earned all-American honors with a third-place finish in the 2,000-meter run.

The Badgers also finished ninth in the AIAW outdoor championship.

WISCONSIN TIME LINE

1980: The U.S. announced it would boycott the Moscow Olympic Games to protest the Soviet Union's invasion of Afghanistan.

The Council of Ten adopted a resolution to establish a task force to prepare a plan for incorporating women's athletics into the Conference.

Claude Gregory scored 29 points and pulled down 17 rebounds in his last game for Wisconsin.

WISCONSIN HEADLINER

Kris Thorsness
Rowing

A two-time Olympian, Kris Thorsness was a gold medalist in 1984 as a member of the sweep eight. She also participated in the 1988 Olympics in the four with coxswain. Thorsness, a native of Anchorage, Alaska, was a member of five U.S. national teams competing in world championship.During her Wisconsin career, from 1977-82, she led the Badgers to a second-place finish in the varsity eight at the 1980 national championship and fourth-place finish in 1982.

WISCONSIN HEADLINER

Ray Snell
Football

Ray Snell, a native of Baltimore, Maryland, was a first-team all-America selection by *The Sporting News* in 1979. The 295-lb. lineman, known for his speed and agility, blocked for Ira Matthews and Dave Mohapp on Coach Dave McClain's second Badger squad. Snell was the 22nd overall pick by the Tampa Bay Buccaneers in the first round of the 1980 National Football League draft.

LEADING THE WAY

Randy Jablonic
Crew Coach

Randy Jablonic's career as a Badger rower from 1957-60 began a 40-year association with the sport at the University of Wisconsin. A member of the 1959 national champion varsity eight crew, he competed in the 1960 Olympic Trials in the four-person event. Jablonic went on to serve as frosh coach in the program's history at the conclusion of the 1968 season. His crews won the Ten Eyck Trophy—awarded to the school that scores the most points in the National Intercollegiate Rowing Championship—10 times. Jablonic's varsity eight crew won its fifth national collegiate title in 1990 and earned a trip to the Royal Henley Regatta in London. He was name d the Eastern Association of Rowing Colleges Coach of the Year for his achievements. He remains a consultant for the Badger program after retiring in 1997.

Men's Conference Medal of Honor winners

1970
Douglas R. McFadyen

1971
Don Vandrey

1972
Pat Matzdorf

1973
Keith D. Nosbusch

1974
Gary D. Anderson

1975
James R. Dyreby, Jr.

1976
Patrick J. Christenson

1977
Peter W. Brey

1978
Michael Eaves

1979
Steve Lacy

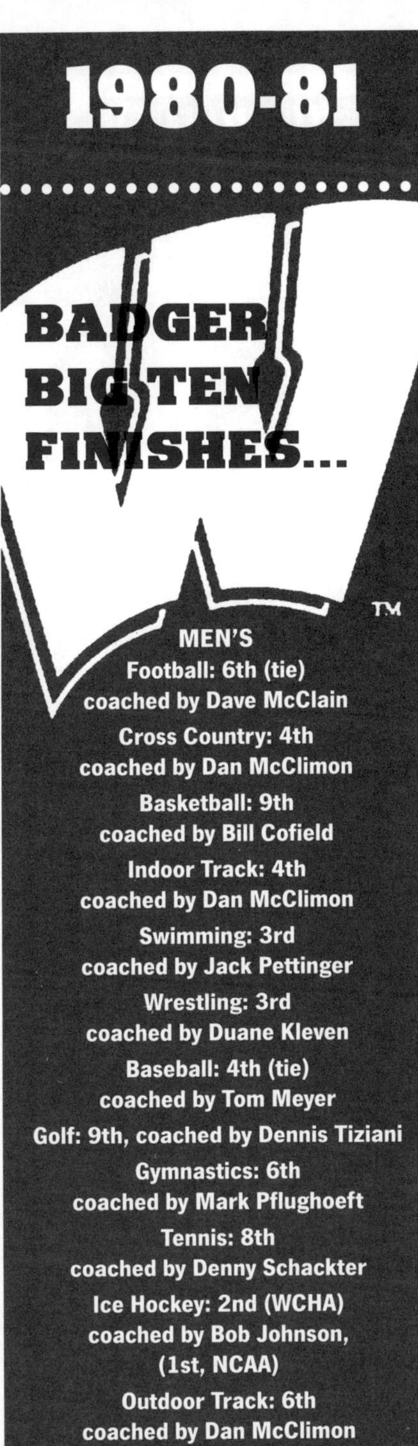

MEN'S
Football: 6th (tie)
coached by Dave McClain
Cross Country: 4th
coached by Dan McClimon
Basketball: 9th
coached by Bill Cofield
Indoor Track: 4th
coached by Dan McClimon
Swimming: 3rd
coached by Jack Pettinger
Wrestling: 3rd
coached by Duane Kleven
Baseball: 4th (tie)
coached by Tom Meyer
Golf: 9th, coached by Dennis Tiziani
Gymnastics: 6th
coached by Mark Pflughoeft
Tennis: 8th
coached by Denny Schackter
Ice Hockey: 2nd (WCHA)
coached by Bob Johnson,
(1st, NCAA)
Outdoor Track: 6th
coached by Dan McClimon

WOMEN'S
Cross Country: 2nd
coached by Peter Tegen
Basketball: 5th (tie)
coached by Edwina Qualls
Indoor Track: 1st
coached by Peter Tegen
Swimming: 4th
coached by Carl Johansson
Volleyball: 7th
coached by Kristi Conklin
Golf: 8th, coached by Jackie Hayes
Outdoor Track: 1st
coached by Peter Tegen

Badgers win third NCAA hockey title

Wisconsin won its third NCAA hockey title on March 28, 1981, in its sixth trip to the national collegiate tournament. The Badgers had posted a 23-13 regular season record and a 17-11 second-place showing in the Western Collegiate Hockey Association. In fact, they had dropped three of their last five regular season games and had been eliminated by Colorado College in the WCHA playoffs.

Picked for the NCAA tourney as an at-large entry, the Badgers responded, beating Clarkson College 9-8 in a total goal series in the NCAA quarterfinals. In the national semis, at Duluth, Minnesota, Wisconsin defeated Northern Michigan 5-1, setting up a rematch with a Minnesota team that had beaten the UW in three of four regular season games. They stunned the heavily favored Gophers 6-3 for their most improbable championship, thus earning the nickname, the "Back Door Badgers."

Goaltender Marc Behrend was named the tournament MVP. It was Coach Bob Johnson's last NCAA title. The veteran coach resigned following Wisconsin's second-place NCAA finish in 1982.

Wisconsin Time Line

1981: Walter Cronkite signed off for the last time as the anchor of the "CBS Evening News."

Nine of the 10 conference universities (with Minnesota as the exception) voted to affiliate their women's athletic programs with the Conference; the first official women's championship was held, in field hockey, in the fall of 1981.

Wisconsin defeated No. 1-ranked Michigan 21-14 in football, and eventually went to the Garden State Bowl, its first bowl appearance in 28 years.

WISCONSIN HEADLINER

Marc Behrend
Hockey

Marc Behrend, a native of Madison (LaFollette H.S.), stayed home to play college hockey and it turned out well for both him and the Badgers. Behrend was in goal for Wisconsin's NCAA championship seasons of 1981 and 1983. He recorded 30 saves in the UW's 6-3 NCAA finals win over Minnesota in the surprising 1981 campaign. In the 1983 NCAA title game, the 6-2 win over Harvard was largely credited to Behrend. The veteran goalie had nine and 10 saves in the first and second periods, respectively, as the Badgers nursed 1-0 and 2-0 leads before blowing the game open in the third period. For his efforts in both of those championship runs, Behrend was named the NCAA tournament MVP as well as the Badgers' most valuable for the '83 season. He finished his Wisconsin career with a 49-8-3 mark for a UW record winning percentage of .842. Behrend had a career 2.64 goals-against average, a .912 save percentage and four shutouts. He was the goaltender for the U.S. Olympic hockey team in 1984 and played three seasons for the NHL's Winnipeg Jets.

WISCONSIN HEADLINER

Ann French &
Claire Allison
Badminton

The 1979 Broderick Award winner for badminton, Ann French was a four-year all-American while competing from 1978-82. She and doubles partner Claire Allison, who competed for the UW from 1980-83, won the 1981 and 1982 Association of Intercollegiate Athletics for Women (AIAW) national title. French also finished among the top eight players in singles competition all four years and earned six all-American honors. French, a native of Elmhurst, Ill., was the UW's inaugural Medal of Honor winner for women in 1982. In addition to winning two AIAW doubles titles, Allison, a native of Montreal, was the runner-up in singles at the 1982 AIAW Championship and won the singles title at the 1983 National Intercollegiate Badminton Championship. She and Sandra Colby won the 1983 NIBC doubles title.

LEADING THE WAY

Duane Kleven
Wrestling Coach

Duane Kleven more than lived up to expectations after he succeeded George Martin as Wisconsin wrestling coach in 1970. In a dozen seasons as the Badgers' mentor, Kleven directed the UW matmen to a 132-48-5 record, guided 26 wrestlers to all-America honors and finished among the Big Ten's top three teams on nine occasions. His teams had six top-10 NCAA finishes, including a school-best fourth place in 1976. In his first season, Kleven led Wisconsin to a 13-4 record, tying the school record for most wins in a season. The National Wrestling Coaches Association named him NCAA coach of the year in 1976-77, a year after the U.S. Wrestling Federation had accorded him similar honors. An outstanding prep wrestler at Stoughton High School, Kleven also competed for the Badgers. He began his coaching career in 1962 with Wisconsin High School in Madison, served in the military and guided Racine Park High School to two state titles. Kleven then coached UW-Oshkosh to a 10-7 mark in 1969 before coming to Madison.

THE LIST

Wisconsin's Olympic Rowers

Men

Mark Berkner, Verona, Wisconsin, 1992
Bob Espeseth, Rockford, Illinois, 1980, 1984, 1988
Neil Haleen, Sheboygan, Wisconsin, 1976
Dave Krmpotich, Philadelphia, 1988
Stewart MacDonald, Belmont, Massachusetts, 1968, 1976
Tim Michelsen, Deerfield, Wisconsin, 1972
Eric Mueller, Cedarburg, Wisconsin, 1996

Women

Chris Cruz, Fond du Lac, Wisconsin, 1980
Cindy Eckert, Brookfield, Wisconsin, 1988, 1992
Yasmin Farooq, Waupun, Wisconsin, 1992, 1996
Carol Feeney, Oak Park, Illinois, 1992
Sarah Gengler, Milwaukee, 1988, 1992
Carie Graves, Spring Green, Wisconsin, 1976, 1980, 1984
Melissa Iverson, Anoka, Minnesota, 1996
Mara Keggi, Middlebury, Connecticut, 1988
Peggy McCarthy, Madison, 1976, 1980
Kim Santiago, Monroe, Wisconsin, 1998, 1992 (alt.)
Kris Thorsness, Anchorage, Alaska, 1984, 1988
Chari Towne, Wild Rose, Wisconsin, 1984
Jackie Zach, Madison, 1976

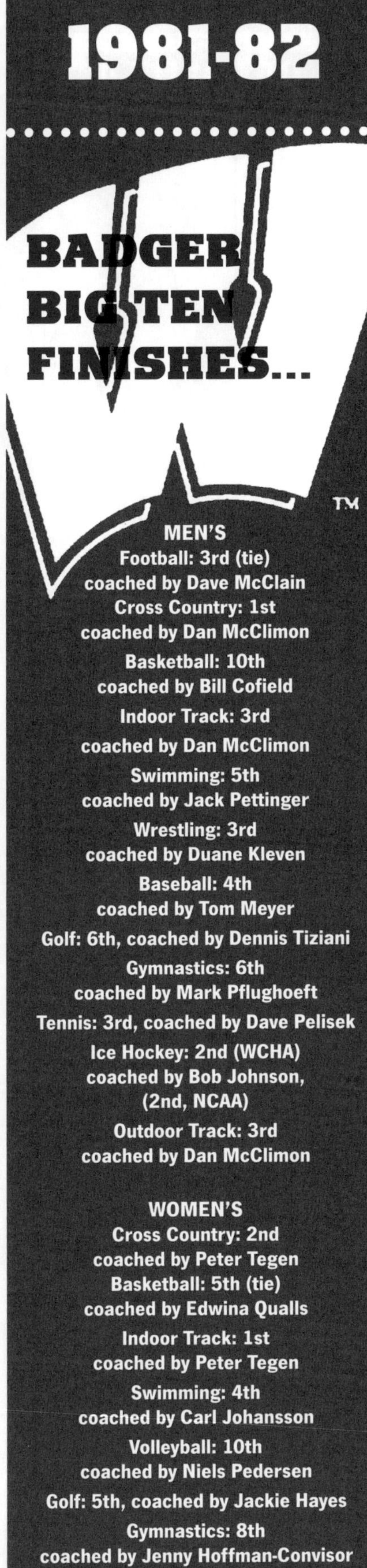

1981-82
BADGER
BIG TEN
FINISHES...
MEN'S
Football: 3rd (tie)
coached by Dave McClain
Cross Country: 1st
coached by Dan McClimon
Basketball: 10th
coached by Bill Cofield
Indoor Track: 3rd
coached by Dan McClimon
Swimming: 5th
coached by Jack Pettinger
Wrestling: 3rd
coached by Duane Kleven
Baseball: 4th
coached by Tom Meyer
Golf: 6th, coached by Dennis Tiziani
Gymnastics: 6th
coached by Mark Pflughoeft
Tennis: 3rd, coached by Dave Pelisek
Ice Hockey: 2nd (WCHA)
coached by Bob Johnson,
(2nd, NCAA)
Outdoor Track: 3rd
coached by Dan McClimon
WOMEN'S
Cross Country: 2nd
coached by Peter Tegen
Basketball: 5th (tie)
coached by Edwina Qualls
Indoor Track: 1st
coached by Peter Tegen
Swimming: 4th
coached by Carl Johansson
Volleyball: 10th
coached by Niels Pedersen
Golf: 5th, coached by Jackie Hayes
Gymnastics: 8th
coached by Jenny Hoffman-Convisor
Tennis: 6th
coached by Kelly Ferguson
Outdoor Track: 3rd
coached by Peter Tegen

Women begin official Big Ten competition

Women's athletics became an official part of the Big Ten Conference during the 1981-82 season. Teams had been competing in unofficial league championships prior to 1981, but these championships are not officially recognized.

In 1981-82, the Big Ten Conference sponsored women's championships in 11 sports—basketball, cross country, field hockey, golf, gymnastics, swimming, softball, tennis, indoor track, outdoor track, and volleyball. Wisconsin won the 1982 Big Ten indoor track championship for its first official league title.

1981-82 also marked a change in the women's athletic program at Wisconsin. Field hockey was dropped after the 1980-81 season with soccer picked as its replacement. Craig Webb was hired as the first women's soccer coach at Wisconsin and he led his team to a 12th-place finish in the AIAW national championship.

Soccer also had its first all-American that year as Karen Lunda earned third-team honors.

1981-82 would also be the last year that Wisconsin women's athletics would compete on the national level under the AIAW banner. The NCAA began offering women's championships in 1981-82 resulting in two national champions in many sports that season. Without the support of a number of larger universities, the AIAW was forced to disband.

Wisconsin Time Line

1982: The space shuttle Columbia was launched on its first commercial mission.

The Big Ten approved an increase in the number of permissible basketball games to 28.

Wisconsin scored 6-0 football win at Ohio State, its first victory in Columbus since 1918.

WISCONSIN HEADLINER

Tim Krumrie
Football

Noseguard Tim Krumrie's play was a primary reason Wisconsin returned to post-season bowl action (in 1981 and 1982) after a 19-year absence. Krumrie, a Mondovi, Wis., native, was a three-time, first-team all-Big Ten performer and helped lead the Badgers to the 1981 Garden State and 1982 Independence bowls (he was voted the game MVP). Krumrie was a consensus all-America choice in 1981 and earned first-team acclaim a year later, as well. He set a then-Wisconsin record for career tackles with 444 and still ranks third all-time at the UW. Krumrie was a Lombardi Award semifinalist twice (1981 and 1982) at Wisconsin and was a 10th-round draft choice of the NFL's Cincinnati Bengals. A two-time Pro Bowl participant, he played 12 years for Cincinnati, including Super Bowl XXIII in 1989.

WISCONSIN HEADLINER

Pat Johnson
Track and Field

Pat Johnson starred at Wisconsin from 1978-82 as one of the mainstays of the Coach Peter Tegen's burgeoning Badger women's track and field program. Johnson, a 20"2 1/4" high school long jumper out of Chicago (DuSable High School), became a three-time national long jump champion and seven-time all-American for the Badgers. Remarkably, she qualified in the long jump for every national meet during her career. She won Association of Intercollegiate Athletics for Women (AIAW) indoor long jump titles in 1980 and 1982 and the AIAW outdoor championship in a record 21'4 3/4" in '82. Johnson won 12 Big Ten titles, including seven of a possible eight in the long jump. She was inducted into the UW Athletic Hall of Fame in 1997.

VandenBoom intercepts three Michigan passes

Matt VandenBoom, a three-year letterwinner for the Badgers from 1980-82, never had a more memorable game than in Wisconsin's season opener September 12, 1981, in Madison. VandenBoom, a junior and former walk-on from Kimberly, Wis., intercepted three passes to key the Badgers' 21-14 upset of top-ranked Michigan. Coach Dave McClain's team won four of its first five games and finished 7-5 after losing to Tennessee in the Garden State Bowl, its first bowl appearance outside the Rose Bowl. VandenBoom, who had six interceptions for the season, is in a 10-way tie for second on the Wisconsin record board for most interceptions in a game. Clarence Bratt had four against Minnesota in 1954.

State's top four distance runners come to UW

Wisconsin track coach Dan McClimon had a coach's dream come true in 1981, when the top four distance runners in the state—and four of the best in the nation—all signed letters of intent to compete at Wisconsin. John Easker of Wittenberg-Birnamwood, Tim Hacker and Joe Stintzi of Menomonee Falls (North) and Scott Jenkins of Kenosha (Bradford) all had credentials aplenty, with Easker, Hacker and Jenkins with state prep titles under their belts. All went on to stellar careers at Wisconsin, with each earning multiple all-America honors. All were key to the Badgers' 1982 NCAA cross country title, with Hacker and Jenkins finishing fourth and fifth in the race. Hacker, Jenkins and Stinzti also ran on the UW's NCAA title-winning 1985 team, with Hacker taking Wisconsin's second-ever NCAA individual crown.

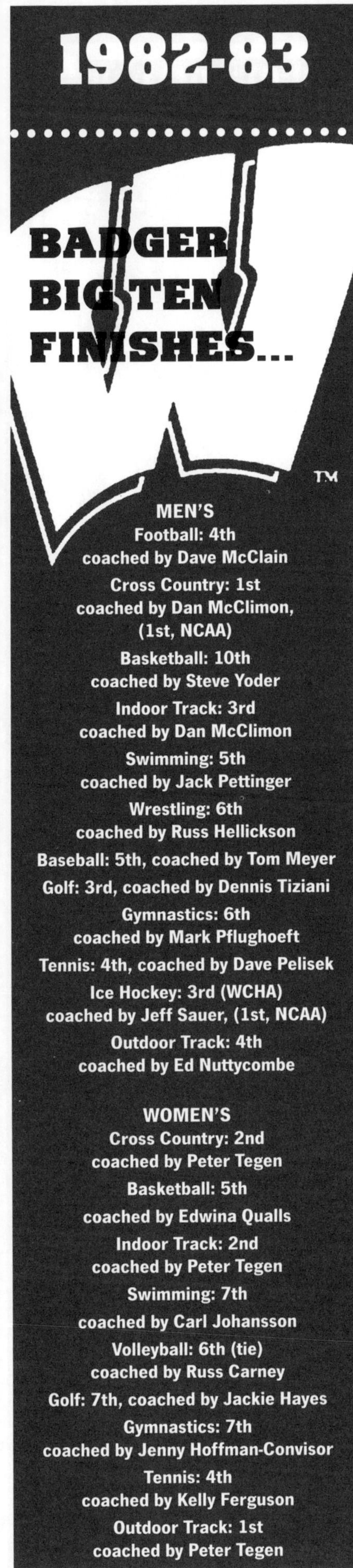

MEN'S
Football: 4th
coached by Dave McClain
Cross Country: 1st
coached by Dan McClimon, (1st, NCAA)
Basketball: 10th
coached by Steve Yoder
Indoor Track: 3rd
coached by Dan McClimon
Swimming: 5th
coached by Jack Pettinger
Wrestling: 6th
coached by Russ Hellickson
Baseball: 5th, coached by Tom Meyer
Golf: 3rd, coached by Dennis Tiziani
Gymnastics: 6th
coached by Mark Pflughoeft
Tennis: 4th, coached by Dave Pelisek
Ice Hockey: 3rd (WCHA)
coached by Jeff Sauer, (1st, NCAA)
Outdoor Track: 4th
coached by Ed Nuttycombe

WOMEN'S
Cross Country: 2nd
coached by Peter Tegen
Basketball: 5th
coached by Edwina Qualls
Indoor Track: 2nd
coached by Peter Tegen
Swimming: 7th
coached by Carl Johansson
Volleyball: 6th (tie)
coached by Russ Carney
Golf: 7th, coached by Jackie Hayes
Gymnastics: 7th
coached by Jenny Hoffman-Convisor
Tennis: 4th
coached by Kelly Ferguson
Outdoor Track: 1st
coached by Peter Tegen

Badgers win NCAA titles in cross country and hockey

Wisconsin won its first ever title in men's cross country and its fourth national collegiate hockey title in the 1982-83 season. Coach Dan McClimon's harriers earned their first hill-and-dale win in November, 1982, at Bloomington, Indiana, scoring 59 points to defeat runner-up Providence, which had 138. Wisconsin became the first champ from the Big Ten since Michigan State in 1959.

Pacing the Badgers were sophomores Tim Hacker and Scott Jenkins, who finished fourth and fifth, respectively, in the 10,000-meter race. The three other Wisconsin scorers also earned all-American honors. John Easker placed 16th, Joe Stintzi 23rd and Jim Brice 26th. Randy Berndt (47th) and Don Volkey (84th) rounded out the Badger finishers. It was, unfortunately, Coach McClimon's only national title with his prize recruits of 1981. He was killed in a plane crash the following spring.

It was another success on ice in March 1983 as the Badgers claimed their fourth NCAA championship with a 6-2 win over Harvard. It was the first NCAA title for Coach Jeff Sauer, who had been named to succeed Bob Johnson just nine months earlier.

Wisconsin's tournament advance wasn't easy at first. Chris Chelios and Paul Houck scored the tying and game-winning goals as the Badgers beat North Dakota 6-5 in triple overtime—the longest game in school history—to advance to the WCHA championships. Two wins over Minnesota gave the UW the WCHA win and top West seed in the NCAA. A win over St. Lawrence moved the Badgers into the NCAA semifinals against Providence which they beat 2-0 to move into the title game. Senior goaltender Marc Behrend was named NCAA tournament MVP for the second time in his career.

WISCONSIN TIME LINE

1983: The OPEC oil cartel cut its per-barrel price from $34 to $29, the first price cut in its 23-year history.

The first *Big Ten Women's Records Book* was published.

Al Toon set a Big Ten record with 252 yards receiving in Badgers' 42-38 win at Purdue.

WISCONSIN HEADLINER

Rose Chepyator-Thomson
Cross Country, Track

Rose Chepyator-Thomson, who began running at Wisconsin as a 25-year-old mother with two children, became one of the best distance runners in Wisconsin's illustrious women's track and cross country history. An 11-time all-American from 1979-83, Chepyator-Thomson was a two-time NCAA champ at 1500 meters and six times won Big Ten track titles. She also won three Big Ten cross country crowns and in 1983 won the UW Big Ten Medal of Honor and was named an NCAA post-graduate scholarship winner. In 1987, Chepyator-Thomson won the 800-meter run at the National Indoor Masters' Championships. She completed her master's degree in physical education in 1986, added a second in educational and policy studies in 1988 and in 1990 earned a doctorate in physical education from the UW. Inducted into the UW Athletic Hall of Fame in 1994, Chepyator-Thomson is currently a professor of education and men's and women's cross country coach at SUNY-Brockport.

WISCONSIN HEADLINER

Cindy Eckert &
Carol Feeney
Rowing

Cindy Eckert (1983-87) and Carol Feeney (1984-86) were silver medal winners in the 1992 Olympics. The duo were members of the women's four without coxswain that finished second. Eckert, a native of Brookfield, Wisconsin, was a seven-year member of the U.S. national team. She also participated in the 1988 Olympics in the women's four with coxswain that finished fifth. At Wisconsin, Eckert was a member of the varsity eight boat that won the 1986 national title. She also won two Eastern Sprint titles and the 1986 San Diego Crew Classic championship. Feeney, from Oak Park, Illinois, was a four-year member of the U.S. national team. At Wisconsin, she was a member of the varsity eight boat that won the 1986 national title.

WISCONSIN HEADLINER

Theresa Huff
Women's Basketball

The only UW woman to have her jersey (No.21) retired, Theresa Huff was a four-time MVP for the Badger womenís basketball team from 1979-83. Huff, who led Milwaukee Riverside High School to the 1978 and 1979 WIAA state tournaments, at one time held 30 Wisconsin records. A finalist for the 1983 Wade Trophy, Huff amassed 62 double-doubles (double figures in points and reounds) in 118 career games. Huff led Wisconsin to its first post-season appearance to end the 1981-82 season as the Badgers reached the quarter-finals of the Association of Intercollegiate Athletics for Women national tournament. Huff became Wisconsin's first professional women's player and the first American woman to play on a Spanish professional league in 1983-84. She was named to Wisconsin's all-decade team in 1991 in conjunction with the Big Ten Conference's observance of 10 years of women's sports competition. Huff was inducted into the UW Athletic Hall of Fame in 1998.

WISCONSIN HEADLINER

Megan Scott
Volleyball, Basketball,
Track

The only three-sport letterwinner in Wisconsin women's athletics history, Megan Scott lettered in volleyball, basketball and track in just two seasons in Madison. The Platteville, Wisconsin, native transferred to the UW after playing basketball at the University of Kansas for two years. She played volleyball at Wisconsin for two years, earning all-Big Ten honors as a senior. Scott led the Badgers in kills and blocks per game. Scott turned to basketball at the UW for one year and earned second-team all-Big Ten honors. She led the teams in rebounding and ranked third in scoring as the Badgers finished second in the Big Ten. Scott wrapped up her UW career in track by finishing fifth in the discus at the 1984 Big Ten outdoor championship.

WISCONSIN HEADLINER

Tim Gillham
Fencing

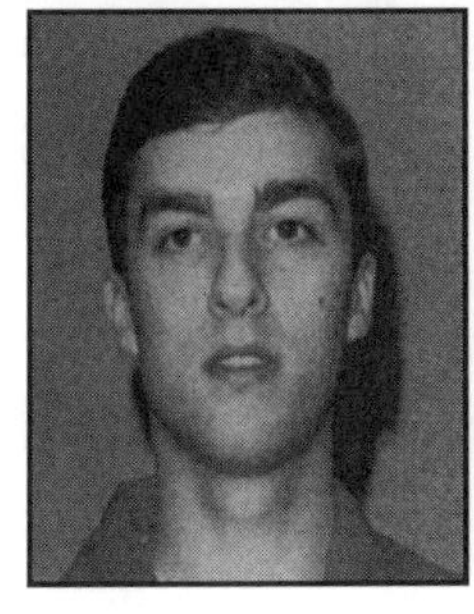

Tim Gillham wasted no time in establishing himself on the Big Ten and national fencing scene. The son of Wisconsin coach Tony Gillham won the Big Ten epee title in his first season and went on to place third in the NCAA championships. He was the Badgers' most valuable fencer on a team that finished second in the Big Ten and 10th nationally. Gillham repeated his victories in the 1984 and 1985 Big Ten meets—becoming the first fencer to win more than two titles in 61 years of Conference fencing competition—and again earned all-America honors in both of those seasons. He never got a chance to try for a fourth Big Ten title and all-America honors; fencing was discontinued as a Big Ten sport prior to the 1985-86 season.

LEADING THE WAY

Dan McClimon
Track and
Cross Country Coach

Dan McClimon, who guided Wisconsin to its first NCAA men's cross country title in 1982, guided Badger teams for 12 seasons before his death in a plane crash in 1983. "Mac" was named NCAA cross country coach of the year three times and began a still-ongoing streak in 1972 that has seen Wisconsin qualify for every NCAA championship meet. McClimon coached 51 NCAA track and cross country all-Americans and three NCAA individual champions. He posted a 52-6 dual meet record in cross country, including a 30-meet winning streak. His teams won Big Ten titles from 1977-79 and again in 1981 and 1982 as well as five NCAA District IV championships. Seven of his teams recorded top-10 NCAA finishes, including a third in 1978 and a fourth in 1981 in addition to the UW's first NCAA title a year later.

UW Swimming Hall of Fame

Wisconsin's swimming and diving program has recognized the following individuals for their contributions:

Robert Baker (1951-53)—team captain, outstanding team leader

Johnson Bennett (1922-23)—three-time Big Ten champion

Bud Blanchard (1964-66)—six-time all-American

Tracy Bush (1970-73)—national finalist

D'Lynn Damron (1969-73)—1973 national three-meter diving champion

Jack Hoaglund (1953-55)—team captain, Big Ten and NCAA finalist

Brad Horner (1973-76)—three-time all-American, Pan American gold medalist

Winston Kratz (1926-27)—200-meter breaststroke national champion

Chuck LaBahn (1946)—for extraordinary service and contributions to the UW and to the swimming program

Peggy (Anderson) Meyer (1974-77)—national three-meter diving champion, five-time all-American

Paul Pohle (1940-42)—for exceptional contribution and service to Wisconsin swimming

Jerry Smith (1949-51)—team captain, outstanding team leader

Fred Westphal (1957-59)—NCAA 50-yard freestyle champion, Big Ten champion, all-American

George Taylor (1913-15)—four-time Big Ten champion

Badgers vs. Big Ten football opponents

Opponent	UW record	Last UW win
Chicago	19-16-5	1937, 27-0
Illinois	28-33-7	1997, 31-7
Indiana	28-16-2	1997, 27-26
Iowa	35-36-2	1997, 13-10
Michigan	10-42-1	1994, 31-19
Michigan State	15-24-0	1995, 45-14
Minnesota	42-57-8	1997, 22-21
Northwestern	51-29-5	1997, 26-25
Ohio State	13-48-5	1992, 20-16
Penn State	3-2-0	1995, 17-9
Purdue	34-27-8	1996, 33-25

1983-84

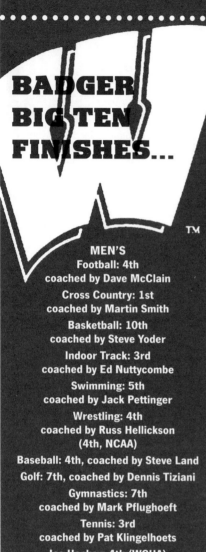

BADGER BIG TEN FINISHES...

MEN'S
Football: 4th
coached by Dave McClain
Cross Country: 1st
coached by Martin Smith
Basketball: 10th
coached by Steve Yoder
Indoor Track: 3rd
coached by Ed Nuttycombe
Swimming: 5th
coached by Jack Pettinger
Wrestling: 4th
coached by Russ Hellickson
(4th, NCAA)
Baseball: 4th, coached by Steve Land
Golf: 7th, coached by Dennis Tiziani
Gymnastics: 7th
coached by Mark Pflughoeft
Tennis: 3rd
coached by Pat Klingelhoets
Ice Hockey: 4th (WCHA)
coached by Jeff Sauer
Outdoor Track: 1st
coached by Ed Nuttycombe

WOMEN'S
Cross Country: 1st
coached by Peter Tegen
Basketball: 2nd
coached by Edwina Qualls
Indoor Track: 1st
coached by Peter Tegen
Swimming: 6th
coached by Carl Johansson
Volleyball: 7th (tie)
coached by Russ Carney
Golf: 8th, coached by Jackie Hayes
Gymnastics: 6th
coached by Jenny Hoffman-Convisor
Tennis: 5th
coached by Kelly Ferguson
Outdoor Track: 1st
coached by Peter Tegen

Badger women win Big Ten "triple crown" in cross country, indoor and outdoor track

Wisconsin won its first Big Ten Conference "triple crown"—conference titles in cross country, indoor track and outdoor track during the same season—for women's sports in 1983-84.

The cross country team started it out by winning its first conference title in four years. Wisconsin scored 52 points to easily outdistance Purdue, which finished second with 71 points. Cathy Branta won her second consecutive Big Ten individual championship covering the 5,000-meter course in Champaign, Illinois, in 16:26.2.

The Badgers continued their winning ways during the 1984 indoor track season, winning the Big Ten indoor title with 104 points. Indiana finished a close second with 99.5 points. Branta was again the star of the meet, winning the mile in 4:38.31 and the two mile in 9:52.77. She set Big Ten meet records in both events and was named the Athlete of the Championship. Other event winners were Katie Ishmael in the three-mile run in a meet record of 15:19.70; Sharon Dollins with a meet record 40'0" triple jump; and Dorothea Brown with a 20'3 1/2" long jump.

Wisconsin completed its Triple Crown sweep at the Big Ten outdoor meet, scoring 124 points to win by 10 points over Indiana. Branta and Ishmael both won two events to lead the team. Branta set meet records of 4:16.47 in the 1500 meters and 9:15.30 in the 3000 meters. Ishmael won the 5000 meters in a meet record of 16:23.57 and the 10,000 meters in 34:24.1.

Dollins and Brown again claimed the horizontal jumps with Dollins winning in a meet record of 41'1/4" and Brown taking the long jump at 20'10 1/2".

WISCONSIN TIME LINE

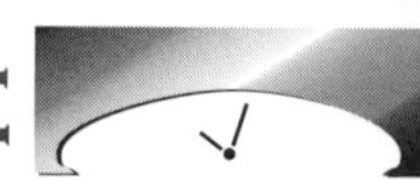

1984: The Games of the XXIIIrd Olympiad opened in Los Angeles, minus a Soviet-led bloc of 15 nations.

Athletic directors approved a 10-week double round-robin volleyball schedule for 1985.

The UW's fourth straight seven-win football season ended with 20-19 loss to Kentucky in the Hall of Fame Bowl.

WISCONSIN HEADLINER

Al Toon
Football, Track

Al Toon's speed and agility made him a major force on Wisconsin football and track teams of the early 1980s. He was twice named an all-Big Ten first-team selection in football and twice won Big Ten triple jump titles in track. Toon, who came to Madison from Newport News, Virginia. (Menchville High School), earned six "W" awards in his two sports. Toon still holds Badger records for top receiving yardage in a game (252 vs. Purdue) and in a career (2,103 yards). And he still tops the UW list for career receptions (131) and is second in receiving touchdowns (19). Toon was twice the Badgers' MVP and played in the post-season in the Hall of Fame Bowl, the Japan Bowl and the Hula Bowl; in the latter, he was the offensive MVP with 10 receptions for 124 yards and 2 touchdowns. An all-American in the triple jump in 1982, Toon set a Big Ten record of 54'7 1/4". Following his Badger days, Toon went on to a distinguished NFL career with the New York Jets from 1985-92. He was inducted into the UW Athletic Hall of Fame in 1995.

WISCONSIN HEADLINER

Isabelle Hamori
Fencing

Isabelle Hamori recorded the best finish ever for a UW woman fencer at the NCAA championship. The New Orleans native finished second at the 1987 championship, leading the Badgers to a ninth-place team finish. Hamori also finished 12th as a sophomore and as a junior. Hamori was a three-time Big Ten champion, leading the Badgers to the team title as a sophomore, junior and senior. She was named a four-time team MVP for Wisconsin.

Top 15 crowds at Camp Randall

Attendance	Opponent	Year
80,024	Michigan	1978
79,940	Ohio State	1978
79,864	Iowa	1997
79,806	Michigan	1997
79,607	Penn State	1996
79,579	Ohio State	1976
79,576	Northwestern	1996
79,521	Iowa	1976
79,507	Ohio State	1995
79,327	Illinois	1997
79,253	Ohio State	1980
79,203	Michigan State	1970
79,111	Purdue	1976
79,026	Iowa	1979
79,023	Iowa	1985

Badgers post best record at home

Wisconsin's women's basketball team chalked up a 12-1 home record and had its best-ever Big Ten Conference finish at 13-5 under Coach Edwina Qualls. Season highlights included a 79-70 win at home over eventual Conference champion Ohio State and a three-game winning streak to end the season and ensure a runner-up finish.

LEADING THE WAY

Peter Tegen
Track and
Cross Country Coach

After 24 seasons as women's track and cross country coach at Wisconsin, it's safe to say that Peter Tegen could retire any time and his place as a legend would be secure. But the native of Hanover, Germany, a fixture on the UW and national track scene since 1974, shows no sign of slowing down. Tegen has coached more than 40 national champions in cross country and track and his athletes have garnered all-America honors more than 200 times. Tegen has coached the Badgers to two NCAA cross country titles, 21 top-10 national finishes in cross country and 20 top-10 NCAA placings in track. Thirty-six times the Badgers have won Big Ten team titles under his direction. Included in that list are an unprecedented three straight "triple triples"—wins in Conference cross country, indoor and outdoor track—from 1983-86. Most noted among Tegen's athletes are the three Olympians he's coached: Cindy Bremser (1984), Suzy Favor Hamilton (1992 and 1996) and Kathy Butler (1996).

LEADING THE WAY

Dave McClain
Football Coach

Dave McClain's sudden death by heart attack in April, 1986, shocked and saddened those who had witnessed the fine job he did in reviving the Badger football program, as well as those who knew him as a good family man and an enthusiastic, committed coach. McClain came to Wisconsin in December, 1977, and guided the Badgers to a 46-42-3 record that included three bowl appearances. The first coach to take Wisconsin to back-to-back bowl games (1981 Garden State Bowl and 1982 Independence Bowl), he also coached the UW to the '84 Hall of Fame Bowl. McClain, a native of Upper Sandusky, Ohio, came to Wisconsin from Ball State and, four years into his tenure in Madison, had the Badgers, consistent losers for more than a decade, in a bowl game. The UW's indoor practice facility is named after McClain.

Men's Conference
Medal of Honor winners

1980
Thomas G. Stauss

1981
David C. Goodspeed

1982
David Mohapp

1983
David Farley

1984
John Johannson

1985
John Easker

1986
Tim Hacker

1987
J.J. Weber

1988
Paul Gruber

1989
Dave Lee

Badger harriers finish 1-2-3 in Big Ten

John Easker led a 1-2-3 sweep finish for Wisconsin in the 1983 Big Ten men's cross country championship, the first time a UW harrier squad had accomplished the feat. With Scott Jenkins placing second and Joe Stintzi third, Coach Martin Smith's Badgers coasted to a 19-point victory, their third straight Conference title. That total was the second-lowest in the meet's history, trailing only a 1959 Michigan State that also went 1-2-3, and its 52-point margin of victory over Michigan was the second-greatest in meet annals. The 1991 UW team would equal its predecessor's feat.

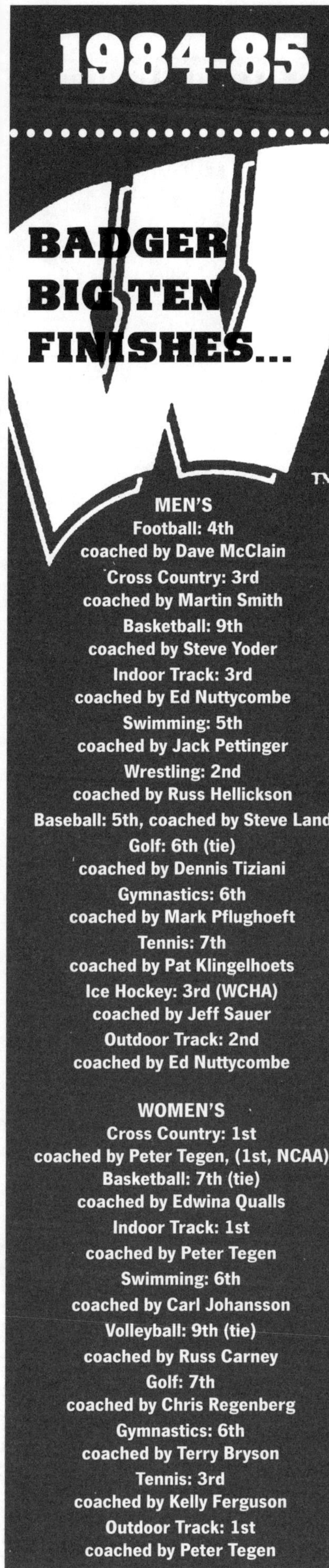

1984-85

BADGER BIG TEN FINISHES...

MEN'S
Football: 4th
coached by Dave McClain
Cross Country: 3rd
coached by Martin Smith
Basketball: 9th
coached by Steve Yoder
Indoor Track: 3rd
coached by Ed Nuttycombe
Swimming: 5th
coached by Jack Pettinger
Wrestling: 2nd
coached by Russ Hellickson
Baseball: 5th, coached by Steve Land
Golf: 6th (tie)
coached by Dennis Tiziani
Gymnastics: 6th
coached by Mark Pflughoeft
Tennis: 7th
coached by Pat Klingelhoets
Ice Hockey: 3rd (WCHA)
coached by Jeff Sauer
Outdoor Track: 2nd
coached by Ed Nuttycombe

WOMEN'S
Cross Country: 1st
coached by Peter Tegen, (1st, NCAA)
Basketball: 7th (tie)
coached by Edwina Qualls
Indoor Track: 1st
coached by Peter Tegen
Swimming: 6th
coached by Carl Johansson
Volleyball: 9th (tie)
coached by Russ Carney
Golf: 7th
coached by Chris Regenberg
Gymnastics: 6th
coached by Terry Bryson
Tennis: 3rd
coached by Kelly Ferguson
Outdoor Track: 1st
coached by Peter Tegen

Badger harriers win UW's first women's NCAA title

Wisconsin's first NCAA title for women came in 1984 when the Badgers won the NCAA Cross Country Championship.

Led by individual champion Cathy Branta, top-ranked Wisconsin scored 63 points to run by Stanford, which totalled 89 points. Branta covered the 5,000 meters on the Penn State University campus in a course record of 16:15.6. The senior from Slinger, Wisconsin, finished almost seven seconds ahead of second-place Shelly Steeley of Florida, who crossed in 16:22.3.

Junior Katie Ishmael finished sixth overall in 16:37.7 to earn her second all-American honor. Also gaining all-America status were sophomore Kelly McKillen, who finished 17th in 16:56.3; and sophomore Birgit Christiansen, who was 28th in 17:05. All five Badger scorers finished among the top 45 runners with freshman Stephanie Herbst crossing in 17:17.6 as the fifth scorer. Other finishers were sophomore Stephanie Bassett, who was 58th in 17:28.5; and junior Holly Hering, who finished 67th in 17:34.6.

"Can you imagine four all-Americans and a national championship?" said UW coach Peter Tegen, who was named the NCAA Coach of the Year. "I don't know what to think yet.Everything has happened so fast. It just hasn't sunk in yet, but I can say, it's the finest thing that's ever happened to Wisconsin women's cross country."

Wisconsin had finished among the top 10 teams in seven AIAW championships and two NCAA championships prior to winning its first national title.

Wisconsin Time Line

1985: Patty Cookset became the first female jockey to ride in the Preakness.

Athletic directors approved an increase in the football travel squad from 60 to 70.

Mary Ellen Murphy was named the third coach in Wisconsin's women's basketball history.

WISCONSIN HEADLINER

Cathy Branta-Easker
Cross Country, Track

Five-time NCAA and 11-time Big Ten champion Cathy Branta-Easker won just about every track honor possible in 1984 and 1985, her last two years at Wisconsin. The Slinger, Wisconsin, native in 1985 won the Jumbo Elliott Award, the Jesse Owens Award, the Broderick Award and the Big Ten Medal of Honor. A three-time winner of the Wisconsin Athlete of the Year award from 1983-85, Branta-Easker won NCAA championships in cross country (1984), in the 3,000-meter run indoors (1984), the 3K outdoors (1984) and both the 1500 and 3,000 in the 1985 outdoor meet. She was also a three-time U.S. national champ. In 1985, she also won the 3,000 at the World University Games and at the U.S. Olympic Festival. She was runner-up in the 1984 World Cross Country Championships and an alternate for the 3K for the 1984 U.S. Olympic team. She was named to the UW Athletic Hall of Fame in 1993. Married to former Wisconsin men's distance all-American John Easker, they live on a dairy farm outside Wausau with their three children.

WISCONSIN HEADLINER

John Easker
Cross Country, Track

A key member of Wisconsin's first men's cross country national championship team in 1982, John Easker was a four-time cross country and three-time all-America distance runner in track. A native of Birnamwood, Wisconsin, Easker was a five-time Big Ten track champion. He was the Big Ten cross country champion in 1983 and won the District IV cross country title in 1983 and 1984. He finished 16th overall during the Badgers' 1982 NCAA championship performance and came back the next two years to finish fourth and third, respectively, at the NCAA meet. Easker went on to become a runner-up in the 1984 USA Senior Men's International Cross Country Trials and helped lead the U.S. to a second-place finish in the World Cross Country Championships. He and his wife, former five-time UW national women's distance champ Cathy Branta, operate a dairy farm outside Wausau.

WISCONSIN HEADLINER

Richard Johnson
Football

Three-time "W" award winner Richard Johnson was named to numerous all-America teams following the 1984 season. A speedy defensive back, he was named *Sports Illustrated's* national defensive player of the week following Wisconsin's 35-34 win on the road over Missouri in 1984. In that game, Johnson blocked two kicks, intercepted a pass and recovered a blocked punt for a touchdown. He also set the UW career mark for blocked kicks (9). The Houston Oilers picked him in the first round of the 1985 National Football League draft.

Women's Conference Medal of Honor winners

1982
Ann French

1983
Rose Thomson

1984
Janet Huff

1985
Cathy Branta

1986
Lisa Fortman

1987
Amy Justeson

1988
Chris Gilles

1989
Maureen Hartzheim

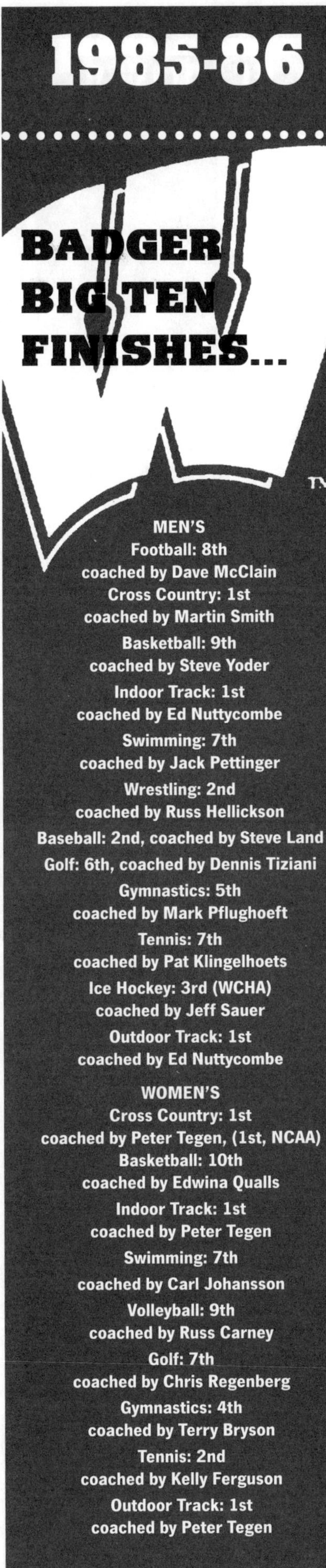

1985-86
BADGER
BIG TEN
FINISHES...
TM
MEN'S
Football: 8th
coached by Dave McClain
Cross Country: 1st
coached by Martin Smith
Basketball: 9th
coached by Steve Yoder
Indoor Track: 1st
coached by Ed Nuttycombe
Swimming: 7th
coached by Jack Pettinger
Wrestling: 2nd
coached by Russ Hellickson
Baseball: 2nd, coached by Steve Land
Golf: 6th, coached by Dennis Tiziani
Gymnastics: 5th
coached by Mark Pflughoeft
Tennis: 7th
coached by Pat Klingelhoets
Ice Hockey: 3rd (WCHA)
coached by Jeff Sauer
Outdoor Track: 1st
coached by Ed Nuttycombe
WOMEN'S
Cross Country: 1st
coached by Peter Tegen, (1st, NCAA)
Basketball: 10th
coached by Edwina Qualls
Indoor Track: 1st
coached by Peter Tegen
Swimming: 7th
coached by Carl Johansson
Volleyball: 9th
coached by Russ Carney
Golf: 7th
coached by Chris Regenberg
Gymnastics: 4th
coached by Terry Bryson
Tennis: 2nd
coached by Kelly Ferguson
Outdoor Track: 1st
coached by Peter Tegen

Wisconsin wins men's, women's NCAA cross country titles

The UW men's and women's cross country teams made history in the NCAA championships in November, 1985, at Dretzka Park in Milwaukee. Coach Martin Smith's men and Coach Peter Tegen's women notched wins in the NCAA cross country meet, the first time men's and women's teams from one school had won in the same year.

Leading Wisconsin was senior Tim Hacker, from nearby Menomonee Falls, who won his first NCAA title by sprinting away from Iowa State's Yobes Ondieke and Marquette's Keith Hanson in the final 1 1/2 miles to become the UW's second NCAA champ in the sport. The Badgers, unbeaten and ranked first all year, placed five runners among the top 43 finishers to score 67 points and upend defending champion Arkansas (104). Joe Stintzi (11th), Scott Jenkins (24th), Kelly Delaney (26th) and Rusty Korhonen (43rd) were the other UW scorers. Hacker, Stintzi, Jenkins and Delaney earned all-America honors.

The women's victory—the second straight by Tegen's team—was almost as impressive. Led by Big Ten and NCAA District IV champion Stephanie Herbst's seventh-place finish, the Badgers scored 58 points to Iowa State's 98. Joining Herbst as all-Americans were Katie Ismael in 15th and Lori Walter in 22nd. Other members of the squad were Michelle Lumley, Holly Hering, Stephanie Bassett, Kelly McKillen and Birgit Christiansen.

Wisconsin Time Line

1986: Kodak lost a patent suit to Polaroid and abandoned the instant-photo market.

The Big Ten and the Pac-10 entered into an agreement with ABC-TV for the televising of college football games through the 1990 season.

Wisconsin took eventual NCAA champ Indiana to three overtimes before losing 86-85 at the Field House.

Suzy Favor won the first of her nine NCAA track and field championships, running 4:41.69 in the mile at the NCAA indoor meet at Oklahoma City.

WISCONSIN HEADLINER

Jim Jordan
Wrestling

The winningest wrestler in Wisconsin history, Jim Jordan compiled a 156-28-1 (.846) record during his four-year career. Jordan, one of only three multiple NCAA wrestling champions in Badger annals, won national titles at 134 pounds in 1985 and 1986. A native of St. Paris, Ohio, Jordan compiled a 47-4-0 mark in 1984-85, including a 7-4 win over Oklahoma State's John Smith in the national title match. He followed that with a 49-3-1 slate (still the winningest season in UW history) in 1985-86 that included his second NCAA crown. Jordan was a three-time all-American, two-time Big Ten champion and National Wrestling Coaches Association All-Star in 1985. Jordan was named to the Amateur Wrestling News Freshman All-American team a year after completing a stellar high school career during which he registered a 154-1 record and four state titles.

WISCONSIN HEADLINER

Roddy Kirschenman
Swimming

Roddy Kirschenman is one of just six men's swimmers in Wisconsin history to earn at least four all-America honors. The Omaha, Nebraska, native swam for the Badgers from 1986-89. In 1987, he finished eighth in the 1650 freestyle to earn his first all-America distinction. His second all-America honor came a year later when he was 16th with the 800 freestyle relay team. Kirschenman took home a pair of all-America accolades his senior year ('89), finishing 15th in the 500 freestyle and 16th with the 800 freestyle relay team. He earned all-Big Ten mention in 1987. Kirschenman set the school record in the 1650 freestyle in '87, as well. He also set two UW Natatorium/SERF pool records in the 1650 freestyle and with the 800-yard freestyle relay team. Kirschenman was on the U.S. National Team that placed third in the 1500 at the 1987 World University Games.

WISCONSIN HEADLINER

Tony Granato
Hockey

Tony Granato was the first of the three hockey-playing Granato brothers to play at Wisconsin. Now a 10-year veteran of the National Hockey League, Granato played at the UW from 1983-87. He is the school's fourth all-time leading scorer with 100 goals and 120 assists for 220 points in 152 games. He is third in career goals at Wisconsin. A native of Downers Grove, Illinois, Granato was a 1987 Hobey Baker Award finalist as college hockey's player of the year and was a second-team all-American that season. He played for the 1988 U.S. Olympic Team. A two-time all-Western Collegiate Hockey Association selection, Granato was an inspiration to the entire NHL when he came back to play the 1996-97 season after undergoing brain surgery in February, 1996. He earned the NHL's prestigious Bill Masterton Trophy for "perseverance, sportsmanship and dedication to hockey."

WISCONSIN HEADLINER

Tim Hacker
Cross Country, Track

Wisconsin has won three NCAA team men's cross country titles and Tim Hacker, a native of Menomonie Falls, Wisconsin, was an integral part of two of them. A nine-time all-American in cross country and track, he finished fourth nationally to lead the Badgers to the 1982 NCAA cross country crown and came back three years later to win the individual NCAA title as the Badgers again grabbed the team championship in '85. Hacker, who later was an assistant coach for the Badgers from 1987-92, won Big Ten titles in 1981, '84 and '85. Hacker anchored the UW's distance medley relay NCAA champion at the indoor championships in 1985. He was a three-time winner of Wisconsin's Tom Jones Most Valuable Runner award and won both the Don Gehrmann Leadership Award and Dan McClimon Memorial Award in 1985. Now a college professor and still an active runner, Hacker most recently won the U.S. national cross country title in 1997.

WISCONSIN HEADLINER

Stephanie Herbst Cross Country, Track & Field

Stephanie Herbst made her mark in the UW record books as one of the nation's top distance runners. A former collegiate record holder in the 10,000 meters, Herbst won three NCAA titles. She won the 3000 meters at the 1986 indoor championship and was a double winner at the 1986 outdoor championship taking the 5000 and the 10,000 meter titles.

Herbst was a six-time all-American and a seven-time Big Ten champion including two cross country titles. She led the Badgers to the 1985 NCAA cross country title and nine Big Ten championships. Herbst was named the 1986 Suzy Favor-Big Ten Female Athlete of the Year and was also nominated for the Broderick Award in track and cross country. The Chaska, Minnesota, native was a two-time Academic all-American and two-time Academic all-Big Ten honoree majoring in business.

WISCONSIN HEADLINER

Yasmin Farooq Rowing

Yasmin Farooq has the distinction of being named to the U.S. National Rowing Team eight years. The coxswain from Waupun, Wisconsin, was named to the 1992 and 1996 U.S. Olympic teams and has competed in six World Championships. Her crew won the gold medal at the 1995 World Championship. She has medaled nine times in international competition.

At Wisconsin, Farooq coxed two national championship crews—the freshman eight in 1985 and the junior varsity eight in 1986. She earned Academic all-Big Ten honors as a senior.

WISCONSIN HEADLINER

Tim Madden Tennis

The second-winningest men's tennis player in Wisconsin history with 112 victories, Tim Madden earned all-Big Ten honors three times during his four-year career under Coach Pat Klingelhoets. A product of Lewiston, Illinois, Madden put together a career record of 112-43 (.723) and led the Badgers in wins three times (23-5 in 1985-86, 17-7 in 1986-87 and 30-15 in 1987-88). Madden, who teamed with Jack Waite to compile a 1-1 record in doubles at the 1988 NCAA Championships, twice served as team captain for the Badgers and earned the team's Sportsmanship Award each of his four years. He was also named Big Ten Sportsman of the Year in 1987-88 and again in 1988-89. Madden was named Wisconsin's MVP in 1986-87 and 1987-88. He has been Purdue's men's tennis coach since 1994.

WISCONSIN HEADLINER

Andy Rectenwal Soccer

The career scoring leader in Wisconsin men's soccer history, forward Andy Rectenwal completed his four years as a Badger with a school-record 46 goals and 28 assists for 120 points. He is second all-time in assists and game-winning goals (11) for the Badgers. He also is the UW's all-time leader in shots with 240 (53 more than the next player on the list). Rectenwal, a native of Bloomington, Minnesota, was a two-time all-Mideast selection (1986 and 1987) and a first-team all-Big Ten choice in 1987. Rectenwal, who captained the Badgers that year, still holds the UW single-season record for points with 45 in 1986. He also holds school records for goals in a game (four vs. Michigan in 1986) and points in a game (eight vs. Michigan in 1986).

WISCONSIN HEADLINER

Rick Olson
Basketball

Madison native Rick Olson stayed home to play his college ball and became one of the best players in school history. Olson, who fell just 10 points short of becoming Wisconsin's all-time scoring leader when his four-year career ended in 1986 (he scored 1,736 points), remains the Badgers' all-time leader in minutes played (3,962) and is tied with Michael Finley in career starts (112). Olson, in fact, started every game during his four years at Wisconsin. He is the UW's career free throw percentage leader (.870) and set a then-Big Ten record for consecutive free throws made when he connected on 36 straight during 1984 and 1985. A third-team all-Big Ten selection in 1985-86, he was an honorable mention all-league choice in 1984-85. He was selected in the seventh round of the 1986 NBA draft by the Houston Rockets.

LEADING THE WAY

Martin Smith
Men's Cross Country Coach
Assistant Track Coach

Martin Smith's 15-year run as head coach of the Wisconsin men's cross country program was marked by nothing but success. Smith, who also was an assistant track coach for the Badgers, guided the Badgers to two (1985 and 1988) NCAA cross country titles, 12 Big Ten team championships and 10 District IV crowns. His Wisconsin squads finished in the top five at the NCAA meet nine times. Among the student-athletes he coached, four have won Big Ten individual championships, 33 have earned all-America accolades, 38 have been named all-Big Ten and another 51 have been academic all-Big Ten honorees. The Badgers' eight straight Big Ten cross country titles from 1985-92 tied for the sixth-longest dynasty in Big Ten history in any sport. Smith was named head track coach and cross country coach at Oregon in August, 1998.

Retired Football Numbers

35
Alan Ameche, two-time all-American and 1954 Heisman Trophy Winner.

40
Elroy Hirsch, nicknamed "Crazylegs," ran for 786 yards in Wisconsin's 8-1-1 season in 1942.

80
Dave Schreiner, two-time all-American named Big Ten player of the year in 1942.

83
Allan Shafer, a quarterback who was fatally injured in the 1944 Wisconsin-Iowa game and in whose memory the "Living Memorial" scholarship is awarded.

Big Ten Athlete of the Year Wisconsin Women's nominees

1983
Cathy Branta, track and cross country

1984
Cathy Branta, track and cross country

1985
*Cathy Branta, track and cross country

1986
*Stephanie Herbst, track and cross country

1987
Suzy Favor, track and cross country

1988
*Suzy Favor, track and cross country

1989
*Suzy Favor, track and cross country

* won award

1986-87

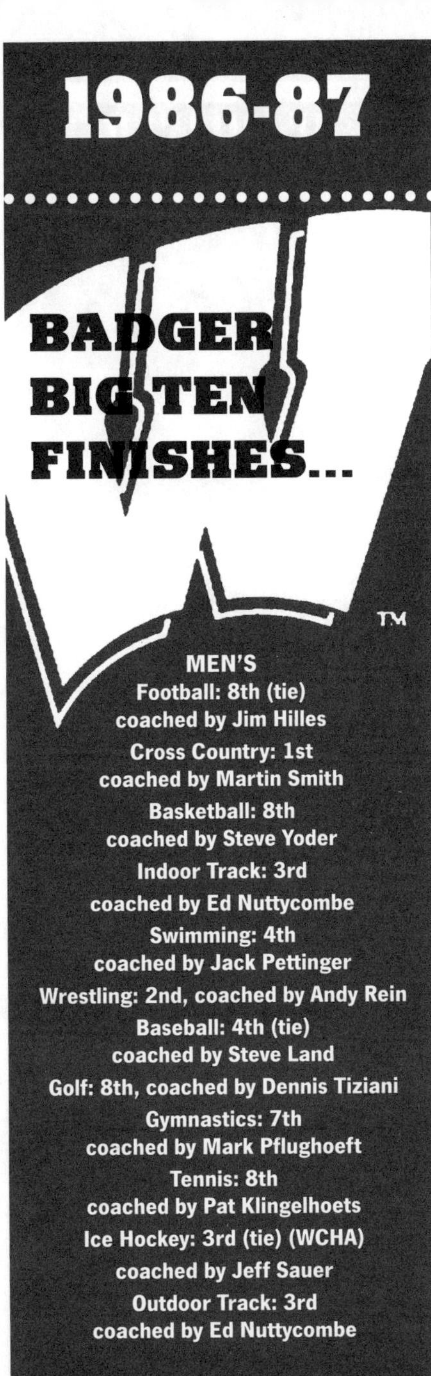

BADGER BIG TEN FINISHES...

MEN'S

Football: 8th (tie)
coached by Jim Hilles

Cross Country: 1st
coached by Martin Smith

Basketball: 8th
coached by Steve Yoder

Indoor Track: 3rd
coached by Ed Nuttycombe

Swimming: 4th
coached by Jack Pettinger

Wrestling: 2nd, coached by Andy Rein

Baseball: 4th (tie)
coached by Steve Land

Golf: 8th, coached by Dennis Tiziani

Gymnastics: 7th
coached by Mark Pflughoeft

Tennis: 8th
coached by Pat Klingelhoets

Ice Hockey: 3rd (tie) (WCHA)
coached by Jeff Sauer

Outdoor Track: 3rd
coached by Ed Nuttycombe

WOMEN'S

Cross Country: 1st
coached by Peter Tegen

Basketball: 8th (tie)
coached by Mary Murphy

Indoor Track: 1st
coached by Peter Tegen

Swimming: 4th
coached by Carl Johansson

Volleyball: 8th (tie)
coached by Steve Lowe

Golf: 8th
coached by Chris Regenberg

Gymnastics: 6th
coached by Terry Bryson

Tennis: 3rd
coached by Kelly Ferguson

Outdoor Track: 4th
coached by Peter Tegen

Suzy Favor becomes youngest NCAA track champ

Suzy Favor, less than a year removed from Stevens Point High School, became Wisconsin's youngest national collegiate champion when she won the mile in the NCAA indoor track and field championships in March, 1986, at Oklahoma City.

Favor, already touted as one of the nation's premier women distance runners as a freshman, won the mile in 4:41.69. She also won the 1500-meter run in a meet record 4:09.85 that spring in the NCAA outdoor meet that at Baton Rouge, Louisiana.

Favor won at least one title in seven of the eight NCAA meets in which she competed from 1987-90 and amassed nine NCAA crowns. She also won 21 Big Ten Conference track championships and ran on two winning relay teams. The Big Ten-Suzy Favor Athlete of the Year Award is presented annually to the top female athlete in the Big Ten.

WISCONSIN TIME LINE

1987: Chrysler Corp. announced it would buy financially ailing American Motors Corp.

Athletic directors approved a move from baseball divisional play to a 28-game schedule, with the top four teams advancing to the Conference tournament.

Suzy Favor was named Big Ten Female Athlete of the Year—the first of three times she won the award which eventually bore her name.

WISCONSIN HEADLINER

Suzy Favor Hamilton
Cross Country, Track

Suzy Favor Hamilton's career at Wisconsin epitomizes excellence in athletics. That she has been paired with no less a track legend than Jesse Owens speaks volumes for her. Competing as Suzy Favor, not only was she one of the most accomplished athletes in Wisconsin history, but also in the annals of the NCAA. The Stevens Point native six times earned athlete of the meet honors at Big Ten Conference track or cross country meets and five times was named by coaches as Athlete of the Year for one of her two sports. Her championship numbers are nothing short of staggering—9 NCAA individual track titles, 23 Big Ten track titles, 14 all-America honors in track and cross country, 7 UW records, 40 straight wins in finals races and only 2 losses in 56 collegiate finals. She won an unprecedented three straight Jesse Owens-Big Ten Female Athlete of the Year awards, prompting the Conference to name the award after her, and other national and collegiate honors too numerous to mention. Twice a U.S. Olympian (1992, 1996), Hamilton still is a nationally ranked distance runner. She was inducted into the UW Athletics Hall of Fame in 1996.

WISCONSIN HEADLINER

Paul Gruber
Football

One of the best offensive linemen in Wisconsin history, Paul Gruber earned first-team all-America honors from The *Sporting News* in 1987. A player with tremendous size, strength and speed, he was regarded by some as the top offensive lineman in college football in 1987. A native of Prairie du Sac, Wisconsin, Gruber was a first-team all-Big Ten selection and team captain that year. He started 32 of 33 games during his four-year (1984-87) Badger career. Gruber was a first-round draft choice of the Tampa Bay Buccaneers in 1988 and went on to become a first-team all-rookie selection. An all-league player several times during his 10-year career with the Buccaneers, he missed only four games due to injury and holds Tampa Bay records for most games played (151) and started (151).

UW Hockey Coaches' Records

Coach (Seasons)	Record
Robert Blodgett (1923-24)	3-9-1
W.R. Brandow (1926-27)	1-9-0
Spike Carlson (1930-31)	4-6-1
John Farquhar (1927-30)	21-20-7
Kay Iverson (1924-26)	9-10-5
Bob Johnson (1966-82)	267-175-23
John Riley* (1963-66)	34-19-3
Bill Rothwell** (1975-76)	12-24-2
Jeff Sauer (1982-Present)	405-244-33
Art Thomsen* (1931-35, 1963-64)	17-24-4
A.C. Viner (1921-23)	3-13-3

*co-coaches during 1963-64

**coached while Bob Johnson was on leave to coach Olympic team

Big Ten championships won by Wisconsin women's teams

Cross Country
1983, 1984, 1985 1986, 1987, 1988, 1991, 1995, 1997

Fencing
1986, 1987

Golf
1994

Tennis
1996

Indoor Track
1982, 1984, 1985, 1986, 1987, 1990, 1996

Outdoor Track
1983, 1984, 1985, 1986, 1990, 1991, 1996

Volleyball
1990, 1997

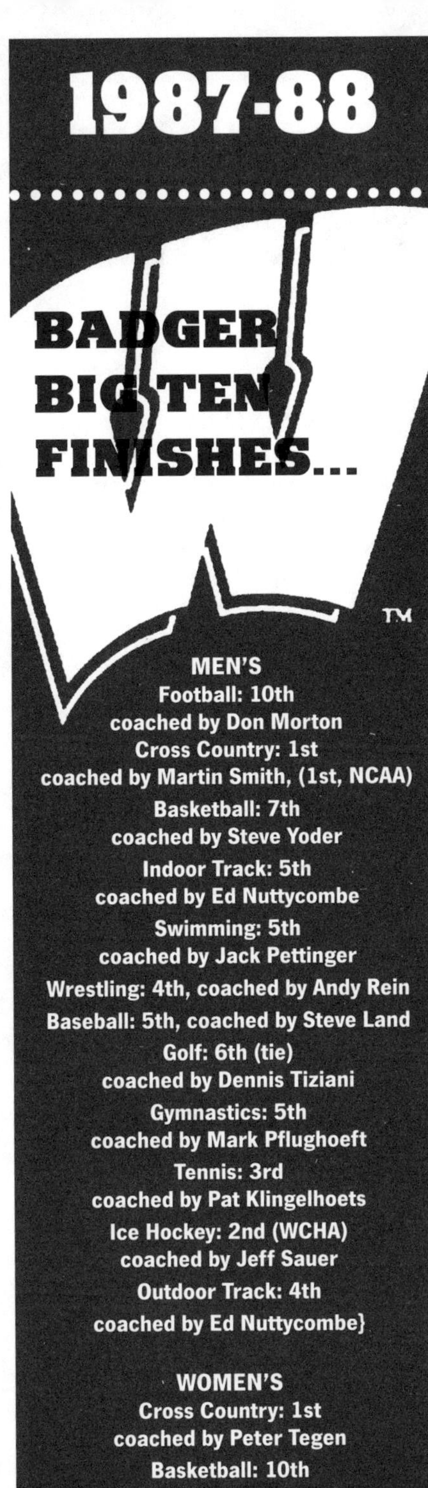

1987-88

BADGER BIG TEN FINISHES...

MEN'S
Football: 10th
coached by Don Morton
Cross Country: 1st
coached by Martin Smith, (1st, NCAA)
Basketball: 7th
coached by Steve Yoder
Indoor Track: 5th
coached by Ed Nuttycombe
Swimming: 5th
coached by Jack Pettinger
Wrestling: 4th, coached by Andy Rein
Baseball: 5th, coached by Steve Land
Golf: 6th (tie)
coached by Dennis Tiziani
Gymnastics: 5th
coached by Mark Pflughoeft
Tennis: 3rd
coached by Pat Klingelhoets
Ice Hockey: 2nd (WCHA)
coached by Jeff Sauer
Outdoor Track: 4th
coached by Ed Nuttycombe}

WOMEN'S
Cross Country: 1st
coached by Peter Tegen
Basketball: 10th
coached by Mary Murphy
Indoor Track: 5th
coached by Peter Tegen
Swimming: 10th
coached by Carl Johansson
Volleyball: 5th (tie)
coached by Steve Lowe
Golf: 6th
coached by Chris Regenberg
Gymnastics: 5th
coached by Terry Bryson
Tennis: 2nd
coached by Kelly Ferguson
Outdoor Track: 2nd
coached by Peter Tegen

Tegen wins 25th Big Ten title as UW coach

Coach Peter Tegen earned his 25th Big Ten Conference championship in women's track or cross country when his harriers won the 1987 Big Ten Conference cross country title.

The Badgers placed all five scorers among the top 11 finishers to score 42 points, half the number of points of second-place finisher Iowa. And the team did it without all-Americans Stephanie Herbst and Lori Wolter who quit the team prior to the start of the season.

Sophomore Suzy Favor paced the Badgers with a third-place finish in 17:03. Minnesota's Eileen Donaghy won the individual title in 16:58. Freshman Kim Kauls earned all-Big Ten honors with a sixth-place finish in 17:29. Senior Carole Harris finished ninth in 17:43, Tammy Breighner was 10th in 17:45 and Mary Hartzheim finished 11th in 17:46.

The Wisconsin women earned a berth in the NCAA Championship by winning the NCAA IV meet with 56 points. Harris was the top UW finisher coming in sixth in 17:11.2.

The Badgers wrapped up their season with a sixth-place finish in the NCAA championship. Oregon won the team title with 98 points while Wisconsin scored 155 points. For the second year in a row, Favor led the individual effort for the Badgers, earning all-American honors with a 21st-place finish. Favor covered the 5,000-meter course in 16:47.6. Harris also earned all-American honors crossing in 16:49.1, good for 24th place. Other scorers were Gordy Hartzheim, 49th in 17:13.4; Mary Hartzheim, 52nd in 17:15.2; and Breighner, 76th in 17:37.5.

WISCONSIN TIME LINE

1988: The 15th Olympic Winter Games opened in Calgary, Alberta, Canada.

Wayne Duke announced his intention to retire as Big Ten commissioner.

The Badgers made their first NIT basketball appearance—and first post-season play since 1947—defeating New Orleans 63-61 at the Field House.

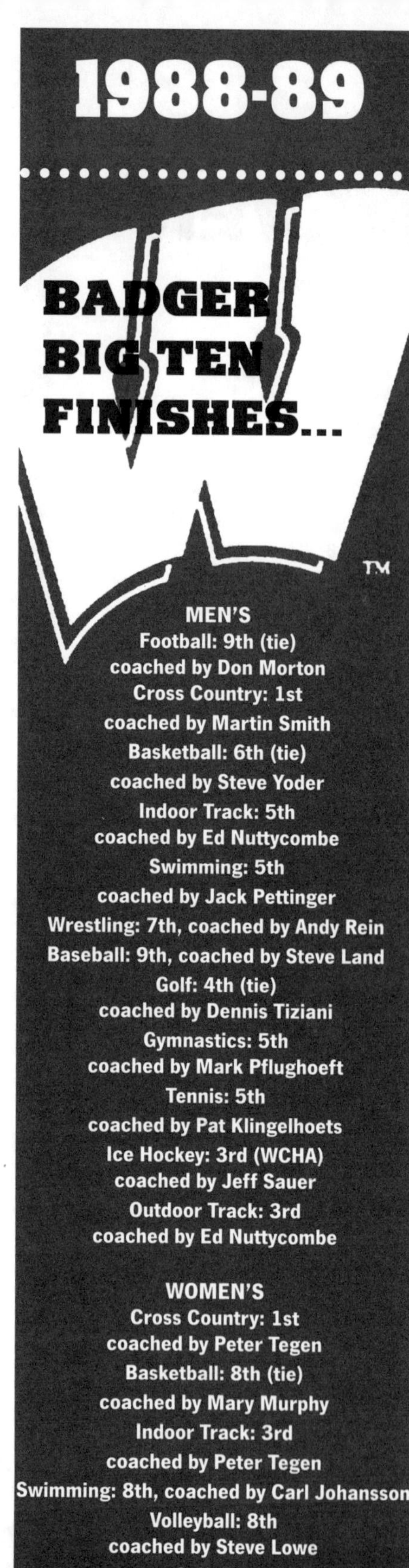

1988-89

BADGER BIG TEN FINISHES...

MEN'S
Football: 9th (tie)
coached by Don Morton
Cross Country: 1st
coached by Martin Smith
Basketball: 6th (tie)
coached by Steve Yoder
Indoor Track: 5th
coached by Ed Nuttycombe
Swimming: 5th
coached by Jack Pettinger
Wrestling: 7th, coached by Andy Rein
Baseball: 9th, coached by Steve Land
Golf: 4th (tie)
coached by Dennis Tiziani
Gymnastics: 5th
coached by Mark Pflughoeft
Tennis: 5th
coached by Pat Klingelhoets
Ice Hockey: 3rd (WCHA)
coached by Jeff Sauer
Outdoor Track: 3rd
coached by Ed Nuttycombe

WOMEN'S
Cross Country: 1st
coached by Peter Tegen
Basketball: 8th (tie)
coached by Mary Murphy
Indoor Track: 3rd
coached by Peter Tegen
Swimming: 8th, coached by Carl Johansson
Volleyball: 8th
coached by Steve Lowe
Golf: 7th
coached by Chris Regenberg
Gymnastics: 6th
coached by Terry Bryson
Tennis: 2nd
coached by Kelly Ferguson
Outdoor Track: 2nd
coached by Peter Tegen

Men's basketball makes NIT

It had been awhile—42 years, to be exact. Coach Steve Yoder's 1988-89 UW men's basketball team returned to post-season play for the first time since 1947 when the Badgers compiled a 17-11 regular-season record to qualify for the National Invitation Tournament.

The 1988-89 Badgers got an early jump on the season with an 8-0 mark on a two-week summer tour of Denmark, Finland and Sweden. Wisconsin returned from overseas and proceeded to register an 8-2 mark in non-conference play, capturing the First Bank Classic in Milwaukee with a 70-55 win over state-rival Marquette in the title game. UW senior Danny Jones earned tournament MVP honors. The Badgers later defeated Marquette, 61-59, to complete a season sweep of the Warriors.

Wisconsin opened Conference play with a come-from-behind win over Minnesota at the UW Field House. Four straight losses followed before the Badgers played themselves back into post-season contention by winning six of their next eight for a 7-6 record with five league games left to play. The UW, however, dropped four of its last five to finish the league campaign in a sixth-place tie with Purdue at 8-10.

Though bypassed by the NCAA, the Badgers gained entry to the NIT and defeated New Orleans in a first-round game at the Field House, 63-61, before being eliminated by St. Louis in the second round.

The Badgers' 18 victories were the most at Wisconsin since 1940-41. Yoder was named District XI and Midwest Coach of the Year. Jones and Trent Jackson earned second-team all-Big Ten mention.

Wisconsin Time Line

1989: The Supreme Court ruled that burning the American flag as a form of political protest is protected by the 1st Amendment.

James E. Delany became the Big Ten's fifth commissioner.

Danny Jones snapped Wisconsin's career scoring mark with his first basket in a game against Ohio State; he ended his career with 1,854 points.

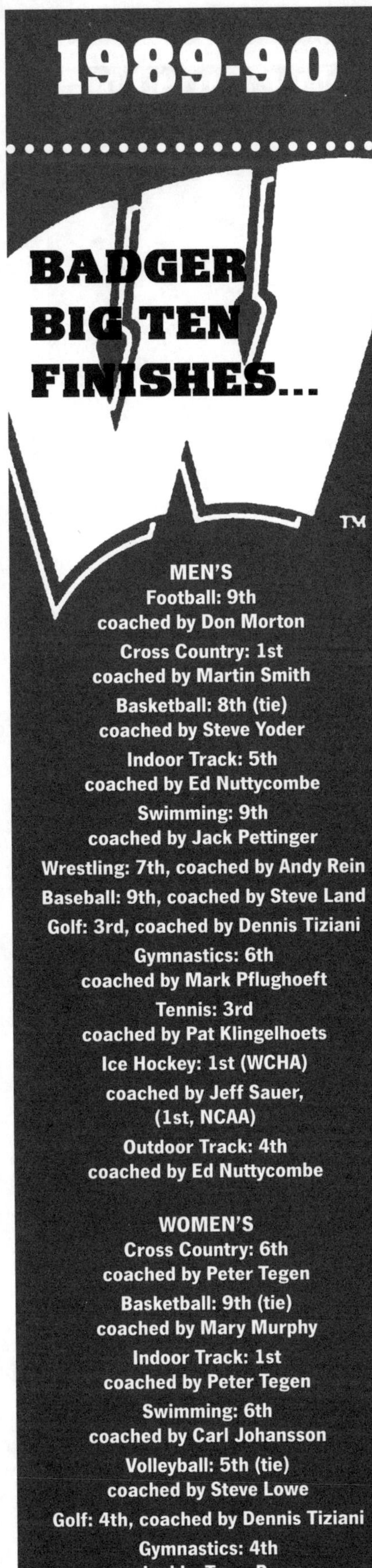

MEN'S
Football: 9th
coached by Don Morton
Cross Country: 1st
coached by Martin Smith
Basketball: 8th (tie)
coached by Steve Yoder
Indoor Track: 5th
coached by Ed Nuttycombe
Swimming: 9th
coached by Jack Pettinger
Wrestling: 7th, coached by Andy Rein
Baseball: 9th, coached by Steve Land
Golf: 3rd, coached by Dennis Tiziani
Gymnastics: 6th
coached by Mark Pflughoeft
Tennis: 3rd
coached by Pat Klingelhoets
Ice Hockey: 1st (WCHA)
coached by Jeff Sauer,
(1st, NCAA)
Outdoor Track: 4th
coached by Ed Nuttycombe

WOMEN'S
Cross Country: 6th
coached by Peter Tegen
Basketball: 9th (tie)
coached by Mary Murphy
Indoor Track: 1st
coached by Peter Tegen
Swimming: 6th
coached by Carl Johansson
Volleyball: 5th (tie)
coached by Steve Lowe
Golf: 4th, coached by Dennis Tiziani
Gymnastics: 4th
coached by Terry Bryson
Tennis: 3rd
coached by Kelly Ferguson
Outdoor Track: 1st
coached by Peter Tegen

Hockey wins NCAA title

Led by a strong core of seven seniors, Coach Jeff Sauer's eighth Wisconsin hockey team rolled to the WCHA regular-season and playoff titles before capping a 36-9-1 season with the school's fifth NCAA championship.

Sauer's squad was fortunate to have all the ingredients necessary for a championship team—talent and leadership being two of the most noticeable. The Badgers, with a senior class that included Tom Sagissor, John Byce, Chris Tancill, Gary Shuchuk, Rob Mendel, Mark Osiecki and captain Steve Rohlik, finished the campaign by going 18-1-1.

Wisconsin jumped out to a 9-1 mark to start the season, but was just 9-8 over its next 17 games, including a 4-3 loss at Northern Michigan on January 19. The Badgers, however, bounced back the next night against the Wildcats—winning 10-1—and went on to sandwich two nine-game winning streaks around just one loss at Minnesota and one tie with North Dakota.

The Badgers clinched the league title with a 5-4 OT win over North Dakota on February 24 and notched the WCHA playoff crown on March 12 with a 7-1 win over arch-rival Minnesota. The UW swept an NCAA Tournament quarterfinal series from Maine, defeated Boston College 5-4 in the semifinals and Colgate 7-3 in the title game at Detroit's Joe Louis Arena behind a Byce hat trick.

Shuchuk earned first-team all-America honors, while Tancill was named the NCAA Tournament MVP.

Wisconsin Time Line

1990: The Dow Jones Industrial Average ended the day above 2800 for the first time, at 2810.15.

Pennsylvania State University was admitted to the Big Ten.

Don Davey became first four-time first-team academic all-American in NCAA Division I football history.

WISCONSIN HEADLINER

Gary Shuchuk
Hockey

Wisconsin's Big Ten Athlete of the Year nominee in 1990, forward Gary Shuchuk helped lead the Badger hockey team to a 36-9-1 overall record and a 7-3 win over Colgate in the '90 NCAA title game at Detroit's Joe Louis Arena. Shuchuk, a native of Edmonton, Alberta, earned first-team all-America honors that season after leading the Badgers in scoring with 41 goals and 39 assists for 80 points. Named the Badgers' MVP, Shuchuk served the team as an assistant captain. He finished his Wisconsin career with 85 goals (seventh on the all-time UW list) and 91 assists for 176 points in 177 games. Shuchuk went on to play three seasons apiece for the National Hockey League's Detroit Red Wings and Los Angeles Kings. He played in Switzerland during the 1997-98 season.

WISCONSIN HEADLINER

Danny Jones
Basketball

Wisconsin's career scoring leader for five years from 1990-95, Danny Jones is now the UW's second-leading scorer with 1,854 career points. Jones, a forward from Rockford, Illinois, was an Associated Press honorable mention all-American in 1989 after helping lead the Badgers to the NIT (the school's first post-season appearance since 1947). Jones, a two-time, second-team all-Big Ten choice, was also a two-time Badger team captain. He led the Badgers in scoring in 1988-89 and '89-90 and in rebounding in '87-88 and '88-89. Jones set a then school-record for points in a season when he scored 611 in 1988-89. He scored in double figures in 91 games for the Badgers, including a stretch of 33 straight. Jones ranks in the top three in nine different career statistical categories at Wisconsin.

WISCONSIN HEADLINER

Lisa Boyd
Volleyball

Lisa Boyd became Wisconsin's first volleyball all-American in 1990 after leading the Badgers to their first-ever Big Ten Conference title and NCAA tournament appearance. She was named the Big Ten Player of the Year and also earned all-region selection that year. The 6-2 middle blocker led the Big Ten in blocks per game and ranked among the conference leaders in a number of other categories. The Dolton, Illinois, native earned honorable mention all-Big Ten honors as a sophomore and as a junior. She led the volleyball team to its first post-season appearance ever when the Badgers won the inaugural National Invitational Volleyball Championship in 1989.

LEADING THE WAY

Andy Rein
Wrestling, Wrestling Coach

Andy Rein contributed to the Wisconsin wrestling program as both an athlete and coach. Rein wrestled for the Badgers from 1977-80, serving as team captain in each of his last two seasons. A three-time all-American, he capped his career by going undefeated (40-0) as a senior and winning the NCAA title at 150 pounds with a 4-2 win over Oregon's Scott Bliss in the finals. Rein posted a 115-19-1 career mark and won Big Ten titles in 1978 and 1980. A gold medal-winner at the 1979 Pan American games, he won a silver medal at 149.5 pounds as a member of the 1984 U.S. Olympic team. Rein coached the Badgers from 1987-1993 and compiled a 69-35-3 record that included honors as 1987 Rookie Coach of the Year by *Amateur Wrestling News* and 1992 Big Ten Coach of the Year. Rein coached 14 all-Americans and three national champions at Wisconsin.

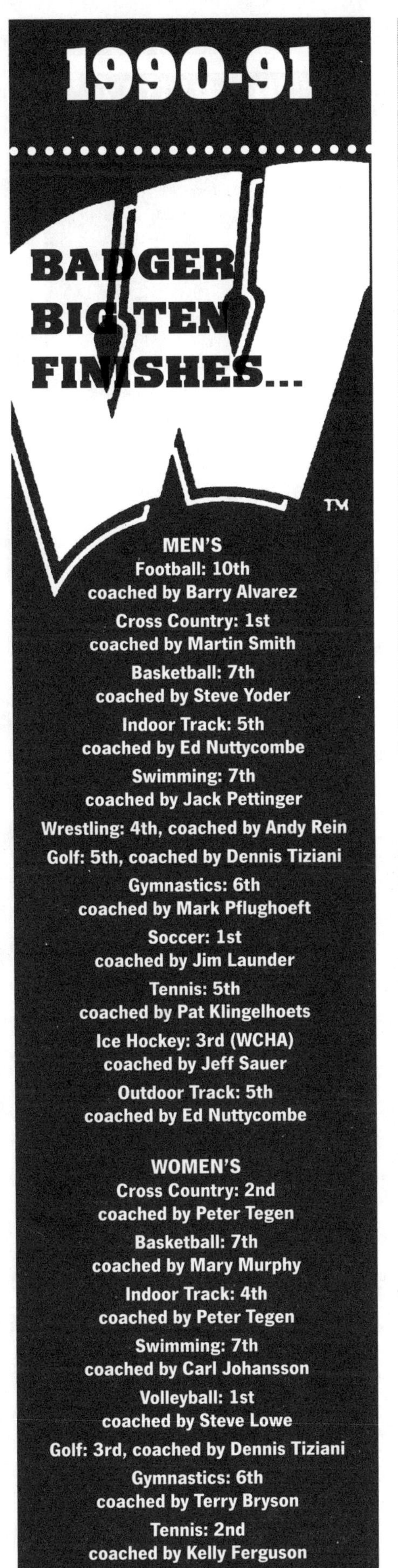

1990-91
BADGER
BIG TEN
FINISHES...
MEN'S
Football: 10th
coached by Barry Alvarez
Cross Country: 1st
coached by Martin Smith
Basketball: 7th
coached by Steve Yoder
Indoor Track: 5th
coached by Ed Nuttycombe
Swimming: 7th
coached by Jack Pettinger
Wrestling: 4th, coached by Andy Rein
Golf: 5th, coached by Dennis Tiziani
Gymnastics: 6th
coached by Mark Pflughoeft
Soccer: 1st
coached by Jim Launder
Tennis: 5th
coached by Pat Klingelhoets
Ice Hockey: 3rd (WCHA)
coached by Jeff Sauer
Outdoor Track: 5th
coached by Ed Nuttycombe
WOMEN'S
Cross Country: 2nd
coached by Peter Tegen
Basketball: 7th
coached by Mary Murphy
Indoor Track: 4th
coached by Peter Tegen
Swimming: 7th
coached by Carl Johansson
Volleyball: 1st
coached by Steve Lowe
Golf: 3rd, coached by Dennis Tiziani
Gymnastics: 6th
coached by Terry Bryson
Tennis: 2nd
coached by Kelly Ferguson
Outdoor Track: 1st
coached by Peter Tegen

Badgers win women's Big Ten volleyball crown

Nineteen-ninety was a year of firsts for the Wisconsin volleyball team. The Badgers won their first Big Ten Conference title, made their first NCAA tournament appearance, earned their first Big Ten Player of the Year honor, named their first all-American and had their first Big Ten Coach of the Year.

Wisconsin wrapped up its first Conference title on the road with a win at Michigan State to finish with a 16-2 league record. Senior Lisa Boyd was named the Big Ten Player of the Year with juniors Arlisa Hagan and Liz Tortorello also being named to the first team. Steve Lowe was named the Big Ten Coach of the Year.

The Badgers defeated Illinois in the first round of the NCAA tournament in front of a record crowd of 10,935 in the UW Field House. The record crowd made Wisconsin one of the nation's leaders in attendance as the Badgers averaged 2,199 spectators per match to lead the Big Ten.

Wisconsin lost to Penn State in the semifinals of the NCAA Mideast Regional to end its season 29-8. Boyd and Hagan earned all-region honors with Boyd being named Wisconsin's first all-American, earning second-team honors.

The Badgers also suffered a greater loss in August, 1991, when Lowe passed away from complications due to lung cancer.

Wisconsin Time Line

1991: The U.S. and allies launched an assault against Iraqi troops in Kuwait.

The Big Ten-SEC Challenge in women's basketball was held at Iowa, with Iowa, Purdue, Auburn and Georgia the participating teams.

Wisconsin women partcipated in their first NCAA basketball tournament, losing 85-74 to Montana in a first-round game.

WISCONSIN HEADLINER

Don Davey
Football

Defensive end Don Davey typified the term "student-athlete" during his four-year (1987-90) career as a football player at Wisconsin. Davey was the first four-time academic all-American (university division) in history. A native of Manitowoc, Wisconsin, Davey was also a four-time academic all-Big Ten choice. He set a then-school record for career tackles for loss with 49 and completed his Badger career with 267 total tackles. He led the Big Ten in sacks with seven to earn first-team all-league honors in 1990. A team captain in 1990, Davey earned bachelor's and master's degrees in mechanical engineering. Davey was a third-round choice of the Green Bay Packers in 1991 and played in Green Bay from 1991-94. He spent the 1995-97 campaigns with the Jacksonville Jaguars. He has played in 92 games, including 40 starts, in the NFL.

WISCONSIN HEADLINER

Jack Waite
Tennis

Waukesha, Wisconsin, native Jack Waite is the winningest men's tennis player in Wisconsin history. Waite, who played for Coach Pat Klingelhoets from 1988-91, racked up a 131-47 (.736) mark during his four-year career. He was 31-14 in 1988-89, 40-5 in 1989-90 and 38-17 in 1990-91. Wisconsin's Big Ten Medal of Honor winner for 1990-91, Waite was a two-time all-Big Ten player and was named Big Ten Player of the Year in 1991. He played singles in the 1991 NCAA Championships and came away with a 1-1 mark. Waite was a three-time academic all-Big Ten selection, three-time Badger MVP and three-time winner of Wisconsin's Sportsmanship Award. He was named Big Ten Sportsman of the Year in 1989-90.

WISCONSIN HEADLINER

Troy Vincent
Football

Although he played just one year of high school football, Troy Vincent became one of the nation's top cornerbacks and punt returners for Barry Alvarez's first two Wisconsin teams. A 1991 all-America selection, Vincent was also honored that year as the Big Ten's co-Defensive Player of the Year. He was runner-up for the Jim Thorpe Award, given to the nation's top defensive back. Vincent was selected by the Miami Dolphins as the seventh overall choice in the 1992 National Football League draft.

WISCONSIN HEADLINER

Patrick Tompkins
Basketball

Patrick Tompkins was Wisconsin's top rebounder in 1990 and 1991, earning first-team all-Big Ten honors as a senior. He also was the Badgers' most valuable player. In 1990, Tompkins pulled down an average 6.4 rebounds per game, a stat that improved to 8.8 per game in 1991. He had 14 "double-doubles" (double figures in points and rebounds in a game) in his career. Tompkins was a key player for Coach Steve Yoder on two National Invitation Tournament teams.

WISCONSIN HEADLINER

Heather Taggart
Soccer

The only two-time first-team all-American in women's soccer, goalkeeper Heather Taggart lead the Badgers to a 17-3 record and a second-place finish at the 1991 NCAA Championship. Wisconsin appeared in four consecutive NCAA tournaments during Taggart's years. The four-time all-region selection was named the 1991 Adidas Goalkeeper of the Year and was a finalist for the Adidas Soccer Player of the Year award. Taggart set UW career records for shutouts (52.5), fewest goals allowed (37) and saves (310). A Chancellor's Scholar and Golden Key National Honor Society member, Taggart majored in biochemistry and molecular biology at Wisconsin. She was a 1992 first-team academic all-American and three-time Academic All-Big Ten selection. Taggart, a native of Omaha, Nebraska, was named Wisconsin's Female Athlete of the Year and UW Big Ten Medal of Honor recipient in 1992. She received an NCAA Postgraduate Scholarship in 1992 which she used to attend medical school at the University of Nebraska.

LEADING THE WAY

Steve Lowe
Women's Volleyball Coach

With Steve Lowe at the helm, the Badger volleyball program burst onto the national scene. Unfortunately, that dream burst when Lowe unexpectedly passed away in 1991 from complications due to cancer. Lowe was named the UW volleyball coach in 1986 and built the program into a national power. In 1989, he directed the Badgers to the title in the inaugural National Invitational Volleyball Championship, their first post-season appearance ever. The following year he steered Wisconsin to its first Big Ten title and guided the Badgers to their first NCAA tournament appearance and first national ranking, finishing 10th in the final 1990 NCAA poll. Lowe also produced Wisconsin's first volleyball all-American with Lisa Boyd earning second-team honors in 1990. Lowe, who had a 108-64 career record in five years at Wisconsin, earned 1990 Big Ten and AVCA Mideast Coach of the Year honors.

LEADING THE WAY

Cheryl Marra
Associate Athletic Director

In her eight years as an associate athletic director, Cheryl Marra has been the catalyst in bringing three NCAA Championships to the University of Wisconsin. In 1993, the NCAA Division I women's volleyball championship was held in Madison and garnered the highest attendance in the history of women's collegiate volleyball. One of the most successful NCAA women's golf tournaments was held in Madison in 1998 while the volleyball championship will return in 1998. Marra has been instrumental in hosting a number of successful Big Ten and NCAA tournaments at Wisconsin. Marra, who came to Wisconsin from Denison University where she served as the women's athletic director from 1983-90, supervises men's and women's basketball, men's and women's golf, men's and women's swimming and diving, and volleyball. She also serves as the primary women's athletic administrator to the Big Ten Conference and the NCAA. Marra has a bachelor's degree in physical education and health and a master's degree in physical education from Ohio State.

First Big Ten volleyball title

The 1990 season was one of firsts for the Wisconsin volleyball team. The Badgers won their first Big Ten Conference title, made their first NCAA tournament appearance, earned their first Big Ten Player of the Year honor, named their first all-American and had their first Big Ten Coach of the Year. Wisconsin won its first league crown with a 16-2 league record. Senior Lisa Boyd was named the Big Ten Player of the Year and Arlisa Hagan and Liz Tortorello also were named to the first team. Steve Lowe was named the Big Ten Coach of the Year.

The Badgers defeated Illinois in the first round of the NCAA tournament before a record crowd of 10,935 in the UW Fieldhouse. Wisconsin lost to Penn State in the semifinals of the NCAA Mideast Regional to end its season 29-8. Boyd was named Wisconsin's first all-American, earning second-team honors. The Badgers also suffered a loss in August of 1991 when Lowe passed away from complications due to lung cancer.

1991-92

MEN'S

Football: 8th (tie)
coached by Barry Alvarez

Cross Country: 1st
coached by Martin Smith

Basketball: 9th
coached by Steve Yoder

Indoor Track: 3rd
coached by Ed Nuttycombe

Swimming: 6th
coached by Jack Pettinger

Wrestling: 2nd
coached by Andy Rein, (7th, NCAA)

Golf: 3rd, coached by Dennis Tiziani

Soccer: 1st, coached by Jim Launder

Tennis: 5th
coached by Pat Klingelhoets

Ice Hockey: 2nd (WCHA)
coached by Jeff Sauer, (2nd, NCAA)

Outdoor Track: 3rd
coached by Ed Nuttycombe

WOMEN'S

Cross Country: 1st
coached by Peter Tegen

Basketball: 3rd
coached by Mary Murphy

Indoor Track: 2nd
coached by Peter Tegen

Swimming: 9th
coached by Carl Johansson

Volleyball: 3rd (tie)
coached by Margie Fitzpatrick

Golf: 5th, coached by Dennis Tiziani

Tennis: 2nd
coached by Kelly Ferguson

Outdoor Track: 2nd
coached by Peter Tegen

UW women 2nd in NCAA soccer tournament

The Wisconsin women's soccer team made its fourth consecutive appearance in the NCAA tournament in 1991 and advanced to the championship game.

The Badgers lost to nine-time champion North Carolina, 3-1, to finish second in the nation, the highest finish ever in the 11-year history of the program.

Wisconsin received a first-round bye and defeated seventh-ranked Hartford 1-0 in the quarterfinals. At the NCAA Championship, the Badgers defeated second-ranked Colorado College 1-0 before losing to the Tar Heels to finish 17-3.

Senior Heather Taggart became Wisconsin's only two-time first-team all-American and was also named the adidas Goalkeeper of the Year. The Omaha, Nebraska, native was nominated for the Hermann Trophy, honoring the women's soccer player of the year. Senior Kari Maijala also earned first-team all-American honors.

Wisconsin Time Line

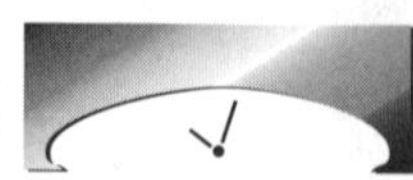

1992: Democrat Bill Clinton won the presidency over incumbent President George Bush.

The Conference approved a cross-licensing merchandising program.

Wisconsin reached the NIT basketball tournament for the third time in five years, but lost 77-73 to Rice in a first-round game at the Field House.

WISCONSIN HEADLINER

Matt Demaray
Wrestling

Matt Demaray is one of just three multiple NCAA champions in Wisconsin wrestling history. A 150-pound native of Apple Valley, Minnesota, Demaray won back-to-back NCAA titles in 1991 and 1992. The second-winningest wrestler in Wisconsin history with 150 victories, Demaray went 42-0 en route to his first title win, 4-3, over Iowa State's Steve Hamilton in 1991. A year later Demaray defeated Penn State's Troy Sunderland 5-2 for his second national crown. Demaray's record during his last two seasons was 80-3. A two-time Big Ten champion, he competed in two National Wrestling Coaches Association All-Star meets. Demaray was Big Ten Wrestler of the Year in 1991. He also earned first-team academic all-America honors from the National Wrestling Coaches Association in 1991-92. Demaray was Wisconsin's Big Ten Medal of Honor recipient as a senior.

WISCONSIN HEADLINER

Duane Derksen
Hockey

The winningest goaltender in Wisconsin hockey history with an 80-40-6 career record, Duane Derksen helped lead the Badgers to four straight NCAA Tournaments (1989-92), including two championship game appearances and one title (1990). Derksen was the all-NCAA Tournament goalie in 1990. A product of Morden, Manitoba, Derksen was a second-team all-American and finalist for the Hobey Baker Award as college hockey's player of the year in 1991-92. He is first in career games (126) and minutes (7,444) played at Wisconsin and second in career saves (3,222). Derksen was named Western Collegiate Hockey Association Player of the Year in 1992 and earned selection to the all-WCHA second-team twice and first-team once. Derksen was a 1988 draft choice of the National Hockey League's Washington Capitals.

LEADING THE WAY

Paula Bonner
Assistant Athletic Director

Paula Bonner was always an advocate of women's sports. In 1983, she was appointed assistant athletic director in charge of women's athletics.Bonner administered the complete operation of the sport program until leaving in 1989 for a position with the UW Alumni Association. Under Bonner, the women's athletic program was ranked among the top 20 in the nation. The program included several nationally ranked teams which won four national championships. Her research on gender equity issues helped get additional funding for women's athletics with a budget increase from $780,000 to $1.2 million. Bonner, a native of South Carolina, was the chair of the UW Athletic Board's Women's Sports Committee. She was a charter member of the Wisconsin Task Force on Women's athletics and served as a co-host of the Badger Women's Sports Show.

Hockey All-Americans
(first team)

Forwards

Mike Eaves (1977, 1978)
Mark Johnson (1978, 1979)
John Newberry (1982)
Patrick Flatley (1983)
Paul Ranheim (1988)
Gary Shuchuk (1990)

Defensemen

John Jagger (1970)
Jeff Rotsch (1972)
Brian Engblom (1975)
Craig Norwich (1976, 1977)
Theran Welsh (1980)
Bruce Driver (1982)
Paul Stanton (1988)
Barry Richter (1993)
Brian Rafalski (1995)

Goaltenders

Julian Baretta (1977)
Roy Schultz (1980)

1992-93

BADGER BIG TEN FINISHES...

MEN'S

Football: 6th (tie)
coached by Barry Alvarez

Cross Country: 1st
coached by Martin Smith

Basketball: 8th (tie)
coached by Stu Jackson

Indoor Track: 3rd
coached by Ed Nuttycombe

Swimming: 6th
coached by Jack Pettinger

Wrestling: 6th, coached by Andy Rein

Golf: 1st, coached by Dennis Tiziani

Soccer: 2nd, coached by Jim Launder

Tennis: 9th
coached by Pat Klingelhoets

Ice Hockey: 2nd
coached by Jeff Sauer

Outdoor Track: 4th
coached by Ed Nuttycombe

WOMEN'S

Cross Country: 4th
coached by Peter Tegen

Basketball: 10th
coached by Mary Murphy

Indoor Track: 2nd
coached by Peter Tegen

Swimming: 9th
coached by Nick Hansen

Volleyball: 7th
coached by John Cook

Golf: 5th, coached by Dennis Tiziani

Tennis: 2nd
coached by Kelly Ferguson

Outdoor Track: 3rd
coached by Peter Tegen

Wisconsin men win Big Ten golf tournament

Wisconsin won its second Big Ten golf championship—and first since 1957—with a seven-stroke victory over Ohio State on Indiana's course in Bloomington. Coach Dennis Tiziani's team totaled 1,159 strokes for the 72-hole tournament. The score equaled the sixth-best in Big Ten golf history.

Leading the Badgers was Jason Fitchett, who carded a 287 off rounds of 70, 76, 74 and 67 to finish second by five strokes to Iowa's Brad Klapprott. Finishing among the top five in the Conference in a fifth-place tie at 288 were Jim Pejka (71-75-74-68) and Ben Walter (70-75-70-73). Also scoring for Wisconsin was Joe Ring, with a 302, while Mark Scheibach carded a 303.

The Badgers had been building toward a title, having placed in the Big Ten's first division the four previous seasons. The tee-to-green success continued for the Badgers in 1994 as they again topped the Big Ten standings with a 1,151 stroke total and three-stroke margin over Northwestern in the tournament at Ann Arbor.

Walter shot a 274 to become Wisconsin's fourth Big Ten medalist. He set Big Ten records for lowest 36-hole score (65-65-130) and lowest 54-hole score (65-65-70-200) en route to the win. Tiziani was named Big Ten Coach of the Year for both 1993 and 1994.

WISCONSIN TIME LINE

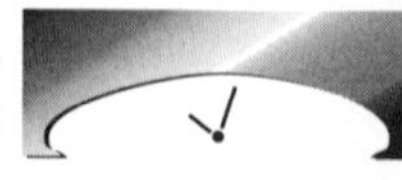

1993: Tennis Hall-of-Famer and rights advocate Arthur Ashe died at age 49 of complications from the AIDS virus.

The Conference extended Commissioner James E. Delany's contract through 1998.

Wisconsin shared the Big Ten football title and beat UCLA 21-16 in the 1994 Rose Bowl.

WISCONSIN HEADLINER

Donovan Bergstrom
Cross Country, Track

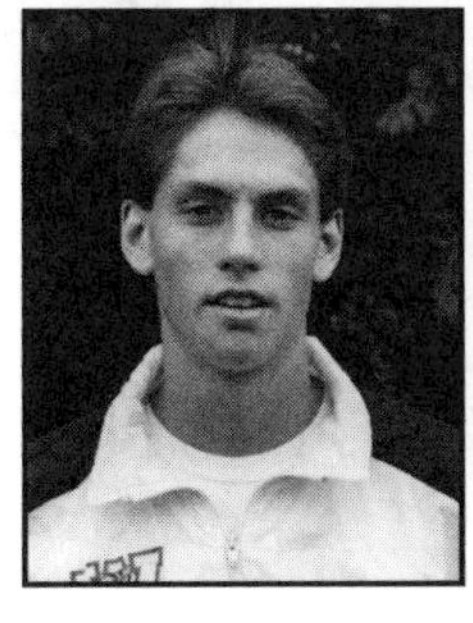

A two-time cross country and three-time track all-American, Donovan Bergstrom was another in a long line of great Wisconsin runners. A native of Elgin, Minnesota, Bergstrom won the 1993 NCAA 3,000-meter steeple-chase title after finishing fourth in 1990 and second in 1992. Bergstrom won the Big Ten steeplechase in 1992 and 1993. Wisconsin won the 1990, '91 and '92 Big Ten cross country titles with Bergstrom. A cross country all-American in 1991 and 1992, he was named the UW's Most Valuable Runner in 1990 and 1991 and served as the Wisconsin team captain in 1992. Bergstrom was Wisconsin's 1993 Conference Medal of Honor winner as well as its nominee for Big Ten Athlete of the Year. A psychology major, Bergstrom was a three-time academic all-Big Ten selection in track and cross country and the first student-athlete named three times to the U.S. Cross Country Coaches Association all-academic team.

WISCONSIN HEADLINER

Clare Eichner
Track

Four-time NCAA champion Clare Eicher starred for Coach Peter Tegen's women's track teams from 1988-93. A seven-time all-American, Eichner made 1993 her special season, winning both the mile and the 3,000-meter run at the NCAA indoor championships. She repeated the double at the outdoor meet, taking wins in both the 1500 and 3000. After her senior season, Eichner won the 3K at the World University Games. She first earned all-America honors at the 1991 NCAA outdoor meet with a sixth in the 3,000. By the next season, Eichner improved to second in the indoor 3K and fifth in the outdoor race. A 10-time Big Ten champion, she won three consecutive 1500-3000 doubles at the outdoor meet and two straight mile-3000 doubles indoors. Eichner was named 1993 Wisconsin Female Athlete of the Year and was nominated for the 1993 Honda Award in track and field.

Men's and Women's Conference Medal of Honor Winners

1990
John Byce and Susan Temple

1991
Jack Waite and Elaine Demetroulis

1992
Matt Demaray and Heather Taggart

1993
Donavan Bergstrom and Kim Sherman

1994
Louis Hinshaw and Susie Holt

1995
Jeff Gold and Dana Tzakis

1996
Scott Lamphear and Lauren Gavaris

1997
Alastir Steel and Kathy Butler

1998
Eric Raygor and Katie Voigt

Record crowd for NCAA volleyball at Field House

Wisconsin hosted the NCAA Division I volleyball championship at the Field House. Madison quickly gained a reputation as a hotbed for collegiate volleyball when 11,155 fans attended the finals session. More than 21,000 attended all the sessions.

1993-94

MEN'S
Football: 1st (tie)
coached by Barry Alvarez

Cross Country: 2nd
coached by Martin Smith

Basketball: 7th
coached by Stu Jackson

Indoor Track: 5th
coached by Ed Nuttycombe

Swimming: 8th
coached by John Davey

Golf: 1st, coached by Dennis Tiziani

Soccer: 3rd (tie)
coached by Jim Launder

Tennis: 4th
coached by Pat Klingelhoets

Ice Hockey: 3rd
coached by Jeff Sauer

Outdoor Track: 3rd
coached by Ed Nuttycombe

WOMEN'S
Cross Country: 4th
coached by Peter Tegen

Basketball: 9th
coached by Mary Murphy

Indoor Track: 3rd
coached by Peter Tegen

Swimming: 5th
coached by Nick Hansen

Volleyball: 5th, coached by John Cook

Golf: 1st, coached by Dennis Tiziani

Soccer: 2nd (tie)
coached by Dean Duerst

Tennis: 4th
coached by Kelly Ferguson

Outdoor Track: 3rd
coached by Peter Tegen

Badgers share Big Ten football title, win Rose Bowl

After eight straight losing season, the Badgers were back in a big way in 1993 ... back to the top of the Big Ten and back to Pasadena for the first time sine 1963. Picked to finish in the middle of the Big Ten pack, Coach Barry Alvarez's football team posted a school record 10-1-1 mark and a 6-1-1 Big Ten record en route to a share of the Conference championship with Oho State (which tied the Badgers, 14-14).

More importantly, the Badgers made a return trip to the Rose Bowl, in which they had last played in 1963 following that Conference championship season. Powered by Big Ten MVP Brent Moss's 158 rushing yards and two touchdowns as well as a tenacious defense, the UW beat UCLA 21-16, holding the Bruins without a touchdown until the fourth quarter.

More than 70,00 Wisconsin fans cheered the Badgers on. Wisconsin finished the season ranked fifth in the CNN/USA Today poll and sixth in the Associated Press poll, the highest post-season rankings ever for a Badger team.

Wisconsin Time Line

1994: Comic actor John Candy died at 43 while filming a western comedy in Durango, Mexico.

The first Big Ten women's soccer champion was determined in an eight-team championship tournament at Wisconsin.

Wisconsin claimed its second straight bowl win, a 34-20 victory over Duke in the Hall of Fame Bowl.

WISCONSIN HEADLINER

Valter Kalaus
Swimming

Valter Kalaus, a native of Budapest, Hungary, was one of Wisconsin's top men's swimmers during the early 1990s. Kalaus set school records in the 200-yard freestyle, 500-yard freestyle and was part of the UW's school record-setting 800-yard freestyle relay team. Named to the all-Big Ten team in 1992, Kalaus earned three all-America selections that season, finishing fifth in the 500 freestyle and 14th in both the 1650 freestyle and 800 freestyle relay. A marketing major, Kalaus was a two-time academic all-Big Ten choice (1993 and 1995). Prior to coming to Wisconsin, Kalaus competed for Hungary at the 1988 Olympics in Seoul, South Korea, finishing 10th in the 400-meter freestyle and 13th in the 1500-meter freestyle. He was a 15-time Hungarian national champion. He earned three gold and two silver medals at the 1985 and '86 Junior European Championships.

WISCONSIN HEADLINER

Brent Moss
Football

Wisconsin football returned to prominence in 1993 and one of the primary reasons was the play of tailback Brent Moss. The 5-9, 205-pound native of Racine, Wisconsin, earned the Silver Football, given to the Big Ten MVP, as well as garnering recognition as a second-team all-American and first-team all-Big Ten choice. Moss carried 312 times for a then-UW-record 1,637 yards and 16 touchdowns as a junior in '93, leading the Badgers to a share of the Big Ten title and a berth in the Rose Bowl for the first time since 1963.Moss completed his outstanding campaign by rushing for 158 yards and two touchdowns to help the Badgers defeat UCLA in Pasadena on New Year's Day in 1994. He became the first Badger to lead the Big Ten in rushing since Billy Marek in 1974. Moss finished his career as Wisconsin's second all-time leading rusher with 3,428 yards.

WISCONSIN HEADLINER

Amy Wickus
Track & Field

Baraboo native Amy Wickus had a storybook career for Coach Peter Tegen's women's track and field squad from 1992-95. Wickus won eight individual Big Ten titles, ran on three winning relay teams during that span. She won four straight outdoor 800-meter championships and claimed 800-1500 doubles in both the 1994 and 1995 outdoor meets. Wickus still hold Badger records at 600 meters (1:27.77) and 800 meters (a collegiate record 2:01.65) and is second on the all-time UW list at both 400 meters and 1500 meters. Wickus was hardly less successful in NCAA competition, winning four NCAA individual titles, including the 1995 outdoor 1500 and three straight indoor 800 titles from 1993-95. She also anchored Wisconsin's winning 4 x 800 relay quartets in the 1992 and 1993 indoor nationals. She was named the 1994 Big Ten indoor and outdoor athlete of the year and won similar honors for the 1995 indoor season.

WISCONSIN HEADLINER

Ben Walter
Golf

When Ben Walter fired his 10-under-par-274 at the Big Ten Championships in Ann Arbor, Michigan, in 1994, he became Wisconsin's first conference medalist in men's golf since 1963. Walter, a native of Menomonie, Wisconsin, led the Badgers to their second consecutive Big Ten title with his record-setting performance. His 274 was just three strokes off the Big Ten record of 271 set by Ohio State's Joey Sindelar in 1981. Walter's 36-hole score of 130 (65-65) and his 54-hole score of 200 (65-65-70) both set Big Ten records. A two-time (1993 and 1994) all-Big Ten selection for Coach Dennis Tiziani's Badgers, Walter advanced to the NCAA Championship as an individual after qualifying with a tie for sixth place at the NCAA Central Regional in Oklahoma City. He missed the cut at the NCAA Championship.

LEADING THE WAY

Barry Alvarez
Football Coach

In seven years in Madison, football coach Barry Alvarez has rebuilt a program and begun a new tradition of high expectations for Wisconsin. Coupled with that has been a revitalization of student, alumni and public interest in the Badgers' fortunes. The only coach in Wisconsin history to lead the Badgers to consecutive January bowl victories, Alvarez took the 1993 Badgers to a Big Ten co-championship and 21-16 Rose Bowl win over UCLA. His 1994 squad posted an 8-3-1 mark, including a 34-20 win over Duke in the 1995 Hall of Fame Bowl. Alvarez is one of only two coaches in Conference history to turn last-place programs their first year into Big Ten champs. That Alvarez has turned Wisconsin around is no surprise to those who know the enthusiastic and energetic coach's philosophy, which preaches togetherness, toughness, discipline, focus and a no-nonsense approach. Alvarez came to Madison in 1989 after stops at Notre Dame (as assistant head coach and defensive coordinator, at Iowa and in the high school ranks.

LEADING THE WAY

Sue Ela
Women's Rowing Coach

Sue Ela was involved with the UW women's rowing program for 25 years. A 1975 horticulture graduate, Ela was a Wisconsin oarswoman from 1972-75. She served as the assistant rowing coach for three years, prior to her appointment to the women's head coaching position in 1979. Ela was associated with three national championship teams at Wisconsin. As a member of the 1975 national championship rowing team, she brought home the first Wisconsin women's varsity eight trophy. As a coach, she brought the varsity title back to Wisconsin in 1986. Her junior varsity eight boat also won a national title at the 1986 regatta in Cincinnati, In addition to her national championships, Ela's varsity crews have finished in the top four nationally 11 times. In 1989, Ela was recognized by US Rowing as the "Woman of the Year," and in 1990 received a special achievement award from the Madison Pen and Mike Club. She was also recognized as the 1995 EAWRC Coach of the Year.

LEADING THE WAY

Dennis Tiziani
Golf Coach

Dennis Tiziani has been head men's golf coach at Wisconsin for 21 years and head women's coach for nine and, during that time, has guided both programs from obscurity to national prominence. He has taken the men's team to two (1990 and 1992) NCAA Championship tournaments and led the Badger women to their first NCAA Regional appearance in 1994. Tiziani has been named men's Big Ten Coach of the Year twice (1989 and 1993) and women's coach of the year once (1994). Wisconsin's men's squad won the Big Ten title in 1993 and then, a year later, Tiziani coached both the men and women to the conference title. Tiziani played three years on the PGA Tour and participated in the U.S. Open four times. Two of his children, Nicki and Mario, were four-year golf letterwinners at Wisconsin. Nicki is married to PGA golfer Steve Stricker.

Winning football seasons

Ten Badger football teams have had 10 winning seasons in the past 33 years.

Year	Record	Pct.	Bowl	Coach
1997	8-5-0	.615	Outback	Barry Alvarez
1996	8-5-0	.615	Copper	Barry Alvarez
1994	8-3-1	.708	Hall of Fame	Barry Alvarez
1993	10-1-1	.875	Rose	Barry Alvarez
1984	7-4-1	.625	Hall of Fame	Dave McClain
1983	7-4-0	.636	–	Dave McClain
1982	7-5-0	.583	Independence	Dave McClain
1981	7-5-0	.583	Garden State	Dave McClain
1978	5-4-2	.545	–	Dave McClain
1974	7-4-0	.636	–	John Jardine

1994-95

BADGER BIG TEN FINISHES...

MEN'S
Football: 3rd
coached by Barry Alvarez

Cross Country: 1st
coached by Martin Smith

Basketball: 9th
coached by Stan Van Gundy

Indoor Track: 1st
coached by Ed Nuttycombe

Swimming: 8th
coached by Nick Hansen

Wrestling: 7th
coached by Barry Davis

Golf: 8th, coached by Dennis Tiziani

Soccer: 1st (tie)
coached by Jim Launder

Tennis: 10th
coached by Pat Klingelhoets

Ice Hockey: 2nd (tie) (WCHA)
coached by Jeff Sauer

Outdoor Track: 1st
coached by Ed Nuttycombe

WOMEN'S
Cross Country: 2nd
coached by Peter Tegen

Basketball: 3rd
coached by Jane Albright-Dieterle

Indoor Track: 2nd
coached by Peter Tegen

Swimming: 4th
coached by Nick Hansen

Volleyball: 5th, coached by John Cook

Golf: 9th, coached by Dennis Tiziani

Soccer: 2nd, coached by Dean Duerst

Tennis: 3rd
coached by Patti Henderson

Outdoor Track: 2nd
coached by Peter Tegen

Badger men sweep Big Ten cross country and track titles

The 1994-95 Badgers of Ed Nuttycombe and Martin Smith achieved a rarity in Big Ten history, a sweep of the cross country, indoor and outdoor track championships. It marked the second time in a decade that the UW had swept all three Conference titles; the Badgers had also turned the trick in the 1985-86 season.

Smith's cross country team, led by all-Americans Jason Casiano and James Menon, scored a low 42 points at Iowa City in the fall of 1994 to hold off Michigan by 12 points. It also gave the Badgers a measure of revenge against the Wolverines, who had snapped Wisconsin's eight-year Big Ten win streak a year earlier.

In the indoor meet at Champaign, Nuttycombe's trackmen were unfriendly guests, scoring 101 points to hold off Illinois by 1-1/2 points. Four Badgers—hurdler Reggie Torian, middle-distance man Carlton Clark, distance runner Casiano and heptathlete James Dunkleberger—won individual Big Ten crowns and the distance medley relay team also triumphed.

The outdoor Big Ten Championships at Minneapolis gave the Badgers just a bit more breathing room, as the UW tallied 123 points to outlast Michigan (112 1/2) and Illinois (109). Casiano was a double winner, taking the 5,000 and 10,000-meter runs, while steeplechaser Pascal Dobert won his first Big Ten title in his specialty.

WISCONSIN TIME LINE

1995: The federal building in Oklahoma City was bombed, with 267 people dying in the blast.

The Big Ten Conference marked its centennial anniversary.

Michigan and Illinois kicked off the 100th season of Big Ten football competition on September 2.

Wisconsin made its second appearance in the NCAA women's basketball tournament after a third-place Big Ten finish.

WISCONSIN HEADLINER

Michael Finley
Basketball

Thought by many to be the greatest player in school history, Michael Finley is Wisconsin's career scoring leader with 2,147 points and helped rejuvenate the program during the early 1990s. A three-time honorable mention all-America choice and two-time, first-team, all-Big Ten selection, Finley teamed with Tracy Webster and Rashard Griffith to help guide the Badgers to the second round of the 1994 NCAA Tournament—the school's first appearance in the "Big Dance" in 47 years. The only player in Wisconsin history to score 500 points in three different seasons and the only Badger ever to average more than 20 points in three separate campaigns, Finley still ranks first or second in 11 different UW career statistical categories. He was selected in the first round (21st overall) of the 1995 NBA draft by the Phoenix Suns and currently is a standout with the Dallas Mavericks.

WISCONSIN HEADLINER

Cory Raymer
Football

Cory Raymer in 1994 became Wisconsin's first consensus all-American in 13 years. Raymer, a four-year starting center, earned first-team honors from the Associated Press, United Press International, the American Football Coaches Association, Walter Camp, *The Sporting News*, *Football News* and *College Sports* magazine. He allowed just one-half of a sack in his last three seasons. Also a two-time all-Big Ten selection, Raymer played a major role in increasing the Badgers' team rushing average from 94 to 244 yards per game during his career. He was a second-round pick of the Washington Redskins in the 1995 National Football League draft.

LEADING THE WAY

Ed Nuttycombe
Men's Track and Field Coach

During his 15 years as Wisconsin's head men's track and field coach, Ed Nuttycombe has developed one of the most successful programs in the nation. A three-time Big Ten Indoor and Outdoor Coach of the Year (1995-97), Nuttycombe also has earned two (1995 and 1997) District IV Coach of the Year honors. The Richmond, Virginia, native has teamed with Coach Martin Smith's Wisconsin cross country program to win four "triple crowns" (Big Ten titles in cross country, indoor track and outdoor track all in the same season), including three straight, the most by any Big Ten school or coach. He has guided the Badgers to nine Big Ten titles (four indoor and five outdoor). Nuttycombe's squads also have recorded a pair of top-10 finishes at the NCAA Outdoor Championships, with the UW's third place in 1997 its best-ever NCAA effort. He has produced more than 75 all-Big Ten, 60 all-America and 30 academic all-Big Ten selections.

Griffith debuts with 27 points

Center Rashard Griffith made his first performance at the Wisconsin Fieldhouse one that Badger fans would long remember. The highly touted freshman showed why he was so heavily recruited, scoring 27 points against Wright State. That still stands as a UW freshman record. He also pulled down 12 rebounds and had six assists. Griffith, who lettered at Wisconsin in 1994 and 1995 before leaving school, helped second-year coach Stu Jackson's team to an 18-11 overall mark and 8-10 slate in the tough Big Ten. The NCAA tournament selection committee recognized the strength of the league when it picked the Badgers as an at-large entry in the tournament. It was Wisconsin's first NCAA appearance since 1947. Griffith set a school record for NCAA tournament rebounds with 15 in the Badgers' 80-72 first-round win over Cincinnati. His 13.9 scoring average and 8.5 rebounding average are each the fourth-best freshman marks in Wisconsin history.

1995-96

BADGER BIG TEN FINISHES...

MEN'S

Football: 7th (tie)
coached by Barry Alvarez

Cross Country: 1st
coached by Martin Smith

Basketball: 8th
coached by Dick Bennett

Indoor Track: 1st
coached by Ed Nuttycombe

Swimming: 10th
coached by Nick Hansen

Wrestling: 8th
coached by Barry Davis

Golf: 2nd, coached by Dennis Tiziani

Tennis: 10th, coached by Pat Klingelhoets

Ice Hockey: 6th (WCHA)
coached by Jeff Sauer

Outdoor Track: 1st
coached by Ed Nuttycombe,
(6th, NCAA)

WOMEN'S

Cross Country: 1st
coached by Peter Tegen

Basketball: 3rd
coached by Jane Albright-Dieterle

Indoor Track: 2nd
coached by Peter Tegen

Swimming: 2nd
coached by Nick Hansen

Volleyball: 7th
coached by John Cook

Tennis: 1st
coached by Patti Henderson

Outdoor Track: 1st
coached by Peter Tegen

Men's soccer team wins NCAA championship

Coach Jim Launder's UW soccer team to its first NCAA soccer championship in 1995 off the strength of seven consecutive shutouts to close the season. Only the second team in school history to reach the NCAA quarterfinals, the UW swept through tournament play, stopping Duke 2-0 in the championship game at Richmond, Virginia, after edging Portland 1-0 in the national semifinals.

In the championship game, Wisconsin outshot the Blue Devils 15-6 and one-time reserve goalkeeper Jon Belskis saved both Duke shots that reached him. Lars Hansen scored the game-winner 8:12 into the first half; it was his fourth game-winning goal of the season and third in the '95 tournament. The Badgers completed the season with a 20-4-1 mark, setting a school record for victories. They also had 17 shutouts in 25 games, five more than the previous record.

The Badgers started the season 9-2, losing only to Miami of Ohio (1-0) and to 18th-ranked Creighton 2-0 in a game in Wisconsin outplayed the Bluejays. In fact, only Michigan State would score more than one goal on Wisconsin for the rest of the season. The UW dropped Penn State 2-0 to seal the Big Ten regular season title and then avenged a 2-1 overtime loss to MSU with a 2-0 win in the blizzard-shortened Big Ten championship title game.

Pacing Wisconsin in its championship season were co-captains Scott Lamphear, a first-team all-America selection, and Mike Gentile, a third-team pick. Launder was named national coach of the year.

Wisconsin Time Line

1996: Wisconsin won five of its last six football games, including a 38-10 Copper Bowl win over Utah.

Wisconsin had three men's NCAA track and field champions: James Dunkelberger (decathlon), Reggie Torian (110-meter hurdles) and Pascal Dobert (steeplechase).

The Big Ten announced that its first-ever men's post-season basketball tournament would be held after the 1997-98 season at the United Center in Chicago.

President Bill Clinton was re-elected, becoming the first Democrat elected to two terms since Franklin D. Roosevelt.

WISCONSIN HEADLINER

Kathy Butler
Cross Country, Track & Field

In only three years, Kathy Butler became one of the Badgers' most decorated athletes. A transfer from the University of Guelph in Canada, Butler won five NCAA titles, earned 13 all-American honors and won 17 Big Ten titles in only two years of competition in cross country and three years of competition in track. The Waterloo, Ontario, native won three consecutive NCAA Outdoor 3000-meter titles. She also won titles as a member of the distance medley relay at the 1996 NCAA Indoor meet and was the 1995 NCAA cross country champion. Butler was named the 1995-96 Honda Sports Award winner and the U.S. Track Coaches Association Athlete of the Year for cross country. She was also named the USTCA Indoor Track Athlete of the Year in 1997. On the Big Ten level, she was named the 1997 Big Ten/Suzy Favor Female Athlete of the Year. She is a five-time Big Ten Athlete of the Year in track and cross country. A 1996 Olympian, Butler finished 24th in the 5000 meters in Atlanta. She is the three-time Canadian national cross country champion and has competed in four World Cross Country championships finishing as the top Canadian twice.

WISCONSIN HEADLINER

Barb Franke
Basketball

The leading scorer in UW women's basketball history, Barb Franke concluded her career in 1996 with 1,994 points. She was a two-time honorable mention all-American, two-time All-Big Ten selection, three-time team MVP and 1992 Big Ten Freshman of the Year. A 6-2 forward, Franke led the Badgers to three consecutive 20-win seasons and three NCAA tournament appearances. Franke led the Badgers in scoring, rebounding and blocks for three years in a row even after coming back from knee surgery after her freshman season. She was also a member of the William R. Jones Cup team that won a gold medal in 1994. A former Miss Iowa Basketball from Cedar Falls, Franke continued her playing career after college. She played in France following graduation, but returned to the states after another knee injury. Franke was drafted in 1998 by the Chicago ABL team.

WISCONSIN HEADLINER

Jason Casiano
Cross Country, Track

Wisconsin's male athlete of the year in 1994-95, distance runner Jason Casiano was a four-time cross country all-American and a five-time all-American in track and field. A member of three Big Ten cross country championship teams and four (two indoor, two outdoor) conference championship track squads, the Portage, Ind., native won six Big Ten titles (two indoor, four outdoor) and finished second three times and third once in his four appearances at the Big Ten cross country championship. Casiano won the NCAA indoor 5,000-meter title in 1996. He was named Athlete of the Championship at the 1993 Big Ten Indoor Championship and was 1991 Big Ten Cross Country Freshman of the Year.

WISCONSIN HEADLINER

Amy Lee
Volleyball

Amy Lee goes down in the UW history books as one of its best all-round volleyball players. She ranks among the top 10 in six career categories, including setting UW career records for kills and total attack attempts. The 6-0 outside hitter finished with 1,661 kills and 4,129 attack attempts in her career. Lee earned all-American and all-region honors as well as unanimous selection as an all-Big Ten pick in 1998. The Badgers won the Big Ten title in 1998 and advanced to the NCAA Central Regional final, the farthest a UW team has advanced. As a senior, the Milwaukee native led the team in kills, ranked second in service aces and third in blocks.

WISCONSIN HEADLINER

Scott Lamphear
Soccer

Scott Lamphear, a native of Livonia, Michigan, finished in a second-place tie behind Ohio State football player Eddie George in the voting for 1995-96 Big Ten male athlete of the year. Lamphear anchored the defense for Wisconsin's 1995 NCAA champion soccer team and, in the process, earned first-team all-America, all-Midwest and all-Big Ten honors. A four-year starter at sweeper for the Badgers, Lamphear set school records for games played and starts. With Lamphear's help, the 1995 Badgers recorded shutouts in 17 of 25 games, including an unprecedented run of five straight whitewashes in the NCAA Tournament. The '95 Badgers were the only team in NCAA soccer tournament history to shut out all five opponents en route to the title. Lamphear also was a GTE Academic All-America first-team selection in 1995-96.

LEADING THE WAY

John Cook
Women's Volleyball Coach

John Cook recently completed his sixth and most successful season as the women's volleyball coach at Wisconsin. In 1997, the Badgers won the Big Ten championship, advanced to the finals of the NCAA Central Regional and ended the season ranked fifth in the nation. Cook, a 1979 graduate of the University of San Diego, was named the 1997 AVCA District 2 Coach of the Year and the Big Ten Conference Co-Coach of the Year. In six years, Cook has led the Badgers to five post-season tournament appearances and four consecutive 20-win seasons. He has coached three all-Americans, seven all-District and seven all-Big Ten honorees at Wisconsin. Cook has also had 17 academic all-Big Ten selections during his six years. Cook came to Wisconsin after serving as an assistant coach with the bronze medal-winning U.S. men's volleyball team at the 1992 Olympics. He also served as an assistant at the University of Nebraska.

LEADING THE WAY

Jane Albright-Dieterle
Women's Basketball Coach

Jane Albright-Dieterle has turned "BadgerBall" into a national phenomenon. She recently completed her fourth season as the women's basketball coach leading the Badgers to three 20-win seasons in the last four years and three NCAA tournament appearances. "Badger Ball" has also brought in the fans with Wisconsin ranking among the top three teams in the nation in attendance the last two years. Albright-Dieterle was named the 1995 and 1996 WBCA District IV Coach of the Year by her peers, and also the 1995 Big Ten Coach of the Year. After four years of coaching in high school, Albright-Dieterle moved to Tennessee as an assistant in 1981, became an assistant at Cincinnati in 1983 and a year later became head coach at Northern Illinois, where she guided the Huskies to four NCAA appearances and became NIU's all-time winningest basketball coach. Albright-Dieterle coached the gold medal-winning South team at the 1991 U.S. Olympic Festival. During the summer of 1996, Albright-Dieterle was the head coach of the R. William Jones Cup team that won the gold medal in Taiwan.

THE LIST

Women's Big Ten Outdoor Track Championship Seasons

Wisconsin's women have won Big Ten outdoor track titles at every conference location except Ann Arbor and Iowa City.

Year	Points	Site
1976	194	East Lansing, Michigan
1978	174	Evanston, Illinois
1979	172	Champaign, Illinois
1980	157 2/3	Minneapolis, Minnesota
1981	182	East Lansing, Michigan
1983	94	West Lafayette, Indiana
1984	124	Columbus, Ohio
1985	138	Evanston, Illinois
1986	130	Madison
1990	155	Champaign, Illinois
1991	127	Columbus, Ohio
1996	149	State College, Pennsylvania
1997	121	Champaign, Illinois

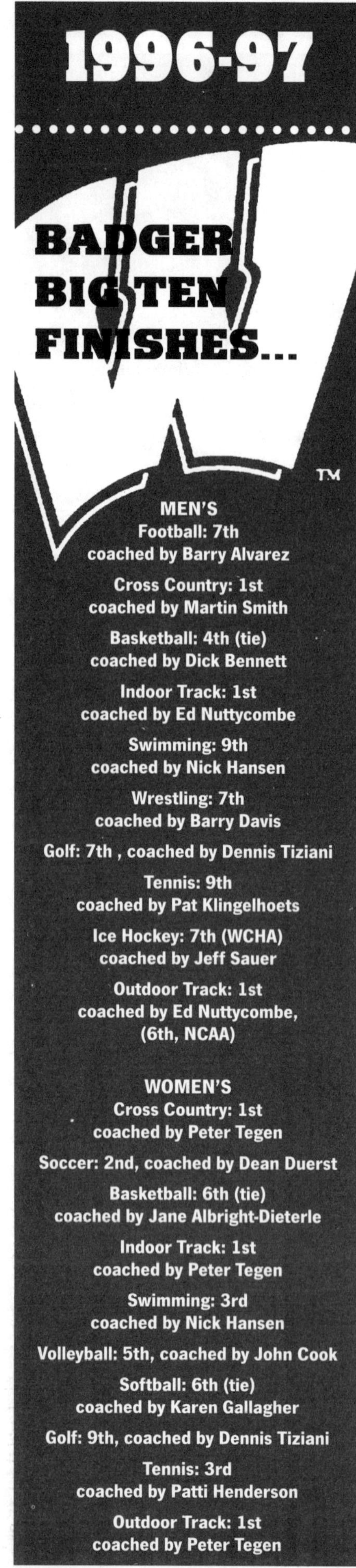

1996-97

BADGER BIG TEN FINISHES...

MEN'S

Football: 7th
coached by Barry Alvarez

Cross Country: 1st
coached by Martin Smith

Basketball: 4th (tie)
coached by Dick Bennett

Indoor Track: 1st
coached by Ed Nuttycombe

Swimming: 9th
coached by Nick Hansen

Wrestling: 7th
coached by Barry Davis

Golf: 7th, coached by Dennis Tiziani

Tennis: 9th
coached by Pat Klingelhoets

Ice Hockey: 7th (WCHA)
coached by Jeff Sauer

Outdoor Track: 1st
coached by Ed Nuttycombe, (6th, NCAA)

WOMEN'S

Cross Country: 1st
coached by Peter Tegen

Soccer: 2nd, coached by Dean Duerst

Basketball: 6th (tie)
coached by Jane Albright-Dieterle

Indoor Track: 1st
coached by Peter Tegen

Swimming: 3rd
coached by Nick Hansen

Volleyball: 5th, coached by John Cook

Softball: 6th (tie)
coached by Karen Gallagher

Golf: 9th, coached by Dennis Tiziani

Tennis: 3rd
coached by Patti Henderson

Outdoor Track: 1st
coached by Peter Tegen

Badger men record first cross country and track "triple-triple"

Records, it's said, are made to be broken, but Wisconsin's accomplishments in cross country, indoor and outdoor track over a three-season span culminating with the 1996-97 campaign may be a long time in being equaled, let alone exceeded.

The men's cross country and track teams, coached by Martin Smith and Ed Nuttycombe, respectively, recorded the first "triple-triple" in Big Ten annals, winning championships in each of three consecutive years in the sports. The cross country team, which has advanced to the NCAA meet every year since the start of NCAA district qualifying in 1972, again won the Big Ten crown and finished XX nationally, its XX straight top XX finish. And the 1997 season may have been Wisconsin's best season ever by what is arguably its best team ever.

Indoors, the Badgers had three champions in four events—Reggie Torian in the 55-meter dash and the 55-meter high hurdles; Carlton Clark in the 600; and Matt VanderZanden in the triple jump—as they won their third straight crown. Three UW athletes won outdoor Big Ten titles—hurdler Torian, sprinter Tony Simmons in the 100 and decathlete Greg Gill.

And at the NCAA outdoor championships, Wisconsin finished in a fourth-place tie with 31 points, equal to the Badgers' 1938 finish as the school's best ever and a great follow-up to the sixth place NCAA effort of 1996. The UW's three individual titles—by Torian in the hurdles, James Dunkleberger in the decathlon and Pascal Dobert in the steeplechase—were the most by any school in the meet.

Wisconsin Time Line

1997: Bill Clinton is inaugurated for a second term as president of the United States.

The Big Ten and Nike entered into a five-year agreement to assist women's sports.

The UW and Colorado College played collegiate hockey's longest men's game at 5 hours, 24 minutes. The Tigers scored at the 9:30 mark of the fourth overtime to win 1-0.

WISCONSIN HEADLINER

Reggie Torian
Track and Field

One of only eight Badgers ever to earn all-American honors five times in track and field, Reggie Torian put together one of the most impressive seasons in UW history in 1996-97. It culminated with his victory in 110-meter high hurdles in the NCAA outdoor championships that helped the Badgers to a third place finish. The Markham, Illinois, native established himself as one of the world's top hurdlers, setting a new collegiate 60-meter hurdle record indoors with a time of 7.47 which was the 10th-fastest in world history (sixth among Americans). He followed that performance with a win in the 60-meter hurdles at the USATF Indoor Championships in Atlanta, Georgia, over a field that included four Olympians. Torian won the 55-meters and 55-meter hurdles at the '97 Big Ten indoor meet and the 100-meters and 110-meter hurdles at the '97 conference outdoor meet. He was named Big Ten Indoor and Outdoor Athlete of the Year.

WISCONSIN HEADLINER

Ron Dayne
Football

Few athletes in any sport have enjoyed success in their first two years quite like running back Ron Dayne. The 5-10, 260-pounder from Berlin, New Jersey, did not start until his fifth game as a freshman, yet he still became only the 11th player in NCAA history to rush for 2,000 yards in a season. Dayne carried 325 times for 2,109 yards and 21 touchdowns as a rookie, en route to third-team Associated Press all-America honors. He followed up his astounding freshman year with a 1,457-yard, 15-touchdown campaign as a sophomore despite missing 12 quarters during the season. His two-year total of 3,284 yards rushing was second-most in NCAA history behind the legendary Herschel Walker. Dayne entered his junior year fourth on the NCAA career rushing average list (153.4). He needed only 144 yards to pass Bill Marek to become Wisconsin's career rushing leader.

WISCONSIN HEADLINER

Melissa Zimpfer
Tennis

Melissa Zimpfer became Wisconsin's first singles all-American in women's tennis in 1996 after advancing to the round of 16. The Dayton, Ohio, native has the distinction of being the highest ranked player in UW history being ranked as high as fifth during the 1996-97 season. During the 1997 NCAA Championship, Zimpfer teamed with Colleen Lucey in 1997 to earn all-American honors in doubles. The duo set the UW season record for most wins in a season with 33 and also hold the UW career record for wins with 57.

Zimpfer was named the Big Ten Conference Player of the Year in 1996 leading the Badgers to their first team title. She set the UW season record for highest winning percentage (.857) in 1996 after finishing with a 36-6 record. Her 36 wins also tied the UW record for most wins in a season. Zimpfer wrapped up her career with the highest winning percentage in singles at .845. Zimpfer is a two-time first-team all-Big Ten selection. She played two years at Wisconsin after transferring from the University of Tennessee.

WISCONSIN HEADLINER

Gina Panighetti
Swimming

Heading into her junior season, Gina Panighetti is already the most decorated UW women's swimmer. She is a four-time all-American, three-time honorable mention all-American, three-time Big Ten champion and the 1998 Big Ten Conference Swimmer of the Year.

The Chico, California, native finished among the top six swimmers in the the 100-yard butterfly and 200-yard butterfly at the NCAA Championship as a freshman and as a sophomore. As a freshman, Panighetti was the first UW women's swimmer to earn all-American honors in an individual event and the first to capture all-American honors in two individual events during the same year.

As a sophomore, Panighetti was named the Big Ten Conference Swimmer of the Year after winning the 100 fly and 200 fly at the Big Ten Championships. She also set Conference records in those two events during the season and holds UW records in six individual events or relays.

WISCONSIN HEADLINER

Tarek Saleh
Football

Twice an all-Big Ten first-team selection at defensive end, Tarek Saleh earned all-America honors from Football News following his 1996 senior season. The 240-lber. paced the Big Ten in quarterback sacks in both 1995 and 1996. He also led the Conference in tackles for loss as a junior and was third in that category as a senior. For his Wisconsin career, Saleh finished as the school's record-holder in tackles for a loss (58), yardage (283), quarterback sacks (33) and yardage (227). He also set Wisconsin records for tackles (14) and yardage (97) during the 8-5 campaign. Saleh was named most valuable player of the 1996 Copper Bowl, a 38-10 Wisconsin win over Utah.

LEADING THE WAY

Patti Henderson
Women's Tennis Coach

Patti Henderson has guided the Wisconsin women's tennis team to its first-ever Big Ten Conference championship and three consecutive NCAA tournament appearances. Wisconsin won the Big Ten title in 1996, earning its first NCAA team berth. The Badgers advanced to the quarterfinals and had their first singles all-American. Henderson led the Badgers to the NCAA Championship again in 1997, this time earning three all-American honors. Henderson, who came to Wisconsin from Northern Illinois, has coached five all-Americans, 10 all-Big Ten selections and 13 Academic all-Big Ten honorees. A 1986 graduate of Florida State, Henderson has been instrumental in keeping the USTA/ITA Women's National Indoor Team Tennis Championship in Madison. This national championship features 16 of the top teams in the nation and takes place in Nielsen Tennis Stadium in Madison.

LEADING THE WAY

Dick Bennett
Men's Basketball Coach

The hiring of Dick Bennett as Wisconsin's men's basketball coach in the spring of 1995 raised doubts in the minds of some observers who wondered if the former mentor at UW-Stevens Point and UW-Green Bay could succeed in the rugged and highly competitive Big Ten. It took Bennett less than one year to erase those doubts. In his first season he masterfully guided a team most felt would struggle to win 10 games to a 17-15 overall record and an appearance in the second round of the NIT. Bennett coached his second Wisconsin squad to the school's first 18-win regular season since 1915-16, its first 11-win Conference campaign since 1941 and a spot in the NCAA Tournament for only the fourth time in school history. After losing three starters from the '96-97 squad, the Badgers dipped to 12-19 overall in 1997-98, but Bennett entered his fourth season with more wins—47—than any three-year coach in school annals.

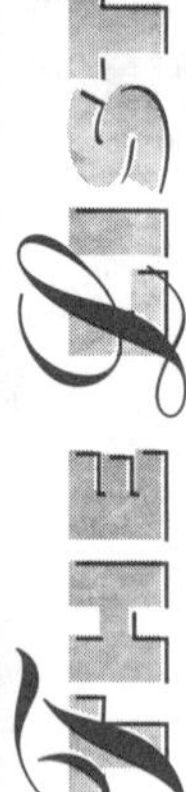

Wisconsin's Big Ten Jesse Owens and Suzy Favor "Athlete of the Year" Award Nominees

1990: Gary Shuchuk, hockey
*Suzy Favor, track & cross country

1991: Matt Demaray, wrestling
Lisa Boyd, volleyball

1992: Troy Vincent, football
Heather Taggart, socer

1993: Donovan Bergstrom, track & cross country
Claire Eichner, track & cross country

1994: Brent Moss, football
Amy Wickus, track & cross country

1995: Jason Casiano, track & cross country
Amy Wickus, track & cross country

1996: Scott Lamphear, soccer
Kathy Butler, track & cross country

1997: Ron Dayne, football
*Kathy Butler, track & cross country

*denotes Big Ten—Suzy Favor "Athlete of the Year"

1997-98

BADGER BIG TEN FINISHES...

MEN'S
Football: 5th
coached by Barry Alvarez
Cross Country: 2nd
coached by Martin Smith
Soccer: 4th (tie)
coached by Kalekeni Banda
Basketball: 9th (tie)
coached by Dick Bennett
Indoor Track: 2nd
coached by Ed Nuttycombe
Swimming: 8th
coached by Nick Hansen
Wrestling: 5th
coached by Barry Davis
Golf: 8th, coached by Dennis Tiziani
Tennis: 6th
coached by Pat Klingelhoets
Ice Hockey: 2nd (WCHA)
coached by Jeff Sauer
Outdoor Track: 2nd
coached by Ed Nuttycombe

WOMEN'S
Cross Country: 1st
coached by Peter Tegen
Soccer: 4th (tie)
coached by Dean Duerst
Basketball: 6th
coached by Jane Albright-Dieterle
Indoor Track: 2nd
coached by Peter Tegen
Swimming: 4th
coached by Nick Hansen
Volleyball: 1st (tie)
coached by John Cook
Golf: 8th, coached by Dennis Tiziani
Softball: 8th (tie)
coached by Karen Gallagher
Tennis: 3rd
coached by Patti Henderson
Outdoor Track: 2nd
coached by Peter Tegen

Kohl Center opens

A six-year plan came to fruition on January 17, 1998, with the opening of the Kohl Center on the Wisconsin campus as the Badgers hosted Northwestern in men's basketball. In 1992-93, athletic department officials had concluded that the venerable Wisconsin Fieldhouse, home to UW basketball, wrestling and myriad other events since 1930, could no longer adequately serve the needs of growing athletic, university and community constituencies.

Named after Sen. Herb Kohl, whose $25 million gift—the largest single donation in the university's history—provided the primary funding for the $76.4 million facility, the Kohl Center seats 17,142 for basketball, more than 15,000 for hockey and from 14,000-17,000 for concerts. It's the second largest arena in the Big Ten. Other major benefactors were Albert (Ab) and Nancy Nicholas, whose $10 million donation was critical, and the Kellner family—Jack F. and sons Ted and Jack W.—which contributed $2.5 million. The Nicholas-Johnson Pavilion and Plaza as well as the Nicholas Suites are named for Ab and Nancy while the Kellner Concourse is named after that family.

The multipurpose facility has been funded entirely through private support from UW alumni and friends as well as through program revenues generated by the Division of Intercollegiate Athletics. The state issue bonding authority for $27 million of the cost, which will be paid off through revenues generated by Kohl Center. The remaining $49.4 million was through private gifts.

Wisconsin Time Line

1998: India and Pakistan tested hydrogen bombs and drew global condemnation led by the United States.

The Big Ten Conference held its first post-season men's basketball tournament to determine the Conference's automatic qualifier to the NCAA tourney. Michigan won.

The Badgers lost 33-6 to Georgia in the Outback Bowl at Tampa, Florida. It was Coach Barry Alvarez's first bowl loss after three victories.

WISCONSIN HEADLINER

Barbara Urbanska
Tennis

Barbara Urbanska became the first UW women's tennis player to earn all-American honors in singles and doubles in the same year in 1998. Urbanska advanced to the round of 16 at the NCAA Championship and with doubles partner Marjon Copier, advanced to the round of eight to earn all-American honors in both categories. Urbanska is a three-time all-Big Ten selection and three-time team Sportsmanship Award winner. She is a two-time Academic all-Big Ten selection and was named to the 1997 Academic all-District team. Urbanska, who still has a year of competition remaining, is one of the top UW singles players of all time with 73 career victories. She and Copier are also tied for fifth on the UW season list for doubles wins with 24.

LEADING THE WAY

Pat Klingelhoets
Men's Tennis Coach

Continuing to keep the Wisconsin men's tennis program competitive in the Big Ten, Pat Klingelhoets completed his 16th season as head coach in 1997-98 by taking the Badgers to the NCAA Regionals (the school's first-ever appearance). Klingelhoets, who played tennis for the Badgers from 1969-72, has compiled a 224-189 career mark and has coached players to all-Big Ten status 20 times. He has coached eight of the 10 winningest players in school history. The Badgers have recorded 20 wins three times under Klingelhoets' direction and have finished in the Big Ten's upper division eight times, including a streak of five straight from 1987-92. Klingelhoets, a native of Monona, Wisconsin, still plays tennis competitively and won the men's title at the 1994 Wisconsin Open. He was ranked No. 1 among state amateurs in 1994.

THE LIST

Kohl Center by the numbers

460,000	Size in square-feet
17,142	Capacity for basketball
13,344	Capacity for hockey
14,025	Capacity for end-stage concerts
17,300	Maximum capacity for other events
1,827	Capacity of Nicholas-Johnson Pavilion
333	Wheelchair and wheelchair companion locations
6	TDD telephones
26	Public restrooms
7	Family (unisex) restrooms
36	Luxury suites
18	Concession stands
2,400	Square-footage of retail store
14	Ticket sales windows
8	Locker rooms for home and visiting teams, officials and tournament (2)
835	Size of media work room in square-feet

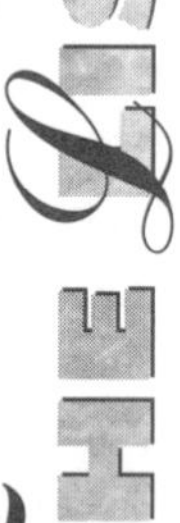

THE LIST

Men's Big Ten Cross Country Championship Seasons

Wisconsin has won 33 Big Ten team championships, more than twice as many as Indiana and Michigan State, despite going 26 years (from 1951-76) without winning. The Badgers won a record eight straight titles from 1985-92.

1910
1912
1913
1915
1918
1924
1925
1926
1927
1939
1944
1945
1948
1949
1950
1977
1978
1979
1981
1982
1983
1985
1986
1987
1988
1989
1990
1991
1992
1994
1995
1996

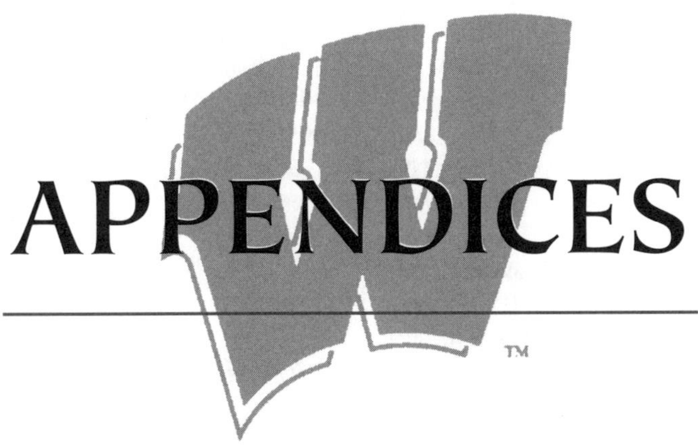

APPENDICES

UNIVERSITY OF WISCONSIN ATHLETICS ADMINISTRATORS AND COACHES

Faculty Representatives

1896 C.R. Barnes
1896-1899 E.A. Birge
1899-1905 C.S. Slichter
1905-1906 T.S. Adams
1906-1909 C.P. Hutchins
1910-1912 G.W. Ehler
1912-1931 J.F.A. Pyre
1932-1935 A.T. Weaver
1936-1947 William F. Lorenz
1947-1951 Kenneth Little
1951-1954 Kurt F. Wendt
1954-1959 George Young
1959-1970 Frank Remington
1970-1971 George Young
1971-1986 Frank Remington
1981-1987 Diane Lindstrom
1986-1987 David Tarr
1987-1989 Jane Voichick
1987-1991 Ted Finman
1989-1992 Cyrena Pondrom
1991-Present James Hoyt
1992-1994 Jane Robbins
1994-1996 Barbara L. Wolfe
1996-Present Robin Douthitt

Athletic Directors

1920-1924 Tom E. Jones (acting)
1925-1932 George Little
1933-1935 Walter Meanwell
1936-1950 Harry Stuhldreher
1950-1955 Guy Sundt
1955-1969 Ivan Williamson
1969-1987 Elroy L. Hirsch
1987-1989 Ade Sponberg
1989-Present Pat Richter

Women's Athletics Administrators

1974-83 Kit Saunders-Nordeen
women's athletic director
1983-89 Paula Bonner
associate athletic director
1986-89 Kit Saunders-Nordeen
primary women's administrator
1990-Present Cheryl Marra
associate athletic director and senior women's administrator

Sports Information Directors

1923-1929 Les Gage
1929-1941 George Downer
1941-1946 Bob Foss
1946-1956 Arthur G. Lentz
1956-1957 James A. Mott (acting)
1957-1966 George L. Lanphear
1966-1990 James A. Mott (men's)
1975-1977 Phyllis Krutsch (women's)
1977-Present Tamara Flarup (women's)
1990-Present Steve Malchow (men's)

Baseball Coaches

1900-1901 Phil King
1902-1903 Oscar Bandelin
1904-1905 Bemis Pierce
1907 C.P. Hutchins
1908-1911 Tom Barry
1912 Gordon (Slim) Lewis
1913 William Juneau
1914-1917 Gordon (Slim) Lewis
1918 Guy Lowman
1919-1920 Maurice A.. Kent
1921-1932 Guy Lowman
1933-1934 Irvin Uteritz
1935-1936 Robert Poser
1937-1939 Lowell Douglas
1940-1970 Arthur Mansfield
1971-1984 Tom Meyer
1984-1991 Steve Land

Men's Basketball Coaches

1899-1905 James Elsom
1905-1908 Emmett Angell
1909-1911 Haskell Noyes
1912-1917 Dr. Walter Meanwell

1918-1920	Guy Lowman
1921-1934	Dr. Walter Meanwell
1935-1959	Harold Foster
1960-1968	John E. Erickson
1969-1976	John Powless
1977-1982	Bill Cofield
1983-1992	Steve Yoder
1993-1994	Stu Jackson
1994-1995	Stan Van Gundy
1995-Present	Dick Bennett

Women's Basketball Coaches

1974-1976	Marilyn Harris
1976-1986	Edwina Qualls
1986-1994	Mary Murphy
1994-Present	Jane Albright-Dieterle

Men's Cross Country Coaches

1909	J.C. Elsom
1910-1911	Charles Wilson
1912	Clarence Cleveland
1913-1914	Thomas E. Jones
1915	Fred G. Lee
1916	Irvin A. White
1917	Thomas E. Jones
1918-1920	George T. Bresnahan
1921-1925	Meade Burke
1926-1947	Thomas E. Jones
1948-1949	Guy Sundt
1950-1959	J. Riley Best
1960	Tom Bennett
1961-1963	Charles Walter
1964	Tom Bennett
1965-1967	Charles Walter
1968-1970	Robert Brennan
1971-1982	Dan McClimon
1983-1997	Martin Smith
	Jerry Schumacher

Women's Cross Country Coach

1974-Present	Peter Tegen

Diving Coaches

1951-1964	Art Krueger (men's)
1964-1994	Jerry Darda
1994-Present	Jim Fischer

Fencing Coaches

1911	Walter Meanwell
1912-1914	H.D. MacChesney
1915	George Breen
1916-1917	H.D. MacChesney
1918-1919	No Team
1920-1926	Fred Schlatter
1927-1951	Arpad L. Masley
1952-1972	Archie Simonson
1972-1990	Tony Gillham
1990-1991	Jerzy Radz

Football Coaches

1889	Alvin Kletsch
1890	Ted Mestre
1891	Herb Alward
1892	Frank Crawford
1893	Parke Davis
1894-1895	H.O. Stockney
1896-1902	Phil King
1903-1904	Art Curtis
1905	Phil King
1906-1907	C.P. Hutchins
1908-1910	J.A. Barry
1911	J.R. Richards
1912-1915	W.J. Juneau
1916	Paul Withington
1917	J.R. Richards
1918	Guy Lowman
1919-1922	J.R. Richards
1923-1924	Jack Ryan
1925-1926	George Little
1927-1931	Glenn Thistlewaite
1932-1935	Dr. C.W. Spears
1936-1948	Harry Stuhldreher
1949-1955	Ivan B. Williamson
1956-1966	Milt Bruhn
1967-1969	John Coatta
1970-1977	John Jardine
1978-1985	Dave McClain
1986	Jim Hilles
1987-1989	Don Morton
1990-Present	Barry Alvarez

Men's Golf Coaches

1926	Joe Steinauer
1927-1931	George Levis
1932-1951	Joe Steinauer
1952-1969	John Jamieson
1970-1977	Tom Bennett
1977-Present	Dennis Tiziani

Women's Golf Coaches

1975-1976	Jane Eastham
1976-1984	Jackie Hayes
1985-1989	Chris Regenberg
1989-Present	Dennis Tiziani

Men's Gymnastics Coaches

1902-1905	J.C. Elsom
1906-1907	Emmett Angell

1908-1909	J.C. Elsom
1910	Felix Zeidelhack
1911-1917	H.D. MacChesney
1918	Joe Steinauer
1919-1922	Fred Schlatter
1923	Frank Leitz
1924-1926	Fred Schlatter
1927-1935	Arpad L. Masley
1936-1947	No Team
1948-1959	Dean Mory
1960-1961	George Bauer
	Gordon Johnson
1962-1971	George Bauer
1972-1978	Raymond Bauer
1978-1991	Mark Pflughoeft

Women's Gymnastics Coaches

1974-1978	Marian Snowdon
1978-1984	Jenny Hoffman-Convisor
1984-1991	Terry Bryson

Ice Hockey Coaches

1916-1919	Joe Steinauer
1922-1923	Dr. A.K. Viner
1924	Robert Blodgett
1925-1926	Kay Iverson
1927	W.R. Brandow
1928-1930	John Farquhar
1931	Spike Carlson
1932-1935	Art Thomsen
1936-1963	No Team
1963-1964	Art Thomsen
	John Riley
1965-1966	John Riley
1967-1975	Bob Johnson
1975-1976	Bill Rothwell (acting)
1977-1982	Bob Johnson
1983-Present	Jeff Sauer

Men's Rowing Coaches

1894	Andrew W. Marston
1895-98	Andrew W. O'Dea
1899	C.C. McConville
1900-1906	Andrew W. O'Dea
1907-1910	Edward Ten Eyck
1911-1928	Harry "Dad" Vail
1929-1934	George "Mike" Vail
1935-1940	Ralph Hunn
1941-1942	Allen Walz
1943	George Rea
1944-1945	none
1946	Allen Walz
1947-1968	Norm Sonju
1969-Present	Randy Jablonic

Women's Rowing Coaches

1974-1979	Jay Mimier
1979-Present	Sue Ela

Men's Soccer Coaches

1977-1981	Bill Reddan
1982-1996	Jim Launder
1997-Present	Kalekeni Banda

Women's Soccer Coaches

1981-1986	Craig Webb
1986-1994	Greg Ryan
1994-Present	Dean Duerst

Softball Coaches

1996-Present	Karen Gallagher

Men's Swimming Coaches

1912-1913	Chauncey Hyatt
1914-1919	Harry H. Hindman
1932-1951	Joe Steinauer
1951-1969	John Hickman
1970-1994	Jack Pettinger
1994	John Davey (acting)
1994-Present	Nick Hansen

Women's Swimming Coaches

1973-1974	Jack Pettinger
1974-1977	Roger Ridenour
1977-1992	Carl Johansson
1992-Present	Nick Hansen

Men's Tennis Coaches

1919-1922	George E. Linden
1923-1925	Arpad Masley
1926-1930	William Winterble
1931	Loren Cockrell
1932-1935	Arpad Masley
1936-1937	William Kaeser
1938-1939	Roy Black
1941-1943	Carl Sanger
1944-1945	Harold A. Taylor
1946-1947	Carl Sanger
1947-1951	Al Hildebrandt
1952-1962	Carl Sanger
1963	David G. Clark
1964-1968	John Powless
1969-1972	John Desmond
1973-1981	Denny Lee Schackter
1982-1983	Dave Pelisek
1983-Present	Pat Klingelhoets

Women's Tennis Coaches

1974-1976	Pam McKinney
1976-1977	Laurel Holgerson
1977-1978	Katie Munns (acting)
1978-1981	Laurel Holgerson
1981-1994	Kelly Ferguson
1994-Present	Patti Henderson

Men's Track and Field Coaches

1893	R.G. Booth
1894	M.J. Gillen
1895	W.B. Overson
1896	Charles Craigie
1897	E.W. Moulton
1898	James Temple Charles Craigie
1899	John T. Moakley
1900-1904	C.H. Kilpatrick
1905	James Temple
1906	George Downer Emmett Angell
1907-1908	Emmett Angell
1909	E.W. Moulton
1910	Charles Hutchins James Lathrop
1911-1912	Charles Wilson
1913-1948	Thomas E. Jones
1949-1950	Guy Sundt
1951-1960	Riley Best
1961-1969	Charles Walter
1970-1971	Robert Brennan
1972-1977	Bill Perrin
1978-1983	Dan McClimon
1983-Present	Ed Nuttycombe

Women's Track and Field Coach

1974-Present	Peter Tegen

Volleyball Coaches

1973-1975	Kay Von Guten
1975-1978	Pat Hielscher
1978-1981	Kristi Conklin
1981-1982	Niels Pedersen
1982-1985	Russ Carney
1986-1991	Steve Lowe
1991	Margie Fitzpatrick
1992-Present	John Cook

Wrestling Coaches

1914-1916	Fred Schlatter
1917-1918	Arthur Knott
1919-1920	Joe Steinauer
1921-1933	George Hitchcock
1934-1935	Paul Gerlin
1936-1942	George Martin
1943	John Roberts
1944	Jim Dailey Frank Jordan
1945	Frank Jordan
1946-1970	George Martin
1971-1982	Duane Kleven
1983-1986	Russ Hellickson
	Andy Rein and Barry Davis

UNIVERSITY OF WISCONSIN OLYMPIANS

Men's Crew

Bob Espeseth, Jr.	1976, 1980, 1984, 1988
Neil Halleen	1976
Randy Jablonic	1972
Tim Mickelson	1972
Norm Sonju	1964
Curt Drewes	1972

Women's Crew

Chris Cruz	1980
Cindy Eckert	1988, 1992
Yasmin Farooq	1992
Carol Feeney	1992
Carie Graves	1976, 1980, 1984
Mara Keggi	1988
Peggy McCarthy	1976, 1980
Kim Santiago	1988, 1992
Kris Thorsness	1984, 1988
Chari Towne	1984
Jackie Zoch	1976

Hockey

Steve Alley	1976
Marc Behrend	1984
Chris Chelios	1984
Bruce Driver	1984
Pat Flatley	1984
Tony Granato	1988

Sean Hill	1992
Jim Johansson	1988, 1992
Coach Bob Johnson	1976
Mark Johnson	1980
Ed Lebler	1984, 1988
Bob Lundeen	1976
Mike Richter	1988
Bob Suter	1980
John Taft	1976

Speed Skating

Beth Heiden	1980
Eric Heiden	1980

Men's Track and Field

Emil Breitkreutz	1904
Don Gehrmann	1948
Coach Tom Jones	1948
Lloyd LaBeach	1948
Steve Lacy	1980, 1984
Mike Manley	1972
Charles McGinnis	1928
Arlie Mucks	1912, 1916
George Poage	1904
Arlie Schardt	1920
Frank Waller	1904
Coach Charles "Rut" Walter	1964

Women's Track and Field

Cindy Bremser	1984
Suzy Favor Hamilton	1996

Wrestling

Jim Haines	1976
Russ Hellickson	1976, 1980
Lee Kemp	1980
Andy Rein	1984

UNIVERSITY OF WISCONSIN NCAA CHAMPIONS

Men's

Basketball

Team (1)

1941: UW 39, Washington State 34 (Coach Bud Foster)

Boxing

discontinued as NCAA championship sport after 1960

Team (8)

1939: UW, 25 points (Coach John J. Walsh)
1942: UW, 23 points (Coach John J. Walsh)
1943: UW, 32 points (Coach John J. Walsh)
1947: UW, 24 points (Coach John J. Walsh)
1948: UW, 45 points (Coach John J. Walsh)
1952: UW, 27 points (Coach John J. Walsh)
1954: UW, 19 points (Coach John J. Walsh)
1956: UW, 47 points (Coach John J. Walsh)

Individuals (38)

1936: Robert Fadner, 125 lbs.
1939: Gene Rankin, 135 lbs.
1939: Omar Crocker, 145 lbs.
1939: Woodrow Swancutt, 155 lbs.
1939: Truman Torgerson, 175 lbs.
1940: Woodrow Swancutt, 155 lbs.
1940: Nick Lee, Hwt.
1941: Gene Rankin, 135 lbs.
1942: Gene Rankin, 135 lbs.
1942: Warren Jollymore, 145 lbs.
1942: Cliff Lutz, 155 lbs.
1942: George Makris, 175 lbs.
1943: Cliff Lutz, 145 lbs.
1943: Don Miller, 155 lbs.
1943: Myron Miller, 165 lbs.
1943: George Makris, 175 lbs.
1943: Verdayne John, Hwt.
1947: Cliff Lutz, 145 lbs.
1947: John Lendenski, 165 lbs.
1948: Donald Dickinson, 148 lbs.
1948: Steve Gremban, 148 lbs.
1948: Calvin Vernon, 176 lbs.
1948: Vito Parisi, Hwt.
1951: Dick Murphy, 155 lbs.
1951: Bob Ranck, Hwt.
1952: Bob Morgan, 147 lbs.
1952: Bob Ranck, Hwt.
1953: Pat Sreenan, 147 lbs.
1953: Ray Zale, 178 lbs.
1954: Bob Meath, 156 lbs.
1956: Dean Plemmons, 112 lbs.
1956: Dick Bartman, 139 lbs.
1956: Vince Ferguson, 156 lbs.
1956: Orville Pitts, 178 lbs.
1956: Truman Sturdevant, Hwt.
1959: Charles Mohr, 165 lbs.
1960: Brown McGhee, 132 lbs.
1960: Jerry Turner, 156 lbs.

Cross Country

Team (3)

1982: UW, 59 points (Coach Dan McClimon)
1985: UW, 67 points (Coach Martin Smith)
1988: UW, 105 points (Coach Martin Smith)

Individual (2)

1939: Walter Mehl, 20:30.9 (4 miles)
1985: Tim Hacker, 29:17.88 (10,000 meters)

Ice Hockey

Team (5)

1973: UW 4, Denver 2 (Coach Bob Johnson)
1977: UW 6, Michigan 5 (OT) (Coach Bob Johnson)
1981: UW 6, Minnesota 3 (Coach Bob Johnson)
1983: UW 6, Harvard 2 (Coach Jeff Sauer)
1990: UW 7, Colgate 3 (Coach Jeff Sauer)

Rowing

Team (11)

1900: Freshmen, 2 miles, 9:45.4
1907: Freshmen, 2 miles, 9:58.0
1951: Varsity, 2 miles, 7:50.5
1959: Varsity, 3 miles, 18:01.7
1964: Freshmen, 2000 meters, 6:49.4
1966: Varsity, 3 miles, 16:03.5
1972: Freshmen, 2000 meters, 6:19.8
1973: Varsity, 2000 meters, 6:21.0
1973: Jr. Varsity, 2000 meters, 6:28.5
1973: Freshmen, 2000 meters, 6:35.1
1974: Varsity, 2000 meters, 6:33.0

Individuals (2)

1927: Winston Kratz, 200-yard breaststroke, 2:46.3
1959: Fred Westphal, 50-yard freestyle, 22.3

Soccer

Team (1)

1995: UW 2, Duke 0 (Coach Jim Launder)

Swimming

Individuals (2)

1927: Winston Kratz, 200-yard breaststroke, 2:46.3
1959: Fred Westphal, 50-yard freestyle, 22.3

Indoor Track and Field

Individual (7)

1967: Ray Arrington, 1,000-yard run, 2:07.8
1968: Ray Arrington, 1,000-yard run, 2:09.3
1969: Ray Arrington, 1,000-yard run, 2:08.0
1970: Mark Winzenreid, 880-yard run, 1:51.7
1971: Mark Winzenreid, 880-yard run, 1:50.9
1971: Pat Matzdorf, high jump, 7'2"
1996: Jason Casiano, 5,000-meter run, 13:50.08

Relays (2)

1976: Two-mile relay (Mark Randall, Steve Lacy, Mark Sang, Dick Moss), 7:26.79
1985: Distance Medley Relay (Pat Ames, Robert Hackett, John Easker, Tim Hacker), 9:39.40

Outdoor Track and Field

Individuals (16)

1921: Lloyd Wilder, pole vault, 12í0î
1937: Chuck Fenske, mile run, 4:13.9
1938: Walter Mehl, 2 mile run, 9:11.1
1944: Bob Ray, javelin throw, 174í 5/8î
1948: Don Gehrmann, 1,500-meter run, 3:54.3
1949: Don Gehrmann, mile run, 4:09.6
1950: Don Gehrmann, mile run, 4:12.4
1952: Walter Deike, 10,000-meter run, 32:25.1
1970: Pat Matzdorf, high jump, 7í1î
1971: Mark Winzenreid, 880-yard run, 1:48.8
1973: Skip Kent, 880-yard run, 1:47.2
1980: Randy Jackson, 3,000-meter steeplechase, 8:22.81
1993: Donovan Bergstrom, 3,000-meter steeplechase, 8:29.08
1997: Pascal Dobert, 3,000-meter steeplechase, 8:31.68
1997: James Dunkleberger, decathlon, 7,924 points
1997: Reggie Torian, 110-meter hurdles, 13.39

Wrestling

Individual (15)

1974: Rick Lawinger, 142 lbs.
1976: Jack Reinwand, 126 lbs.
1976: Lee Kemp, 158 lbs.
1976: Pat Christenson, 167 lbs.
1977: Lee Kemp, 158 lbs.
1978: Lee Kemp, 158 lbs.
1978: Ron Jeidy, 190 lbs.
1977: Jim Haines, 118 lbs.
1980: Andy Rein, 150 lbs.
1985: Jim Jordan, 134 lbs.
1986: Jim Jordan, 134 lbs.
1989: Dave Lee, 167 lbs.
1991: Matt Demaray, 150 lbs.
1992: Matt Demaray, 150 lbs.
1996: Jeff Walter, Hwt.

Women's

Badminton

Team (1)

1983: National Intercollegiate Badminton Championship

Individuals (4)

1981: Ann French/Claire Allison, AIAW Doubles Champions
1982: Ann French/Claire Allison, AIAW Doubles Champions
1983: Claire Allison, NIBC Singles Champion
1983: Claire Allison/Sandy Colby, NIBC Doubles Champions

Cross Country

Team (2)

1984: UW, 63 points (Coach Peter Tegen)
1985: UW, 58 points (Coach Peter Tegen)

Individual (2)

1984: Cathy Branta, 16:15.6 (5,000 meters)
1995: Kathy Butler, 16:51 (5,000 meters)

Rowing*

Team (10)

1975: Varsity 8, 1000 meters, 3:07.3
1979: Novice 8, 1000 meters, 3:13.7
1980: Jr. Varsity 8, 1000 meters, 3:15.2
1980: Novice 8, 1000 meters, 3:12.8
1980: Middleweight 4 with coxswain, 1000 meters, 3:30.30
1985: Novice 8, 1500 meters, 5:39.2
1986: Varsity 8, 2000 meters, 6:53.28
1993: Novice 4, 2000 meters, 7:55.81
1995: Novice 4, 2000 meters, 7:18.2
1996: Novice 4, 2000 meters, 7:53.2

*National Collegiate Rowing Championships

Swimming & Diving

Individual (4)

1970: #D'Lynn Damron, 1-meter diving
1970: #D'Lynn Damron, 3-meter diving
1973: *D'Lynn Damron, 1-meter diving
1976: *Peggy Anderson, 3-meter diving

#National Association of Girls' and Women's Sports
*Association of Intercollegiate Athletics for Women (AIAW)

Indoor Track and Field

Individual (14)

1980: *Pat Johnson, long jump, 21í4 æî
1981: *Pam Moore, 400-meter dash, 53.88
1981: *Pat Johnson, long jump, 20í10î
1984: Cathy Branta, 3,000-meter run, 9:04.81
1986: Stephanie Herbst, 3,000-meter run, 8:58.68
1987: Suzy Favor, mile run, 4:41.69
1989: Suzy Favor, mile run, 4:30.63
1990: Suzy Favor, mile run, 4:38.19
1990: Suzy Favor, 3,000-meter run, 9:02.30
1993: Amy Wickus, 800-meter run, 2:04.80
1993: Claire Eichner, mile run, 4:38.64
1993: Claire Eichner, 3,000-meter run, 9:09.66
1994: Amy Wickus, 800-meter run, 2:02.05
1995: Amy Wickus, 800-meter run, 2:04.86

Relays (5)

1981: *4x800-meter relay (Sue Beischel, Maryann Brunner, Ellen Brewster, Sue Spaltholz), 8:44.26
1983: Two-mile relay (Ellen Olson, Mary Anne Brunner, Sue Spaltholz, Rose Thomson), 8:53.5
1992: 3,200-meter relay (Sarah Renk, Julie Cote, Sue Gentes, Amy Wickus), 8:28.41
1993: 3,200-meter relay (Julie Cote, Sarah Renk, Kim Sherman, Amy Wickus), 8:26.77
1996: Distance Medley (Markesha McWilliams, Jenni Westphal, Janet Westphal, Kathy Butler), 11:08.91

*Association of Intercollegiate Athletics for Women (AIAW)

Outdoor Track and Field

Individuals (19)

1982: *Pat Johnson, long jump, 21í 4 æî
1984: Cathy Branta, 3,000-meter run, 8:59.57
1985: Cathy Branta, 1500-meter run, 4:12.64
1985: Cathy Branta, 3,000-meter run, 9:08.32
1986: Stephanie Herbst, 5,000-meter run, 15:42.36
1986: Stephanie Herbst, 10,000-meter run, 32:32.75
1987: Suzy Favor, 1500-meter run, 4:09.85
1988: Suzy Favor, 1500-meter run, 4:13.91
1989: Suzy Favor, 1500-meter run, 4:15.83
1990: Suzy Favor, 800-meter run, 1:59.11
1990: Suzy Favor, 1500-meter run, 4:08.26
1992: Sue Gentes, 1500-meter run, 4:16.38
1993: Kim Sherman, 800-meter run, 2:02.99
1993: Clare Eichner, 1500-meter run, 4:20.12
1993: Clare Eichner, 3,000-meter run, 9:03.06
1995: Amy Wickus, 1500-meter run, 4:14.53
1995: Kathy Butler, 3,000-meter run, 9:09.02
1996: Kathy Butler, 3,000-meter run, 9:16.19
1997: Kathy Butler, 3,000-meter run, 9:01.23

Relays (1)

1981: *4x800-meter relay (Sue Beischel, Maryann Brunner, Ellen Brewster, Sue Spaltholz), 8:53.44

*Association of Intercollegiate Athletics for Women (AIAW)

UNIVERSITY OF WISCONSIN BIG 10 TEAM CHAMPIONS

Men
includes co-championships

Baseball
1902, 1912, 1930, 1946, 1950

Basketball
1907, 1912, 1913, 1914, 1916, 1918, 1921, 1923, 1924, 1929, 1935, 1941, 1947

Cross Country
1910, 1912, 1913, 1915, 1924, 1925, 1926, 1927, 1939, 1944, 1945, 1948, 1949, 1950, 1977, 1978, 1979, 1981, 1982, 1983, 1985, 1986, 1987, 1988, 1989, 1990, 1991, 1992, 1994, 1995, 1996

Fencing
1955, 1957, 1959, 1967, 1976, 1978, 1979, 1982, 1984, 1985

Football
1896, 1897, 1901, 1906, 1912, 1952, 1959, 1962, 1993

Golf
1957, 1993, 1994

Gymnastics
1902, 1905, 1908, 1913, 1915, 1916, 1923

Ice Hockey
1972, 1973, 1974, 1977, 1978

Indoor Track
1927, 1930, 1949, 1962, 1965, 1967, 1968, 1969, 1970, 1971, 1986, 1995, 1996, 1997

Outdoor Track
1915, 1916, 1931, 1964, 1969, 1984, 1986, 1995, 1996, 1997

Women
includes co-championships

Cross Country
1983, 1984, 1985, 1986, 1987, 1988, 1991, 1995, 1996, 1997

Fencing
1986, 1987

Golf
1994

Tennis
1996

Indoor Track
1982, 1984, 1985, 1986, 1987, 1990, 1996

Outdoor Track
1983, 1984, 1985, 1986, 1990, 1991, 1996

Volleyball
1991, 1997

ALL-TIME WISCONSIN LETTERWINNERS

This list is as complete as possible, but undoubtedly some omissions have occurred. Please address corrections or additions, as appropriate, to either the Men's or Women's Sports Information Offices, University of Wisconsin, 1440 Monroe Street, Madison, Wisconsin 53706.

Men's Baseball

A

Ackeret, James	1945
Ackeman, John	1957
Adler, Charles	1964
Adler, Michael	1971-72
Aehl, John	1955-57
Ambelang, Phillip	1961
Amundson, Roland	1939-40
Amundson, Ross	1966-67
Andrews, LaVern	1951
Andringa, Rob	1989-90
Amentrout, Joseph	1984-86
Auman, Lloyd	1945

B

Bailey, Marlyn	1961
Baillie, Geoffrey	1968-69
Bakken, James	1960
Barbian, Ronald	1951, 53
Barker, Michael	1985-88
Barsness, Bradley	1982, 1984-86
Barwick, James	1981-83
Bauer, Ernest	1950
Bauman, Lee	1972-75
Baumgarten, Theodore	1952
Beckerman, Eric	1988-89
Biese, Grant	1964-66
Bennett, Steven	1973-76
Bentheimer, Michael	1981-82, 1984-85
Berkes, David	1977
Berling, Gregory	1977
Bietila, Walter	1938-39
Billy, David	1970
Binder, John	1979-81
Bixby, Ken	1939-41
Blang, Darin	1988-90
Blaskowski, Mike	1986-89
Block, Ronald	1949-mgr
Boese, Howard	1942, 1946
Borchardt, Todd	1987-89
Borcherding, Lyle	1951
Boschulte, R.D.	1968-70
Brandt, Harold	1964-65
Brick, John	1958-59
Brinker, Merlin	1944
Brown, Craig	1986-89
Brozovich, Rob	1990
Bryant, David	1975-77
Buchholz, William	1965-66
Buker, Cyril	1938-40
Burger, Robert	1955
Burmeister, Brian	1981-82
Burks, Frank	1960
Buss, Gary	1969
Butcher, Edward	1942-43, 47
Buuch, Thomas	1985
Byce, John	1986-89

C

Calabrese, Nick	1940
Calkins, Michael	1982-86
Campbell, Arnold	1952
Campion, Dennis	1986-89
Cannon, Edward	1958-59
Carlson, Craig	1971
Carpenter, Richard	1945
Carter, Craig	1981
Carter, Paul	1953-54
Cepicky, Scott	1986-89
Chartaw, Edward	1966-68
Christianson, Glenn	1950
Cincotta, August	1955-56
Clark, Alan	1976-77
Coluccy, Johnm	1985
Compton, Craig	1990
Cook, Robert	1946-48
Cooper, Thomas,	1951-53
Crorkin, Pat	1984-86
Cunningham, William	1940
Curry, Steven	1976
Cvengroe, Patrick	1956
Czaplewski, William	1982-85

D

Dahle, Thomas	1938-mgr
Davis, Danny	1981
Davis, Jeff	1984
Davis, John	1987
Defnet, Michael	1980-83
DeMerit, John	1956-57
Derkson, Robert	1981-82
Dickmann, K.J.	1984, 86
Dilley, Mark	1961
Dismeier, Russell	1938-40
Dobrowski, Rick	1988
Domnitz, Lawrence	1974-75
Domski, Dan	1972-74
D'Orazio, Nello	1938-40
Doudna, Brian	1985, 88-89
Doudna, Irvin	1937
Dunbar, Robert	1978
Dzurak, Jon	1977-80

E

Eckl, Robert K.	1963
Eckl, Robert K. Jr.	1985-88
Edlefson, James	1978
Eichorst, Tim	1984-85
Eisenach, Robert	1943
Elliot, Bruce	1948-50
Ellison, Richard	1940-42
Engdahl, Charles (Chip)	1990
Englebretson, Robert	1941-42, 47
Enlund, James	1969-71
Erickson, Bruce	1968-70
Evans, Gene	1948-50

F

Fahey, Thomas	1972
Fellows, Forest	1942
Fenn, Harold	1964
Fenn, Richard	1966
Ferris, Stanley	1937
Fink, Sheldon	1949-51
Fjelstad, Kenneth	1938-39
Fischer, Tom	1986-88
Flanagan, Mark	1989-90
Ford, Robb	1949
Forman, Jack	1941
Fox, Leo	1937
Freitag, Brant "Dusty"	1989-90
Friske, Edward	1943
Fronke, Roy	1947
Fuchs, Daryl	1971-74
Fuhs, James	1958
Fuller, Scott	1986-88
Furseth, Paul	1949-51

G

Gaestel, Melvin	1950-51, 1954
Galli, Lon	1969-71
Garman, Houston	1944
Gassman, Albert	1944
Gerlach, John	1937-38
Gillet, James	1943, 47-mgr
Giovinetti, Gene	1980
Goldstein, Bernard	1948-mgr
Graboski, Jim	1980-83
Grahn, Bill	1990
Granitz, Frank	1942, 1946
Gustavson, Duane	1974-76

H

Haas, James	1943, 46
Hackbart, Dale	1959-60
Haines, Tim	1983-85
Hamilton, Mark	1987-90
Handford, Thomas	1961-62
Hart, Michael	1981-82
Hash, David	1952-53
Hatch, Michael	1952-53
Hemming, Richard	1962
Henricks, Robert	1937-39
Hense, Richard	1964-65
Hess, William	1961
Hestnes, Steve	1983-84
Hilliard, Greg	1990
Hnath, John	1975-78
Hoglund, Paul	1944
Holt, Walter	1956-58
Hoosen, John	1963
Howe, Dennis	1962-63
Hrlevich, Richard	1954-55
Huebner, Phillip	1982
Huset, Thomas	1966-67

Hyne, James	1981

J

Jahnke, John	1953
Jaroch, Eugene	1944-47
Jaskulski, Lawrence	1969
Jeffers, Robert	1974-76
Johnson, Michael	1970-71
Johnson, Thomas	1968-70
Johnson, Ward	1958-59
Jones, Edward D.	1942
Jordan, Jeffrey	1978-80
Juntunen, Todd	1981

K

Kallies, Ralph	1974
Kasper, John	1942, 46-47
Keating, Edward	1949-50
Keenen, J. Douglas	1962
Kelliher, Wayne	1956-57
Kenefrick, Don	1951
Kent, LaVern	1937
Kilinski, Richard	1970
Kipper, Thomas	1946, 49-50
Kitzman, Eric	1944-45
Klein, Mark	1977
Kleinschmidt, John	1961-63
Knoll, Ronald	1957-58
Kopfer, Ros	1989-90
Koth, Terry	1986-87
Krafft, Harlan	1965-67
Kraft, Gary	1966-67
Krajewski, LeRoy	1962, 64
Kresbach, Thomas	1963
Krohn, Ronald	1961-63
Kronenberg, Harold	1946
Krumrei, David	1968-69
Krysa, Stanley	1953
Kuenn, Harvey	1951-52
Kumlein, Gregg	1970

L

Laatsch, Michael	1975-76
Laesch, Jeff	1990
Lamboley, Luke	1962
Lanphear, George	1937
Larsen, Richard	1974-77
Larson, James	1977-78
Larson, Mike	1984-87
Lautenbach, Walter	1943-43, 47
Lawrence, James	1946-48
Lemke, Douglas	1946, 48
Lenahan, Raymond	1950
Leve, Floyd	1946-49
Lewis, Richard	1946
Liebenstein, Eric	1985-89
Locklin, Ronald	1954-55
Locklin, Stuart	1947-48
Lowe, Charles	1946-49
Lynch, Greg	1988-89
Lyon, William	1960

M

Maas, Albert	1944
Macken, Mike	1981-84
Mackey, Scott	1973-76
Magee, Kirk	1977-80
Mahlberg, Gregory	1970-73
Mallat, William	1958-59
Malecha, Jeff	1990
Manns, Mark	1982-85
Marik, Frank	1958-60
Marriott, John Francis	1937
Marsden, Steve	1977-80
Marshall, William	1960
Mathews, Robert	1982-85
Mayer, Kevin	1990
McKenzie, Gary	1983
McKeon, Brian	1988
Merlet, James	1963
Messman, Craig	1983-85
Milkewitz, Bernard	1941-mgr
Miller, Glenn	1965
Miller, Richard	1955
Moore, Darrell	1978-81
Moore, Ronald	1951
Moran, David	1953-54
Morenz, Paul	1964-66
Moriarty, David	1958-59
Morley, Stanley	1971, 74
Mueller, Dwight	1974
Mueller, Russ	1958-60
Mulry, Kenneth	1978-81
Murphy, Daniel	1943, 45-46
Myers, Rodney	1988-90

N

Nau, Alan	1962-64
Negus, Frederick	1943
Nelsen, John	1973, 1975-76
Nelson, Phillip	1944-45
Neuhauser, Charles	1954-55
Nickels, Michael	1967-69
Nieman, Ronald	1956-58
Noble, Anthony	1978-79
Noelke, Mike	1986-88
Nord, Ronald	1949
Norvell, Merritt	1961
Nowicki, James	1967
Nowka, Elwood Jack	1954-56
Nygaard, Joseph	1946-47

O

Oakley, Steven	1966, 68
Oberdorfer, Jon	1975
O'Brien, George	1977-78
O'Brien, George E.	1952
O'Brien, Gregory	1970-72
Olle, David	1972-74
Olsen, Phillip	1955
Olson, Norman	1937-38
O'Neill, Tom	1989-90
Osterberg, Thomas	1954-mgr
O'Toole, James	1957
Otting, Andrew	1972-75

P

Padgham, Jack	1950-mgr
Painter, Lance	1986-90
Palmiter, Albert	1937
Pavlik, Ronald	1952-53
Pearson, Wallace	1944-45
Pelowski Scott	1986-89
Pennington, Leslie	1968, 1970
Perthel, Robert	1944-45
Peters, James	1964
Petersen, James	1973, 75
Phillips, Monte	1978-80
Pinnow, Gary	1965-67
Plagenz, Lyle	1959, 62
Plietz, Ronald	1948-49
Ploetz, Steven	1974-76
Poser, John	1966-68
Popovics, Thomas	1963-64
Pribyl, Brian	1979-81
Primeau, Charles	1953
Primis, Lance	1967-68
Puls, Otto	1953-54
Purull, Leonard	1975-76

Q

Quandt, Harlan	1948, 1950
Quantrill, Paul	1987-89

R

Radder, Howard	1937-38, 40
Radke, Florian	1937-38
Raether, Harold	1952-54
Randall, Steve	1972-73
Randolph, Eugene	1980-83
Refling, David	1971-72
Regan, James	1946
Reich, Lance	1966
Reichardt, Rick	1963-64
Reinhart, William Roger	1937
Rennebohm, Robert	1943
Rennicke, Dean	1979-81
Rennicke, Randall	1975-77
Richards, William	1958-60
Richter, Pat	1961-63
Rizzi, Arthur Jr.	1947
Robichaud, William	1954-55
Robinson, John	1945
Rodel, Thomas	1972-74
Rogneby, James	1958-59
Roman, Tim	1985-88
Romary, Joseph	1963-65
Romoren, Peter	1978-79
Rosenblum, Mark	1964-66
Rosplock, Jim	1986
Roth, Robert	1941
Rowlands, David	1958
Rubin, William	1955-57
Rudolph, Chester D., Jr.	1937-mgr
Rusch, Sheldon	1954-56
Russell, James	1944

S

Sabo, Scott	1982-84
Sadowkski, Carey	1987-90
Sager, Tim	1981, 83-84
Sawallich, Keith	1972
Saxer, John	1939-41
Saxer, William	1941
Schaak, James	1961
Schachte, Norbert	1954-56
Schaefer, Mark	1985
Schawel, Randy	1971-74
Scheid, James	1978
Schider, Russell	1979
Schilling, Robert	1938-40
Schinke, Thomas	1967-68
Schlosser, David	1975
Schmid, George	1956-58
Schmidlkofer, Michael	1965
Schmidt, Vince	1979-80
Schmitz, Joel	1990
Schneider, James	1970
Schneider, Lloyd	1941-42
Schnurr, John	1951
Schroeder, Harold	1937
Schten, Eric	1984
Schubeck, Peter	1947
Schultz, James	1955-57
Schultz, Steven	1977
Schumann, Merlin	1964-65
Schuppe, Samuel	1949
Schuring, Kenneth	1961, 63
Schyvinck, Jeff	1984-87
Scime, Joe	1979-83
Scully, John	1968
Seegers, Patrick	1976-78

Selbo, Glen	1947
Sepich, James	1955, 57
Setzer, Michael	1967-69
Shandling, Paul	1970-71
Shea, Robert	1949-50
Shellenback, Frank	1978-80
Sherman, John	1981
Shipley, Thomas	1972-74
Silampa, Thomas	1972-74
Simon, John	1959-60
Skalecki, Daniel	1969-71
Slotten, Kenneth	1951
Slotten, Royal	1951
Smith, Andrew	1938-40
Smith, Harold	1964-65
Smith, Robert	1938, 40-41
Smyth, Jon	1966
Sobush, Dennis	1971
Spitzer, Arthur	1937-mgr
Sprindis, Gary	1962
Spytck, Fred	1971-73
Steiner, Ronald	1960
Stephan, Clarence	1939-40
Stillman, Martin	1959-60
Stivers, Richard	1957, 59-60
Strand, Melford	1961, 63
Sullivan, Robert	1941-43
Sund, Michael	1959
Suter, Allen	1952-53
Sutton, Robert	1944-45
Sweeney, Dennis	1965-66
Sweet, Leonard	1941
Szulczewski, James	1952

T

Tadevich, Stephen	1964-65
Tadych, Rhinert	1948-49
Temp, James	1952-55
Tennant, John	1949
Thaler, Arthur	1940-mgr
Thielen, Paul	1977
Thompson, James	1946-48
Thompson, Jerome	1945-46
Thome, James	1968
Tobert, Lance	1963-65
Tomkins, Reginald	1985, 87
Torresani, Robert	1956-57
Tourek, Charles	1946
Townsend, Kenneth	1956
Trebbin, James	1967-69
Treger, Gerald	1959
Trotta, Richard	1953
Turco, Peter	1942, 46-mgr
Tuttle, Lawrence	1953
Twite, Bruce	1976
Tymus, Dave	1962-64

U

Unke, Ronald	1951-53

V

Van Dien, James	1951
Van Eerden, Richard	1959-61
Van Eerden, Robert	1951
Van Proosdy, James	1977-80
Van Sickle, Robert	1940-42
Vergetis, Gust	1952-54
Verkuilen, David	1980-83
Vilet, Tom	1989-90
Voight, Stuart	1969-70

W

Wagner, Carlyle	1953-55
Wagner, Stanley	1960, 1962
Waity, Charles	1946
Wald, Gary	1968-69
Walsh, Thomas	1971-72
Wandschneider, Ross	1958
Wegner, Brian	1984-87
Weisensel, Peter	1963
West, Thomas	1975-76
Wheeler, Mark	1977
Whitmore, Scott	1990
Wierschem, Joseph	1943
Willding, Robert	1940-42
Williams, Russell	1960, 62
Wilson, Jim	1988-89
Wilson, Robert	1947-50
Winn, Harry	1943
Wolff, Brian	1987-90
Wolff, Robert	1952
Woodring, William	1980-mgr
Wyngarden, Brett	1990

Y

Yoder, Chris	1990

Z

Zahradka, Robert	1964
Zauft, Gibbs	1943

Zeinert, Brad	1984
Zimmerman, Michael	1977-79
Zimmerman, Orvell	1944-45
Zirbel, Craig	1977-80
Zuehls, George	1937
Zydowsky, Edward	1971-73

Men's Basketball

A

Adams, James	1911
Adams, Lloyd	1970
Affeldt, George	1943
Alwin, Robert	1940-41-42
Anderson, Dean	1976
Anderson, Gary	1972-73-74
Anderson, George	1914
Anderson, Orrin	1925
Anderson, Peter	1951-52
Anderson, Walter	1939-40
Andrews, Charles	1926-27-28
Arthur, Frank	1907
Aslakson, Charles	1965
Auriantal, Hennsy	1996-97

B

Bachman, Willis	1945
Badura, Robert	1955-56
Bailey, John	1979-80-81-82
Bain, Frank	1925
Barao, Thomas	1970
Barlow, Millard	1919
Barnard, Samuel	1958
Barnes, Kenneth	1964-65-66
Barnes, Robert	1985
Barneson, Robert	1958-59-60
Barnum, Rollie	1925-26-27
Bartlett, Edwin	1902-03
Barwig, Byron	1923-24-25
Baumgarten, David	1971
Behr, Louis	1926-27-28
Bell, Byron	1937-38-39
Bencriscutto, Fred	1950, 51
Bender, John	1933
Bickelhaupt, William	1910
Biggs, James	1959-60-61
Birch, Albert	1909-10-11
Birch, Frank	1918
Bishop, Warren	1900-01
Blackwell, Cory	1982-83-84
Bloor, James	1946
Bohen, James	1963-64-65
Borland, Glenn	1956-57-58
Bowers, Dale,	1949
Breitkreutz, Emil	1904-05
Brens, John	1962-63-64
Brey, Peter,	1975-76-77
Brock, Harold	1918
Brooks, Henry	1925-26
Buechl, William	1951
Bunke, Richard	1945
Burdick, William	1899-1900
Burington, Keith	1968-69
Burkemper, David	1996-97
Burks, Frank	1960
Bush, James	1904-05-06

C

Cable, Richard	1952-53-54-55
Calderwood, Ty	1997
Cannon, Patrick	1971
Carl, Adam	1993
Carlin, Michael	1966-67-68
Carlin, Shawn	1995-96
Carlson, George	1918
Carpenter, Edward	1952
Cary, David	1983
Ceaser, Carl	1920-21-22
Chandler, William	1916-17-18
Chmielewski, Ed	1929-30-31
Chrnelich, Joseph	1977-78-79-80
Clinton, James	1951-55
Clow, Fred	1958-59-60
Colbert, Brian	1975-76
Coleman, Booker	1995-96-97
Conger, Chris	1993-94-95
Conlon, Dennis	1970-71
Cook, Robert	1946-47-48
Coyne, Willia	1937

D

Dahlke, Charles	1951-52
Daly, Michael,	1953-54
Dandridge, Greg	1980-81-82-83
Daugherty, Sean	1995-96-97
Davis, Ernest	1937-38
DeCremer, James	1970-71
DeMark, Nick	1934-35-36
DeMerit, John	1957
Deppe, Ted	1941
Dick, Donald	1944
Diebold, Marshall	1923-24-25
Dougan, Trevor	1926
Douglass, Billy	1989-90-91-92
Downs, Edward	1943
Doyle, John	1928-29
Drayton, Dwight	1970
Duany, Duany	1997
Dupee, David	1937-38-39
Dutrisac, Richard	1959-61
Dykstra, Clarence	1944

E

Ellenson, John	1989-90-91
Ellerman, Raymond	1928-29
Elsom, Kendall	1923-24
Ely, Louis	1991-92-93
Englund, Gene	1939-40-41
Englund, Gene Jr.	1962
Epperson, Charles	1940-41-42

F

Falk, Robert	1975-76-77
Falls, Richard	1947-48
Fanning, Willis	1920
Fraber, Maurice	1929-30
Farwell, Knight	1924
Faurote, Gerald	1976-77
Finley, Michael	1992-93-94-95
Fleming, Sean	1987
Floden, Tuve	1915
Folz, Daniel	1953-54-55-56
Fossum, Bruce	1948-49
Foster, Harold	1928-29-30
Franklin, Joseph	1966-67-68
Frasor, Robert	1970-71-72
Frey, Mannie	1937-38
Fuller, Gordy	1935-36-37

G

Gage, Leslie,	1922-23
Gaines, Arnold	1977-78-79-80
Gallagher, John	1939-40
Gallagher, Robert	1944
Galle, Fred	1927
Gardner, Thomas	1966
Garrott, William	1935
Gharrity, Martin	1960
Gibson, Douglas	1922-23-24
Gillespie, James	1989
Godfrey, Roger	1953-54
Goering, Vince	1945
Golston, Carl	1982
Good, Brian	1989-90-91-92
Grams, David	1963-64
Grant, Paul	1997
Gregory, Claude	1978-79-80-81
Gregory, James	1977-78
Griffith, Rashard	1994-95
Grimm, Kurt	1944-45-46
Griswold, Harry	1930-31-32
Gross, Raymond	1957-58-59
Gustafson, Kenneth	1964-65-66
Gwyn, Thomas	1961-62-63

H

Haarlow, Robert	1946-47-48-49
Haas, Mel	1914-15-16
Hackbart, Dale	1959
Hall, Jeremy	1996
Hamann, Ray	1933-34-35
Hardy, Emir	1975
Harget, Edmund,	1926
Harper, Carl	1912-13-14
Harper, Hugh	1906-08-10
Harrell, Damon	1990-91-92-93
Harris, Bob	1937
Hastings, Daniel	1978-79-80-81
Haukedahl, Stanley	1937
Hearden, Donald	1962-63-64
Heineman, Michael	1984-85-86-87
Helmholz, Henry	1900-02
Hemming, Victor	1917
Henderson, Dwight	1912
Hendrickson, Eino	1967-68-70
Henry, Albert	1969-70
Herreid, Carl	1952
Hertz, Gilman,	1943-47
Hippen, Jack,	1982-83-84-85
Hirschberg, Walter	1899-1900-01
Hisle, Larry Jr.	1990-91
Holcomb, Douglas	1947
Hollinger, Robert	1945
Holt, Walter	1957-58
Hoskins, Darnell	1994-95
Hotchkiss, George	1926-27-28
Howard, Leon	1971-72-73
Hughbanks, Thomas	1960-61-62
Hughes, Kerry	1972-73-74
Hughes, Kim	1972-73-74

J

Jackson, Ronald	1961-62
Jackson, Trent	1986-87-88-89
Jacobson, Steve	1982
Jefferson, Ivan	1959
Jenkins, Robert	1978-79-80
Johnsen, Jason	1991-92-93-94
Johnson, Allen	1912-13
Johnson, Bobbie	1963-64
Johnson, Grant	1991-92-93-94
Johnson, James	1967-68-69
Johnson, Robb	1966-67
Johnson, Robert	1975-76
Johnson, William	1944-45
Johnson, Silas Jr.	1951-52
Jones, Charles	1935-36-37
Jones, Danny	1987-88-89-90
Jorgensen, Richard	1955-56

K

Kelley, Brian	1992-93-94-95

Kilbride, Andy 1992-93-94-95
Knake, Robert 1933-34
Knapp, Harold 1918-19-20-21
Koehler, Dale 1973-74-75-76
Korth, John 1983
Kosolcharoen, Michael 1996-97
Kotz, John 1941-42-43
Kowalszyk, Henry 1927-29
Kreklow, Mike 1980-81
Krueger, Robert 1943-47
Kuechenmeister, Hugo 1914
Kulas, Brian 1957-58-59

L

Lange, E.O. 1914-15
Laszewski, Jay 1983-84-85-86
Lautenbach, Walter 1942-43-47
Leichtfuss, David 1957
Lenheiser, Ray 1941
Levis, George 1915-16-17
Lindemann, Walter 1908
Litzow, Robert 1956-57-58
Locum, Tim 1988-89-90-91
Lotzer, Mark 1976
Luchsinger, Robert 1973-74-75
Lynch, John 1941-42

M

Mack, Thomas 1955-56
Mader, Robert 1947-48-49-50
Maisel, Lawrence 1918
Malinowski, Erik 1996
Manwarring, Craig 1972
Mapel, Charles 1902
Markham, Marshall 1949-50-51
Mason, Sean 1995-96
Mathews, Eugene 1945-46
Matthews, Wesley 1978-79-80
Matthusen, Carl 1929-30
Mayberry, Craig 1969-70
McCallum, James 1967-68
McCauley, Bruce 1973-74-75
McConochie, Stewart 1903-04
McCoy, Marcus 1973-74-75
McDonald, Gilbert 1933-34-35
McDuffie, Otto 1992-93
McGee, Carlton 1991-92-93
McIntosh, Charles 1917
McIntosh, Clarence 1919-23
Meiners, Matt 1997
Menzel, Exner 1946-47
Merkel, Ralph 1925-26-27
Meyers, Paul 1916-17
Miller, David 1983-84
Miller, Fred 1933
Miller, Godfrey 1925
Miller, Lycan 1927-28-29
Miller, Richard 1954-55-56
Miller, William 1967
Mills, David 1959
Mills, Edward 1943-47-48
Mitchell, Keith 1979-80-81-82
Mitchell, Lee 1935-36-37
Mitchell, Thomas 1967-68-69
Molaski, Tom 1986-87-88-89
Moore, Earl 1948-49-50
Moore, Howard 1993-94-95
Morenz, Paul 1965-66
Morrow, J. Paul 1952-53-54
Mueller, Curtis 1954-55-56
Murray, Richard 1959-60

N

Nagle, Charles 1967-68-69
Nelson, Douglas 1930-31-32
Nelson, George 1926-27-28
Neprud, Carl 1912
Newburg, Mark 1976-77-79-80
Nicholas, Albert 1950-51-52
Nickoli, Rober 1946
Niemuth, Wallace 1946-48
Nord, Ronald 1950
Nwachukwu, Osita 1995-96

O

Oaks, Leroy 1932
O'Brien, Leland 1944
Ockershauser, Karl 1934
Okey, Sam 1996-97
Oler, Lee 1970-71-72
Olsen, Harold 1915-16-17
Olson, Rick 1983-84-85-86
O'Melia, Michael 1962-63-64
Ostrom, Lonnie 1961-62-63

P

Page, Donald 1949-50
Pamperin, John 1958
Parker, John 1954-55-56
Paterick, Timothy 1973-75-76
Patterson, Donald 1963
Patterson, Ray 1942-43-44-45
Paul, John 1929-30-31
Paust, Benjamin 1904
Pearson, William 1975-76-77-78
Pease, Harlow 1919-20
Peters, Jay 1991-92
Petersen, Jeff 1992-93-94
Peterson, Mosezell 1995-96-97
Petty, Larry 1978-79-80-81
Phelps, Marion 1912
Piacenza, Richard 1973-74-76
Plondke, Scott 1984
Ploss, John 1982-83-84-85
Poker, Lawrence 1947-48-49
Portmann, Kurt 1987-88-89-90
Poser, John 1930-31-32
Poser, Rolf 1933-34-35
Potter, John 1901-02-03
Powell, Howard 1936-37-38
Powers, Edward 1926
Powers, Robert 1961
Preboski, Felix 1934-35

Q-R

Quest, Matt 1997
Radke, Steven 1957-58
Rebholz, James 1967
Rebholz, Russ 1931
Reddick, Melvin 1969
Rehfeldt, Donald 1947-48-49-50
Rehm, Frederick 1941-42-43
Reinhart, Roger 1935-36
Remstad, Robert 1951
Renfroe, Dwayne 1981
Rewey, Stanley 1932
Richgels, Glen 1971
Richter, Pat 1961-62-63
Ripley, Rodney 1984-85-86-87
Rippe, Russel 1946-47-48
Rizzi, Arthur 1946-47
Roberts, David 1964-65-66
Roberts, Jalil 1994
Robertson, Pollis 1986-87-88-89
Robinson, Byron 1988-89-90
Rogers, Douglas 1946-47-48-49
Rogers, Harlan 1906-07-08
Rogneby, James 1957-58-59
Rohan, Patrick 1971-72
Rooney, George 1936-37-38
Rossin, Robert 1959-60
Roth, Robert 1941
Roth, Scott 1982-83-84-85
Ruckel, Robert 1946
Rudd, Allen 1976
Rundell, John 1938-39-40
Ryckman, Kenneth 1932
Ryser, Albert Jr. 1944

S

Sands, Albert 1913-14
Scheiwe, Edward 1940-41-42
Schell, Jay 1992
Schell, John 1967-68-69
Schmitt, Gustav 1904
Schneider, Fredric 1948-49-50
Schneider, Harvey 1930-31-32
Schoeneck, Thomas 1965
Schofield, Harvey 1902-03-04
Schrage, Warren 1941-42
Schubring, Darin 1986-87-88-89
Schuhmacher, Troy 1997
Schwartz, John 1950
Schwartz, Robert 1939
Scott, Harlo 1941-42
Scoville, Walter 1910-11-12
Scribner, Charles 1905-06-07
Selbo, Glen 1944-47
Sellers, Brad 1982-83
Serbiak, Robert 1958-59
Severin, Max 1903-04
Shafer, Adam 1997
Sherrod, Clarence 1969-70-71
Siebel, Kenneth 1961-62-63
Siefert, Charles 1952-53
Simms, Willie 1989-90-91
Simpson, Eber 1917-18
Smith, Desmond 1944-45
Smith, James 1979
Smith, James III 1976-77-78
Smith, Jim 1983
Smith, Robert 1946
Smith, Shelton Jr. 1985-86-87
Smith, Thomas 1933-34
Smith, William 1976-77
Spika, Daniel 1954
Spooner, A. Dwight 1923-24
Stack, John 1958-59
Stangel, Otto 1912
Steen, Marvin 1931-32
Stege, Edward 1934-35-36
Steinhaus, Gregg 1983-84-85-86
Steinmetz, Christian 1902-03-04-05
Steinmetz, Christian R. 1931
Stelter, Keith 1965
Stephens, Steven 1957-58
Stoll, George 1925-26-27
Stoltz, Oscar 1914
Stover, Paul 1898-1900-01
Stracka, Anthony 1952-53-54
Strain, William 1939-40-41
Strickler, Palmer 1946
Sullivan, Robert 1945
Sullivan, Robert 1941-42-43
Sweeney, Dennis 1965-66-67
Swenholt, Helmer 1907-08-09
Swenson, Edwin 1918
Sydnor, Raymond 1977-78

T

Tapp, Rodney 1987-88
Taylor, Warren 1920-21-22

Tebell, Gustaf 1921-22-23
Tenhopen, Elmer 1927-28-29
Terwilliger, Emmett 1935
Timmerman, Donald 1940-41
Timmerman, Greg 1993
Tompkins, Patrick 1988-89-90-91
Tornowske, Russell 1931

U
Ulwelling, John 1960
Uphoff, Rodney 1971

V
Vander Meulen, David 1960-61
Van Dien, James 1950-51
Van Gent, Eugene 1912-13-14
Van Riper, John 1911-12-13
Varney, F. Carleton 1924-25
Voigt, Theodore 1967-68-69
Vraney, Brian 1995-96-97

W
Wackman, Ralph 1924-25
Ward, Thomas 1951-52-53
Watson, Gary 1971
Weaver, LaMont 1972-73-74
Weber, Jeffrey 1984-85-86-87
Weber, Robert 1953-54
Webster, Tracy 1992-93-94
Wegner, Fred 1934-35-36
Weigandt, Robert 1937-38-39
Weisner, Ronald 1952-53-54
Wendlund, Russell 1944
Weston, Frank 1919-20
Wickman, Ray 1931-32-33
Wilhelm, Steve 1972-73-74
Willey, Rob 1986-88-89
Williams, John 1921
Williams, Rolland 1921-22-23
Winn, Harry Jr. 1964-65
Wise, John 1946-49
Witt, William 1908-09-10
Wittig, Robert 1963
Woellaeger, Edwin 1903
Worthman, Robert 1949-50

Y
York, Claude 1940
Young, Francis 1960

Z
Zeiger, Richard 1955-56
Zink, David 1968-69-70
Zinkgraf, Gary 1979-82
Zorn, Willis 1945-48-49
Zubor, Mark 1964-65-66
Zulfer, Anthony 1918-19
Zuppke, Robert 1904-05

Men's Cross Country

A
Abbott, Allen C. 1901
Agger, Sean 1996
Agger, Todd 1995-96
Ancuauz, Brian 1980
Arrington, Raymond 1966-67
Avila, Al 1976

B
Bachhuber, Gregory J. 1935-36
Baird, Jerome E. 1942
Baker, Charles 1970-71
Bakke, Gary 1959
Baldwin, Dick 1977
Balistreri, Ted 1984-85-86-87
Barrett, Lawrence 1953-54-55
Bauer, Jerome J. 1942
Baumgarth, Verlin, H. 1943
Beck, Richard J. 1949-50
Becker, J. A. 1912-13
Bergstresser, John 1924
Bergstrom, Donovan 1989-90-91-92
Berndt, Randall J. 1982-83
Bertles, William M. 1906
Bertrand, Kenneth J. 1929-30-31
Blankenagel, John C. 1907
Borsa, Chris 198- 86-87-88
Bosley, Andy 1993-94-95-96
Bradish, Chas B. 1912
Brady, Branch 1966-67-68
Braaten, Eric 1972-73-74
Bresnahan, George T. 1912-13
Brice, James 1979-81-82
Brinen, Scott 1995-96
Brothers, Wellington 1918-19-20
Bullamore, Charles 1927
Burgess, William T. 1927, 29
Buxton, Edward F. 1938-39

C
Carroll, Thomas F. 1936
Casiano, Jason 1991-92-93-94
Chandler, Kensal R. 1942-43
Chandler, Pete 1975-76-77-78
Chapman, Victor 1925-26
Connors, James 1962
Cooke, Lloyd 1935-36
Cordes, John 1969
Corrigan, Thomas M. 1938-40
Cortright, Harry M. 1929-30-31
Costanza, Samuel D. 1950
Crummy, James H. 1931-32

D
Dallas, Calvin 1971-72-73
Dalton, Jon W. 1953-54-55
Dameworth, Bryan 1991-92-93-94
Dani, Mark 1986
Dayton, Willard L. 1917
Deignan, Mike 1984
Deike, Walter, D. 1947, 50-51
Delaney, Kelley 1983-84-85
Dennis, Henry 1994
Des Jarlais, Gerald 1951
Devlin, Robert 1957-58-59
DiJoseph, Jason 1990
Diley, Chester 1928
Dobert, Pascal 1992-94-95-96
Dooley, Donald 1959-60-61
Dorow, Bruce 1980
Downin, Matt 1996
Downs, Phil 1992-93-94
Duis, Frank R. 1951
Dunwiddie, David T. 1948

E
Easker, John W. 1981-82-83-84
Elsom, Bernado W. 1917-18
Escarcega, Tony 1994-95-96
Estick, Dick 1957
Evans, Jon 1993

F
Farin, William G. 1937-38-39
Fein, Steve 1996
Felton, Hilbert O. 1915
Fenske, Charles H. 1935-36-37
Fink, Delmar S. 1927-28-29
Finkle, George H. 1921, 23
Firchow, Donald A. 1949-50-51
Fleming, James 1971-72, 74-75
Follows, John W. 1929
Folsom, Howard 1929
Fraser, Bruce 1964-65-66
Fry, Scott 1985-86-87-88

G
Gard, Gregory 1962
Gehrmann, Donald A. 1946-47-48-49
Golden, Demmer 1915, 17
Goldie, William B. 1912-13
Goldsworthy, Vernon 1928-29-30
Gombar, Francis 1919
Gordon, Robert 1966-67-68
Greenlee, Samuel E. 1950
Gruber, John 1977
Gumbreck, Lawrence G. 1925-26

H
Hacker, Jeff 1978-79-80-81
Hacker, Timothy 1981-82-84-85
Hanson, J. Bradley 1967-68
Harvey, William D. 1913
Healey, Claude S. 1912
Hean, Clarence S. 1905
Heen, Robert 1987-88
Henrich, David 1962
Herdt, Kris 1984-85
Herold, Glenn 1969-70-71-72
Hoffman, Jack 1980
Howison, William K. 1920
Huffman, Mike 1984, 86-87-88

I-J
Inda, William 1952
Jackson, Arnold S. 1943-44
Jackson, Randy 1976-77-78-79
Jacobson, John 1983-84
Jaeger, Peter 1991-92-93-94-mgr.
Jahnke, Urban E. 1941
James, Evan W. 1935
Jenkins, Scott A. 1982-83-84-85
Jensen, Alvin J. 1945
Jesse, Dick 1974-mgr.
Johnson, Mark 1973-74-75-76
Johnson, Richard 1970-71-72-73

K
Kaines, Joel 1989, 90, 92
Kammer, Jack 1944, 46-47-48
Kane, Bart 1988
Kane, Mike 1970
Kennell, Charles 1976, 78-79
Kijowski, Dennis W. 1982
Kirk, Laurence R. 1930-31
Kleinschmidt, Karl W. 1934-35
Knox, Howard E. 1938-39-40
Knutson, Arthur M. 1921
Koening, Thomas 1956-57-58
Korhonen, Jay "Rusty" 1985-86-87-88
Kowal, Dan 1972-73-74
Krueger, Paul M. 1933
Kubley, Ray R. 1924-25

L
Lacy, Steve 1974-75-76, 78
LaHeurte, Phil 1978-79-80
Lands, Fred 1968-69
Larson, Mark 1969-70-71
Lashway, Henry C. 1934
Latigo-Olal, Kenneth 1965-66

Lawson, William 1944
Leverenz, Erwin F. 1945-46
Lewis, Chris 1989-90
Link, Walter 1924
Logan, Fred 1963
Lohr, William H. 1941
Loker, Donald 1960-61-62
Long, John 1987-88-89-90
Loomis, Porter L. 1918
Lueck, Eric 1987-88, 90-91
Lueck, Wayne J. 1982-83
Lyndgaard, Dan 1972-73-74-75

M
Mackesey, Dave 1974
Maddux, Troy 1986-87-88
Manley, P. Michael 1961-62-63
Mann, John P. 1943
Marcks, Brian 1960-61
Martell, Dean 1968-69-70
Mauer, Bruno 1952-53-54
McHugh, William P. 1952
McKinney, Daniel 1957-58
McLaughlin, Donald 1952
McNeel, Wakelin Jr. 1948
Mehl, Walter J. 1938-39
Menon, James 1992-93-94
Merrill, Henry B. 1914-15
Metzker, Carl W. 1946-47-48-49
Meyer, Bernard E. 1919
Meyer, Richard 1955-56
Miehe, Mark 1974, 76-77-78
Miller, Richard 1959-60-61
Mohrhusen, Jerome W. 1934
Monfore, Thomas E. 1952-53-54
Moorhead, Douglas M. 1922
Morin, Jeff 1975
Morrison, Eric 1990-91-92
Munson, John B. 1946-47
Murphy, Steve J. 1951
Muskat, John 1933

N
Nayer, Richard 1978
Nelson, Alfred 1973-74-75-76
Nelson, Raymond F. 1913
Nelson, William A. 1975
Nelson, William R. 1967
Nielsen, Rolf 1961

O
Ocock, Robert 1929
Ofansky, Joe 1976

P
Palmer, David 1965
Patterson, Arthur 1944
Payne, John J. 1926
Peterson, Barney 1964-65
Peterson, Richard 1962-63
Pick, Philip E. 1936
Poole, Rickey 1965
Pruski, Joseph 1961

Q-R
Quigley, Tom 1979-80-81-82
Rakocy, James 1964
Randall, Mark 1974-75-76-77
Randolph, E. Richard 1948-49-50
Randolph, Jeff 1975-76-77-78
Reierson, Robert J. 1947
Reitan, Tor 1962
Risch, Ronald 1955-56
Ritchie, Josh 1993
Rossmeissel, Carl 1922
Rudersdorf, Ward J. 1942
Ruenzel, Norman 1934-35
Runzheimer, Kurt 1991

S
Sang, Mark 1975
Sauer, Terry 1974
Savage, Rob 1977, 79-80
Schardt, Arlie A. 1914-15-16
Scharnke, Robert 1969-70-71
Schoenike, Howard G. 1940
Schoenfelder, Jay 1996
Schoensee, Phil 1984-85-86, 88
Schrock, Virgil E. 1945
Schumacher, Jerry 1990-91v92
Schumacher, Thomas 1971-72-73-74
Schutt, George A. 1926
Schutte, Harry 1979
Schwalback, James 1931-32-33
Seaton, Edward A. 1911-12
Shaffer, William 1968
Seibold, Dirk 1972
Sisson, Mark 1980-81, 83
Slater, Thomas 1971-72-73
Smith, Howard W. Jr. 1946
Smith, Jerome 1959-60-61
Stabb, Eric 1988-89-90
Stanke, Craig 1975-mgr.
Sternberg, Carroll 1950-51-52-53
Stintzi, Jim 1976-77-78-79
Stintzi, Joseph 1981-82-83, 85
Sultze, Eugene 1952-53-54

T
Taylor, Bill 1984
Thomas, J. Thomas 1967, 69
Thompson, A. McClure 1930
Thompson, Chris 1980
Thornton, Gary 1967
Toabe, Sidney L. 1942
Towle, William Bradford 1936-37-38
Tshudy, Lionel 1922
Tullberg, Steven 1962-63-64
Tulledge, Stewart 1957

U-V
Urquhart, James 1948-49-50
Valley, Lloyd 1922
Vandrey, Donald 1968-69-70
Vicklund, Clarence A. 1943
Volkey, Donald K. 1982-83
Voss, Alan 1967-68-69

W
Wade, Gerald C. 1920, 22
Wall, Mark H. 1920-21
Wall, Willard W. 1927
Ward, Kenneth 1968
Ward, Thomas R. 1949-50-51
Webster, E. Knight 1942, 44-45
Weeks, Glenn R. 1947-48-49
Weinert, James 1963-64
Wigglesworth, Richard 1955-56
Wixon, Darvey W. 1929
Wohlgemuth, John 1929
Wright, George L. 1930-31-32

Y-Z
Younglove, Michael 1980-81
Zobel, Raymond L. 1943-44, 34 **(?)**
Zola, John 1925-26-27
Zolin, Byron I. 1941
Zubrod, Lee 1989-90-91

Men's Football
A
Abbott, Allen 1900-01-02-03
Ace, Norris 1951
Ackert, James 1944
Adam, Tyler 1990-91-92-93
Adamov, Bob 1995-96
Addy, Henry 1976
Ahara, Edwin 1890-91
Ahrens, Dave 1977-78-79-80
Alberts, Rodger 1964-65
Albright, Edward 1968-69-70
Albright, William 1948-49-50
Alexander, Arthur H. 1911-12-13
Alexander, Brian 1995
Alexander, Walter A. 1894-95, 99
Alford, Harry 1969
Allen, John 1957
Allen, Maynard 1906
Altmann, Robert 1957-58-59
Ambrose, Steven 1955-56
Ameche, Alan 1951-52-53-54
Amundsen, Norman 1953-54
Anderson, Ashley 1941-42, 46
Anderson, Brian 1985-86-87-88
Anderson, Dave 1975
Anderson, Dave 1994-95
Anderson, Earl 1895, 97-98-99
Anderson, Ross 1978-79-80
Anderson, Sidney 1909
Andrykowski, Ervin 1951-52
Anthony, Thomas 1960
Anthony, Todd 1993
Antonie, William 1987-88-89
Apkarian, Gregory 1973
Armentrout, Joe 1983-84-85-86
Armstrong, Brett 1981-82-83
Arneson, Dave 1983-84
Arpin, H.A. 1911
Artley, Marvin 1985-86-87-88
Ashby, Solomon 1986
Atkinson, W. 1896
Aulik, David 1965
Austin, Tim 1972
Austin, Willie 1996

B
Bachhuber, James 1972-73
Bachman, J. Cary 1951
Backus, August 1928-29
Baer, Richard 1960-61
Baffico, Steve 1994-95
Bahlow, Ed 1944
Bailey, Raymond 1975-76
Baine, W.M. 1903
Ballweg, Charles 1970
Bakken, Jim 1959-60-61
Banaszak, John 1987-88-89
Bandor, Gary 1965
Bangert, Donald 1960
Barber, Greg 1976-77-78
Barker, Mike 1990
Barkley, Matt 1990
Barnes, Harry 1920
Barnum, Rolland 1924-25-26
Baron, Daniel 1972
Barr, Wallace 1919-20, 22
Barryman, C. 1895
Barrios, Richard 1972-73
Barth, George 1892
Bartholomew, Ken 1928
Basten, Jim 1988-89-90
Batsch, Dan 1987-88-89-90
Baumann, Robert 1940-41-42

Baxter, Richard	1982-83
Becker, Michael	1972-74
Becker, Robert	1933-34
Beddell, M.	1898
Begel, William	1931
Behr, Samuel	1928-29-30
Belcher, Kevin	1982-83-84
Belin, Chuck	1989-90-91-92
Bellford, Russ	1983-84
Bellile, Ken	1938
Bellin, Roy	1936-37-38
Bellows, Frank	1912-13-14
Below, Martin	1918, 22-23
Bender, John	1933-34
Bendrick, Ben	1945-46-47-48
Bennett, Tom	1946-47-48
Bennett, Steve	1948-49
Benninger, Michael	1973-74
Bentson, Harold	1923
Benz, Fred	1935-36-37
Benzschawel, Scott	1985, 87
Berg, David	1965-66
Berg, M.J.	1916
Berger, Louis	1912
Bergold, Scott	1982-83-84
Bernard, Giscard	1994-95-96
Berndt, Charles	1950-51-52
Bernet, Lee	1962-63-64
Berriman, Daniel	1982
Bertke, Wilson	1902-03-04
Bestor, Glenn	1955-56
Bestor, Scott	1986-87-88
Bevell, Darrell	1992-93-94-95
Beyers, Dow	1915
Bichler, David	1960-61
Bieberstein, Adolph	1922-23-24
Bingham, James	1933
Binish, Stanley	1928-29
Blackbourne, Lisle	1946-47-48-49
Blackburn, Bill	1889
Blackman, Thane	1923-24-25
Blackmun, Gil	1956
Blair, E.R.	1899
Blake, Rex	1967-68
Blaskowski, Curt	1978-79-80
Bleyer, Charles	1906
Bliss, Donald	1965-66-67
Bloedorn, Arthur	1956
Bobo, Frederick	1985-86
Boggs, Bryn	1995
Bohlig, Gregg	1972-73-74
Boliaux, Guy	1978-79-80-81
Bondi, Hobart	1917
Boodry, Kevin	1976
Booher, Martin	1953-54, 56
Booker, Earl	1979-80, 82
Boots, Richard	1966
Bonner, Brian	1983-84-85
Borders, John	1967-68
Borgerding, Mike	1977
Borland, Kyle	1979-80-81-82
Bosold, Edward	1971-72-73
Bourne, Jim	1990-91-92
Botham, Richard	1944
Bowers, Dale	1946
Bowman, Kenneth	1961-62-63
Boyajian, John	1966-67
Boyke, Scott	1989
Boykins, Michael	1983-84-85-86
Boyle, F.E.	1907-08
Boyle, Pat	1941-42
Brader, James	1918-19-20-21
Bradley, Henry	1898
Brady, Donny	1993-94
Braker, Thomas	1977-78-79
Branaman, Lance	1983-84-85
Brandstat, R.	1910-11
Brandt, Harold	1962-63-64
Brandt, William	1974-75
Bratt, Clarence	1953-54
Bratton, Charles	1930-31
Braun, Robert	1971-72-73
Breckenridge, William	1912-14
Brekke, Brad	1988-89-90
Brekke, Michael	1987
Breuscher, Terry	1976-77
Brewer, Chester	1896
Brhely, Michael	1978
Bridgeman, John	1955-56
Brigham, Thomas	1964-65
Bright, George	1910-11-12
Briggs, Thomas	1968
Brin, Michael	1995
Brindly, Thaddeus	1904-05
Brockett, John	1966
Brodhagen, Eugene	1936-37-38
Bronson, Paul	1940-41
Brooks, W.L.	1889
Brown, Aaron	1989-90-91-92
Brown, Clarence	1968
Brown, Demetrius	1996
Brown, Jamel	1991-92-93-94
Browne, Tom	1990-91
Browning, Keith	1986
Bruce, Andrew	1889-90-91
Bruhn, Peter	1962
Brumder, W.C.	1889
Brumm, Roman	1918, 21
Brunston, Jevon	1993
Bryan, Mike	1991-92
Bryant, Onjai	1996
Bucci, Frank	1933
Bucciarelli, Gale	1965-66
Buck, Howard	1913-14-15
Budde, John	1935
Budde, Robert	1982
Bunge, G.C.	1919-20-21
Bunge, George W.	1893-94
Bunker, Eugene	1909-10
Burgess, Yusef	1990-91-92-93
Burke, Tom	1995-96
Burks, Archie Roy	1950-51-52
Burks, David	1987-88
Burney, Richard	1979
Burns, Jason	1991-92-93-94
Burrus, Jefferson	1924-25-26
Burt, Charles	1965-67
Burt, Michael	1975,77-78
Buser, Alfred	1910-11-12
Bush, James	1902-03-04, 06
Buss, Gary	1968-69-70
Buss, Lynn	1966-67-68
Buss, Ronald	1970-71-72
Buss, Terry	1973-74-75
Butler, Nathaniel	1968-69-70
Butler, Robert	1911-12-13

C

Cabral, Armand	1977-78-79
Callahan, Russell	1934
Calligaro, Len	1941-42
Cameron, Don	1925-26-27
Cammett, Stuart	1977
Campbell, Joe	1944
Campbell, LaMar	1994-95-96
Campbell, Tyrone	1989
Canada, Larry	1973-74-75-76
Canny, Thomas	1952
Canonie, Tony	1966
Cantrell, Branden	1994-95-96
Carl, DuWayne	1957
Carl, Harland	1951-52-53
Carlson, Ronald	1956-57
Carney, Theo	1992-93-94
Carolan, Penn	1943
Carpenter, Charles	1916-17, 19
Carpenter, Marcus	1996
Carr, Kemal	1983-84
Carroll, Mike	1975-76
Carter, Daryl	1993-94-95-96
Carter, Fred	1910
Cascadden, Chad	1993-94
Case, Charles	1892
Casey, George	1928-29-30
Casey, Michael	1978, 79
Casper, Gary	1989-90-91-92
Castle, Lewis	1912
Castro, Cayetano	1993-94-95-96
Catlin, Mark	1930-31
Cavill, Michael	1966-67-68
Cepicky, Scott	1984-85-86-87
Chaconas, George	1990
Chamberlain, Alonzo	1898-99-00, 03
Chamberlain, H.R.	1898-99
Chambers, C.C.	1911
Chandler, Patrick	1967
Chaney, Charles	1945
Charles, David	1976-77-78
Chavez, Phil	1993
Christensen, Gwynn	1948-49
Christenson, Dennis	1978-79
Christianson, Carl	1921
Christianson, Edward	1934-35-36
Christian, Richard	1975-76
Chryst, George	1957-58
Chryst, Paul	1986-87-88
Cibik, Vince	1938
Cinelli, Rocco	1956
Cisler, James	1986
Clark, B.N.	1889
Clark, F.	1903-04, 06
Clark, John	1964
Clarke, Robert	1943
Clauss, Joseph	1935-36
Clawson, Larry	1973
Claypool, Tywin	1989
Cleary, Pat	1990
Coatta, John	1949-50-51
Cochems, Ed	1897-98-99-00-01
Cochems, Henry	1894
Cohee, Kevin	1977-78
Cole, Jess	1980-81
Cole, Wallace	1926
Cole, Walter	1935-36-37
Coleman, Harry H.	1891
Collias, Nicholas	1944, 47-48
Collins, Pat	1974-75-76
Collins, William	1918-19-20
Collins, Willie	1981
Commander, Azree	1994-95-96
Comstock, N.	1894-95-96-97-98
Cone, Robert	1939
Connor, Charles	1943
Connor, Gordon	1926-27-28
Connors, Phillip	1972
Conry, Clifford	1928
Cooper, F.	1907
Cooper, Myron	1956-57
Corcoran, Gordon	1957
Cory, W.	1896
Cox, John	1977
Cox, T.A.	1944, 46-47-48

Craine, James 1952
Cramer, Herbert 1916
Crawford, Lionell 1988-89-90, 92
Crenshaw, T.P. 1892
Criter, Kenneth 1966-67-68
Crofoot, Edwin 1925-26-27
Crooks, Daniel 1969-70
Crossen, David 1975-76-77-78
Cruickshank, Dave 1996
Cuccia, Henry 1965-66
Cuisinier, Frank 1927-28
Cullen, Mark 1972-73-74
Culver, Harry 1907
Cummings, Leo 1913-14-15
Cunningham, C.J. 1906-07-08
Currier, Charles 1964-65
Currier, Ken 1942, 46-47
Curtin, Joseph 1906
Curtis, Arthur 1898-99-00-01
Curtis, H. 1906
Curtis, Louis 1987
Cusack, Donald 1944
Cuthbert, Donald 1931
Cvengros, Jerome 1955
Cwayna, Michael 1953
Czech, Dave 1990-91
Czechowicz, Bob 1974-75-76-77
Czechowicz, Thomas 1975-76

D

Dal Sasso, Anthony 1943-44
Damos, Ted 1940-41
Darby, James 1994-95-96
Daum, R. 1901
Davey, Allen 1917, 19-20
Davey, Don 1987-88-89-90
Davey, John 1943-44
Davidson, T.R. 1907-08
Davis, A. 1893
Davis, Anthony 1972
Davis, Carl 1973
Davis, Christopher 1971-72-73
Davis, Chucky 1979-81-82
Davis, Ralph 1946
Davis, Raymond 1934
Davies, James 1927-28
Davies, William 1936, 38
Davy, George 1913
Dawkins, J.C. 1992-93-94
Dawkins, Joseph 1968-69
Dayne, Ron 1996-97
Dean, James 1908-09-10
Dean, Joseph 1897
Deanovich, George 1933-34
Deerwester, Charles 1972-73
Dehnert, George 1934
Delaney, Pat 1980
Dellenbach, Jeff 1981-82-83-84
DeLisle, James 1968-69-70
DeRamus, Lee 1991-92-93
Derby, Glenn 1985-86-87
Derleth, Henry 1958,-59-60
Dering, Charles 1900-01, 04-05
Diatelevi, Pete 1993-94-95-96
Dickinson, Henry 1893-94-95
Dickert, Gary 1972-73-74
Dierks, Robert 1941-42
DiSalvo, Steve 1976
Dittman, Fred 1906-07
Dittman, J. 1906
Dittrich, John 1954-55
Dixon, John 1952-53
Dixon, John 1980
Dixon, Ken 1975-76
Doar, Fred 1943
Doerger, Jerome 1978-79-80-81
Dohmeier, Thomas 1976
Donaghey, James 1918
Donaldson, James 1934
Donnellan, Dave 1947
Donovan, Louis 1904-05
Dooney, Ray 1943
Door, J. 1900
Doran, Mark 1980-81-82
Domres, Thomas 1965-66-67
Dornburg, Roger 1951-52-53
Dorsch, Albert 1937-38-39
Downham, Thomas 1960
Downing, Robert 1948-49
Doyle, John 1937-38-39
Drews, John 1948
Dreutzler, C. 1908
Dreyer, Wally 1946-47v48
Driver, Earl 1899-00-01-02
Drummond, William 1974-75
Dudley, Anthony 1977
Dunaway, Don 1929
Durkin, Joseph 1952
Dyer, Warren 1965-66-67

E

Eagleburger, Leon 1922-23
Eckl, Robert 1937-38-39
Edler, Ray 1916
Edwards, Clarence 1931-32
Eggebrecht, Otto 1920
Eggers, Virgil 1930
Egloff, Ronald 1974, 76
Eicher, Donny 1995
Ellerson, Gary 1982-83
Elliott, Alvah 1919-20-21
Elliott, Bruce 1944-47-48-49
Elliot, Anthony 1977
Ellis, Fred 1941
Ellison, Kevin 1990
Embach, James 1947-48-49
Embick, Dick 1938-39-40
Emery, Larry 1983-84-85-86
Engelke, Robert 1931
Engle, Bob 1944-45
Engler, Derek 1994-95-96
Erdmann, Scott 1975-76-77-78
Esser, Clarence 1943-44-45-46
Esser, Norbert 1952-53
Eulberg, John 1943
Evans, Gene 1946-47-48-49
Ezerins, Elmars 1960, 62

F

Fabry, John 1962
Fagerstrom, Eric 1939
Farmer, Ralph 1963-64
Farris, Tom 1939-40-41
Faverty, Harold 1945, 48, 50-51
Fawley, Charlie 1984-85-86
Fedenia, James 1969-70
Fee, John 1944
Felker, Eugene 1950-51
Ferguson, John 1933
Ferguson, Rufus 1970-71-72
Fields, Leonard 1967-68
Fields, Russell 1983-84-85
Filiatraut, John 1990
Filtzer, Robert 1915-16
Findlay, Albion 1902-03-04-05
Fischer, Sid 1943
Fish, John 1933-34-35
Fisher, Orville 1939
Fixmer, Mike 1980
Fladoes, Martin 1919
Flanigan, Brian 1994-95-96
Fleischer, O.J. 1904
Fleming, Neil 1961
Fletcher, Eddie 1988-89-90-91
Fletcher, Terrell 1991-92-93-94
Flower, L.B. 1891
Flowers, Otis 1987-88
Floyd, Rufus 1975
Fogg, Joseph 1901-02-03
Fontaine, Thomas 1933-34
Ford, Eric 1987
Forrest, H.G. 1895, 97
Fortino, Victor 1985-86-87-88
Fowee, John 1970
Fowler, Carlos 1990-91-92-93
Fox, John 1962
Fox, Orville 1939
Frain, Ronald 1962-63-64
Frank, Arthur 1906, 09
Franz, James 1973-74-75
Fraser, James 1957-58
Fredrick, Craig 1980-81
Freeman, Damone 1988v89
Freeman, John 1890-91-92-93
Frei, Jerry 1942-46-47
Freimuth, Robert 1963
Freis, Randal 1971
Freund, Robert 1946-47
Fricke, Harry 1944-45
Fritz, Steve 1983
Fritz, William 1965-66-67
Froelich, Kevin 1973
Frokjer, Randy 1972-73-74
Fronek, David 1963-64-65
Fucik, Robert 1907-08-09-10
Fuchs, George 1945-46
Fugitt, C.T. 1897
Fulco, Frank 1982
Fullington, Tim 1985

G

Gaatz, David 1983-84-85
Gable, William 1948-49, 51
Gage, Fred 1938-39-40
Gales, Kenny 1993-94
Gallagher, John 1946
Galletti, Mike 1994-95-96
Galvin, M.E. 1914
Gamber, Jeff 1985
Gantenbein, Milton 1928-29-30
Gardner, M.L. 1914-15-16
Garnsey, E.G. 1916
Garrot, William 1938
Gaskill, Glenn 1967
Gassner, Kevin 1974-75
Gavre, Vince 1936-37-38
Gay, Al 1994-95
Gehler, William 1956-57
Gelbach, Warren 1905-06
Gelein, E.A. 1912-13
George, Wray 1944-45-46-47
Gerber, Ervin 1923
Ghidorzi, Chris 1996
Gibson, Aaron 1996
Gibson, Edward 1920-21-22
Gilbert, Harry 1948, 50-51
Gile, Gordon 1938-39-40
Gill, Ralph 1921
Gillette, Edmund 1910-11-12
Gingrass, Robert 1953-54
Girard, Earl 1944, 47
Gladem, Wendell 1981-82-83

Glavin, Terry	1992, 94
Glenn, Damon	1994-95
Gnabah, Walter	1930
Godfrey, Rick	1989-90
Goeke, James	1965
Goldenberg, Charles	1930-31
Golemgeske, John	1933, 35-36
Goodman, Robert	1965
Gordon, Greg	1975-76-77-78
Gorman, Michael	1985
Gosa, Gerald	1974
Gotstein, John	1927
Gotta, John	1959-60
Gould, Harry	1897
Gould, Stevens	1917, 19, 21
Grabow, Brad	1982-83-84
Gradisnik, Anthony	1937-38-39
Graf, Rick	1983-84-85-86
Graff, Neil	1969-70-71
Graham, Robert	1977
Grams, Eric	1996
Granitz, Frank	1941, 46
Graper, Leslie	1916
Gray, Wells	1954-55
Green, Charles	1975, 77-78-79
Green, Gerald	1979-80-81-82
Greenwood, David	1979-80-81-82
Gregg, John	1895, 97
Gregoire, Todd	1984-85-86-87
Gregory, William	1968-69-70
Greyer, Neovia	1969-70-71
Grice, Michael	1974-75
Grimm, Richard	1960-61
Grinde, Roger	1936
Grisley, William	1966-67
Grogan, Francis	1904
Gross, Michael	1962
Gross, Trent	1996
Grossman, Robert	1965-66
Gruber, Paul	1985-86-87
Grudzinski, James	1964
Grundy, Jack	1981
Gulseth, Wendell	1952-53
Gunderson, B.C.	1915

H

Haas, Michael	1972
Habeck, Milton	1971
Haberman, Hal	1945, 48-49
Hable, Bernard	1979
Hable, Burton	1952
Hackbart, Dale	1957-58-59
Hackbart, Vernon	1965
Haese, Jack	1944
Hady, Patrick	1979-80-81-82
Hagberg, Earl	1956
Hall, John	1993-94-95-96
Hallberg, John	1986
Halleran, Timothy	1976
Haluska, James	1952, 54-55
Halverson, Charles	1949
Hammen, Edwin	1917
Hammerson, E.J.	1901
Hammond, James	1949-50-51
Hannah, Albert	1969-70-71
Hancock, Howard	1915-16-17
Hanke, Del	1944
Hanley, Bob	1945, 47-48
Hansen, David	1950-51
Hanssen, Robert	1972-73
Hanzel, Lawrence	1948-49
Hanzlik, Bob	1941
Harder, Pat	1941-42
Harmon, Doyle	1924-25-26
Harmon, Leo	1924-25
Harney, Brian	1971-72-73
Harot, Henry	1929
Harrington, Michael	1973
Harris, Welton	1922-23-24
Harrison, Marck	1982-83-84
Hart, Edward	1957-58-59
Hartlieb, Andy	1986-87-88
Hartman, Edward	1937
Haukedahl, Stan	1934, 36
Haworth, Richard	1931-32-33
Hayes, Donald	1994-95-96
Hayes, Neil	1927
Hazard, William	1974
Hazzard, William	1897
Hearn, Napolean	1961
Heath, Stan	1946
Hecker, Robert	1944
Heckl, Joe	1962-63
Hegg, Troy	1995
Hegseth, Stuart	1976
Hegwood, Ronald	1976
Hein, Chris	1991-92-93-94
Heineke, James	1957-58-59
Heineke, John	1957
Heinz, Lawerence	1943
Helt, Mark	1985
Henderson, Jimmy	1989
Hennig, James	1964
Henrici, Ronald	1962
Henry, Robert	1940
Herrington, Mike	1979-80, 82-83
Hertel, William	1955
Hess, William	1960-61
Higgins, Peter	1967, 69
Hildreth, Harry	1943
Hile, Charles	1893
Hill, Early	1956-57-58
Hiltgen, Chris	1989
Hintz, Eldridge	1946-47
Hirsbrunner, Paul	1940-41-42
Hirsch, Elroy	1942
Hobbs, Jon	1956-57-58
Hobbs, William	1957-58-59
Hodges, Dennis	1943
Hoeffel, J. Merrill	1910-11-12
Hoegh, Mark	1952-53
Hoehn, Armand	1946-47
Hofer, Kenneth	1956
Hoffman, Brian	1984-85
Hoffman, Duncan	1964
Hoffman, Edward	1966-67-68
Hoffman, John	1971
Hohfield, Rudolph	1921-22
Hohman, Jon	1962-63-64
Holland, Louis	1961-62-63
Holland, Louis Jr.	1985
Holloway, Robert	1938-39
Holm, Kurt	1977-78
Holmes, George	1944
Holmes, Harvey	1897-98
Holmes, James	1957-58
Holstein, William	1901
Holt, Reggie	1990-91-92-93
Holzwarth, Karl	1957, 59
Hoppman, Dave	1976
Hoskins, Mark	1940-41-42
Hosler, H.	1906-07
Hotchkiss, George	1927
Houston, Thomas	1977, 80
Hovland, Lynn	1935, 37-38
Howard, David	1954-55-56
Howard, J.	1906, 08
Howard, Larry	1962, 64
Howard, Michael	1984-85-86
Howay, Gregory	1963
Howell, Daniel	1987, 89
Hubbard, Tom	1945
Hudson, Craig	1986-87-88-89
Huggett, Jerry	1991
Hughes, Paul	1981
Humphries, Anthony	1985
Hunt, Fred	1904
Hunt, Leon	1986-87-88-89
Hunter, Malvin	1987-88-89-90
Huntley, Kevin	1994-95-96
Huntley, Lee	1906-07
Husting, Berthold	1898
Hutchinson, William	1950-51-52
Huxhold, Kenneth	1948-49-50
Huxhold, Terry	1958-59-60
Hyland, Richard	1968-69-70

I

Iakisch, Robert	1907-08
Irish, Russell	1922-23
Isom, Adolph	1968-69

J

Jackson, Brandt	1967-68
Jackson, Keith	1993-94
Jackomino, Bradley	1976-77-78
Jacobazzi, Roger	1962-63-64
Jacobi, Gustav	1917, 19
Jacobs, H.H.	1892-93-94-95
Jacobson, Carl	1910
Jaeger, Roger	1969-70-71
Jakious, Richard	1972-73-74
Janek, Chris	1996
Jankowski, Eddie	1934-35-36
Jankowski, Thomas	1964-65-66
Jansen, Brian	1985
Janule, Victor	1966
Jax, James	1961
Jefferson, Theodore	1970
Jenkins, Lowell	1957-58-59
Jenkins, Michael	1972-73-74
Jenkins, Nathan	1965
Jensen, Howard	1929-30
Jensen, Paul	1934-35-36
Jenson, Joel	1964
John, Rex	1938, 45
Johnson, Albert	1905-06
Johnson, Bob	1963
Johnson, Duane	1972, 75
Johnson, Ervin	1936
Johnson, Eugene	1945
Johnson, Farnham	1942
Johnson, Gregory	1969-71
Johnson, James	1968, 70
Johnson, Lawrence	1976-77-78
Johnson, Leon	1986-87-88-89
Johnson, Malcolm	1990
Johnson, Richard	1982-83-84
Johnson, Robert	1972-73-74
Johnson, Ron	1992-93-94
Johnson, Scott	1987-88
Johnston, Robert	1984-85-86
Joki, Matthew	1988
Joliffe, W.M.	1897-98-99
Jones, Bryan	1994
Jones, George	1904
Jones, James	1963-64
Jones, Michael	1981-82-83-84
Jones, Rex	1974-75
Jones, Theodore	1898, 1903
Jones, Thomas	1976
Jones, Timothy	1985

Jordan, Lynn	1933-34-35
Jordan, Tim	1982, 84-85-86
Josten, John	1978, 80, 82
Joyce, Leo	1979-80-81
Juneau, William	1899-00-01-02
Jung, Louis	1964-65
Jurewicz, Bryan	1993-94-95-96

K

Kabat, Greg	1930-31-32
Kalasmiki, Mike	1978-79
Kaltenberg, Thomas	1975-76-77
Karel, John	1892, 94-95-96, 98
Kasiska, Robert	1924-25-26
Kavanagh, Scott	1996
Kaye, Jesse	1964-65
Keeler, Ray	1912-13-14
Keeling, David	1982
Keenan, Joe	1943
Keigher, Greg	1995
Kelich, Joe	1982-83
Kellogg, William	1960
Kelly, Joseph	1947-48-49
Kelly, Michael	1975-76
Kelly, Pat	1977-78
Kelly, W.M.	1914, 16-17
Kemp, Nikki	1994
Kempthorne, Dion	1961-62
Kennedy, Brant	1985-86-87
Kennedy, Chris	1993
Kennedy, Martin	1913-14
Kennedy, Robert	1950-51-52
Kerr, James	1889-90
Kessenich, Paul	1949
Ketelaar, William	1927-28-29
Keyes, Bud	1985-86-87
Keyes, Orton	1917
Kieckhefer, Herbert	1916-17
Kiessling, Oscar	1921
Kiltz, John	1978
Kindt, Don	1943, 45-46
King, Troy	1979-80-81-82
Kissling, Dan	1986-87-88-89
Kittel, Tom	1945, 47-48
Klinzing, Vern	1945
Klosek, Timothy	1971
Kmet, James	1983-84-85-86
Knapp, George	1891-92
Knauff, Donald	1946-47-48-49
Knobel, F.	1898
Knoeck, Tim	1986-87-88-89
Kobza, Robert	1983-84
Koch, Thomas	1971-72
Koch, Walter	1915-16
Kocourek, David	1956-57-58
Koeck, Rich	1972-73-74
Koehler, Harold	1941
Koenig, William	1932-33
Kolbusz, Don	1939
Kolian, Richard	1955-56
Konovsky, Robert	1954-55
Kopina, Dan	1974-75
Kostka, Wayne	1966
Kouba, Steve	1994
Kowalski, Tim	1989
Krall, David	1976-77-78
Kralovec, Arthur	1916-17
Kranhold, Harvey	1931-32
Kreger, Jeffrey	1969
Kreick, Ray	1939-40-41
Krein, Joel	1979
Krepfle, Mike	1978-80
Kresky, Joe	1926-27-28
Kreuz, Louis	1914-15-16
Kreuz, Robert	1925-26
Kron, Gary	1968
Kroner, Gary	1961-62
Krueger, Lee	1990,-91-92-93
Krueger, Matt	1991
Kruger, Kenneth	1929,-30-31
Krugman, John	1970-71
Krumrie, Tim	1979-80-81-82
Kuenzler, John	1943
Kuhlemeier, James	1966
Kulcinski, Gerald	1958-59-60
Kull, Fred	1891-92-93-94-95
Kummer, Milt	1932-33-34
Kundert, Kenneth	1933-34
Kunesh, Ervin	1960
Kurek, Ralph	1962-63-64
Kusa, James	1943-44

L

La Bun, Vladimir	1974-75
LaCroix, Richard	1965-66
Ladewig, Fred	1940
Lager, Dennis	1965
Laird, Ken	1943
Lamia, Vincent	1973-74-75-76
Lamphere, Robert	1953
Landsee, Bob	1982-83, 85
Lane, William	1949-50-51
Lange, Raymond	1911-12-13
Lanphear, George	1936
Lanphear, Dan	1957-58-59
Larson, Albert	1898-99-00-01
Larson, Lloyd	1924-25
Laubenheimer, Roger	1943-44
Leafblad, Ronald	1962-63-64
Leaper, Wesley	1918
Lee, Donald	1943, 46
Lee, Rory	1990
Lehman, C.	1945
Leitl, Lester	1925-26
Leppla, Robert	1975
Lerro, Joe	1977
Lerum, Arnie	1899-00-01
Letz, Robert	1943
Leu, Robert	1950-51
Levenhagen, Mark	1972
Levenhagen, Michael	1973
Levenhagen, Pat	1954-55-56
Levenick, Dave	1977-78-79-80-81
Levine, Jason	1993
Levisee, Lester	1905
Lewis, Danny	1955-56-57
Lewis, Greg	1973-74-75
Lewis, Richard	1980
Lick, Dennis	1972-73-74-75
Lick, James	1983
Lick, Steven	1975-76-77
Liethen, Alois	1929
Liljequist, Lawrence	1902-03
Linden, John	1928-29
Lindsey, Scott	1969
Linfor, Joe	1930-31-32
Little, Gary	1972
Little, James	1967
LoCascio, Guy	1974
Locklin, Ronald	1952-53-54
Locklin, Stuart	1946
Loehrke, John	1936-37, 39
Loepfe, Dick	1941, 46-47
Logemann, R.	1889
Lokanc, David	1970-71-72
London, Michael	1964,65
London, Michael	1991-92-93, 95
Long, F.	1902
Long, Thomas	1924-25
Lonnborg, Thomas	1971-72
Loope, T.E.	1889
Lopp, Frank	1941, 46
Lorenz, Albert	1938-39-40
Lorenz, Don	1978-79
Losse, Gary	1969-70
Lossow, Rodney	1985-86-87
Loukas, Anthony	1964-65-66
Lovshin, Leonard	1933, 35-36
Lovshin, Ralph	1931-32
Lowe, Dean	1943
Lowe, William	1954-55v56
Lowery, Tony	1987-88-90-91
Lowman, M.	1907-08
Lubratovich, Milo	1928-29-30
Lucas, Richard	1975
Luko, Jeffrey	1979, 81
Luksik, Franklin	1957
Lund, Gary	1970-71-72
Lurtsema, Rob	1993
Lusby, William	1928-29-30
Lutz, John	1943
Lyle, J.T.S.	1897
Lyles, Kevin	1993-94-95-96
Lysek, David	1994-95-96
Lyman, F.S.	1899
Lyman, T.U.	1892-93-94
Lynch, Brendan	1988-89-90-91
Lyons, Eugene	1940-41-42
Lyons, Terry	1974-75-76

M

Macias, Jay	1991-92-93-94
Mack, Jeffrey	1972-73-74
Mackmiller, William	1901, 10-11
Magazzeni, Joe	1988-89
Mahnke, Allan	1934-35
Mahone, Tyrone	1989-90
Makris, George	1941-42
Maksen, Bill	1991
Malesevich, Bronko	1936-37
Malesevich, Emil	1936
Malone, Wally	1982
Mals, Ray	1945
Mangum, Mark	1990
Manic, Dennis	1972-73
Maniecki, Jason	1991, 93-94-95
Manley, Korey	1990-91-92
Mann, Berthold	1918
Mansfield, Arthur	1928
Mansfield, Bob	1948, 50
Mansfield, Von	1980-81
Marcin, Raymond	1963, 65
Marconi, Joseph	1985
Marek, Billy	1973-74-75
Margoles, Harry	1918, 20
Marks, Randall	1968-69-70
Marrow, Brian	1981-82-83
Marsh, Charles	1902
Marshall, Albert	1900-01
Martin, Carl	1952
Martin, Cecil	1995-96
Martin, James	1937
Martin, Jay	1913
Martine, Jim	1978-79
Maselter, William	1964-65
Maternowski, Curt	1989-90-91-92
Mather, Israel	1898
Matthews, Ira	1975-76-77-78
Mauerman, J.F.	1898
Maves, Earl	1946-47
May, William	1943
Mayer, Michael	1970-71-72

Mayo, Brad	1987-88-89
McAndrews, Harry	1924-25
McCauley, Thomas	1966-67-68
McClish, Michael	1969
McConnell, Philip	1989
McConnell, Tim	1974-75-76
McCormick, Henry	1925
McCoy, James	1977-78
McCrory, Raymond	1915-16
McCullough, Carl	1993, 95-96
McFadden, Thad	1980-81, 83-84
McFadzean, Jim	1940-41-42
McGettigan, Pat	1989-90-91-92
McGiveran, Stanley	1924
McGovern, T.Y.	1892
McGuire, Walter	1930-31-32
McIntosh, Chris	1996
McKaskle, Herman	1927
McKay, Bob	1940-41-42
McKinney, Gerald	1961
McKinnon, Kyle	1981
McLaughlin, Paul	1943
McMaster, Paul	1913-14
McMillin, James	1962
McNamara, William	1953-54-55
McNaught, J.H.	1890
McPherson, Charles	1896
Mead, Jack	1941,44 -45
Mearlon, James	1968
Mehring, Robb	1988
Melka, Jim	1981-82-83-84
Melzner, Arthur	1904
Merritt, Ahmad	1996
Messina, Angelo	1972
Messenger, Daniel	1979-80
Messenger, Jeff	1991-92-93-94
Messmer, John	1906-07-08
Messner, Gary	1953-54
Meyer, Martin	1944-45
Meyer, Robert	1943
Meyers, C.M.	1889
Meyers, Paul	1915-16, 19
Meyers, Tilden	1948-49-50
Mialik, Lawrence	1969-70-71
Michuda, Andrew	1974-75-76
Mielke, David	1983-84
Mietz, Robert	1974
Miklusak, Neil	1994-95-96
Milaul, Frank	1941
Mileager, Richard	1975-76-77
Milek, Joseph	1964
Millar, William	1933
Miller, Carl	1922-23-24
Miller, Charles	1906, 08
Miller, Chester	1928
Miller, Don	1939-40-41
Miller, James	1953-54-55
Miller, Jeff	1988-89-90
Miller, Kerry	1988-89-90
Miller, Ronald	1960-61
Miller, William	1953
Minter, Alan	1975-76-77
Moeller, Ralph	1937-38-39
Moffatt, William	1901-02
Moffett, Harold	1912
Mohapp, Dave	1978-79-80-81
Molinaro, Frank	1930-31-32
Moll, John	1908, 10-11
Momcilovic, Milan	1987
Monk, Robert	1964
Monroe, Brad	1969
Montgomery, Ken	1962
Montgomery, Mark	1990-91-92-93
Montgomery, Steven	1977
Montoute, Sankar	1980
Monty, Pete	1993-94-95-96
Moon, Lancelot	1970-71
Moore, Brian	1959-60-61
Moore, James	1976-77-78
Morgan, Michael	1974-75-76-77
Morris, Melvin	1956-57
Mortell, Emmett	1935
Moss, Brent	1991-92v93
Motl, Kevin	1979-80
Mucklestone, R.W.	1907-08
Mucks, Arlie Sr.	1914
Muegge, Walter	1926
Mueller, Herb	1934
Mullen, Mike	1990
Murphy, Donald	1967-68-69
Murphy, Merritt	19x00
Murphy, Peter	1907-08, 11
Murray, Jack	1937-38-39
Muschinske, Bruce	1977
Myers, Bobby	1996

N

Namnick, Steve	1978
Nault, Jeffrey	1981-82
Neal, Marvin	1979-80-81, 83
Negus, Fred	1942, 46
Nellen, James	1934-35

Nelson, Gordon	1920-21
Nelson, Oscar	1893-94, 96
Nelson, Parnell	1931
Nelson, Paul	1923-24-25
Nelson, Robert	1958-59
Nelson, Robert	1993, 95
Nelson, Scott	1990-91-92-93
Nelson, Todd	1986-87-88
Nena, Gerald	1960
Nettesheim, Dave	1945
Nettles, James	1961-62-63
Newell, Robert	1987-88-89-90
Nichols, Thomas	1922-23-24
Nicolazzi, Richard	1957
Nines, Richard	1945
Nordwig, Todd	1971
Norvell, Aaron	1989-90-91-92
Norvell, Merritt	1960-61-62
Norwick, Joseph	1974-75
Nosbusch, Keith	1970-71-72
Novak, Clarence	1972,73,74
Nowak, James	1967, 69
Nowka, Pete	1985-86-87-88
Null, Robert	1934-35
Nyquist, Matt	1992-93-94-95

O

O'Brien, George	1950-51-52
O'Brien, John	1902, 04
O'Brien, John P.	1936-37-38
O'Dea, Pat	1896-97-98-99
O'Donahue, Pat	1949-50-51
O'Donnell, Jody	1979-80-81-82
O'Neill, Ed	1947
Odomes, Nate	1984-85-86
Ofstie, Harold	1911-12-13
Olsen, Harold	1916
Olshanski, Hank	1947
Olson, William	1917
Oman, Tury	1928-29-30
Onstad, Erick	1891
Orlando, Todd	1991-92-93
Orlich, Dan	1945
Orszula, Mark	1979,80
Osswald, Chris	1981, 83-84
Osthoff, Oscar	1907-08-09
Otterback, Harold	1946-47-48-49
Otto, Tim	1988
Owens, Fred	1987-88-89

P

Paar, Ronald	1962-63
Pacetti, Mario	1932-33-34
Pacetti, Nello	1929, 31-32
Pagel, John	1972
Panos, Joe	1991-92-93
Parish, Forest	1948
Parish, Steven	1979
Parks, John	1927-28-29
Partington, Paul	1986-87-88
Paskvan, George	1938-39-40
Passini, Michael	1971-72
Patterson, Brian	1993-94
Paul, Herbert	1937
Peabody, Alvin	1972-73-74
Peak, Vern	1935-36-37
Pearce, James	1967
Pearse, Benjamin	1922
Pearson, Bret	1981-82-83-84
Peele, H.J.	1896-97, 99
Perkins, Ronald	1958-59-60
Perry, C.S.	1903-04
Peters, Kenton	1951-52
Peters, Shawn	1988
Peters, Thomas	1955, 57
Peterson, Clarence	1936
Peterson, Donald	1939-40
Peterson, H.	1903
Peterson, Keith	1985-86, 88
Peterson, Marv	1932-33
Peterson, Phillip	1966
Peterson, Robert	1939
Petruska, Robert	1948-49-50
Phillip, Clifford	1940
Pickens, Robert	1963
Pierce, Brad	1983-84
Pierce, Brady	1988-89-90
Pierce, Maurice	1910-11
Pike, Harry	1933
Pillath, Roger	1961-62-63
Pinnow, Gary	1964-65
Pinnow, John	1946-47-48
Piper, Robert	1943
Piraino, Albert	1964
Pittleman, Irving	1944
Pizer, Gordon	1934
Pluff, Gary	1968
Pohl, Neil	1934, 36-37
Poindexter, William	1970-71
Polaski, Steve	1922,24-25
Polczinski, Nick	1989-90
Pollard, Ronnie	1973-74-75-76
Pollex, Eric	1995
Pollock, Chester	1911
Pophal, Raymond	1944
Popp, Anton	1935
Porett, Leo	1933
Pottinger, Earl	1945
Powell, Thomas	1912
Powell, Walter	1912-13
Prael, F.W.	1889
Pratt, Sylas	1993-94
Prchlik, Arthur	1951-52
Price, Art	1983-84
Price, Arthur	1928
Price, Edgar	1944, 47-48
Price, J.	1903
Price, William	1949
Prins, Richard	1943
Proctor, Thomas	1952
Propsom, Michael	1969
Prusinski, Michael	1976
Purnell, James	1961-62-63
Pyre, J.F.A.	1891, 95-96

Q-R

Quaerna, Arnold	1963
Rabas, Greg	1980-81
Rabas, Thomas	1955
Radcliffe, Robert	1948-49-50
Raddatz, Craig	1983-84-85-86
Rader, Mike	1994-95-96
Radke, Fred	1925
Rafko, Nick	1990-91-92-93
Ramlow, Richard	1943
Rapps, David	1988-89-90
Rasmussen, Jeff	1991-92
Rasmussen, John	1974-75-76
Rau, Harold	1914-15
Ray, Bob	1940-41-42
Raymer, Cory	1991-92-93-94
Reber, Thomas	1980
Rebholz, Harold	1927-28-29
Rebholz, Harold Jr.	1953
Rebholz, Russ	1930-31
Reddick, Melvin	1967-68-69
Reese, Dwight	1991-92
Regan, Jim	1942
Reich, Robert	1943
Reichardt, Rick	1962-63
Reid, Michael	1983-84-85-86
Reimer, John	1974-75
Reineck, Gary	1966-67-68
Reinke, James	1954-55-56
Reise, Steven	1973
Relich, Daniel	1976-77-78
Remp, R.W.	1903-04
Rendtorff, Edmund	1893
Rennebohm, Robert	1946-47
Rhodes, Rodney	1972-73
Rhymes, John	1993
Rice, Eric	1964-65-66
Richards, John	1892-93-94-95
Richards, Marshall	1980
Richardson, Charles	1972
Richardson, Curtis	1980-81
Richardson, Seth	1900
Richter, Bob	1964-65-66
Richter, Pat	1960-61-62
Ridlon, Walter	1966-67
Rieger, Harry	1914-15
Riewer, Frank	1941
Riordan, James	1937
Riordan, J.P.	1895-96-97, 00
Ritcherson, Lewis	1969
Roan, Michael	1991-92-93-94
Roberson, Royce	1994-95
Roberts, George	1941
Roberts, Jacques	1968
Roberts, John	1940, 42
Roberts, Ronald	1953
Robertson, Arthur	1943
Robinson, Bradbury	1903
Robinson, Rafael	1988-89-90-91
Rodgers, James	1957
Rodriguez, Joe	1976-77
Roedel, John	1965
Rogenski, Theodore	1960
Rogers, C.	1899
Rogers, Harlan	1906-07-08
Rogers, James	1959
Rohde, John	1994
Rohde, Kevin	1982-83
Rooney, Harold	1941
Rosandich, Ron	1955
Rose, Eugene	1926-27-28
Rose, Randy	1974-75-76
Roseth, Leonard	1905, 09
Rosga, Tim	1996
Ross, James	1985-86-88
Ross, John	1933
Rothbauer, Joe	1978-79-80
Rowe, Charles	1943
Rudat, Karl	1967-68
Rudolph, Joe	1992-93-94
Ruetz, Howard	1978-79-80
Russell, James	1992
Rustman, Karl	1947-48
Rutenberg, Bill	1980
Rutenberg, William	1952
Rux, Steve	1986-87
Ryan, John	1966-67-68
Ryan, John E.	1893-94, 96-97

S

Sachen, Michael	1964-65
Sachtjen, Kenneth	1948-49-50
Safranek, Randy	1972
Saleh, Tarek	1993-94-95-96
Salen, Gregory	1973
Salmons, David	1968
Samp, Edward	1910-11-12

Samuel, Mike	1995-96
Sanger, Art	1972-73-74
Sanger, Carl	1933
Sanger, Fred	1925
Sauter, Kendall	1939
Savage, Corey	1981
Sawicki, Mark	1978
Schade, Donald	1959-60-61
Schaefer, Jerry	1948-49
Schaffner, Donald	1966, 68
Scheid, Terry	1970
Schenk, James	1961-62
Schernecker, Edward	1922
Schick, William	1983-84-85
Schieble, Dan	1976-77-78
Schiller, Robert	1931-32-33
Schinke, Thomas	1965-66-67
Schleisner, Bill	1950-51
Schlicht, Kurt	1983
Schliksbier, Karel	1975
Schmidt, Edward	1914
Schmidt, Rudy	1968-69
Schmitsch, Richard	1966-67
Schmitz, Bill	1937-38-39
Schneck, Dan	1995
Schneck, Mike	1996
Schneider, Alfred	1923
Schneider, James	1969
Schneider, Paul	1992
Schneider, W.H.	1904
Schneller, John	1930-31-32
Schnetzky, Rick	1993v94
Schoessow, Wallace	1966-67-68
Schofield, Harvey	1902-03
Schoonover, Alan	1957, 59
Schrader, David	1970, 72
Schreiber, William	1900-01
Schreiner, Dave	1940-41-42
Schremp, Thomas	1977-78-79
Schroeder, Daniel	1973
Schuelke, Karl	1933-34, 38
Schuette, Paul	1926
Schwartz, John	1944
Schwarze, Herbert	1924
Schymanski, James	1971-72-73
Scott, Ralph	1917, 19-20
Scribner, Charles	1907-08
Seamonson, Al	1980-81
Searcy, Henry	1990,-91-92-93
Seelinger, Len	1941-42
Seifert, Michael	1971-72-73
Seis, Dean	1980
Self, Clarence	1943, 46-47-48
Senczyszyn, David	1990
Senn, Ed	1980
Senn, George	1898-99-00-01
Severson, Peter	1981-82
Shackerford, Lamark	1990-91-92-93
Shafer, Allan	1944
Sharp, Duer	1988-89-90-91
Sharron, Scott	1985
Shea, Bob	1945, 47-48
Sheehan, William	1929
Sheldon, Walter	1889, 92, 95-96
Shelton, Rodney	1991
Shinnick, Thomas	1968-69-71
Shoemaker, Lawrence	1927, 29
Shong, A.C.	1898
Shorney, Gordon	1919
Shumate, Mark	1979-80-81-82
Shwaiko, Paul	1952, 54-55, 58
Silverwood, T.P.	1895-96
Silvestri, Carl	1962-63-64
Simala, Jay	1992
Simcic, John	1948-49-50
Simkowski, George	1950-51-52
Simmons, Douglas	1930-31
Simmons, Haywood	1994-95
Simmons, Ken	1973-74-75
Simmons, Tony	1994-95-96
Simonson, Richard	1956
Simpson, Eber	1915-16-17
Simpson, George	1915
Sims, Clint	1979-80-81-82
Sims, Darryl	1980-81-82, 84
Sivyer, Benjamin	1917
Sklare, Scott	1975
Skow, Emil	1900-01
Skrzypchak, Eric	1996
Slaughter, B.K.	1924
Smith, Brian	1982
Smith, Frederick	1918-19
Smith, Harold C.	1928, 32-33
Smith, Harold, F.	1929-30-31
Smith, Jerome	1950-51
Smith, John B.	1972-73
Smith, John H.	1967-68
Smith, Leonard	1922
Smith, Lewis	1927-28-29
Smith, Lynwood	1914-15
Smith, Ronald	1962-63-64
Smith, William	1961-62-63
Smolich, Michael	1970-71
Snell, Ray	1977-78-79
Snell, Robert	1968
Sobocinski, Phil	1964-65-66
Sondrup, Ryan	1995-96
Soukop, Rudolph	1906-07
Souza, Wayne	1977-78
Spaeth, Tony	1989-90-91-92
Sparger, David	1985-86
Spencer, Troy	1985
Spiller, Rod	1993-94-95-96
Sprague, Charles	1958
Springer, Ernest	1906, 08
Spurlin, Larry	1979-80-81
Staiger, David	1949-50
Stalcup, Jerry	1957-58-59
Staley, Ronald	1960-61
Stangel, C.G.	1898
Stanger, Dirk	1996
Stanley, Henry	1935
Starch, Ken	1973-74-75
Stark, Harold	1917
Stark, Howard	1919-20
Stark, Steve	1992-93-94-95
Stassi, Mike	1982
Stauss, Tom	1977-78-79
Stavrum, Edwin	1913-14-15
Stecker, Aaron	1995-96
Steffen, Joe	1996
Stein, Jeffrey	1987
Steiner, Ronald	1957-58-59
Steiner, Rudy	1971-72
Steinmetz, George	1950-51-52
Stejskal, Dennis	1975-76-77
Stellick, Jack	1955
Stensby, Clarence	1951-52-53-54
Stephenson, Dennis	1969-70
Steverson, Ron	1980-81
Stewart, Jon	1973
Stiehm, Ewald	1906-07-08
Stieve, Terry	1973-74-75
Stills, Ken	1983-84
Stipek, Ray	1923-24-25
Storck, Robert	1970-71-72
Stout, Ward	1930-31
Stracka, Tim	1978-79-80, 82
Strain, Clair	1931-32, 34
Straubel, Austin	1924-25-26
Street, Lester	1896
Strehlow, Rollie	1949-50-51
Striefel, Rick	1986
Stroede, Terrence	1978-79
Strongquist, Luther	1904
Strop, Todd	1989, 91
Stupka, Bob	1942
Subach, Mark	1980-81-82
Suits, William	1960
Suminski, David	1950-51-52
Sumner, Louis	1889-91-92
Sundt, Guy	1918-19-20-21
Surber, Gordon	1947
Suttle, Jason	1994-95-96
Swalve, Gary	1966-67-68
Swan, Scott	1981
Swiderski, Edward	1930
Swopes, Aaron	1987
Sydnor, Eric	1985-86
Sydnor, Raymond	1978-79
Sykes, Robert	1922, 27

T

Taft, Merrill	1922-23
Tams, Mike	1989-90
Tandberg, Alvin	1911-12-13
Tansor, Dave	1986
Tarrell, Lucius	1904-05
Tarzetti, Kenneth	1944
Taulien, John	1985
Taylor, George	1913-14
Taylor, Glenn	1915-16
Taylor, John	1919
Taylor, Leonard	1995-96
Taylor, Robert	1982, 84-85-86
Teague, Robert	1949
Tebell, Gustaf	1920-21-22
Teckemeyer, Oscar	1923-24
Teets, Richard	1985-86
Temp, James	1952-53-54
Tennant, John	1938-39-40
Terrell, Melvin	1980, 84
Teteak, Richard	1956-57-58
Teteak, Deral	1949-50-51
Thiele, R.C.	1891
Thomas, Charles	1954-55
Thomas, Greg	1987-88-89-90
Thomas, Vaughn	1979-80-81-82
Thompson, Alan	1969-70-71
Thompson, Donnel	1996
Thompson, George	1895
Thompson, Jerry	1944-45
Thompson, Jim	1945-46
Thompson, Mike	1991-92-93-94
Thompson, Patrick	1990-91-92
Thompson, Rich	1988-89-90-91-92
Thornally, Dick	1940-41-42
Thurner, George	1930-31-32
Tietz, John	1966-67
Tobias, Dave	1930-31-32
Todd, Wayne	1966-67-68
Toepfer, Jim	1947
Tommerson, Clarence	1934-35-36
Tompkins, Reginald	1985-86
Toon, Al	1982, 83, 84
Torian, Reggie	1994-95
Tormey, Albert	1912-13
Tormey, Thomas	1900
Tornow, Elmer	1938-39
Torpfer, Jim	1947
Tratt, Paul	1897-98-99-00
Tratt, W.F.	1892

Trautman, George 1894-95
Trautman, H. 1896
Trotta, Lee 1968
Tucker, Melvin 1990-91-92, 94
Turk, Daniel 1983-84
Turturro, Ralph 1978

U

Underwood, Pete 1987
Underwood, Steven 1960-61-62
Unverzagt, Eric 1991, 93-94-95
Ursin, Donald 1952-53-54
Usher, Edison 1918

V

Vance, Jerry 1980-81
VandenBoom, Matt 1980-81-82
Vanderboom, E.J. 1902-03-04-05
Vanderhoof, William 1950
Vander Kelen, Ron 1962
VanderVelden, Donald 1960-61
Vanderveldt, Jamie 1993-94-95-96
VandeZande, Chad 1985-86-87-88
VanGent, Conrad 1911, 13
VanRiper, John 1911-12
VanRoo, Todd 1992
Vaughn, Harold 1917
Veit, Sam 1991-92-93-94
Veith, Steven 1977-78-79
Vergetis, Gus 1953
Vernon, Calvin 1948
Versnik, Ron 1980-81-82
Verstegen, Mike 1991-92-93-94
Vesel, Charles 1960
Vesperman, Michael 1973-74
Vincent, Troy 1988-89-90-91
Vinci, Steven 1986-87-88
Vine, Jeffrey 1976-77-78-79
Vogds, Evan 1941-42
Vogt, Hugo 1943
Voigt, Stuart 1967-68-69
VonBremer, George 1925-26-27
Von Heimburg, Ernest 1962, 64
Voss, Donald 1951-52
Vranesh, George 1941

W

Waerig, John 1995-96
Wagner, Jeffrey 1985-86, 88
Wagner, John 1977
Wagner, Robert 1978
Wagner, Rube 1926-27-28
Wagner, Scott 1996
Wagner, Steve 1973-74-75
Walgenbach, Gene 1941
Walker, Albert 1957
Walker, Averick 1983-84
Walker, Carlton 1980-81
Walker, David 1891-92
Walker, Elbert 1969-70-71
Walker, Melvin 1967
Walsh, Jeffrey 1977
Walter, Ted 1980
Ware, Tim 1989-90-91-92
Warren, Ebert 1927-28-29
Wartinbee, Bob 1948
Washburn, Cliff 1943
Washer, Charles 1903
Washington, Lee 1976-77
Washington, Selvie 1973-74
Wasikowski, Paul 1978
Wasserbach, Lloyd 1940-41-42
Watrud, James 1977
Watters, Philip 1986
Weber, Bernard 1943-44
Webster, Michael 1971-72-73
Weems, Cyril 1993-94-95-96
Wegner, Edmund 1938-39-40
Weigandt, Bob 1937-38
Weiger, Ralph 1943
Weimar, Albert 1913-14-15
Weiske, Bob 1944, 47-48
Weiss, Howard 1936-37-38
Welch, George 1977-78-79
Welch, Gerald 1957
Welch, Myron 1926-27
Wernicke, C.F.G. 1912
Wescott, Ward 1901
Wesley, James 1971-72
Westedt, Paul 1933
Weston, Frank 1917, 19-20
Westphal, John 1980-81
Weyker, Jeff 1988
Wheeler, Mark 1984
Wheeler, Sam 1965-66-67
White, Jeff 1974
White, LaMarr 1987-88-89-90
Whitmore, Alba 1907
Whitmore, Joseph 1907
Whittaker, Elmer 1906-07, 09
Whittaker, Terry 1969-70-71
Wiener, M.R. 1890
Wiesner, Tom 1958-59-60
Wilce, John 1907-08-09
Wilder, Lee 1969-70
Wilke, Earl 1925-26
Willding, Robert 1939-40
Williams, Bill 1986-87-88, 90
Williams, Brandon 1996
Williams, Charles 1996
Williams, Dean 1893
Williams, Edward 1923
Williams, John 1979-80-81-82
Williams, John L. 1989
Williams, Robert 1985, 87
Williams, Robert 1989-90-91
Williams, Roland 1920-21, 23
Williams, Sid 1956-57-58
Williams, Stanley 1972-73-74
Williams, Tony 1996
Willson, Milo 1932
Wilmarth, George 1899
Wilson, Glen 1953-54
Wilson, J. Donald 1935
Wilson, J. Robert 1925-26-27
Wilson, Robert 1946-47-48-49
Wilson, Sean 1989-90
Wimmer, Hugo 1952
Wimmer, James 1930
Wimpress, James 1974
Winckler, Bob 1979-8081-82
Windward, Erwin 1935-36
Winfrey, Carl 1968-69-70
Wings, David 1985-86-87-88
Wink, Jack 1942, 46-47
Winslow, George 1982-83
Wirth, Jeff 1990-91-92-93
Withers, Edward 1949-50-51
Witkus, Douglas 1976-77
Witt, Gerald 1951-52-53
Wittig, Richard 1961
Wojdula, Andy 1961-62-63
Wojtowicz, George 1978
Wolf, Jeffrey 1987-88
Wood, John 1966
Woodford, Bruce 1977
Woods, James 1920-21
Wrabetz, Voyta 1903-04-05
Wright, James 1935
Wright, Randy 1981-82-83
Wuhrman, Jerald 1952-53
Wunsch, Jerry 1993-94-95-96

Y

Yanakos, William 1966-67-68
Yarborough, William 1968-69-70
Yderstad, Charles 1948-49-50
Yeager, Clive 1898-99
Yocum, Chad 1991-92-93, 95
York, Claude 1938-39
Young, Richard 1969
Young, Scott 1993-94-95
Young, Stephen 1962-63
Yourg, Daniel 1979

Z

Zakula, Mark 1972-73-74
Zeisler, George 1906
Zeman, Robert 1957-58-59
Ziemetz, Arthur 1974
Ziese, Edgar 1927
Zimmerman, John 1973-74-75
Zinke, Arthur 1913
Zoelle, Charles 1947
Zouvoas, Peter 1957, 59
Zullo, Vince 1991-92-93-94
Zych, Lester 1943

Men's Hockey

A

Addison, Donald 1964-67
Akervik, Andy 1985-88
Alley, Steve 1972-77
Althaus, Jeff 1990-93
Alward, Charles 1964-65
Anderson, Craig 1995-96-97-98
Andersson, Dean 1984-88
Andringa, Jeff 1980-83
Andringa, Rob 1987-91
Arundel, Dave 1970-74
Auger, Jacques 1990-91

B

Balkovec, Maco 1991-95
Baretta, Julian 1975-79
Baxter, Gary 1982-86
Behrend, Marc 1980-83
Benson, Brad 1980-81
Bentley, Lloyd 1969-73
Bianchi, Joe 1995-96-97-98
Bjornlie, Dan 1996-97-98
Blaisdell, Mike 1979-80
Boyd, James 1968-71
Bradley, E.J 1995-96-97-98
Bunz, Garry 1984-87
Burroughs, Charles 1967-70
Buss, Matt 1990-94
Busse, Robert 1963-65
Buzza, Paul 1980-81
Byce, John 1986-90

C

Campbell, Brian 1977-80
Capouch, Mark 1974-78
Carlson, Jeff 1965-68
Carey, Jim 1992-94
Carroll, Tom 1979-83
Carter, Shawn 1992-96
Chelios, Chris 1981-83
Cherrey, Norm 1969-73
Chuckel, Thomas 1969-72

Clegg, Raymond	1964-65
Connor, Dean	1967-69
Cowan, Michael	1966-69
Coyne, John	1973-74

D

Danielson, Jan-Ake	1981-84
Daubenspeck, Kirk	1993-97
Decker, Joe	1987-91
DeHate, Delbert	1966-70
Derksen, Duane	1988-92
De Saint Phalle, Jacques	1982-83
Deprez, Don	1971-75
Dibble, Mike	1973-78
Doers, Mike	1991-94
Doner, Lexi	1980-84
Dool, Timothy	1969-73
Dougherty, John	1979-81
Driver, Bruce	1980-83
Duffy, James	1963-64
Durocher, Chuck	1979-80

E

Eaves, Mike	1974-78
Elick, Mickey	1992-96
Ellis, Charles	1963-67
Engberg, Gary	1970-71
Engblom, Brian	1973-75
Englehart, Brad	1994-95-96-97-98
Enrico, Rick	1994-95-96-97-98
Erickson, Brian	1969-72
Ethier, Pat	1979-83
Exarhos, Chris	1995-97

F

Fairchild, Kelly	1991-94
Faust, Eric	1982-87
Fitzgerald, Mark	1966-69
Flatley, Pat	1981-83
Folk, Al	1969-72
Ford, Pat	1984-88
Francisco, Jason	1989-93
French, Thomas	1963-65

G

Geisness, Todd	1985-87
Gilchrist, Daniel	1968-71
Gleffe, Michael	1966-69
Gorowsky, Dan	1977-81
Grafton, Kenneth	1963-64
Graham, Robert	1980-81
Granato, Don	1987-91
Granato, Rob	1992-94
Granato, Tony	1983-87
Grauer, Les	1975-79
Graveline, Paul	1983-87
Gregory, John	1974-78
Gremore, Jamey	1978-81
Griffin, Ron	1976-80
Gruden, Luke	1995-96-97-98
Gusak, Yuri	1995-96-97-98
Gwozdecky, George	1973-77

H

Haley, Darren	1994-97
Hall, Ben	1964-67
Harwell, Joe	1989-92
Heatley, Murray	1968-71
Hedlund, Todd	1991-94
Helgeson, Jon	1987-92
Hendrickson, Stu	1968-71
Heppner, Rick	1982-84
Herbst, Dave	1974-77
Hill, Sean	1988-91
Hinkley, Stan	1970-74
Houck, Paul	1981-85
Houston, Paul	1981-85
Howard, Troy	1992-96
Hudon, Gilles	1978-79

J

Jagger, John	1968-71
Jeffries, James	1973-75
Jefferies, Mark	1974-76
Jensen, Chris	1987-89
Johannson, Jim	1982-86
Johannson, John	1980-84
Johnson, Brad	1974-78
Johnson, Jack	1972-73
Johnson, Mark	1976-79
Johnson, Murray	1974-78
Johnson, Peter	1978-82
Johnston, James	1969-73
Joseph, Curtis	1988-89

K

Katlaps, Ulvis	1992-94
Kavolinas, Clark	1975-79
Keeley, Richard	1964-67
Keller, Randy	1978-81
Kelso, Douglas	1969-73
Kennedy, Charles	1965-66
Keryluk, Ken	1978-82
Kleisinger, Terry	1980-84
Klipsic, Richard	1967-70
Krug, Tim	1993-97
Kuk, Dustin	1996
Kuklinski, Gary	1969-72
Kuklinski, Thomas	1972-73
Kurtz, Brett	1988-92

L

Lambie, John	1985-89
Lannan, Pat	1969-72
LaPlante, Mike	1995
Lebler, Ed	1978-81
Lecy, Scott	1977-81
Lecy, Todd	1979-83
Leevers, Robert	1966-68
Leszcynski, Ron	1963-66
Lundeen, Dave	1973-77
Lundeen, Paul	1977-78
Lundeen, Robert	1971-75
Lundeen, Tom	1975-77

M

Macdonald, Doug	1988-92
Machowski, Thomas	1971-75
MacKenzie, Ken	1984-87
Makey, Jim	1970-73
Maley, Dave	1982-86
McFadyen, Douglas	1967-70
McFarlane, Jay	1978-81
McGrath, Mike	1983-85
McIntosh, Norm	1974-78
McKenzie, Steve	1980-82
McNab, Dave	1973-78
Meeker, Mike	1975-77
Mellanby, Scott	1984-86
Mendel, Rob	1986-90
Metro, Tony	1965-68
Michelizzi, Jon	1989-93
Mill, Gary	1982-84
Miller, Sterling	1963-64
Moore, Blaine	1990-94
Moran, John	1965-68
Moreau, T.R	1996
Morgan, Jon	1977-81
Mullen, Brian	1980-82
Mullens, Brad	1974-78

N

Nate, Jeff	1980-84
Nelson, Chris	1988-92
Nelson, Gregory	1966-69
Newberry, John	1980-82
Norwich, Craig	1974-77

O

Obrodovich, Thomas	1965-68
Olmstead, Dennis	1972-74
Osiecki, Mark	1987-90
Ostapina, Mark	1977-79
Otness, David	1973-74

P

Parker, John	1986-91
Passalino, Mark	1982-86
Pay, David	1972-74
Pearson, Ted	1980-84
Pendleton, Kip	1978-81
Perkins, Richard	1971-75
Perrin, Ian	1974-79
Peterson, Larry	1966-68
Peterson, Matt	1994
Petruzates, James	1964-67
Phippen, Tim	1976-79
Plante, Dan	1990-93
Poffenroth, Robert	1967-70
Poss, Greg	1986-89

R

Rafalski, Brian	1991-95
Ragatz, Frederick	1963-65
Rahko, Richard	1964-65
Ranheim, Paul	1984-88
Raygor, Erik	1994
Reay, Bill Jr.	1970-74
Reed, William	1963-65
Reinprecht, Steve	1996-12
Repins, Ed	1980-82
Revak, Glenn	1984-88
Richter, Barry	1989-93
Richter, Mike	1985-87
Riley, John	1964-67
Rohlik, Steve	1986-90
Romanchuk, Rod	1975-79
Rothering, Tim	1995
Rotsch, Jeff	1969-72
Russo, John	1963-66
Rutlin, Ronald	1965-68
Ryan, Tom	1982-86

S

Sabo, Scott	1980-84
Sabo, Steve	1994-95-96-97-98
Sabol, Shaun	1986-88
Sager, Tim	1980-84
Sagissor, Tom	1986-90
Sanderson, Jeff	1989-94
Sanderson, Scott	1992-96
Sauer, John	1994-95
Scheid, Jim	1976-80
Scheid, Tony	1984-88
Semandel, Kurt	1985-89
Shaughnessy, Robert	1970-74
Shier, Andrew	1990-94
Shuchuk, Gary	1986-90
Schultz, Roy	1978-80
Siren, Niki	1996
Skille, Lee	1975-76
Smith, David	1967-70

Smith, Mark 1994
Snedden, Dennis 1987-91
Soper, Jake 1994
Speer, Dave 1978-80
Spencer, Jamie 1991-95
Stanton, Paul 1985-89
Strobel, Mark 1991-95
Strobel, Mike 1991-96
Sundby, Jon 1964-65
Suter, Bob 1975-79
Suter, Gary 1983-85
Suter, John 1973-78
Sykes, Rodger 1987-91

T
Taft, John 1972-77
Talafous, Dean 1971-74
Tancill, Chris 1986-90
Tanner, Bert 1963-64
Thomas, Tim 1981-86
Thomas, Wayne 1968-80
Tochterman, Mat 1968-72
Tok, Chris 1991-95
Tompkins, Dan 1993-95
Tschipper, Steve 1982-86
Tucker, Chris 1990-94
Tuomie, Tray 1989-91
Tuttle, Steve 1984-88

U
Uihlein, Phil 1970-72
Ulseth, Tom 1974-78

V
Valley, Mike 1996
Van Dyke, John 1963-64
Vargas, Ernie 1982-86
Vincent, Ron 1978-82
Vroman, Robert 1967-70

W
Walsh, Matt 1982-86
Wallace, Bruce 1979-80
Weiss, James 1963-64
Welsh, Theran 1977-81
Whipple, Richard 1964-66
White, Jeff 1983-85
Wiitala, Marty 1982-86
Williams, Max 1992-96
Winchester, Gary 1970-74

Y-Z
Young, Donald 1966
Young, Frank 1963-66
Young, James 1969-72
Zent, Jason 1990-94

Men's Soccer

A
Aal, Kareem 1996
Ackerman, Ron 1991-92-93
Adams, Joel 1983-84
Andresen, Eric 1977-78
Averill, Gerard 1982, 84-85-86

B
Babich, Mark 1979-80-81-82
Bell, Mike 1988-89-90-91
Belskis, Jon 1995-96
Bernstein, Robert 1977
Black, Brad 1981, 83
Boykoff, Jason 1989-90
Broadhurst, Christian 1994-95-96
Bylsma, Derek 1991

C
Carlson, John 1979-80-81-82
Cabalka, Jeff 1980-81
Campbell, Scott 1986
Cole, Chad 1993-94-95-96
Cookson, Zachary 1996

D
Dawson, Brian 1988-89-90-91
DeAmicis, Todd 1992-93-94-95
DeBoer, Darryl 1987-88
Deck, Tim 1991-92-93
Dennis, Mark 1980-81-82-83
Diagne, Amadou 1977
Doctor, John 1983
Doherty, Brian 1994-95-96
Doherty, Jeff 1992-93-94
Donian, Dave 1977-78-79
Douglas, Bruce 1983-84
Duerst, Darryl 1979, 81-82
Duerst, Dean 1981-82-83

E
El-Khamissy, Mohammed 1996
Erturk, Erol 1984-85

F
Faris, Chris 1980
Fine, Dave 1980
Fisher, Adam 1987
Flyr, Josh 1988-89-90-91
Friedrick, Larry 1980-81
Froslid, Jim 1985-86-87-88

G
Gentile, Mike 1992-93-94-95
Goggin, Dan 1984-85
Gold, Jeff 1991-92-93-94
Goldberger, Nick 1987-88
Greelis, Jeremy 1996
Grimm, Bryan 1993-94-95
Grimm, Peter 1977
Grogan, Tom 1977
Gross, Greg 1977
Grosse, Keith 1983-84, 86-87
Grosse, Mike 1981-82-83
Grutzner, Fritz 1980-81, 83

H
Hansen, Lars 1992-93-94-95
Harkin, Chris 1979-80-81-82
Hart, Wes 1996
Haugsdal, Borge 1994
Heiden, Eric 1977-78
Henige, Chris 1980-81-82-83
Hickey, Brad 1985-86-87-88
Hofheimer, George 1988-89-90-91
Hoke, Jason 1990-91-92-93
Holmes, Matt 1991-92-93
Houck, Bill 1977
Huffer, Mike 1978-79-80-81
Hurtig, Elliot 1984-85-86
Huston, Shea 1992-93-94-95
Hynes, Robert 1977-78

I
Ipson, Ron 1980
Isaacson, Cory 1989-90

J
Jaworski, Dave 1984-85-86
Johnson, Blake 1979-80
Johnson, Scott 1978-79

K
Keepers, Tom 1982-83
Kehoe, Ryan 1994-95-96
Keyes, Dan 1988
Kollasch, Bob 1987-88-89-90
Konkol, Blaze 1992-93-94-95
Kottke, Mike 1984-85-86
Kowalski, Adam 1995-96
Krajewski, Scott 1996
Kucha, Tim 1985-86, 88-89
Kullby, Kevin 1982-83-84

L
LaFerrera, Brett 1988-89-90-91
Lamphear, Scott 1992-93-94-95
Land, Mike 1987
LaPorte, Mark 1979-80-81-82
Lavey, Andrew 1989-90-91-92
Lennon, Pat 1987-88
Limbrick, Frank 1985-86
Lindstrom, Erik 1996
Loeffler, Paul 1979
Lombardino, Michael 1977-78

M
Malen, Mike 1995-96
Martini, Jim 1977
Maze, Brett 1977-78
Mehrpuyan, Djahangir 1979, 81-82-83
Mesdjian, Raffi 1980
Metcalf, Chris 1977-78-79-80
Meuer, Kelly 1977-78-79
Mihm, Mike 1987-88-89
Minic, Vlatko 1989-90, 92
Mjaanes, Reuben 1987-88-89
Moynihan, Mike 1987-88-89-90
Mudd, Chuck 1980
Mullen, Jim 1977-78-79

N
Nesbitt, Marc 1990-91-92
Nieuwenhuis, Jared 1990-91-92

O
Obenberger, Jon 1984-85
Oxman, Marc 1977
Ozanne, Brendan 1990-91
Ozanne, Ismael 1989-90, 92-93

P
Pasquarello, Nick 1993-94
Paulsen, Eric 1978
Pedraza, Oscar 1984-85
Perry, Erik 1984-85
Pradham, Rajan 1980
Provan, Josh 1993-94-95-96

R
Rectenwal, Andy 1984-85-86-87
Reddan, John 1986-87-88
Reid, Charlie 1984-85
Reinders, Joel 1990-91-92
Roberts, Jeff 1978-79
Rogan, Dan 1984-85
Rose, Steve 1986-87-88-89
Roy, Travis 1992-93-94-95
Rush, Mike 1978-79-80-81

S
Schiedemeyer, Jeff 1986-87-88-89
Schmid, Kent 1978-79
Schvartzer, Javier 1990

Sella, Roberto 1984, 86-87
Senn, Eric 1978-79-80-81
Seymour, Casey 1991
Sickels, Mark 1989-90
Solarte, Joe 1980-81
Sporcich, Scott 1994-95-96
Stamberg, Josh 1991
Steel, Alastair 1993-94-95-96
Steele, Andy 1994
Stein, Lyle 1977-78
Stevens, John 1984
Storm, Ted 1996

T
Tarjan, Eugene 1988
Thodus, Jason 1981-82
Thomas, John 1985-86-87
Thompson, Rett 1989-90-91
Thorson, Tim 1989
Tiegs, Dan 1980, 82-83
Towne, Tim 1985-86-87

V-W
Von Ruden, Kyle 1994
Watson, Doug 1995-96
Weaver, Paul 1982-83
Wilson, Todd 1994-95-96
Winograd, Jeff 1980-81-82-83

Y-Z
Yoo, Seesun 1984-85-86-87
Zoschke, Todd 1982-83-84, 86

Men's Tennis

A
Aagesen, Nicholas 1921, 23
Anderson, Keith 1957, 58, 59
Annear, Thomas 1981, 82, 83
Arends, Daniel 1982, 83, 84, 85.

B
Ballinger, Todd 1966
Barr, Mike 1975, 76, 77, 78
Barrand, Chester 1942, 43, 47
Bartz, Kenneth 1969, 70 ,71.
Batzle, Willard 1937, 38, 39
Bauhs, Paul 1929
Beamish, John 1942
Becker, Robert 1971
Bishop, Paul 1964, 65, 66
Black, Robert 1967, 68
Black, Roy 1933, 35
Bleckinger, Daniel 1967
Boldenwick, Leo 1926, 27, 28
Borcherdt, Robert 1936, 37, 38
Brodhead, Richard 1943
Bronson, Walter 1970, 71
Brorby, Melvin 1916, 20
Brown, Anthony 1959, 60
Browne, Richard 1979, 80, 81
Bunker, Clifford 1948, 49
Burgess, John 1935
Burr, Christopher 1968, 69, 70

C
Carswell, Jeff 1981
Center, John 1970, 72, 73
Chang, David 1997, 98
Chyle, John 1953
Clark, John 1972, 73, 74
Cohen, Marvin 1961, 62
Colias, James 1968
Colvin, Nick 1997
Conway, John 1965, 66, 67
Conway, Kevin 1970, 71
Cooper, Peter 1975
Coyle, Douglas 1936, 38, 39
Crabel, Robert 1950
Croll, Bobby 1997
Cullen, Eric 1974, 75, 76
Curtis, Donald 1956

D
Dalrymple, Bruce 1939
Damadian, Raymond 1954
Darling, Robert 1958, 59
Davis, John 1943
De Long, William 1944
Deer, Joey 1989, 90, 91, 92
Deloye, James 1950, 51, 52
Dithmar, John 1938
Dowling, Fred 1945
Dubie, Aaron 1992, 93, 94, 95
Duncan, Alex 1994
Durand, Samuel 1925, 26

E
Easum, Donald 1946, 47
Edmonson, Robert 1944
Eiseman, Walter 1962, 64
Elbert, Phillip 1952
Endres, John 1951
Erler, William 1930, 31, 32

F
Fanning, Willis 1920
Feiss, Ferdinand 1948
Finner, Winn 1934
Fraser, Alan 1958, 60
Frautschi, Timothy 1957, 58
Frazer, Alan 1958, 60
Frederickson, Jack 1948
Freeborn, David 1927, 28
Froemming, Robert 1945, 46

G
Giessel, Elmer 1925, 26
Gluck, Geoffry 1965
Go, Adam 1998
Goldin, Martin 1972, 73, 75, 76
Goldstein, Michael 1994, 95, 96, 97
Goodsitt, Harry 1930
Gotfredson, Henry 1920
Gottleib, Aaron 1929
Granert, William 1964, 65
Greeley, David 1933
Grunow, William 1951, 52

H
Hammond, Gerald 1945
Hampton, Larry 1974
Hanson, Harold 1944
Hartz, Jeffrey 1974, 75
Hays, Stanley 1958
Heckrodt, Frank 1945, 46, 49
Hedberg, Joan 1975, 76, 77, 78
Heivilin, Fred 1961, 62, 63
Hentzen, Albert 1956, 57, 58
Hentzen, Herbert 1946, 47, 48, 49
Henschel, David 1995
Hentzen, William 1954
Herrnstadt, Richard 1948
Hertz, Jeffrey 1974
Hewes, Fred 1929
Hoff, Russell 1951
Howes, Robert 1933
Huguelet, Scot 1976

J
Joachim, Frederick 1970
Jones, Craig 1974, 75, 76, 77
Jordan, Todd 1994

K
Kadesch, Philip 1973, 74, 75
Kaesberg, Paul 1944, 45
Kaufman, Robert 1948
Kernjack, Anthony 1931, 32, 33
Kessler, Robert 1971, 72
Kinast, Frank 1946
King, Paul 1962, 64
Kirk, Gary 1963, 64, 65
Klein, Tim 1984, 85, 86
Klingelhoets, Mark 1975, 76, 78, 79
Klingelhoets, Pat 1970, 71, 72
Koehl, Edgar 1939, 40, 41
Koehler, Todd 1993, 94
Kratz, Winston 1927

L
La Borde, George 1928
Larsen, John 1981
Leidel, Donald 1949
Leverentz, Eugene 1950
Loughrin, Mark 1998
Lovett, Steven 1982, 83, 84

M
Mac Innis, Dana 1994
Madden, Timothy 1985, 86, 87
Malik, Jeffery 1995, 96, 97, 98
Marlow, Warren 1942, 43
Maxwell, Bruce 1967, 68, 69
Mcmillen, Robert 1928
Medenwald, David 1959
Meikeljohn, Donald 1929, 30
Meikeljohn, Gordon 1931, 32
Michels, Theodore 1964, 65, 66
Miller, Greg 1993, 94
Miller, Jared 1995
Mirsberger, Dave 1987, 88, 89, 90
Mirsberger, Jim 1988, 89, 90, 91
Moulding, Arthur 1922, 23, 24
Mueller, Warren 1949, 50
Muenz, Russell 1978, 79, 80

N
Negendank, Donald 1950, 51
Negendank, Robert 1941
Nelson, Bryan 1989, 90, 91, 92
Neu, Richard 1947, 48
Niedermeyer, Scott 1974
Nielsen, Arthur 1916, 17, 18
Nielsen, Arthur 1939, 40, 41

O
O'Neil, Junior 1952
Oberlin, David 1962, 63, 64
Oberlin, Thomas 1963, 64, 65
Ohm, Kenneth 1950, 51, 52
Oppenheim, Rob 1989, 90, 91, 92
Ortiz, David 1992, 93, 94

P
Page, Donald 1949, 50
Parker, James 1944
Pease, Richard 1960, 61
Pederson, Tony 1995, 96, 97, 98
Pelisek, David 1978, 79, 80
Perlstein, Scott 1969, 70, 71
Peterson, George 1950
Pilsbury, Eliot 1966, 67, 68

Plotz, Arno 1946, 47
Pollack, Laurence 1970, 71
Pratt, Claude 1939
Puls, Charles 1909
Putterman, Robert 1944

R
Reagan, Robert 1951, 52, 53
Reierson, David 1959, 60
Reist, Stefan 1998
Restuccia, Jon 1984, 85, 86
Richardson, W 1935, 36, 37
Richman, Jordan 1991, 92, 93, 94
Rideout, Vincent 1961, 62, 63
Ringlien, Andy 1980, 81, 82
Ritzenberg, Frank 1968
Roberts, Owen 1953
Roebuck, John 1940
Rogers, William 1945, 47, 48, 49
Rogness, Richard 1965, 66, 67
Romero, William 1953
Rotter, Jerold 1958, 59, 60
Rotter, Marshall 1943
Rubinowitz, Leonard 1963
Rubinowitz, Martin 1960
Rudelius, William 1951, 52, 53
Ruedisili, Lon 1959, 60, 61

S
Sabel, Shane 1996
Sacks, David 1997
Sah, Peter 1924
Schimelfenyg, Paul 1973, 74
Schmidtmann, Jack 1953, 54
Schmitt, John 1950, 54
Schneider, Jim 1986
Schneider, Hubert 1943, 47, 48, 49
Schoen, Armund 1966, 67, 68
Schoenike, Howard 1939, 40, 41
Schudson, Armand 1941, 42
Schumacher, Adam 1997, 98
Schwartz, John 1970, 71, 72
Schwartz, Marc 1987, 88, 89, 90
Schwerdtfeger, Wulf 1964, 65, 66
Seaman, Irving 1903
Semmelhack, Martin 1961
Sessler, Mark 1962, 63, 64
Shepard, David 1956, 57, 58
Siegel, Howard 1929
Siegel, James 1967, 68
Silverman, Daniel 1930, 31, 32
Silverthorn, Rich 1977, 78
Simmons, John 1976, 77
Sobel, Bart 1966, 67
Sorge, Philip 1954
Sperling, Mike 1976, 77, 78
Spiegel, Jodi 1977, 78
Stafford, Willard 1935, 36, 37
Starke, Michael 1977
Stephens, Thomas 1943
Suhm, Clarence 1918

T
Takato, Daisuke 1998
Tank, Robert 1946
Taylor, H 1920
Thomas, Ken 1977, 78, 79, 80
Thomsen, John 1995, 96, 97, 98
Thorne, Malcolm 1994, 95, 96
Tredwell, Thomas 1921, 22, 23
True, Stephen 1973

U-V
Unger, Jeffrey 1967, 68, 69
Van Lieshout, William 1976
Verkins, Earl 1945, 48
Vincent, John 1953, 54

W
Waite, Robert 1988, 89, 90, 91
Wayne, John 1981, 82, 83, 84
Weiss, Jason 1996.
Welch, Don 1983, 84, 85, 86
West, Christopher 1992, 93, 94
Weycer, Joseph 1956, 57
White, Robert 1976, 77, 78, 79
Wilson, Mike 1972, 73, 74, 75
Wingstrom, John 1955, 56, 57
Wright, William 1941

Y-Z
Young, Donald 1967, 68, 69
Zawacki, Ian 1960, 61, 62
Zerweck, John 1985, 86, 87
Ziemer, William 1955, 56
Zuckerman, Jason 1994, 95, 96

Men's Track

A
Abbott, Allen C. 1902, 04
Abendschein, Charles F. 1945
Ackerman, Barry 1963-64
Adams, James Reva 1910
Agger, Sean 1996-97
Agger, Todd 1995-96-97
Agger, William 1967-68
Albrecht, Adam 1994-95-96
Albright, Charles B. 1935
Albright, William C. 1949-50
Ames, Patrick C. 1985-86-87
Anderson, Dalton L. 1946-48
Anderson, Robert J. 1953-54-55
Anderson, Tobin 1986
Andrews, Andrew I. 1917-18-20
Archer, Lee A. 1945
Arend, Jeff 1982-83
Armstrong, Howard 1923
Arne, Peter 1928
Arneson, Arne U. 1946-47
Arrington, Ray 1967-68-69
Ashby, Phillip R. 1951
Atkinson, Loid R. 1950, 52
Atkinson, Thomas J. 1965-66

B
Bachman, Willis D. 1945
Backus, August C. 1929
Baer, Jonathon 1984-85-86-87
Bahnfleth, William 1969-70-71
Baker, Charles 1970-71-72-73
Bal, Bruce 1981
Balistreri, Ted 1985-86-87, 89
Bassett, Norman D. 1913-14
Bassett, Robert C. 1931
Bastian, Ernest 1936
Bauer, Jerome J. 1940, 42-43
Bauman, Walter J. 1912
Beatty, Gerald E. 1964-65-66
Beck, Richard J. 1949, 50
Becker, J.A. 1913
Becker, Robert 1968
Behr, Samuel 1929-30-31
Beierle, Robert 1941-42-43, 47
Belke, Paul 1989-90-91-92
Bell, Buddy F.E. 1958, 60
Bell, James D. 1959-60-61
Benish, George A. 1914-15-16
Bennett, Tom 1947-48-49
Benson, Daniel 1978-79, 81-82
Benson, Glenn 1928-29-30
Bergemann, Brian 1964, 66-67
Bergstresser, John 1924-25
Bergstrom, Donovan 1989-90-91-92-93
Berndt, Randy 1982-83
Bertles, William M. 1907
Bertrand, Kenneth J. 1930-31
Best, J. Riley 1937-38-39
Betts, Russell 1989-90-91-92-93
Bierman, Klaus H. 1958
Bigford, Walter D. 1937
Birkeland, Dag 1973-74, 76
Bishop, Edward 1972-73
Bishop, Warren J. 1900-01
Blackbourn, Lisle Jr. 1947-48
Bleckwenn, Alfred T. 1949-50-51
Bleckwenn, Theodore 1949-50-51
Bliss, Donald 1966, 68
Blodgett, Robert O. 1921
Bobber, Robert J. 1 941
Boe, Nils A. 1933-34
Bolton, Charles 1973-74-75
Bond, Michael 1968-69-70
Booth, George E. 1916
Borsa, Christopher J. 1986, 88-89
Bosley, Andrew 1994-95-96-97
Bowman, Donald 1952
Braaten, Eric 1974
Bradley, James 1972-73-74-75
Brady, Branch 1967-68-69
Brandt, Arthur F. 1929-30-31
Brandt, Robert C. 1937-38
Braun, Jeff 1976-77-78-79
Bredsteen, Joseph 1900
Breitkreutz, Emil W. 1902, 04-05
Brennan, Robert W. 1955-56
Brice, Jim 1982-83
Brinen, Scott 1995,97
Bronk, Ashley 1997
Brown, James 1980
Brown, Keith H. 1944,46
Brown, Kevin 1977-78-79-80
Brown, Terrence 1969-70
Brown, Kenton J. 1944
Buch, Phillip 1973-74
Bulin, Tracy 1986-87-88-89
Bullamore, Charles 1927-28
Bunt, William 1936
Burdick, William C. 1899-1900-01
Burger, Thomas 1992, 94-95-96
Burke, Mead 1915-16-17
Burr, Allen R. 1917, 19
Buser, Alfred L. 1910, 12
Butler, Allen W. 1950
Butler, Michael 1967-68-69
Buxton, Edward F. 1939-40

C
Calabresa, Nick F. 1938
Callender, Richard 1929
Canaan, Harlin E. 1985, 87
Capponi, Ernest L. 1944
Carl, Harland 1952-53
Carlson, Keith R. 1951, 52
Carney, Patrick 1979
Carpenter, Crawford T. 1963-64-65
Carter, Thomas B. 1925
Carter, William 1916
Casey, Thomas 1976-77-78-79
Casey, Thomas B. 1915-16-17
Casiano, Jason 1992-93, 95-96
Cassidy, Clayton G. 1924-25

Name	Years
Cassidy, Paul H.	1929
Chandler, Peter	1978-79
Chandler, Kensal R.	1944-45, 47
Chase, David	1979
Chepyator, Fred K.	1986-87-88-89
Cherne, Alvo R.	1951-52
Christensen, John	1995-96-97
Christianson, Edward G.	1935-36-37
Chritzman, George M.	1913-14
Clark, Carlton	1993, 95-96-97
Clark, Loren J.	1956
Clark, Robert C.	1933-34
Cole, Derek	1982
Collins, Leroy M.	1950-51-52
Consigny, Thomas L.	1955
Cooke, Charles	1992-93
Cooke, Lloyd M.	1936-37
Cooper, Richard L.	1939
Cordes, John	1970, 72-73
Corp, Paul	1931
Cortright, Harry M.	1930-31-32
Cotton, Austing	1957-58
Cotton, John L.	1960, 62
Courtney, Paul	1980
Cox, Justin	1997
Crabb, Jack H.	1943, 47-48
Craig, Glenn W.	1940
Craig, Michael	1976
Crail, Gordon	1971-72
Cranston, Robert W.	1946
Crawford, James A.	1936
Cregan, Thomas P.	1961-62-63
Crites, Gary G.	1965-66
Cronin, Robert	1990
Crowell, Carleton R.	1935-36
Crummy, James H.	1932-33
Crump, Gordon W.	1918, 20
Cunningham, Brandon	1993-94
Curet, Luis	1980, 82
Curtis, Chuck	1971-72-73-74

D

Name	Years
Dahms, Mark	1994
Dakin, Thomas B.	1964-65-66
Dalton, Jon W.	1954, 55, 56
Dameworth, Bryan	1992-93-94-95
Daniells, John E.	1902
Darling, John W.	1939
Davidson, Homer P.	1929-30-31
Deakin, Chris	1981-82-83
De Forest, James	1967-68-69
Diegnan, Michael J.	1985-86-87
Deike, Walter E.	1948, 51-52
Delaney, Kelley	1984-85, 87
Demmin, Lonsdale	1983-84
Dennis, Eugene	1995-96
Dennis, Henry C.	1921
DeRamus, Lee	1993-94
Des Rochers, Daniel	1981
DeVoe, Warren A.	1945
DeYoung, John T.	1944-47-48
Dick, Glenn B.	1967-68, 69
Dick, John	1940
Diehl, Milton L.	1928-29-30
Dilley, Chester	1929
Dix, Eugene E.	1962-63-64
Dixson, LeRoy	1982-83
Dittburner, John	1970-71-72
Dmytrow, David	1992
Dobert, Pascal	1993-94-95-96-97
Dooley, Donald L.	1959-60
Dorow, Bruce	1982
Dorrington, Lewis T.	1934-35
Dorsch, Albert	1938
Dougan, Trevor C.	1927
Downey, Frank E.	1913-14
Downin, Matt	1997
Downs, Phillip	1994-95-96-97
DuBane, Frank J.	1902-03
Duewel, Edward	1953
Duis, Frank R.	1952
Dunkleberger, James	1994-95-96-97
Duquemin, Gordon J.	1944

E

Name	Years
Earle, Thomas B.	1933
Easker, John	1982-83-84-85
Edwards, Roymond C.	1918, 20
Eisele, George	1927, 29
Elsom, Bernardo W.	1918
Embach, James K.	1946
Endres, Otto	1917, 20
Englander, James A.	1950, 52
Englund, Clint	1989-90-91-92
Erickson, John R.	1926-27
Erickson, Thomas	1966-67-68
Erzen, Jerr L.	1961
Escarcega, Tony	1994-95-96-97
Estick, Richard C.	1956-57-58
Euler, Mark	1994
Exum, William G.	1930, 35-36
Ezerins, Elmars P.	1961-62-63

F

Name	Years
Farin, William G.	1938-39-40
Fein, Steve	1997
Felton, Hiblert O.	1916
Fenske, Charles H.	1936-37-38
Fey, James R.	1961
Fink, Delmar S.	1929
Finkle, George H.	1921
Firchow, Donald A.	1950, 52
Firzlaff, Jeff	1988
Fischer, Jeremy	1995-96-97
Fitzgibbon, Thomas M.	1934
Flack, Jeffery P.	1966
Fleming, James	1972-73-74-75
Floyd, Larry	1968-69-70
Flueck, Herbert	1924-25
Follwos, John W.	1929-30
Folsom, Howard	1928-29
Forsberg, Axel C.	1916
Foster, Roger W.	1941, 43, 46
Fox, Henry J.	1931
Frame, William S.	1895-96-97
Fancher, Thomas T.	1967-68
Francis, Neil G.	1925-26
Fraser, Bruce	1965-66-67
Frederick, Tom E.	1946-47
Fredrick, Marcos	1997
Freimuth, Robert M.	1964-65
Freisch, Thomas A.	1952
Fridrich, Arthur J.	1945
Frisch, Arthur W.	1930-31
Froelich, Gary	1979-80-81-82
Fry, Scott D.	1986-87-88-89-90
Fuchs, George J.	1945-46

G

Name	Years
Gafke, Loren	1929-30
Gage, Robert	1971-72, 74
Gannott, Walter C.	1938
Gardner, Robert G.	1938-39-40
Gates, John	1981-82-83-84-85
Gehrmann, Donald	1947-48-49-50
Geib, William J.	1938
Gill, Gregory	1995-96-97
Gillette, Edmund S.	1910
Gilsinger, Jon	1980
Girard, Eland	1953
Gleason, Neil	1972-73
Glendenning, David	1960
Goldberg, Gary	1957
Gloden, Demmer	1918
Goldie, William B.	1913
Goldin, Melvin	1948-49-50
Goldmann, Robert	1987-88-89
Goldsworthy, Vernon	1929-30-31
Gonyon, Harvey L.	1913
Gordon, Robert	1967-68-69
Gordon, James	1972
Gorens, Sherwood W.	1940-41-42
Granby, Walter A.	1930-31
Grant, John	1980-81-82
Greenlee, Samuel	1950-51-52
Greenwood, David	1980-81-82
Gregson, William F.	1917-mgr.
Gross, William	1978
Gruber, John	1978-1979
Gumbreck, Lawrence G.	1926-27
Gwyn, Thomas	1961-62-63

H

Name	Years
Haberman, Warren O.	1940
Hacker, Jeffery	1979-80-81-82
Hacker, Tim	1982, 84-85
Hackett, Robert	1984-85-86-87
Hadley, Lawrence	1941-42, 43-mgr.
Hagemann, Troy	1980-81-82
Haller, Albert E.	1935-36-37
Hammann, William	1923-24
Hammond, Loring T.	1919-mgr.
Hands, Mark	1982
Hands, Richard	1975-76-77-78
Hanson, J. Bradley	1967-68-69
Hanson, Maurice M.	1918
Harrer, Alfred W.	1939-40-41
Harris, Richard	1967
Hartman, Peter	1979-80-81
Harvey, William D.	1914-15-16
Hass, Donald	1944
Hauser, Mark	1995-96
Hausmann, Todd W.	1986
Hawke, Robert	1967-68-69
Hay, Donald C.	1942-43
H'Doubler, Francis T.	1946
Hean, Clarence S.	1903, 06
Hebien, Donald	1954-55-56
Heckel, Lance	1980-81-82
Hedges, Robert N.	1913-14-15
Heineke, James	1959
Heintzen, Harry R.	1916-17
Heise, Leonard H.	1934-mgr.
Heller, Donald E.	1948-mgr.
Helmholz, Henry F.	1900
Hendrick, Charles	1965
Hendrickson, Donald J.	1962-63-64
Henke, William L.	1929-30-31
Henry, Herbert A.	1900
Herdt, Kris M.	1985
Herold, Glenn	1970-71-72-73
Hertz, Gilman W.	1942-43, 47
Heuer, William	1964-65-66
Hewlett, Dial	1968-69-70
Heyde, Marshall R.	1946
Higgenbottom, Elzie L.	1962-63-64
Hill, Harry E.	1925
Hinshaw, Louis	1991-92-93-94
Hirschinger, Louis	1935
Hirsheimer, Earl S.	1921
Hirt, Jeffery J.	1985-mgr.
Hodgell, Robert O.	1942-43, 47-48

Hofer, Kenneth	1955-56
Hoffman, John	1980-81-82
Hoffman, William	1963-64-65
Holden, Bill	1964-65-66
Holland, Louis	1962-63
Holt, Eugene	1959-60
Horn, Ford A.	1949-mgr.
Houden, Richard A.	1949
Hover, William T.	1909-10
Howard, Larry F.	1962, 63
Howard, Levely	1985
Howlett, Andy	1991-92-93
Hsieh, Hsueh Hai	1919
Hubert, Dan	1988-89
Huff, James	1970, 72-73
Huffman, Mike	1985-86-87-88-89
Hunkel, Victor	1928
Huntley, Kevin	1995-96-97
Huston, Harold H.	1915-16
Huxhold, Kenneth	1949-50
Hyatt, Brett	1982-83
Hyland, John	1991-92, 94
Hyland, Richard	1970-71

J

Jackson, Aquine	1967-68
Jackson, David	1980-81, 84
Jackson, Randolph	1977-78-79-80
Jacobsen, Edward	1956-57
Jaeger, Peter	1992-93-mgr. 94mgr.-95mgr.
Jeffay, Henry	1945
Jenkins, Scott	1983-84-85-86
Jenness, Donald	1970-71-72-73
Jensen, Alvin J.	1946, 48-49
Jensen, Howard C.	1930
Jerred, Jack	1946-47-48
Johann, Robert	1945
Johannes, Roland	1974
Johnson, Albert A.	1904, 06-07
Johnson, Deon	1992
Johnson, Edward W.	1921-22-23
Johnson, Erik	1980
Johnson, Gregory	1970-71
Johnson, Lawrence	1976-77
Johnson, Mark	1974-75-76-77
Johnson, Richard W.	1971-72-73-74
Johnson, Robert	1951-52-53
Johnston, Robb	1983
Jones, Bryan	1991-92-93, 95
Jones, Donald H.	1924
Jones, Harold S.	1931-32-33
Jones, Thomas C. Edward	1946-47-48

K

Kaashhagen, Kjell	1978
Kabat, Cyril P.	1940-41-42
Kabat, Gregory	1931-32
Kailas, George W.	1946-47-48-49
Kaines, Joel	1990-91-92-93
Kammer, John	1947-48
Kanalz, Jack	1927-28
Kane, Bar	1988
Kapheim, Joe	1982-83-84
Kartman, Mark	1969-70-71
Kathan, Chris	1994-95
Kauffman, Donald G.	1940
Kauffman, Frank G.	1938-39
Kaufman, Jeff	1975-76-77-78
Kaufman, Thomas	1975-76
Kay, George B.	1935-36
Keachie, George	1902
Keller, John 1978-	79-80-81
Kellman, Richard	1950-51-52
Kellner, Jack F.	1935-36-37
Kelly, Max Edwin	1945
Kemp, Frank F.	1929
Kennedy, Kenneth R.	1924-25-26
Kennell, Charles	1979-80
Kent, Earl (Skip)	1970-71-72-73
Kerr, Spencer H.	1914
Kiesel, Karl H.	1905
Killins, Dale	1995-96-97
Kindt, Donald	1946
Kingstad, Jeffery	1971-72-73-74
Kirk, Laurence R.	1931-32
Klath, Carl	1926-mgr.
Kleinschmidt, Karl W.	1934-35-36
Knox, Merle G.	1942
Knudson, Barney	1913-14
Knutson, David	1976-77-78-79
Kohl, Michael	1978-79
Kommers, William J.	1939
Korhonen, Jay	1986-87-88-89
Kowal, Daniel	1973-74-75
Kreuz, Louis G.	1916
Krieger, Elmer	1923-24-25
Krieger, Herbert D.	1931-mgr.
Krueger, Paul M.	1934
Krueger, Steven T.	1986-87-88-89
Kubly, Ray R.	1925
Kuhls, James	1975

Kulinski, Tim	1997

L

LaBeach, Lloyd B.	1946
Lacy, Steve	1975-76-77-78
Laheurte, Phillipe	1979
Lambert, Walter M.	1942-43, 46-47
Lange, Robert E.	1934
Lanphear, Daniel	1959
Lanos, Fred	1969-70
Larson, Mark	1970-71-72
Larson, Philip	1928-29
Lauzon, Edward	1973-74-75, 77
Latigo-Olal, Kenneth A.	1965-66-67
Lawson, William	1945
Leach, Peter	1992, 94
Learned, Harold N.	1938
Ledman, Eldon D.	1934
Lee, Herbert	1930-31
Lee, Howard J.	1927-mgr.
Legler, Fred M.	1914
Leiske, Roy R.	1935
Lemmer, Kenneth E.	1928
Leverenz, Erwin F.	1946-47-48
Levine, Edward M.	1945
Levy, Robert H.	1929-30
Lewis, Chris	1990
Limberg, Wayne	1924-25
Lione, Richard G.	1951
Liskovec, Joseph J.	1921
Logterman, Jason	1997
Loker, Donald	1961-62-63
Loker, Jeffery	1981-82-83
London, Michael	1993-94
Long, John	1988-89
Loring, Chris	1974-75
Lovshin, Ralph J.	1931-32-33
Lueck, Eric	1988-89, 91-92
Luetzow, Thomas	1981-82
Lunde, Einar H.	1929, 31
Lyndgaard, Daniel	1973-74-75-76
Lysne, Osborne	1929

M

Mack, Tom A.	1954-55
Maddux, Troy	1988
Maercklein, Leslie A.	1960-61
Maleckar, William R.	1918, 20
Malisch, William R.	1938-39-40
Malley, David	1974, 76
Mancheski, Alvin F.	1947
Mangual, Marcel	1971-72-73
Manley, P. Michael	1963-64
Mansfield, David	1972-73
Mansfield, Jack C.	1953-54-55-56
Mansfield, Richard	1979-80-81-82
Mansfield, Robert A.	1949
Mars, Walter A.	1950-51-52
Martell, Dean	1969-70
Martin, Cecil	1997
Martin, Charles	1945
Martin, Paul	1978
Martin, Roderick	1980
Mason, Mason	1899
Matsushima, Glenn	1983
Mattes, Troy J.	1986-87-88-89
Matthews, Austin R.	1915
Matzdorf, Patrick	1970-71-72
Mauer, Bruno J.	1953-54
Mautz, Alex	1996
Mavis, Arnold H.	1949
Mayer, John P.	1927-28, 30
Mayo, Brad	1987-88-89
McAndrews, Harry	1924-25
McClure, Leslie W.	1921
McConnell, Dwight F.	1952
McCullough, Scott	1980-81-82
McDuffie, James	1981-82-83
McEachron, Edgar J.	1901-02-03-04
McFadzean, James C.	1941-42-43
McGinnis, Charles	1925-26-27
McGinnis, Rolland S.	1953
McGinnis, Samuel M.	1957-58
McGiveran, Stanley	1924-25
McGowan, Francis C.	1898-99-1900-01
McGrath, James E.	1963
McHugh, William P.	1953-54
McKinney, Daniel E.	1958-59
Mead, Edwin P.	1923-mgr.
Mecartney, Malcolm	1919-20
Mehl, Walter J.	1937-38-39
Menon, James	1993-94-95-96
Mercer, Joseph D.	1911
Merrick, Dale M.	1920-21-22
Messmer, John	1906-07-08
Mett, Frederick P.	1931-32
Meyer, Edmond F.	1935, 37
Meyer, Tim	1992
Meyers, Tilden P.	1949-50
Michell, Jerome	1931
Miehe, Mark	1975-76-77-78
Milcher, Thomas A.	1953, 55
Miller, Richard J.	1960, 62
Minton, Maurice	1933
Mitchell, Royce	1990-91
Mobley, Basil	1921
Moe, Harold	1928-29
Moeller, Ralph H.	1938-39
Mohr, Charles	1962-63
Mohrhusen, Jerome W.	1935
Molter, Daniel	1978-79
Monfore, Thomas E.	1952-53-54
Montalbano, Alfred J.	1963-64-65
Moody, Ralph E.	1913
Moreau, Richard	1941-42-43
Morrison, Eric	1990-91-92-93
Moss, Richard	1974-75-76-77
Mountain, Josh	1993
Moyar, Timothy	1984
Mucks, Arlie M.	1915-16
Mueller, Paul G.	1907
Muenzer, Richard C.	1933
Mughal, Tariq	1973-74-75-76
Muller, Stephan E.	1962-63
Mulrooney, Robert W.	1976-77-78
Munson, John B.	1946-47-48
Murdaugh, Charles A.	1936
Murei, Michael	1976-77-78
Murphy, Patrick	1969
Murphy, Robert T.	1930-31-32
Murphy, W. Beverly	1928
Myers, Bobby	1997
Mylin, Samuel K.	1956-57-58
Myrland, Arthur L.	1913

N

Nash, Clyde	1918, 20-21
Neely, Lance	1996-97
Nelson, Alf	1976
Nelson, James W.	1961-62-63
Nelson, Leslie V.	1915
Nelson, Vernon A.	1946
Nelson, William R.	1967
Neupert, Lawrence O.	1929
Newberry, William	1995
Newell, Foster S.	1923
Newsome, Tom	1987
Nichols, G.D.	1921
Nichols, Thomas C.	1921-22-23
Nickels, James	1970-71-72
Niemuth, Dave	1983-84-85, 87
Nixon, Jesse	1957-58-59
Novak, Ruissell	1940-41
Nowka, Kurt	1980-81
Nowotny, Glenn J.	1931-32
Nyquist, Matt	1994-95

O

O'Dea, Pat	1897-98
Odomes, Nate	1985-86-87
O'Gara, Michael	1930
Oglesby, Kevin	1987-88
Olson, Roy W.	1957
Onyango, Patrick	1971-72-73
Owens, Fred	1988

P

Padway, Milton	1937-38-39
Pahlmeyer, Ralph B.	1926-27-28
Pamperin, John F.	1958
Pansch, Norman F.	1932-mgr.
Paoli, Joe	1983
Parker, John F.	1959-60
Parker, Ward S.	1934-35-36
Paschong, William G.	1929
Paskvan, George	1940-41
Patrowicz, Bill	1990-91
Patterson, Raymond A.	1944
Patterson, Robert C.	1963-64
Paukner, Robert A.	1943
Payne, John J.	1927
Peat, Arnulfo	1991-92-93-94
Peck, Edward C.	1945
Perry, Claude S.	1914
Perry, Russell L.	1925
Perusse, Roland I.	1943
Petaja, John W.	1927-28
Peters, Adolph C.	1909
Peters, Finsley L.	1951
Peters, Michael J.	1961
Peters, Shawn R.	1986-87-88-89
Peters, Thomas E.	1956, 58
Peterson, Barney L.	1964-65-66
Peterson, David	1968-69-70
Peterson, James D.H.	1918
Peterson, Joel E.	1958
Peterson, Richard A.	1964
Phebus, Doug	1991, 93
Pick, Philip E.	1937
Pickell, Jared K.	1951-52-53
Pierce, Maurice	1910-11
Pingle, Allen	1944
Piper, George A.	1924-25
Pittlemann, Irving W.	1944-45
Pitts, Eugene L.	1941
Pitts, Terrance L.	1960-61-62
Platten, Peter M.	1921-22-23
Plitt, Eugene T.	1955
Plummer, Ross	1976-77-78
Poage, George C.	1902, 04
Polley, Steven	1976
Poole, Rickey L.	1966-67-68
Pratt, George F.	1937-38
Presney, Doug	1983-84
Pride, Douglas E.	1962-63-64
Prosser, Stephan	1970
Purtell, Joseph P.	1929
Pyre, Augustin	1933

Q

Quandt, John G.	1958
Quarles, Charles	1905-06-07

Quigley, Thomas	1981-82-83

R

Raemisch, Mike	1988-89-90-91-92
Rakocy, James E.	1967
Ramsy, Wayne	1920, 22-23
Ramsey, William	1928
Randall, Mark	1975-76-77-78
Randolph, Jeffery	1976-77-78-79
Randolph, Mark	1981
Rappe, Timothy	1973-74-75-76
Ray, C. Harold	1918
Ray, Robert W.	1944
Read, John O.	1924
ReChord, John F.	1959
Reese, Terry	1989-90-91-92
Reid, Walker M.	1949-50
Reierson, Robert J.	1948
Reinhardt, Richard	1971-72, 74
Reinke, James R.	1955
Reitan, Tor V.	1962
Reynolds, Dennis	1978-79
Rich, Howard R.	1935-36-37
Richards, Arch E.	1909-10-11
Rideout, William L.	1906
Riekoff, Harvey	1970
Risch, Ronald R.	1957
Ritt, Steven	1977-78
Roberts, Beckley V.	1948-49-50
Roberts, Bruce	1979-80
Roberts, John C.	1925
Roby, Wayne	1983-84-85
Rodegier, Donald R.	1945
Roden, Edward W.	1931-32-33
Roden, Philip S.	1929
Rodgers, Matt	1997
Rogers, Paul B.	1905-mgr.
Rohn, Chester	1911
Rose, Brody	1996-97
Rossmeissel, Carl	1923
Rotter, Rudolph	1933-34
Rubow, Irving H.	1934-35-36
Ruenzel, Norman	1936
Ruiz, Ricardo	1938
Russell, David G.	1964-65
Ryser, Albert	1944

S

Saari, Howard	1976, 80
Sackett, Norman	1945, 47
Sander, Paul	1995
Sanders, Raymond Y.	1910-11
Sang, Mark	1975-76-77-78
Sather, Robert	1974-75-76-77
Saupe, Kurt	1983-84
Savage, Robert	1978-79
Schafer, William F.	1942
Schaldach, Fred A.	1957
Schardt, Arlie A.	1915-16-17
Scharnke, Robert	1970-71-72
Schauer, Wilbert	1947-mgr.
Schick, Roger D.	1962
Schlanger, Bernard	1935-36
Schley, Percy G.	1912-13-14
Schmidt, Eugene A.	1925
Schmidt, Frank W.	1950-mgr.
Schmidt, Warren	1936-37-38
Schmidt, Warren E.	1965-66
Schneider, Earl E.	1923-24
Schneider, Henry C.	1898
Schoenfelder, Jay	1997
Schoenike, Howard G.	1939-40-41
Schoensee, Phil	1985-86-88-89
Schrader, Roland R.	1926
Schrank, Ed S.	1916
Schuerman, Hilmer G.	1927
Schule, Frederick W.	1900
Schultzee, Max O.	1930
Schulz, Andy	1996
Schumacher, Jerry	1989-90-91-92-93
Schumacher, Thomas	1972-73-74, 76
Schumann, Robert W.	1946
Schutt, George A.	1925
Schwalbach, James A.	1934
Schwarze, Herbert	1925
Schwenger, Robert B.	1926-27
Scott, Alex	1946
Scott, Kim	1974-75-76-77-78
Seales, Maxwell	1995-96
Seaton, Edward A.	1912
Seiberlich, David B.	1964-65-66
Sengstock, David	1995-96
Sengstock, Greg	1979
Shaw, Theo W.	1930-31-32
Shelton, Rodney	1993
Sherburne, Craig B.	1967-68-69
Shomaker, Lawrence W.	1928-29
Shook, Richard W.	1946
Siefert, Jerry R.	1939
Silvis, Steven	1979-80-81
Simmons, H. Douglas	1930-31-32
Simmons, Tony	1994-95-96-97
Simon, Thomas	1997
Sisson, Mark	1980-81-82-83
Skelding, Jerome	1944
Slather, Thomas	1973-74
Smith, Bertram F.	1932-33-34
Smith, Bobby	1996-97
Smith, Carman	1915-16-17
Smith, David T.	1985-86
Smith, Edward J.	1938
Smith, Gilbert J.	1924-27-28
Smith, Ronald	1964
Smith, William R.	1962-63-64
Smithback, Jack P.	1983-84-85-86-87
Smits, Robert Jr.	1995-96
Soe, Donald J.	1950-51-52
Soergel, David G.	1941-42-43
Soutar, Douglas R.	1940
Spafford, Allen	1918-19-20
Springer, Ernest J.	1909
Stabb, Eric	1988-89-90-91
Stafford, Robert R.	1914-mgr.
Stalling, Reginald W.	1965-66-67
Stallworth, Andrew	1972-73-74-75
Stanley, Leotha	1975-76-77-78
Starch, Kenneth	1973-74-75
Statz, Charles W.	1957-58-59
Steenis, John H.	1930
Stelter, Robert M.	1986
Sterfield, James L.	1964
Stevens, Lester B.	1906-07
Stieve, Terrence	1973-74-75
Stiles, Jacy C.	1935-36
Stiles, Phil G.	1915
Stintzi, James	1977-78-79, 81
Stintzi, Joseph P.	1983, 85-86
Stoddard, Brian	1977-78
Stolley, George B.	1921-22
Stowe, Howard L.	1926-27-28
Strickland, David	1980
Stuewe, Herbert A.	1935-36
Sullivan, Scott	1995
Sullivan, William H.	1948-49-50
Sultze, Eugene A.	1953-54-55
Sutton, Daniel	1980
Sweeney, C. Donald	1932
Sykes, David	1980-81
Synold, Scott	1996-97

T

Tauber, David L.	1939-40-41
Taylor, William J.	1985
Terry, Joe	1988-89-90-91
Themar, Michael A.	1986-87-88-89
Theus, Floyd E.	1962-63
Thies, Thomas	1967-68-69
Thomas, Charles R.	1954-55-56
Thomas, Mike	1987
Thompson, A. McClure	1928, 1930-31
Thompson, Bjorn J.	1955-56
Thompson, James G.	1960
Thorton, Gary	1968-69-70
Thorpe, Charles V.	1967-68
Timmerman, Donald L.	1938, 1940-41
Toabe, Sidney L.	1943
Toennies, Mark	1982
Tommerson, Clarence L.	1935-36-37
Toon, Al	1982-83-84
Torian, Reggie	1994-95-96-97
Tormey, Albert	1912
Towle, William B.	1937-38-39
Towle, John O.	1941-42-43, 1946
Tressler, Willis	1926
Trosper, William	1972-73-74
Truschinski, Ryan	1994-95, 97
Tuhtar, Eugene W.	1923-24-25
Tullberg, Steven W.	1963-64-65
Tupurtis, Arnis	1974
Turriff, Rick	1981-82-83-84

U

Urech, Otto J.	1918
Urquardt, James D.	1949, 1951

V

Valley, Lloyd	1923-24-25
Vandermause, Michael	1977-78-79-80
VanderZanden, Matthew	1994-95-96-97
Vanderzee, Gould W.	1906
Vandrey, Donald	1969-70-71
Van Ells, Myron	1923
Vann, James	1974-75-76-77
Vann, Michael J.	1986-mgr.
Van Os, Ron	1979-80
Van Treba, Richard L.	1951
Van Wormer, Glen H.	1960, 1962
Veit, Brian	1995-96
Verbick, Donald J.	1956
Verbick, Robert	1984-85-86
Verbick, Todd E.	1985-86-87-88
Verchota, James W.	1945
Vicklund, Clarence A.	1944
Vierig, Donald A.	1938
Viktor, Joseph	1968-69-70
Vogt, Todd	1989-90-91, 93
Voigt, Stuart	1968-69-70
Volkey, Donald	1984
Voss, Donald P.	1952

W

Wade, Casey	1980-81
Wade, Gerald C.	1923
Wagner, Michael	1976
Wahl, Robert C.	1912-13-14
Wall, Mark H.	1920-21-22
Wallace, Steve	1986-87
Ward, Thomas R.	1951-52
Warriner, Adam	1988-89
Watson, Raymond R.	1946
Webster, Earl K.	1943-44-45
Weeks, Glen R.	1948-49-50

Weinert, James J.	1964-65-66
Weitzel, William W.	1947
Welch, Gerold O.	1950
Wetzel, Roland	1944
Whipple, Richard E.	1946-47-48-49
Whipple, Stephan D.	1965-66-67
White, Burton H.	1922-mgr.
White, Jason	1994
White, Josh	1993-94-95-96
Wiechmann, John K.	1935-36-37
Wilder, Lloyd L.	1921
Wilking, Werner E.	1952-53
Wille, Clarence W.	1922
Williams, Edward B.	1918
Williams, Gary	1972-73-74-75
Williams, Harvey	1945
Williams, Ray E.	1914-15-16
Williams, William F.	1940-41-42
Winzenried, Mark	1969-70-71
Wiskocil, Clement T.	1910
Witt, Gerold O.	1953
Wittig, Robert H.	1961
Wohlgemuth, John	1930
Wolff, Thomas	1972-73
Wright, George L.	1931-32-33
Wright, Kip	1984-85-86-87
Wrucke, Steve C.	1961, 1963
Wurlitzer, Raimund B.	1920-mgr.
Wyckoff, David	1973

Y

Yamada, Yoshio	1949
Yorkson, Thomas L.	1951
Young, Thomas	1970
Younglove, Michael	1981-82

Z

Zilsch, Howard W.	1927
Zobel, Roymond L.	1994-45-46
Zolin, Byron I.	1940-41-42
Zubrod, Lee	1989-90, 1992
Zur, Louis B.	1955

Men's Wrestling

A

Abad, Matt	1989-90
Abbott, James	/1973-74
Alf, Steve	1997
Allen, Patrick	1989-90
Anderson, John	1937-38-39
Anderson, Zach	1996-97
Andreae, Otto, Jr.	1938
Aschebrook, Gordon	1975-76-77
Austin, Stanley	1936-37

B

Babcock, W. J.	1918
Bach, Steven	1965
Bagnall, Lorne	1931
Baker, Robert	1937
Ballweg, Charles	1970
Barbaro, Anthony	1946-47
Barnes, Ervin	1966
Bartkowiak, Donald	1954-55-56
Baudhuin, Jim	1986
Beale, Elmer	1964-65-66
Beebe, Mark	1994-95-96-97
Beecher, Richard	1936
Behling, Dave	1984-85
Behling, Mark	1985
Bell, Nicholas	1980
Benbow, Robert	1923
Bennett, William	1941, 1946-47-48
Benskin, William	1976
Bergsbaken, Carlton	1953
Best, Steve	1993-94-95-96
Bestor, Glenn	1957
Beyer, James	1977
Beiberstein, Adolph	1923-24
Bigger, William	1944
Blackmore, Roger	1941
Boelk, John	1931
Bohman, Michael	1969
Brackett, Max	1927
Brandl, Doug	1994
Brandl, Paul	1958
Breineger, Mike	1978
Bridgeman, R.	1928
Brinkman, Robert	1970
Broming, George	1934
Brotzman, Bruce	1978, 1980, 1982
Burich, Bruce	1970
Busch, Alfred	1941-42

C

Callahan, Carroll	1931
Chada, Harvey	1925
Charland, Jeff	1982
Christenson, Pat	1973-74-75-76
Clauson, Kole	1997
Clayton, Mark	1985-86-87
Clough, Scott	1994, 1996-97
Cole, Allan	1936
Cole, John	1955-56-57
Cole, Wallace	1926
Corp, Paul	1933
Costanza, Samuel	1950-51-52
Coufal, Dusty	1996-97
Culver, Lucian	1920

D

Daemmrich, Otto	1947
Daly, Thomas	1985-86-87
Davies, Frank	1973-74
Davison, Keith	1990-91, 1993-94
De Witte, John	1947, 1949-50
Demaray, Matt	1989-90-91-92
Dolata, Paul	1936
Dowdell, Mike	1994
Drabenstadt, Doug	1987
Duerst, Steve	1979
Duus, Eric	1989
Dzirbik, Edward	1942-43-44

E

Edwards, Earle	1956-57-58
Elfner, Eliot	1960-61
Ensor, Steve	1982-83
Errthum, Mike	1995
Euker, Michael	1980-81-82-83
Evans, David	1976, 1978-79-80
Evans, Steven	1972, 1974-75-76
Evensen, Tony	1986-87-88
Evenson, Dan	1987-88-89-90

F

Falter, John	1950-51-52
Farness, Eric	1986
Farrison, Kim	1978
Ferguson, William	1932-33
Finer, George	1936
Fiore, Nick	1945
Fisher, Keith	1981-82-83
Fisher, Kevin	1981-82-83
Fitzpatrick, Tom	1987-88
Flood, Dan	1989-90-91-92
Flora, John	1958-59
Foster, Randall	1971
Fowler, Oakman	1923
Fox, Theodore	1952-53-54
Framsted, John	1971
Frokjer, Randy	1972

G

Gabert, August	1956, 1959
Galarnyk, John	1982
Geister, Chason	1995-96
Gerling, Paul	1931
Gerten, Henry	1995
Getlin, Lonney	1965-66-67
Gifford, Court	1994-95
Giura, John	1982-83-84-85
Gluck, Michael	1966-67-68
Goemans, George	1953
Goeters, Douglas	1962
Goldstein, Matt	1997
Gonzales, Lawrence	1971-72
Goodspeed, Dave	1979-80-81
Gorman, William	1958-59-60
Gorres, Larry	1969-70-71
Grabot, Thomas	1977
Gregor, George	1924
Grieb, William	1940
Grinde, Bob	1982
Griswold, Mike	1991-92-93
Grudzinski, Scott	1981
Guth, Jerry	1970-71-72-73
Gutknecht, Gary	1975

H

Haase, Randolph	1935-36
Hackbart, Bob	1981-82
Haddon, Steve	1993-94-95-96
Hafeman, Donald	1951
Hager, Earl	1941-42-43
Haines, James	1973-74-75, 1977
Halada, Jerome	1940
Hales, Myron	1929-30-31
Hamel, David	1957-58
Hammer, Ferdinand	1929-30
Hammes, Jack	1953
Hammes, Richard	1955-56-57
Hanley, Norman	1945
Hansen, Ronald	1971
Hanson, Elmer	1925
Hanson, James	1976-77-78-79
Hanutke, Matt	1992-93-94-95
Harms, John	1989-90-91-92
Hass, Gerald	1971
Hatch, Robert	1968
Haugen, Donald	1949
Hauser, Edward	1936
Heine, Kenneth	1968-69
Heinzelman, Joseph	1971-72
Heinzelman, Rick	1966-67-68
Heistad, Stephen	1976
Hellickson, Russ	1967-68-69-70
Helstad, Stephen	1976
Heuer, Wilbur	1923
Heywood, Leland	1929
Hill, Brian	1975
Hill, Donald	1952
Hill, Randy	1978
Hill,William	1945
Hiltbrand, Todd	1987
Hofer, Kenneth	1954
Hoffmann, Steve	1989-90-91-92
Hofman, Robert	1945
Holt, David	1927
Horswill, Craig	1973-74-75-76
Hoyer, Gale	1961

Hughes, Bill 1983-84-85-86
Hull, Marty 1983
Hull, Mitch 1978-79-80
Husted, Tom 1978-79
Huxhold, Terry 1958

I-J

Ianuzzi, John 1981
Innis, James 1959-60
Irick, Charles 1988-89-90-91
Ironside, Larry 1963
Isom, Rudy 1983-84-85
Jeidy, Ron 1974, 1976-77-78
Jerabek, Scott 1979-80
Jetton, Eric 1995-96-97
Jewell, Dennis 1977
Johnson, Brekke 1964-65-66
Johnson, Godfrey 1912
Johnson, Russell 1943
Johnson, Thomas 1940
Jones, Michael 1970-71
Jordan, Jeff 1985-86-87-88
Jordan, Jim 1983-84-85-86

K

Karan, Louis 1926
Karsten, Walter 1930
Kasakaitas, William 1934
Kaseguma, Robert 1953
Keigher, Greg 1996
Kelly, Jon 1990
Kemp, Lee 1975-76-77-78
Kipnis, Dennis 1980
Kissinger, Nyal 1971-72
Kleinhans, Jim 1978-79-80
Knoerr, David 1944
Knott, Arthur 1914
Knutilla, Raymond 1968-69-70-71
Konovsky, Robert 1954-55-56
Kopecky, Bob 1981
Krauss, Richard 1943
Kreuger, Lee 1989-90
Kroner, Ludwig 1968-69-70
Kruchowski, Steve 1978-79
Krueger, Donald 1949-50-51
Kruempelstaedter, James 1955-56-57
Krumrie, Tim 1981

L

Landry, Wallace 1915
Laurenzi, Dino 1951
Lawinger, Paul 1977-78
Lawinger, Rick 1971-72-73-74
Lawinger, Steve 1974-75-76
Lease, Pat 1982
Lederman, Lawrence 1936-37-38
Lee, David 1988-89
Leiskau, Peter 1970-71-72
Lessl, Robert 1949-50-51
Levihn, William 1953
Liegel, Ralph 1985-86-87
Lifsey, Benjamin 1986
Limmex, Dennis 1981-82-83
Limmex,Terry 1979
Lipton, Chad 1995-96-97
Llerandi, Felipe 1949, 1951
Lord, Ryan 1992-93-94-95
Lowe, James 1957, 1959
Loy, Marty 1982-83-84
Ludeman, Charlie 1981-82

M

Madigan, James 1943
Magnan, Cal 1984
Maher, Robert 1947
Mahoney, Joe 1995-96
Mandli, Paul 1950
Mandli, Ray 1981
Manning, Terry 1984-85-86
Marchionda, Rocco 1993-94
Martens, Robert 1940
Martin, Stephen 1963-64
Martino, Scott 1982
Mathews, Edward 1952, 1954-55
Mathias, Walter 1928-29-30
McDonald, Douglas 1988
McInnis, Michael 1970
McKernan, Michael 1987-88
McLeod, John 1960
McMurray, Ora 1921
McNeal, Charles 1958-59
McShane, Paul 1983-84-85, 1987
Mergen, Paul 1962-63
Merry, Donald 1939
Meyer, Harold 1927-28
Meyer, Robert 1979-80, 1982
Milek, Joseph 1963, 1965
Miller, Mike 1987-88-89-90
Minkow, David 192- mgr.
Miyagawa, Richard 1944
Modahl, Gerald 1958-59
Monroe, David 1966
Morris, John 1982-83-84
Morris, Rick 1978-79
Mory, Dean 1934
Mullendore, Arthur 1949
Munson, Earl 1955-56-57
Murphy, Michael 1985-86-87
Murphy, Richard 1955-56

N

Nalley, Richard 1963-64-65
Narveson, Marshall 1978
Neale, Ralph 1954-55-56
Nehrkorn, William 1961
Nettesheim, Dave 1946
Newbury, Kenneth 1937-38-39
Neyer, Neal 1980-81
Nicholas, Robert 1967-68-69
Niemuth, Nathan 1971
Nussbaum, Gerald 1951-52

O

O'Laughlin, Michael 1925
O'Neil, Lawrence 1951
Oberly, Lowell 1943, 1947-48
Oestreich, Berlyn 1934
Olsen, Donald 1957-58
Olsen, Richard 1957-58
Osterhoudt, Walter 1929
Ostrand, Herbert 1949

P

Paar, Ronald 1962-63-64
Paine, Charles 1945
Pape, Daniel 1995-96
Paulsen, Robert 1975
Pedersen, William 1954-55
Penager, Brett 1988-89
Pernat, Daniel 1964-65-66
Peterman, Ivan 1921-22
Peterson, James 1993
Peterson, Joseph 1947-48-49-50
Peterson, Paul 1947-48-49-50
Peterson, Phillip 1947
Pfeiffer, John 1940
Phillips, Chester 1937-38-39
Pieper, Ron 1991-92-93-94
Pillath, Roger 1962-63-64
Plenner, Earl 1924
Popp, William 1957-58-59
Potter, Steven 1967
Powell Robert 1963-64
Prchlik, Arthur 1951-52-53
Premo, Mark 1995
Price, James 1953
Ptacek, Michael 1962-63

Q

Quaglio, Mike 1995
Quale, Duane 1962
Quincannon, Francis 1937-38

R

Radandt, Victor 1951
Rate, John 1967
Rawhouser, Kent 1979-80-81
Reif, Robert 1952-53-54-55
Rein, Andy 1977-78-79-80
Reinwand, Jack 1973, 1975-76
Rhode, John 1933
Rice, Eric 1994
Rice, William 1945
Richards, Kyle 1984, 1986-87
Richman, Mark 1984-85-86
Rittschoff, Fredric 1959-60-61
Ritz, Erwin 1940-41-42
Roberts, Harry, Jr. 1963
Roberts, John 1940-41-42
Roberts, Ronald D. 1952
Robinson, William 1944, 1946-47-48
Roth, E. Walter 1918
Ryan, Donald 1950-51-52

S

Sackerson, John 1963-64
Saggau, Jeffery 1972, 1975
Saichek, Norman 1942
Salisbury, Edgar 1949-50
Sandner, John 1966
Schaefer, Lee 1952-53
Schank, Steve 1994-95
Schiller, Robert 1934
Schilling, Thomas 1982
Schmitz, Mark 1981-82-83-84
Schmook, Gary 1966-67
Schneider, Brian 1994-95-96-97
Schneider, Matt 1996
Schoeneman, Richard 1972
Schuele, David 1934
Schultz, Duane 1982
Sears, John 1958-59-60
Seeber, Luther 1952-53-54-55
Seiler, Todd 1985-86-87-88-89
Self, Clarence 1947-48-49
Shampo, George 1943-44
Sievertsen, Allen 1965-66-67
Silger, Paul 1976, 1977, 1979
Simonson, James 1954-55-56
Skaar, John 1971-72
Smith, Arthur 1927
Smith, Grant 1981-82
Smitz, Louis 1927
Sommer, Gary 1976, 77
Soucie, Laurent 1972-73-74-75
Spellman, Gene 1983-84-85-86
Spicuzza, Robert 1946-47-48-49-50
Spies, Dale 1971-72-73
Spilde, Dan 1990-91-92-93
Splees, William 1925-26
Stark, Aaron 1995-96-97
Stenback, Edwin 1932

Stetson, George 1928-29-30
Steson, Kenneth 1956, 1958
Stipek, Raymond 1925
Suhm, Frederick 1953
Sweeney, Tom 1990, 1993
Swenson, Selmer 1929-30-31

T
Tabet, John 1975-76
Templin, Edward 1921-22-23
Terry, Michael 1977-78-79
Terwilliger, Emmett 1934-35
Thornally, Richard S. 1942
Threinen, C. 1943
Tiffany, Albert 1928, 1930
Toman, Thomas 1960-61
Trachte, Jed 1994-95
Trapino, Robert 1976-77-78
Tyree, Burke 1990

U-V
Upthagrove, James 1957-58
Valley, Philip 1934
Van Dinter, Joey 1986-87
Vasby, Helmer 1934
Vatch, Edward 1972-73-74-75
Viskocil, Eddie 1946
Vissers, Glen 1973-74, 1977

W
Wade, Joseph 1971-72
Wahtola, Charles 1990-91-92-93
Walter, Chris 1992-93-94-95
Walter, Jeff 1992, 1994-95-96
Wanta, David 1985-86
Ward, Jack 1954
Watts, Richard 1971, 1973
Weber, Brian 1982
Weeks, Herbert 1920
Wendorf, Roger 1970-71-72
Wenzel, Fred 1935
Werkheiser, Brett 1995-96
Wilmot, Kevin 1994, 1996-97
Wirnsberger, John 1984, 1986
Witt, Robert 1943
Woods, John 1954
Wyss, Orville 1936

Z
Zander, Jerin 1997
Zimmer, Mark 1980
Zotner, Lyle 1924-25-26
Zur, Louis 1952, 1955

. . . .

Women's Badminton

A-B
Allison, Claire 1980-81-82-83
Bailin, Jill 1975-76-77-78
Biddappa, Meena 1979-80
Boxerman, Cathy 1982-83

C
Clark, Patty 1975-76
Colby, Sandy 1980-81-82-83
Cross, Reenie 1975-76-77-78

D-E
Dempsey, Jessica 1975-76- 77-78
Dirksen, Kathy 1977-78-79-80
Emmerich, Mary 1979-80-81

F
Farmer, Colleen 1974-75
French, Ann 1978-79-80-81-82
French, Linda 1982-83

G
Gage, Linda 1974-75-76-77-78
Gorz, Eileen 1975-76
Gorz, Kathy 1974-75

H
Hensey, Joan 1976-77-78
Hibnick, Andrea 1981-82
Hines, Jennifer 1979-80-81
Hoffman, Paula 1976-77
Hohmann, Mary 1979-80-81-82
Holmes, Debra 1979-80-81-82
Holmes, Janna 1981-82-83
Hosletter, Vicki 1975-76-77
Humes, Joanne 1981-82

J-K
Johnston, Corky 1976-77
Kelly, Colleen 1979-80
Kemberling, Barb 1979-80-81
Kneer, Barbara 1981-82
Kneuer, Cory 1979-80
Kobiship, Marian 1982-83
Kolb, Kris 1981-82
Kopp, Katie 1974-75

L-M
Lira, Rena 1979-80
Masak, Elizabeth 1981-82-83
Masak, Marian 1979-80-81-82
Mass, Joan 1974-75-76-77-78
Matzner, Jo 1981-82
Minda, Kari 1980-81-82
Munson, Peggy 1979-80-81

N-R
Naden, Gail 1974-75
Reilly, Tammy 1977-78-79-80

S-T
Scwarz, Marian 1979-80-81-82
Serwe, Kitty 1979-80
Smith. Jean 1976-77-78
Strell, Barb 1982-83
Tyser, Kimberly 1976-77-78

W-Z
Weis, Loni 1975-76
Wosisowski, Mary Ann 1976-77-78
Zembrosky, Caryn 1977-78

Women's Basketball

A
Adams, Andrea 1981-82-83-84-85
Ambruso, Debbie 1979-80-81
Amend, Stacy 1975-76
Anderson, Keisha 1994-95-96-97

B
Bauer, Amy 1988-89–90
Bertagnoli, Kim 1974-75
Bird, Krista 1997-98
Bolton, Tasha 1974-75
Bonnell, Lisa 1984-85-86-87-88
Bormett, Jean 1974-75-76
Boston, Tanisha 1995-96-97-98
Bostrom, Heather 1988-89-90-91, 1993
Boucher, Nikki 1986-87
Bourne, Michele 1989-90
Buhr, Bev 1974-75
Burkholder, Michele 1994-95-96-97-98

C
Calden, Martha 1974, 76-77
Camp, Kelley 1977-78-79
Cattanach, Karie 1993-94-95-96-97
Christenson, Sally 1974-75
Chrnelich, Mary 1982-83-84
Clark, Mynette 1988-89-90-91-92
Cleary, Christine 1995-96-97-98
Condon, Kristi 1974-75-76

D
Delaney, Julia 1986-87
Dillon, Kesa 1992-93-94-95
Drexler, Margaret 1986-87
Driver, Sheila 1983-84-85-86

E
Ebeling, Judy 1997-98
Edmonds, Gina 1987-88-89-90-91

F
Fahey, Nancy 1977-78-79-80-81
Finchem, Lizbeth 1981-82
Fischer, Michelle 1983-84-85-86-87
Fitzgerald, Lynne 1986-87
Franke, Barb 1991, 93-94-95
Fredrickson, Kay 1987-88-89-90-91
Fredrickson, Kim 1987-88-89-90-91

G
Galligan, Kathy 1975-76
Gough, Linda 1977-78-79-80-81
Grossman, Maike 1985-86

H
Hale, Verdell 1985-86-87-88
Hall, Ann 1978-79-80
Hallisy, Kris 1979-80-81-82-83
Hartwig, Jennah 1993, 95-96-97-98
Hastie, DeLinda 1985-86-87-88
Henkel, Heather 1993-94
Hogans, Phyllis 1977-78-79
Holloway, Maureen 1975-76
Hudson, Camilla 1983-84
Huff, Janet 1980-81-82-84
Huff, Theresa 1979-80-81-82-83
Hunt, April 1977-78

J
Jones, Carol 1979-80-81
Johnson, Becky 1974-75-76-77
Johnson, Faith 1980-81-82, 84-85
Johnson, Janetta 1988-89
Johnson, Sharon 1991-92-93-94-95

K
Kaiser, Kari 1996-97
Kamrath, Kathy 1987-88
Karst, Kerry 1978-79
Kennedy, Katie 1993-94
Klapperich, Ann 1994-95-96-97-98
Klongland, Rachel 1997-98
Konieczny, Missy 1996-97-98
Kozelka, Michele 1988-89-90-91-92
Kroening, Lori 1980-81
Kurilla, Jody 1980-81

L
Landrigan, Amber 1989-90, 92-93
Lawrence, Lisa 1987-88-89-90-91

Lederer, Anne	1983-84
Leet, Rebecca	1990-91-92-93
Leinfelder, Kelly	1985-86-87
Lorenzen, Lorraine	1977-78-79-80
Lowman, Michelle	1978, 80-81-8283

M

Martin, Kim	1992-93
Mason, Ellen	1974-75-76-77
McLean, Liz	1978-79-80
McMullen, Carmella	1984-85
Millhouse, Marsha	1984-85-86
Moore, Pam	1977-78

O-P

O'Malley, Karen	1985-86-87-88
Parduhn, Teena	1975-76
Pate, Dee Dee	1996-97-98
Paulus, Kelley	1996-97-98
Prince, Vicki	1984-85-86-87
Pruitt, Chris	1981-82-83-84-85
Purcell, Joan	1974-75-76-77

R

Rademaker, Dolly	1990-91-92-93-94
Rhodes, Jenny	1994-95-96-97-98
Ricter, Emily	1996-97-98
Riemer, Stacy	1993-94-95-96-97
Rorer, Vivian	1980-81-82
Ross, Carol	1975-76
Rucinski, Shelly	1986-87-88-89-90
Rudigor, Jennifer	1975-76

S

Saeman, Anne	1976-77-78-79
Scott, Carol	1976-77-78
Scott, Megan	1983-84
Scotten, Jennifer	1988-89-90
Shreve, Peggy	1989-90-91-92-93
Sielaff, Linda	1981-82
Sims, LaTonya	1997-98
Skarr, Jane	1983-84
Slovak, Cindy	1982-83-84-85-86
Smith, Carolyn	1977-78
Stoffel, Helen	1986-87
Stuessy, Linda	1982-83-84

T

Theder, Teresa	1981-82-83-84-85
Threatt, Robin	1988-89-90-91-92-93
Tringali, Sue	1975-76

V

Voigt, Katie	1993-94-95-96, 98
Vorwald, Ginny	1976-77-78-79-80
Voss, Kari	1996-97

W

Waterman, Jen	1989-90-91-92-93
Westphal, Jenni	1994-95
Whalen, Dot	1976-77-78-79-80
Wiersma, Amy	1995-96-97-98
Williams, Camille	1991-92-93-94-95
Winkler, Tracy	1992-93-94-95

Y-Z

Young, Inga	1984-85-86-87
Zorr, Cathy	1977-78-79
Zuehlke, Anne	1976-77-78-79

Women's Cross Country

A

Agnew, Sue	1978-79
Alexander, Allegra	1989-90

B

Bassett, Stephanie	1984-85-86-87-88
Bebow, Chris	1978-79
Beer, Tara	1989-90
Benson, Rhonda	1975-76
Billingsley, Marty	1977-78-79
Borgwarth, Nina	1987-88
Branta, Cathy	1981-82-83-84-85
Breighner, Tammy	1987-88-89
Bremser, Cathy	1976-77-78-79
Bremser, Cindy	1974-75-76
Brunner, Maryann	1980-81
Burke, Randee	1974-75
Butler, Kathy	1994-95-96

C

Cheney, Megan	1990-91-92
Christiansen, Birgit	1983-84-85-86
Class, Paula	1977-78
Cote, Julie	1993-94-95
Cote, Nathalie	1993- 94-95

D

Deatherage, Jenelle	1995-96-97-98
Docter, Sarah	1983-84-85
Dressel, Lisa	1989-90-91

E

Eichner, Clare	1988-89-90-91-92-93
Eppers, Agnes	1991-92-93

F

Fairchild, Joan	1978-79
Favor, Suzy	1986-87-88-89-90-91
Frederick. Patti	1982- 83-84
Fredrickson, Sara	1993-94, 96-97-98

G

Gentes, Sue	1989-90-91
Goepel, Chris	1987-88
Grove, Sandi	1979-80, 82-83
Gutierrez, Valerie	1975-76

H

Harris, Carole	1986-87-88-89
Harris, Esther	1987-88
Harris, Karen	1982-83-84-85-86
Hartzheim, Mary	1986-87-88-89-90-91
Hartzheim, Maureen (Gordy)	1986-87-88-89
Heinemann, Beth	1982-83
Herbst, Stephanie	1984-85-86-87
Hering, Holly	1984-85-86-87
Hinton, Pam	1988-89
Hintz, Sarah	1981-82
Houston, Suzie	1977-78-79-80-81
Howe, Amy	1988-89
Howard, Jennifer	1991-92-93-94-95-96

I

Ironside, Heather	1992-93
Ishmael, Katie	1982-83-84-85-86

J

Johns, Amy	1979-80, 82-83
Johnston, Anne	1980-81-82-83

K

Kauls, Kim	1987-88
Kraeger, Jenny	1991-92
Kroeger, Sho	1994-95-96-97-98
Kubly, Nissa	1994-95-96-97
Kujak. Angi	1994-95-96-97-98
Kulbel, Jaime	1995-96

L

Lefebvre, Kathy	1983-84-85-86
Lewis, Marta	1980-81
Luebbering, Teri	1975-76-77-78
Lumley, Michele	1984-85-86

M

McElwee, Marty	1976-77-78-79-80
McKillen, Kelly	1983-84-85-86-87
Millington, Pam	1974-75
Moran, Jane	1977-78
Morin, Lynn	1975-76-77-78-79
Mulrooney, Ann	1976-77-78-79-80

O

Oftedahl, Kiz	1981-82
Olson, Ellen	1981-82-83-84
Ostrem, Francine	1981-82

R

Ranfranz, Lynn	1980-81
Rawling, Heather	1990-91-92
Reneke, Johanna	1983-84-85
Renk, Sarah	1991-92-93
Revak, Julie	1989-90-91- 92-93
Richards, Mary Jane	1996-97
Ripp, Michelle	1992-93-94
Ripp, Sara	1974-75
Rusk, Katie	1974-75-76-77-78

S-T

Schleuter, Nancy	1974-75
Snowbeck, Robin	1993-94
Schaefer, Becky	1996-97-98
Schmidt, Mary	1974-75
Siebers, Carol	1977-78
Spencer, Marybeth	1975-76-77-78-79
Stepka, Mary	1978-79-80-81
Sveum, Angie	1988-89-90
Thomson, Rose	1979-80-81-82-83

V

Van Os, Carol	1981-82
Verway, Anne	1985-86

W

Wagner, Pat	1974-75
Walden, Kathy	1975-76-77
Walsh, Molly	1992-93-94
Walters, Avrie	1997-98
Watson, Jennifer	1993-94
Weltzer, Lisa	1997-98
Westphal, Janet	1994-95-96-97-98
Westphal, Jenni	1995-96-97-98
Wickus, Amy	1992-93-94-95
Wilson, Marta	1980-81-82
Wolter, Lori	1985-86-87-88

Z

Zickert, Pat	1979-80
Zook, Sally	1978-79-80-81

Women's Fencing

A

Al-Attas, Sharifa	1988-89-90-91
Allyn, Julie	1988-89

B

Bartholomew, Candy	1987-88
Beidel, Karen	1974-75-76-77-78
Birnbaum, Nina	1977-78

Both, Margaret	1974-75-76-77-78
Burgo, Sue	1988-89-90-91-92

C-D

Cole, Jenny	1988-89-90-91
Copeland, Mary	1980-81-82-83
Daugherty, C.	1990-91

F-G

Feil, Katherine	1987-88
George, Judith	1987-88
Gibson, Ellen	1976-77
Girard, Lorna	1976-77-78-79-80
Griffin, Maureen	1983-84-85-86

H

Hamilton, Holly	1979-80-81-82-83
Hamori, Isabelle	1983-84-85-86
Hanson, Macayla	1988-89-90-91
Herdeman, Laura	1974-75

J-K-L

Janssen, Margery	1976-77
Kuck, Irene	1985-86
Lardner, Emily	1975-76

M

Menke, Joan	1977-78-79-80-81
Monplaisir, Sharon	1978-79

R

Reeves, Anne	1981-82-83
Ristau, Shelley	1975-76-77
Roth, Jane	1980-81-82-83-84

S-T

Schnurrer, Julie A.	1978-79-80
Seiling, Lisa	1974-75-76
Shier, Liz	1974-75-76
Sperling, Debbie	1985-86-87-88-89
Sperling, Nancy	1983-84-85-86-87
Stenberg, Katherine	1985-86-87-88
Terletzky, Patricia	1986-87

W-Y

Wagner, Jeanne	1988-89-90-91
Warden, Karen	1980-81-82-83-84
Weisgerber, Georganne	1981-82-83
Yee, Jean	1985-86

Women's Field Hockey

B-C

Bormett, Jean	1973-74-75
Cain, Cecelia	1979-80
Canales, Mary	1979-80
Carlson, Michele	1974-75-76-77
Chansky, Linda	1973-74
Christiansen, Sally	1973-74-75
Cook, Mari	1975-76-77-78-79
Cook, Theresa	1975-77-78-79-80
Cox, Ellen	1974-75-76-77
Curtain, Virginia	1975-76-77-78-79

D-E

Dronzek, Laura	1979-80
Elsner, Kate	1976-77-78-79
Ernest, Melissa	1977-78-79-80
Erwin, Trudy	1973-74

F-H

Farmer, Colleen	1973-74-75-76
Firchow, Katherine	1976-77-78
Fischer, Claudia	1973-74
Fox, Nancy	1973-74
Fulton, Gail	1976-77-78-79
Galko, Mary	1978-79
Hagerman, Margaret	1974-75

J-K

Jensen, Carey	1976-77
Knowles, Elizabeth	1977-78-79
Knutson, Debbie	1975-76
Krainik, Sara	1975-76-77-78-79
Kraus, Stephanie	1977-78

L

Langa, Diane	1977-78-79-80
Luehmann, Marlene	1973-74
Lunda, Karen	1977-78-79-80

M

Mallaney, Maura	1977-78-79-80
Mass, Joan	1976-77
Miller, Jeni	1979-80
Murtha, Ellie	1978-79-80

P

Pearce, Helen	1978-79
Peterson, Connie	1974-75

R

Rapp, Maggie	1973-74-75-76
Richardson, Dorah	1974-75
Rivkin, Debra	1979-80
Rynning, Carol	1979-80

S

Schuessler, Julie	1973-74-75-76
Schwabe, Corky	1976-77
Sheehan, Peggy	1976-77

V-Y

Van Winkle, Hope	1973-74-75-76
Waite, Kathy Waite	1973-74
Waite, Robin Waite	1974-75
Yeaton, Susan Yeaton	1978-79-80

Women's Golf

A-B

Amacher, Carrie	1978-79
Becker, Laura	1977-78-79-80-81
Bleyhl, Laura	1991-92-93-94
Blomquist, Allison	1997-98
Bobber, Sheri	994-95-96-97-98
Brewster, Ann	1974-75-76-77
Brown, Erika	1992-93-94-95-96C-D

C-D

Casper, Barb	1980-81-82
DeWulf, Julie	1986-87-88-89-90
Doble, Lisa	1986-87-88-89-90

E-F

Erickson, Dana	1994-95-96
Fitzgerald, Katie	1990-92-93-94
Fox, Jacquie	1984-85-86
Fox, Julie	1985-86
Frohna, Patty	1995-96-97-98

G

Grant, Leslie	1992-93-94
Genda, Sheli	1984-85-86

H

Hackbarth, Jeanne	1982-83-84 85-86
Herron, Alissa	1992-93-94-95
Hockenberry, Cindy	1977-78
Huxhold, Lisa	1979-81-82-83

J

Johnson, Julie	1994-95
Julson, Karen	1974-75-76-77-78

L

Levenhagen, Katy	1981-82, 83-84
Lindsay, Debbie	1974-75

M

Mabie, Rheba	1995-96-97
Macius, Allison	1987-88-89-90
Marting, Beth	1995-86-87-88-89
Mathews, Nancy	1977-78-79
Meeker, Andrea	1996-97-98

N

Narowetz, Erica	1990-91-92-93
Nehs, Holly	1988-89-90-91

P

Pirk, Breinnan	1995-96-97
Plantz, Debbie	1988-89-90
Prieve, Katie	1997-98

R

Ravn, Mary	1975-76-77
Regenberg, Chris	1978-79-80-81-82
Reynoldson, Jill	1975-76
Rudnicki, Connie	1979-80-81-82-83
Rudolf, Liz	1989-90-91-92-93

S

Schnarr, Darby	1994-95-96
Shanahan, Julie	1985-86
Sipla, Marcy	1987-88-89-90-91
Smith, Jennifer	1975-76
Steggerman, Peggy	1976-77

T

Tallard, Chris	1976-77-77-78-79
Tamayo, Monica	1982-83-84-85-86
Tiziani, Nicki	1987-88-89-90-91
Trader, Barb	1975-76
Trapp, Kelly	1996-97-98
Tzakis, Dana	1992-93-94-95
Tzakis, Laura	1996-97

W

West, Karen	1983-84-85-86
White, Cathy	1980-81-82-83-84
Wiese, Rachel	1992-93-94

Z

Zimmerman, Julie	1975-76-77-78
Zimmerman, Kay	1985-86-87-88
Zimmerman, Lori	1983-84-85-86

Women's Rowing

A

Abbott, Jeanne	1979-80
Alioto, Sue	1979-80
Allen, Gail	1980-81
Anderson, Linnea	1990-91-92-93
Aserlind, Kristy	1976-77-78-79

B

Baehmann, Linda	1988-89-90-91-92
Baumgartner, Jill	1996-97-98
Bakken, Val	1997-98
Berger, Chris	1987-88

Berninger, Jo Ann	1979-80-81
Blanding, Mary Beth	1985-86-87-88
Bogdanow, Janet	1982-82-83-84
Bosio, Beth	1975-76-77
Bott, Suzan	1976-77-78
Bradley, Barbara	1977-78
Buckley, Nora	1992-93

C

Calvert, Margaret	1986-87
Canova, Emily	1988-89
Cartwright, Jill	1996-97-98
Clark, Maura	1987-88
Codner, Christy	1996-97-98
Cohen, Sharone	1997-98
Collins, Mary	1997-98
Connell, Mary	1974-75-76-77
Conway, Kara	1996-97
Cox, Sara	1995-96
Cruz, Chris	1977-78-79

D

Daley, Shannon	1992-93
Dinkel, Tamara	1992-93-94-95-96
Dolan, Emily	1988-89
Drissel, Katy	1983-84-1985-86
Dunai, Carey	1987-88-89

E

Ebert, Beth	1978-79
Ebert, Rebecca	1995-96
Eckert, Chris	1984-85-86
Elas, Karen	1974-75-76-77
Ela, Susan	1974-75
Escher, Tiffany	1988-89

F

Fahien, Lisa	1985-86
Falivena, Michelle	1987-88
Farooq, Yasmin	1985-86-87-88
Farrell, Emily	1996-97-98
Feeney, Carol	1983-84-85-86
Folk, Torrey	1995-96-97

G

Gandt, Ellen	1980-81
Gengler, Sarah	1983-84-85-86
Getka, Ann	1995-96-97-98
Gilroy, Jane Kovacevich	1996-97
Gitter, Theresa	1980-81-82
Graf, Laura	1985-86
Graven, Krista	1976-77, 1979-80
Graves, Allison	1981-82-83
Graves, Carie	1974-75-76
Grutzner, Heide	1979-80-81-82
Gundersen, Catherine	1992-93

H

Haberman, Kathy	1984-85-86
Haberman, Rita	1985-86
Hageman, Anne	1982-83
Hageman, Marcia	1982-83
Halvorsonm, Janet	1978-79-80
Haning, Molly	1997-98
Hanson, Julie	1980-81
Harrison, Lois	1977-78
Hartman, Signe	1985-86
Hasz, Barb	1978-79-80
Havice, Elizabeth	1997-98
Hegge, Carolyn	1975-76-77-78
Helke, Katherine	1987-88-89
Heinen, Jenny	1981-82
Herink, Nicosia	1993-94-95-96
Hillmann, Kate	1996-97-98
Holbeck, Kirsten	1997-98
Hope, Katie	1996-97-98
Hope, Kirsten	1996-97-98
Hospel, Mia	1990-91-92-93
Hoyt, Rebecca	1996-97-98
Huang, Wen	1992-93
Huebner, Beth	1995-96
Hughes, Jessica	1995-96
Huhn, Lisa	1995-96
Humphrey, Melissa	1997-98

I-J

Iverson, Melissa	1991-92
Jahnke, Sarah	1986-87-88
Jenz, Jodie	1992-93-94-95
Johnson, Kim	1996-97-98

K

Kacvinsky, Sarah	1993-94-95-96
Kartman, Kari	1990-91
Keggi, Mara	1981-82-83-84
Kelly, Debbie	1977-78-79
Kelly, Judith	1979-80
Kiltz, Linda	1985-86
Knight, Mary Grace	1975-76-77
Konyn, Shannon	1996-97-98
Kouba, Sara	1994-95
Kowal, Mandi	1982-83-84-85
Kraft, Jane	1996-97
Krohn, Amy	1984-85-86

L

Lambrecht, Amy	1994-95
Landry, Carla	1982-83
Lay, Angela	1997-98
Leslie, Deanna	1990-91
Liberman, Lynn	1982-83-84
Luchsinger, Amy	1977-78-79
Ludwig, Jane	1977-78-79-80-81
Lyng, Sara	1997-98

M

Macaulay, Laura	1988-89-90-91-92
Macfarlane, Laura	1996-97-98
Maloney, Ann	1985-86-87
Maloney, Tracey	1994-95
Markwart, Sarah	1994-95
Martin, Amy	1988-89
Mathisen, Amy	1994-95-96
McCarthy, Peggy	1975-76-77-78
McRae, Melissa	1994-95
Mejia, Micaela	1990-91
Menendez, Polly	1980-81
Mesman, Kristine	1979-80
Miller, Tamara	1997-98
Milner, Carol	1974-75
Mintz, Sandie	1985-86-87-88
Mitchell, Andrea	1992-93
Mohs, Sarah	1991-92-93
Montesi, Sue	1984-85-86
Mork, Pamela	1990-91-92-93
Mork, Suzannah	1996-97-98
Morreale, Rose	1981-82-83
Mullen, Karen	1990-91-92-93

N-O

Nelson, Jennifer	1994-95
Nemson, Amy	1995-96-97-98

Norcross, Laurie 1996-97
O'Connor, Mareen 1991-92
Oetzel, Debbie 1974-75-76-77-78
Offerdahl, Susan 1981-82
Olesch, Elizabeth 1985-86

P
Peters, Carrie 1990-91
Phelan, Meghan 1995-96-97-98
Piaquadio, Monica 1978-79
Pingree-Hawkins, Paisley 1995-96
Plac , Kathy 1983-84-85
Plambeck, Erica 1990-91-92-93
Plummer, Melissa 1992-93
Ponti, Catherine 1991-92
Potter, Carolyn 1983-84-85-86

R
Rademacher, Jyll 1997-98
Reis, Charil 1995-96
Rewolinski, Ellen 1996-97
Rodetsky, Rachel 1981-82
Roessel, Stacey 1997-98
Rosenburg, Rebecca 1990-91
Ross, Gail 1980-81
Rudolf, Ulrike 1990-91
Rufenacht, Tynille 1996-97-98

S
Santiago, Kim 1981-82-83-84-85-86
Schaefer, Barb 1974-75
Schindhelm, Jill 1996-97
Schuler, Amy 1983-84
Shonk, Kitty 1994-95
Slewitzke, Ann 1982-83
Smilikis , Katherine 1992-93
Smith, Kristin 1981-82
Stepien, Becky 1980-81
Stetzer, Sallie 1987-88
Steuck, Marge 1977-78-79
Stoddard, Emily 1991-92
Stuckman, Becky 1997-98
Sturino, Jenny 1997-98

T
Thistle, Jodie 1996-97-98
Thoenig, Lucia 1990-91
Thorsness, Kris 1979-80-81-82
Tietjen, Sue 1981-82-83-84
Topp, Kathy 1995-96-97
Towne, Chari 1979-80-81-82
Traci, Beth 1994-95
Traut, Beth 1974-75

U-V-W
Utrie, Gina 1995-96
Vaughn, Anna 1996-97-98
Vrabec, Mary 1982-83
Waschbusch, Kristen 1991-92
Weisbrod, Gwen 1987-88-89
Woelfel, Heidi 1996-97

Y
Yankowski, Marge 1984-85-86
Yankula, Katie 1987-88
Yuan, Vivian 1988-89

Z
Zabkowicz, Tara 1996-97
Zanichkowski, Elizabeth 1974-75
Zink, Kendra 1993-94-95-96-97
Zinniel, Kim 1990-91-92-93
Zoch, Jackie 1975-76

Women's Soccer

A
Afsari, Nahid 1994-95-96-97
Anderson, Jill 1984-85-86
Angevine, Julie 1984-85-86-87
Arndt, Chrissy 1994-95

B
Bakcs, Kim 1986-87-88-89
Barbian, Jaime 1997-98
Baxter, Liz 1988-89-90-91-92
Billet, Jackie 1992-93-94-95-96
Brackett, Mary 1983-84-85-86
Brandt, Gretchen 1992-93
Brennan, Ruth 1994-95-96-97-98
Brown, Shannon 1995-96-97-98
Buckalew, Mary 1984-85

C
Cardelle, Amy 1985-86-87-88-89
Cartes, Allison 1985-86-87
Coats, Chris 1982-83-84
Coole, Michelle 1988-89-90-91-92
Cokins, Becky 1981-82-83-84
Coplin, Kerri 1987-88-89-90-91
Crownhart, Betsy 1981-82

D
De Giovanni, Maria 1995-96-97-98
Detmer, Catharine 1981-82
Dobesh, Megan 1997-98

E-F
Elliott, Katy 1983-84-85-86-87
Falk, Sheila 1983-84-85-86-87
Farnsworth, Amy 1982-83
Fass, Nancy 1981-82-83
Fessel, Chris 1981-82
Fiore, Beth 1981-82
Foy, Morna 1981-82-83-84-85
Frommer, Meredith 1993-94-95-96-97
Fruth, Kathy 1981-82

G
Gallegher, Erin 1982-8384-85-86
Gassert, Emily 1995-96-97-98
Gehrke, Shelly 1987-88-89-90-91
Gjerset, Sue 1985-86-87-88-89
Grafing, Mindy 1984-85-86-87-88
Grussendorf, Chris 1987-88

H
Hackett, Molly 1996-97
Haigh, Jenny 1992-93-94-95-96
Har, Sue 1984-85-86-87-88
Hamblet, Denise 1986-87
Handelman, Erica 1990-91-92-93-94
Hawksin, Michelle 1997-98
Hermberg, Kim 1992-93
Hill, Jennifer 1989-90-91-92
Hoelter, Lindsay 1995-96-97-98
Holmes, Val 1984-85-86-87
Holt, Susie 1990-91-92-93-94
Humphrey, Tina 1982-83-84

J
Johanson, Karen 1984-85-86
Johnson, Chris 1986-87-88-89
Johnson, Julie 1993-94-95-96-97
Johnson, Kris 1988-89-90
Jones, Jennifer 1994-95

K
Keinz, Laura 1985-86-87-88-89
Keller, Jaime 1996-97-98
Kerber, Ann 1995-96-97
Kopmeyer, Margaret 1989-90-91-92
Kraeger, Jenny 1988-89-90-91
Kretchman, Kari 1985-86
Krusing, Jennifer 1986-87-88-89-90

L
Larson, Beth 1983-84-85
Lavers, Ansley 1996-97-98
Lee, Lisa 1983-84-85-86-87
Levine, Becky 1995-96-97
Lewis, Martha 1991-92-93
Little, Nicole 1995-96-97-98
Lubcke, Emily 1996-97-98
Lunda, Karen 1981-82

M
Maier, Carrie 1990-91-92-93-94-95
Maier, Heather 1993-94-95-96-97
Maijala, Kari 1988-89-90-91-92
Malen, Kelly 1988-89-90-91
Mandick, Chris 1981-82
McCaffrey, Kit 1988-89-90-91-92
McKnight, Ursula 1993-94-95-96-97
Mickey, Annette 1986-87-88-89-90
Mickey, Michelle 1984-85-86-87-88
Miguel, Teresa 1990-91
Miller, Jeni 1981-82-83-84-85
Miller, Mandi 1996-97
Miller, Mara 1996-97-98
Miller, Marci 1994-95-96
Moeller, Karen 1987-88-89-90
Moynihan, Sue 1986-87

N
Newinski, Janet 1990-91-92-93-94
Nordman, Cathy 1981-82-83-84

P
Parker, Karen 1982-83-84-85-86
Patraw , Terri 1987-88-89-90-91
Phalen, Helene 1987-88
Phelen, Dorothy 1981-82
Pierson, Holly 1992-93-94
Potter, Leslie 1984-85 86-87
Prestigiacomo, Becky 1994-95-96-97
Priester, Heather 1996-97-98

R
Rademacher, Laura 1993-94-95-96
Reese, Katy 1992-93-94-95-96
Rogosheske, Allison 1997-98
Russ, Tanya 1988-89-90-91-92

S
Sarles, Anne 1981-82
Schaidler, Cathy 1990-91
Scheidler, Mary 1996-97-98
Schwarting, Briget 1996-97-98
Sella, Monica 1981-82
Senn, Theresa 1982-83-84
Serebin, Sandy 1981-82
Shaw, Cathy 1987-88-89-90
Shebesta, Becky 1989-90-90-91-92
Skibski, Cheri 1991-92-93-94-95
Skurnick, Sheri 1993-94-95
Soucek, Linda 1981-982-83 84-85
Sovacool, Jenny 1991-92
Spillane, Katie 1997-98
Stevens, Emily 1996-97-98
Stewart, Jill 1993-94-95-96-97
Stobermann, Melissa 1990-91-9293-94
Strey, Cathy 1994-95-96-97-98

T

Taggart, Heather 1988-89-90-91-92
Torkko, Kari 1992-93-94-95-96
Tomek, Anne-Marie 1984-85
Treichel, Erica 1987-88-89-90-91
Treichel, Janet 1983-84

V

Vance, Amanda 1996-97-98
Vanderbeck, Patricia 1991-99293-94-95

W

Wagner, Allison 1997-98
Walch, Cary 1992-93-94-95-96
Warner, Amy 1987-88-89-91-92
Waterhouse, Cheryl 1986-87-88-89-90
Webb, Kathy 1981-82-83-84
Wegleitner, Heidi 1997-98
Willihnganz, Heather 1993-94-95-96-97
Wirth, Patty 1985-86-87-88-89

Women's Softball

B

Barthe, Lindy 1998
Berg, Amanda 1996-97
Borchard, Julie 1996-97-98
Bouchard, Carin 1996-97-98

C

Cartwright, Susie 1996
Christoff, Nicolle 1996
Coleman, Courtney 1996-97-98
Cummings, Jennifer 1998

E-F

Elliott, Meghan 1996
Fauser, Ashley 1996-97-98

G

Genna, Nicole 1996
Gigen, Becca 1996-97-98
Girard, Jennifer 1997-98
Grill, Jennifer 1998

H

Hartmann, Jennifer 1996-97-98
Hoff, Tara 1996-97-98
Horning, Kym 1996

L-M

LaPerriere, Lisa 1996
Lepinski, Jocelyn 1997-98
Lippert, Sarah 1998
McGee, Keri 1996-97-98

P

Paul, Jennifer 1996
Peltz, Alison 1998
Prickett, Jaime 1996-97-98

Q-R-S

Quinn, Rachel 1996
Riester, Holly 1997-98
Rudolf, Angela 1996
Swartout, Chrissy 1997-98

Women's Swimming

A

Anderson, Amy 1994-95-96-97-98
Anderson, Jody 1986-87
Anderson, Peggy 1974-75-76-77
Aspinwall, Lauren 1988-89-90

B

Baer, Kitty 1982-83-84-85-86
Banholzer, Mary Jo 1978-79-80
Barrett, Tracy 1981-82-83-84-85
Beatty, Brenda 1985-86
Belfor, Jamie 1997-98
Belmonte, Lora 1986-87
Benson, Patricia 1984-85
Beristain, Blanca 1985-86
Berg, Ingrid 1991-92
Berres, Ann 1976-77
Beyler, Jean 1974-75
Biddle, Kristen 1991-92-93-94-95
Biemond, Heather 1988-89-90-91
Binning, Kim 1986-87-88-89-90
Binning, Marcia 1978-79-80-81-82
Bjornaraa, Jaynie 1980-81
Borland, Kathy 1980-81-82-83-84
Bothwell, Dorothy 1984-85
Bova, Gianna 1997-98
Bremel, Debbie 1985-86
Brown, Barb 1975-76
Bryant, Jennifer 1992-93-94
Bull, Kristy 1982-83
Burke, Elizabeth 1975-76-77-78
Burroughs, Gina 1987-88-89-90

C

Carlson, Marlene 1974-75
Caplan, Monica 1994-95-96-97
Chamberlain, Lindsey 1997-98
Chester, Mary 1991-92-93
Clemens, Bobbi 1984-85-86
Coleman, Courtney 1995-996 97-98
Cooper, Carol 1975-76-77-78
Corner, Georgia 1981-82-83-84-85
Corner, Holly 1983-84-85-86
Cripe, Sue 1978-79-80-81-82
Crissinger, Laura 1975-76-77-78

D

Dahler, Cindi 1985-86
Damron, D'Lynn 1970-71-72-73
Davis, Kim 1995-96-97
Deadman, Sue 1983-84-85
Deane, Karen 1976-77-78
DeCloux, Kim 1981-82-83-84-85
DeCroix, Kim 1993-94-95-96-97
Deutsch, Margaret 1976-77-78
DeWall, Alison 1993-94
Dixon, Heather 1984-85-86
DiSalle, Caroline 1996-97-98
Dolmseth, Britten 1986-87-88-89-90
Donhauser, Stephanie 1981-82

E-F

Ehlers, Jean 1980-81-82-83-84
Eklund, Karen 1977-78
Ervin, Jackie 1987-88-89-90
Ervin, Nicole 1988-89-90-91
Esenther, Mary Jo 1980-81-82
Evans, Dana 1977-78
Evers, Leslie 1982-83-84-85
Falk, Mandi 1994-95-96-97-98
Ferris, Elizabeth 1977-78
Fillmore, Anne 1995-96-97-98
Finley, Ann 1983-84-85
Fountain, Janice 1974-75
Fox, Jane 1978-79-80-81-82
Freed, Ann 1987-88-89-90
Freiman, Paige 1992-93-94-95-96

G

Gaertner, Julia 1989-90-91-92-93
Gamelcy, Monique 1974-75-76-77
Gardner, Laurie 1989-90-91-92-93
Garrott, Barb 1974-75
Geiger, Erin 1993- 94-95
Gerenz, Karen 1982-83-84-885-86
Gelting, Sara 1991-92-93
Gibson, Shelly 1989-90
Glaze, Kristi 1983-84-85
Gottinger, Karen 1977-78
Groebner, Martha 1985-86-87-88
Gross, Ann 1976-77
Grossman, Valerie 1978-79-80
Gumtow, Sheila 1976-77
Guenther, Karen 1977-78

H

Hafenstein, Deb 1987-88-89-90
Hamm, Margaret 1978-79-80
Hanton, Mary 1984-85
Hargarten, Anita 1976-77-78
Harmon, Erin 1995-96-97
Hebert, Janice 1978-79-80
Horinek, Susan 1981-82-83-84-85
Howard, Mary 1982-83-84-85
Hrenak, Christy 1988-89-90
Hughes, Penny 1983-84-85-86
Hummel, Paula 1977-78-79-80-81
Hunt, Jody 1981-82-83
Hunter, Hope 1978-79-80-81

I-J

Iverson, Shannon 1995-96-97-98
Jensen, Anna 1993-94
Johannsen, Holly 1996-97-98
Johnson, Jennifer 1991-92
Johnson, Zoe 1978-79-80
Jones, Erin 1988-89-90-91-92
Jones, Marthe 1986-87
Jones, Morgan 1987-88-89-90
Justesen, Amy 1983-84-85-86

K

Kafinger, Barbel 1984-85-86
Kearney, Shannon 1994-95
Kepka, Val 1978-9-80
Kirby, Joy 1984-85
Kjome, Becky 1982-83-84-85-86
Kloke, Robin 1974-75
Krueger, Sarah 1994-95-96-97-98
Krug, Maria 1980-81-82-83-84
Krumplitsch, Kellie 1989-90
Kuehn, Dana 1990-91

L

LaFreniere, Heather 1987-88
Langfeldt, Candy 1975-76
Lanphere, Lisa 1977-78
Lauterbach, Brandie 1994-95-96
Lawler, Erin 1991-92
Lewis, Becca 1993-94
Lueder, Carolyn 1978-79-80
Lueder, Cindi 1982-83-84
Lund, Andrea 1994-95-96-97-98
Lund, Valerie 1996-97-98

M

MacLaren-Meuer, Sally 1977-78-79-80-81
Mallatt, Margaret 1987-88-89-90
Mayer, Beth 1978-79-80
McGahey, Kym 1989-90
McGowan, Kathy 1982-83
McPherson, Jennifer 1989-90-91-92-93
Messner, Sara 1988-89-90-91-92
Mettler, Stacey 1986-87-88-89-90

Miller, Jennifer	1974-75
Miller, Kara	1988-89-90-91-92
Miller, Karen	1977-78
Mitchell, Gigi	1991-92
Mogg, Kirsten	1978-79-80
Mongeon, Betsy	1993-94
Morgenstern, Kathy	1990-91-92-93-94
Mueller, Ghita	1986-87
Munz, Amy	1996-97-98
Murphy, Katie	1991-92-93

N-O

Nelson, Jill	1987-88-89-90
Nelson,Karen	1976-77-78
Neuhold, Zora	1980-81-82-83-84
Newman, Sarah	1991-92-93-94-95
Offerman, Louisa	1993-94-95-96-97
Olds, Sue	1974-75
Olsen, Mary	1976-77-78
Ostby, Laurie	1977-78-79-80

P

Pagach, Tricia	1980-81-82
Panighetti, Gina	1996-97-98
Patee, Lindsey	1995-96-97-98
Paul, Jennifer	1989-90-91-92
Peters, Beth	1977-78-79-80-81
Peterson, Naashom	1991-92-93-94-95
Picl, Jocelyn	1996-97-98
Pisula, Kathy	1989-90-91-92-93
Phle, Erin	1997-98
Poore, Debbie	1978-79-80-81
Premo-Jaeger, Dannielle	1991-92-93-94-95

R

Rasmusson, Annika	1993-94-95-96-97
Reece, Margaret	1990-91-92-93
Reif, Bobbi	1976-77
Reiss, Sheila	1991-92-93
Rogan, Patty	1974-75
Roger, Amy	1979-80-81-82
Roginski, Mary	1985-86-87
Rohloff, Laura	1978-79-80-81

S

Sass, Christine	1995-96-97
Schienle, Jenny	1981-82-83-84-85
Schinke, Heidi	1992-93-94
Schmidt, Julanne	1978-79-80-81-82
Schoeman, Maureen	1984-85-86
Schoeneman, Beth Ann	1978-79-80
Schweiger, Vickie	1976-77
Senn, Ann	1975-76
Serebin, Sandy	1980-81
Seymour, Maria	1991-92-93-94
Shew, Debbie	1976-77-78
Slook, Christine	1989-90
Smith, Rochelle	1987-88-89-90
Solie, Sue	1975-76-77-78
Spilman, Laura	1985-86
Spoehr, Brandy	1991-92
Stark, Stephanie	1988-89-90
Steele, Karen	1977-78
Stelmashenko, Larissa	1985-86-87-88
Stevens, Carrie	1986-87-88-89-90
Stoker, Laura	1976-77
Stonebraker, Ellen	1997-98
Sundquist, Jill	1985-86

T

Tesch, Abby	1997-98
Thoburn, Lisa	1980-81
Tomasik, Cindy	1976-77
Topp, Susie	1995-96-97-98
Toruno, Marina	1992-93-94-95
Troia, Susan	1986-87-88-89-90

U-V

Usher, Jeanne	1976-77-78
Vanderveldt, Kelly	1989-90
Vanderveldt, Tracey	1987-88-89-90
Vick, Lisa	1984-85-87-88

W

Wagner, Julie	1990-91-92-93-94
Walsh, Kathy	1980-81-82-83-84
Walton, Christy	1993-94-95
Walton, Cindy	1978-79-80-81
Weisz, Marti Anne	1992-93-94
Wehr, Kelly	1989-90
Wendricks, Lori	1988-89-90-91-92
Wilder, Carol	1987-88-89-90
Wilkinson, Suzanne	1987-88-89-90
Willett, Mary	1985-86
Wise, Nancy	1974-75
Wolosz, Andrea	1993-94-95-96-97

Y-Z

Young, Judy	1988-89-90
Zeck, Elizabeth	1975-76-77
Zimmerman, Benita	1977-78
Zimmerman, Julie	1974-75-76

Women's Tennis

A

Archbald, Renny	1972-73
Aunan, Patty	1973-74-75-76

B

Bachman, Amy	1977-78-80-81-82
Bachman, Karin	1975-76
Baritot, Dena	1996-97-98
Benz, Stephany	1990-91-92-93-94
Berger, Cheri	1983-84-85-86-87
Berger, Cindy	1975-76
Berger, Debbie	1973-74
Bessey, Claudia	1987-88-89
Birndorf, Sheri	1988-89
Bland, Holly	1979-80-81-82-83
Bormann, Betsy	1976-77-78
Bronson, Wendy	1971-72-73-74-75
Buetow, Betsy	1981-82-83-84-85

C

Carney, Mary	1975-76-77-78-79
Chorney, Doneta	1989-90
Chullino, Jill	1988-89-90-91-92
Copier, Marjon	1993-94, 97-98

D

Dahlgren, Heather	1979-80-81
Demetroulis, Elaine	1987-88-89-90-91

E-F

Erdman, Mary	1971-72
Fenton, Andrea	1972-73-74-75-76
Floreno, Annemarie	1982-83-84-85
Fortman, Lisa	1982-83-84-85-86
Fouret, Jamie	1992-93-94-95

G

Gabler, April	1997-98
Galiene, Jill	1987-88
Gavaris, Lauren	1992-93-94-95-96
Gilles, Chris	1984-85-86-87-88
Gilles, Wendy	1985-86-87-88-89
Ginsberg, Kay	1977-78
Goldfarb, Carolea	1973-74
Goldman, Barbara	1973-74
Gough, Samantha	1986-87-88
Gregersen, Kira	1989-90-91-92-93
Gregory, Amanda	1991-92-93
Groban, Leanne	1977-78-79-80
Grubisic, Tina	1991-92-93-94-95

H

Hargarten, Katy	1985-86
Harris, Holly	1988-89-90-91-92
Hatch, Diana	1987-88-89
Hedberg, Joan	1974-75-76-77-78
Hinderaker, Kathy	1971-72
Holgerson, Laurel	1971-72-73

J-K

Jordan, Gail	1972-73
Kaya, Charlene	1983-84-85-86-87
Kelly, Nancy	1979-80
Kisch, Allison	1985-86-87
Knipp, Danielle	1994-95
Kolb, Karen	1976-77-78-79-80-81

L

Leser, Cathy	1976-77-78
Lucey, Colleen	1993-94-95-96-97

M

McFarland, Molly	1978-79-80
McKinney, Pam	1971-72
Morris, Kathy	1975-76-77-78-79
Morris, Sheri	1978-79-80
Nadell, Joanna	1981-82-83-84
McFarland, Molly	1978-79-80
McKinney, Pam	1971-72
Morris, Kathy	1975-76-77-78-79
Morris, Sheri	1978-79-80

N-O-P

Nadell, Joanna	1981-82-83-84
Andrea Nathan	1996-97-98
Neubauer, Marija	1990-91-92-93-94
Oace, Vicki	1976-77
Poplin, Kate	1980-81-82

R

Rabinowitz, Elyse	1978-79-80-81-82
Reid, Kellie	1982-83-84
Ritt, Elizabeth	1978-79-80-81
Robbins, Wendy	1981-82-83

S

Schmidt, Nancy	1971-72-73
Schumacher, Susan	1975-76
Scott, Carol	1976-77
Shine, Sandy	1982-83
Spiegel, Jodi	1976-77-78-79
Sweeney, Roz	1995-96-97-98

T

Talboys, Chriss	1971-72-73
Thomas, Kristi	1988-89-90-91
Tritchler, Gretchen	1980-81-82-83
Tully, Shannon	1991-92-93-94-95

U-V

Urbanska, Barbara	1995-96-97-98
Van Pelt, Cathy	1983-84-85-86-87
Vastola, Nina	1978-79-80-81

W

Watson, Leslie	1972-73
Williams, Amy	1978-79-80-81-82

Woods, Julie 1995-96-97

Y-Z

Yahr, Kristin 1984-85-86-87-88
Zimpfer, Melissa 1995-96-97
Zobrist, Tracy 1994-95-96-97-98

Women's Track

A

Albert, Bonny 1975-76
Alto, Denise 1990-91-92-93
Anderson, Rachael 1996-97

B

Bassett, Stephanie 1984-85-86-87-88
Beard, April 1996-97-98
Bebow, Mary 1974-75-76
Beischel, Sue 1978-79-80-81-82
Beisner, Brianne 1997-98
Benson, Rhonda 1976-77
Bessert, Lynn 1975-76-77
Billingsley, Marty 1977-78
Boehland, Suzanne 1994-95
Bolenbaugh, April 1994-95-96
Borgwarth, Kathy 1978-79-80-81-82
Borgwarth, Nina 1983-84-85, 87-88
Branta, Cathy 1981-82-83-84-85
Breighner, Tammy 1987-88
Bremser, Cathy 1976-77-78-79
Bremser, Cindy 1974-75
Brewster, Ellen 1977-78-79-80-81
Brockhaus, Joan 1979-80-81
Brown, Dorothea 1982-83-84-85-86
Brown, Jennifer 1985-86-87
Brunner, Maryann 1980-81-82-83-84
Buhr, Bev 1974-75
Burke, Amy 1993-94
Burke, Randee 1974-75-76
Butler, Kathy 1994-95-96-97

C

Cheney, Sarah 1991-92
Christiansen, Birgit 1983-84
Christiansen, Marcia 1983-84-85-86
Christopherson, Kim 1980-81
Chryst, Dolly 1986-87
Cote, Julie 1991-92-93-94-95
Cote, Nathalie 1993-94

D

Davis, Julie 1986-87-88
Deatherage, Jenelle 1995-96-97-98
DeGroot, Jenny 1988-89-90
Dillahunt, Cherie 1984-85-86
Dollins, Sharon 1982-83-84-85-86
Donnally, Erin 1978-79
Douglas, Rose 1996-97-98
Dunlop, Amy 1979-80-81
Dwyer, Jane 1977-78

E

Eichner, Clare 1988-89-91-92-93
Eiring, Kris 1982-83-84-85-86
Eisner, Kiara 1995-96
Eppers, Agnes 1991-92-93
Eppinga, Jennifer 1991-92
Erps, Tina 1992-93-94-95-96-97
Essmann, Cheri 1979-80-81-82

F

Favor, Suzy 1986-87-88-89-90
Ferren, Traci 1986-87-88
Flak, Lisa 1995-96-97-98
Forsell, Anna 1983-84-85
Fredrickson, Sara 1993-94-95-96-97-98

G

Gartzke, Alice 1984-85
Gentes, Sue 1987-88-89-90-91-92
Goepel, Chris 1986-87
Golemb, Lisa 1982-83-84-85-86
Gordon, Sue 1976-77-78-79-80
Gott, Jenny 1994-95
Graf, Laura 1983-84
Green, Aileen 1988-89-90-91-92
Grinaker, Mary 1977-78-79-80

H

Harris, Carole 1984-85-86-87
Harris, Esther 1987-88
Hartzheim, Mary 1986-87-88-89-90-91
Hartzheim, Maureen 1986-87-88-89-90
Heckel, Keli 1975-76
Henschen, Amy 1983-84
Herbst, Stephanie 1984-85-86-87-88
Hering, Holly 1984-85, 87-88
Hinton, Pam 1988-89-90
Hoch, Nancy 1984-85
Holle, Lisa 1992-93
Holtz, Marcia 1974-75
Horney, Sibylle 1987-88-89-90-91-92
Houston, Suzie 1974-75-76-77
Howard, Dot 1975-76-77-78-79
Howard, Jennifer 1991-93-94-95-96
Howe, Amy 1988-89
Hudson, Gilda 1974-75-76-77
Hyland, Heather 1993-94-95-96-97
Hyman, Yvette 1976-77-78-79-80

I-J

Ishmael, Katie 1982-83- 84-85-86
Jackson, Robin 1980-81
Jagelski, Cathy 1977-78
Jahner, Jill 1986-87-88
Jahnke, Sarah 1986-87-88
Jensen, Julie 1974-75-76
Jensen, Sonya 1991-92-93-94-95
Johnson, Angela 1978-79
Johnson, Pat 1978-79-80-81-82
Jones, Crystal 1979-80-81-82
Jones, Darcy 1974-75-76-77
Jones, Renee 1983-84
Joyce, Laura 1997-98

K

Kauls, Kim 1987-88
Kavanaugh, Annette 1983-84-85-86
Keaton, Elva 1987-88-89
Kemnitz, Lori 1978-79-80-81-82
Keskinen, Tammy 1982-83-84-85-86
Kincaid, Lisa 1996-97-98
Kirkpatrick, Kirstin 1990-91-92-93
Kneuer, Cory 1976-77-78
Kraeger, Jenny 1990-91-92
Kroeger, Sho 1995- 96-97
Kropp, Kristi 1982-83-84-85-86
Kubly, Nissa 1994-95-96-97-98
Kujak, Angi 1994-95-96-97-98
Kulbel, Jaime 1997-98

L

Lefebvre, Kathy 1983-84-85-86
Lumley, Michele 1984-85

M

Malone, Jackie 1982-83-84
Mansfield, Sandy 1974-75
Marcell, Stacey 1995-96
Mattes, Tracy 1987-88-89-90
McDonnell, Sue 1987-88-90-91-92
McElwee, Marty 1976 77-78-79-80
McKillen, Kelly 1983-84-85-86
McWilliams, Markesha 1994-95-96-97-98
Melin, Anneli 1995-96-97-98
Metz, Jen 1992-93-94-95-96
Michalski, Kris 1987-88-89-90-91
Millington, Pam 1974-75-76-77-78
Mitchell, Susan 1982-83-84-85-86
Monk, Lori 1974-75
Morin, Lynn 1977-78
Moore, Pam 1977-78-79-80-81
Mortenson, Christy 1990-91-92-93
Mulrooney, Ann 1976-77-78-79-80
Mulrooney, Mary 1980-81-82
Muschitz, Donna 1991-92, 94-95-96
Myers, Julie 1981-82

N

Nagengast, Betty 1977-78-79-80
Nelezen, Michelle 1987-88-89-90
Nitsch, Karen 1981-8283-84-85
Nordstrom, Diane 1980-81-82-83-84

O

Olson, Ellen 1981-82- 83-84
Ostrem, Francine 1980-81-82-83

P

Partoll, Janet 1987-88-89-90-91
Payne, Lisa 1987-88-89-90-91
Paynter, Jennifer 1991-92-93-94-95
Pesch, Stephanie 1996-97-98
Platner, Sue 1975-76

Q-R

Quereshi, Shu 1978-79-80-81
Rabideau, Laurie 1984-85-86-87
Rawling, Heather 1990-91-92
Reneke, Johanna 1983-84
Renk, Sarah 1991-92-93
Revak, Julie 1989-90-91-92-93-94
Ripp, Michelle 1991-92-93
Ripp, Sara 1974-75
Rittmeyer, Charlotte 1990-91-92
Rockweiler, Charlie 1992-93
Ross, Cathy 1997-98
Rucinski, Shelly 1987-88-89
Rusk, Kathleen 1974-75-76-77
Ryan, Karen 1988-89

S

Schaefer, Becky 1995-96-97-98
Schlitz, Julie 1985-86-87- 88-89-90-91
Schleuter, Nancy 1974-75
Schoenike, Jenny 1975-76
Schoo, Patti 1988-89-90-91-92
Schwenck, Tracie 1992-93-94
Schwoeppe, Ann 1986-87-88-89-90
Scott, Carol 1976-77-78-79-80
Scott, Megan 1982-83-84
Scott, Quinn 1997-98
Servi, Jane 1983-84-85-86
Sherman, Kim 1989-90-91-92-93
Snowbeck, Robin 1992-93-94-95-96
Spaltholz, Sue 1979 80-81-82-83-84
Spencer, Marybeth 1976-77-78-79
Stepka, Mary 1979-80-81
Stoffel, Helen 1982-83-84-85-86
Stoop, Martina 1993-94
Suhm, Mindy 1990-91-92-93-94
Sveum, Angie 1987-88-89-90-91

T

Tallard, Sue	1975-76-77-78
Thomson, Rose	1979-80-81-82-83
Thurwachter, Amy	1974-75-76
Tiller, Kim	1987-88-89
Townsend, Lisa	1993-94-95-96-97

V-W

Verway, Anne	1984-85-86
Wagner, Pat	1974-75-76-77
Walrath, Sara	1993-94-95
Walsh, Molly	1991-92
Walter, Avrie	1995-96-97-98
Wasniewski, Carla	1979-80
Wasserburger, Lori	1975-77-78-79
Watson, Jennifer	1992-93-94-95-96
Weltzer, Lisa	1996-97-98
Westphal, Janet	1994-95-96- 97-98
Westphal, Jenni	1995-96-97-98
Wickus, Amy	1991-92-93-94-95
Williams, Bo	1974-75-76-77-78-79
Williams, Camille	1994-95-96
Williams, Jody	1992-93-94
Wilson, Marta	1980-81
Winski, Judy	1980-81-82
Wolter, Lori	1985-86

Z

Zimmerman. Lisa	1986-87
Zook, Sally	1978-79-80

1998-99

BADGER BIG TEN FINISHES...

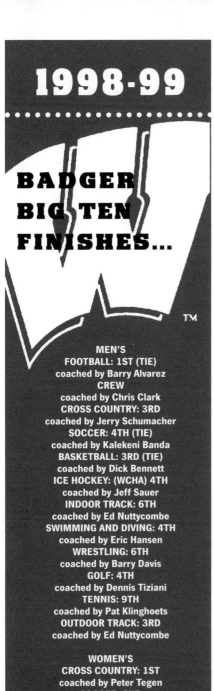

MEN'S
FOOTBALL: 1ST (TIE)
coached by Barry Alvarez
CREW
coached by Chris Clark
CROSS COUNTRY: 3RD
coached by Jerry Schumacher
SOCCER: 4TH (TIE)
coached by Kalekeni Banda
BASKETBALL: 3RD (TIE)
coached by Dick Bennett
ICE HOCKEY: (WCHA) 4TH
coached by Jeff Sauer
INDOOR TRACK: 6TH
coached by Ed Nuttycombe
SWIMMING AND DIVING: 4TH
coached by Eric Hansen
WRESTLING: 6TH
coached by Barry Davis
GOLF: 4TH
coached by Dennis Tiziani
TENNIS: 9TH
coached by Pat Klinghoets
OUTDOOR TRACK: 3RD
coached by Ed Nuttycombe

WOMEN'S
CROSS COUNTRY: 1ST
coached by Peter Tegen
SOCCER: 2ND
coached by Dean Duerst
ROWING
coached by Mary Browning
LIGHTWEIGHT ROWING
coached by Maren Watson
BASKETBALL: 4TH (TIE)
coached by Jane Albright
INDOOR TRACK: 4TH
coached by Ed Nuttycombe
SWIMMING AND DIVING: 4TH
coached by Eric Hansen
VOLLEYBALL: 2ND
coached by Peter Waite
GOLF: 5TH
coached by Dennis Tiziani
SOFTBALL: 6TH
coached by Karen Gallagher
TENNIS: 2ND
coached by Patti Henderson
OUTDOOR TRACK: 2ND
coached by Peter Tegen

THE BIG EVENT

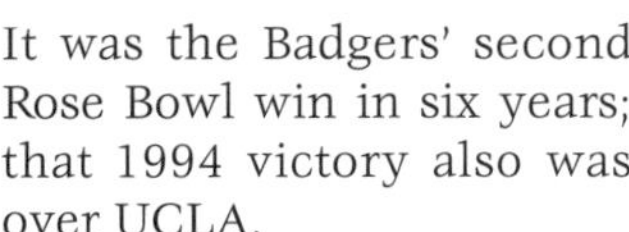

Winningest Badgers claim Rose Bowl, 38-31, over UCLA

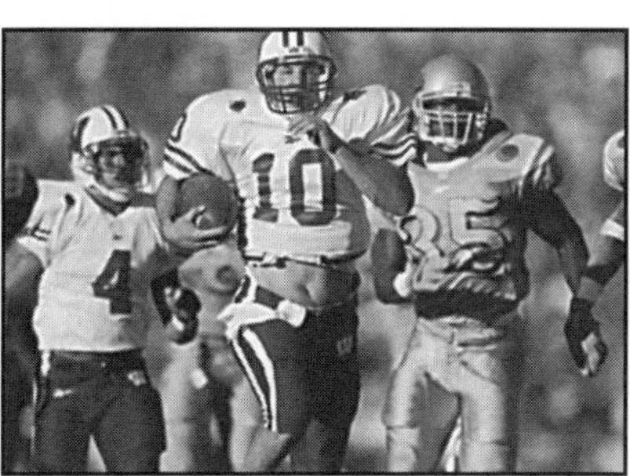

Wisconsin's winningest football team ever (11-1 overall) finished its 1998 season in splendid fashion on New Year's Day 1999 with a 38-31 victory over sixth-ranked UCLA in the 85th Rose Bowl game.

It was the Badgers' second Rose Bowl win in six years; that 1994 victory also was over UCLA.

In its regular-season finale, Wisconsin defeated No. 14 Penn State for the first time since 1959 to earn a share of the Big Ten title at 7-1.

Wisconsin finished the year ranked fifth and sixth, respectively, in the ESPN/*USA Today* coaches' poll and the Associated Press media poll. The UW was ranked every week of the season for only the third time in school history.

Pacing Wisconsin's Rose Bowl win was Ron Dayne, who ran for 246 yards, just one shy of Charles White's Rose Bowl record. Dayne's career-high four touchdowns equaled the game's modern-day record. The game winner came early in the fourth quarter when UW freshman Jamar Fletcher intercepted a Cade McNown pass and returned it 46 yards for a TD and a 38-28 Badger lead.

UCLA cut the lead to seven with a field goal and had yet another chance after the Badgers failed to run out the clock. But Wendell Bryant's sack of McNown on a fourth-down effort stopped the Bruins.

WISCONSIN TIME LINE

1999: The UW men's tennis team hosts the Big Ten singles championship at the Nielsen Tennis Center for the first time.

Wisconsin's men's basketball team defeats Minnesota 61-50 before 17,046 spectators at the Kohl Center, the largest home-game crowd in UW history.

The UW softball team sweeps a doubleheader from Loyola to christen the new Robert and Irwin Goodman Softball Complex.

Badger women win fourth straight conference title

Ho-hum, it was the same old story for Wisconsin's women's cross country team in the fall of 1998.

But it's one that Coach Peter Tegen hopes never ends.

His Badgers won their fourth straight Big Ten cross country title—and 13th overall—in October at Ann Arbor, upending host Michigan 31-36 in one of the closest meets in conference history. And the Badgers weren't even favored—Michigan came in ranked third nationally, Wisconsin eighth.

But a senior and two freshmen came through for Tegen. Freshman Erica Palmer finished second to eventual NCAA champ Katie McGregor of Michigan in 17:22 and earned Big Ten Freshman of the Year honors. Senior Jenelle Deatherage was the second UW finisher, coming in fourth, while another frosh, Bethany Brewster, was fifth. All three earned All-Big Ten honors.

Junior Stephanie Pesch and senior Jenni Westphal were named All-Big Ten second team with their ninth and 11th place finishes, respectively.

Wisconsin went on to win its third successive NCAA qualifying meet two weeks later in the regional at Terre Haute, Indiana, as the Badgers scored 39 points, 14 better than Michigan.

In the NCAA meet at Lawrence, Kansas, Deatherage and Westphal earned All-America honors—the first for Wisconsin since 1995—placing 24th and 30th, respectively. Top runner Palmer was unable to finish the national race because of a case of walking pneumonia, but the Badgers nonetheless finished fifth in the meet.

Wisconsin has participated in 22 national championships and has never been out of the top 10.

UW cagers tie for 3rd in Big Ten, advance to NCAA

Wisconsin's winningest basketball season ever was highlighted by a trip to the NCAA Tournament for the third time in six seasons and the second in four years under Coach Dick Bennett.

Making the 1998-99 season special:

- The UW's 22-10 mark and .688 winning percentage was the best since the 1961-62 team went 17-7 (.708);
- The 22 victories eclipsed the 20-win seasons posted by the 1915-16 and 1940-41 teams;
- The Badgers' third-place finish in the Big Ten at 9-7 was their highest since the 1962 team finished second with a 10-4 record;
- The UW finished the year ranked 18th in the Associated Press poll and became only the second Wisconsin squad—after the 1949-50 team, ranked 16th—to end the season nationally ranked;
- The Badgers' schedule was rated sixth toughest in the nation by the Sagarin Ratings. Wisconsin entered the NCAA Tournament 8-6 against other teams in the tourney;
- Wisconsin's 10-game reversal of fortune—from 12-19 in 1997-98 to 22-10—made the team one of just five in UW history to win at least 10 games more than it had the previous year;
- The Badgers were hot at the start, getting out of the gate 12-1 for the best start by a UW five since 1929-30, and also hot in starting Big Ten play, posting a 7-2 mark;
- Wisconsin led the Big Ten in scoring defense for the second time in Bennett's four seasons, allowing foes just 56.8 points per game, and ranked second nationally in all games at 55.2 ppg, fourth best in school history;
- Honors came in droves, with Mike Kelley the Big Ten's Defensive Player of the Year; Sean Mason and Ty Calderwood second- and third-team All-Big Ten, respectively; and Kelley, Andy Kowske and Hennssy Auriantal Academic All-Big Ten selections;
- Coach Dick Bennett was one of 15 finalists for the Naismith National Coach of the Year Award, one of 10 nominees for the similar Associated Press award and one of six finalists for the Clair Bee Award.

WISCONSIN HEADLINER

Matt Downin
Cross Country

Matt Downin made a big breakthrough in his junior year to chalk up one of the best cross country seasons ever by a Wisconsin runner. The Hampstead, New Hampshire, native placed fourth in the NCAA cross country championships at Lawrence, Kansas, the best finish for a Badger runner since Tim Hacker won the meet in 1985. Downin also won the Big Ten title and was named Big Ten cross country athlete of the year. He set a course record of 24:06 in the meet at Ann Arbor in becoming the first UW runner to win that race since Donovan Bergstrom in 1992. Downin, who also was second in the 1,500- and 5,000-meter runs at the 1999 outdoor track meet, picked up in the fall of 1999 where he left off in 1998. As a senior, he again won the Big Ten harrier crown—becoming only the third UW harrier to win two or more—and again placed fourth in the NCAA meet, leading the Badgers to a second-place finish.

WISCONSIN HEADLINER

Jenelle Deatherage
Cross Country, Track

The 1998-99 Wisconsin female athlete of the year, Jenelle Deatherage was also just about "all-everything" during her collegiate career. The East Peoria, Illinois, native was named the 1999 Big Ten outdoor track athlete of the year following an indoor campaign in which she was the conference meet's top performer. A three-event, three-time All-American in track in 1999, Deatherage was also the Big Ten outdoor champ at 3,000 meters. She finished eighth, fifth and fourth in Big Ten cross country in her final three seasons. She also was a 1998 All-American, twice earned All-Big Ten honors in the sport and three times was an all-region pick. Deatherage won three Big Ten track titles during her career and also was a five-time All-Big Ten academic selection in track and cross country.

LEADING THE WAY

Chris Clark
Men's Crew Coach

International experience has proven a strong suit for Wisconsin men's crew coach Chris Clark since his appointment in 1996. Clark was head coach of the U.S. men's pre-elite rowing team during the summers of 1996-98 and was named Developmental Coach of the Year by the U.S. Olympic Committee in 1997. He served as UW assistant men's rowing coach from 1994-96 and guided his Badger freshman crews to an unbeaten record in cup races during his tenure. Clark's rowing experience reads like a map of the world. Prior to his UW appointment, he was an assistant varsity coach for two years at the U.S. Naval Academy and also coached rowing at Drexel University, Oriel College and University College in Oxford, England. A University of California graduate, Clark has rowed and medaled in regattas in the U.S. and nine other countries since 1979.

The List

Wisconsin's honored athletes

Big Ten Medal of Honor

1998—Erik Raygor, Katie Voigt

1999—Brian Doherty, Shannon Brown

2000—Gina Panighetti, Jay Schoenfelder

Jesse Owens Award nominees

1998—Eric Jetton, wrestling

1999—Matt Downin, track & cross country

2000—Ron Dayne, football

Suzy Favor Award nominees

1998—Angi Kujak, track & cross country

1999—Jenelle Deatherage, track & cross country

2000—Erica Palmer, track & cross country

LEADING THE WAY

Frank J. Remington
Big Ten Faculty Representative

Frank J. Remington served as Wisconsin's faculty representative to the Big Ten and the NCAA from 1959-86. In particular, Remington, a 1947 UW graduate and 1949 Law School graduate, was a strong voice in the NCAA for the development of ice hockey. At the UW, he was an early and strong advocate of a varsity sports program for women. Remington was a member of the Wisconsin Law School faculty for 46 years and was nationally recognized for his pioneering work in criminal law. A continuous member of the UW athletic board, he supported the establishment of the athletic board scholars program in the late 1980s to recognize scholastic achievement by student-athletes. The Frank Remington Scholars Program has been established to honor the graduating male and female student-athlete letter winners with the highest grade-point averages. Remington was inducted into the UW Athletic Hall of Fame in 1999.

WISCONSIN HEADLINER

Walter Lautenbach
Baseball, Basketball

Walter Lautenbach starred for Badger basketball and baseball teams from 192-47, with time for military service interrupting his athletic career. The Plymouth, Wisconsin, native earned major "W" awards in baseball and basketball in 1942, 1943 and 1947. He pitched both games of a 1942 doubleheader against Chicago, winning the opener 10-1 and losing the nightcap 10-5. In 1943, as the Badgers' MVP, Lautenbach defeated Minnesota 2-1 in 13 innings and batted in both runs. He captained the 1947 UW Big Ten basketball champions and was third in team scoring as a starting guard. Lautenbach scored two field goals in the final 13 seconds of play that year to lift the Badgers over Northwestern, 45-44. Following his graduation, he signed a contract with the Oshkosh All-Stars of the National Basketball League. He was inducted into the UW Athletic Hall of Fame in 1999.

WISCONSIN HEADLINER

Carl Holtz
Men's Crew

Carl Holtz starred for Wisconsin crew teams during and after World War II and earned acclaim as the "finest stroke in collegiate rowing" in 1946 and 1947. He captained the 1947 team. The Milwaukee native won major "W" awards in 1942, 1946 and 1947 as the stroke of Wisconsin crews and helped pace Wisconsin to its first national championship in 1946. As a freshman in 1941, Holtz stroked the UW freshman crew to second place at the Poughkeepsie Regatta. He stroked the Badger varsity to second in the 1942 Adams Cup competition before leaving for duty with the U.S. Army Air Corps. Upon his return in 1946, Holtz stroked the crew to the Eastern Sprint Regatta title at Annapolis, Maryland. He was inducted into the UW Athletic Hall of Fame in 1999.

WISCONSIN HEADLINER

Shannon Brown
Soccer

Three-time All-Big Ten selection Shannon Brown, who starred as a defender for the Badgers from 1996-98, had one of the great careers in the annals of Wisconsin women's soccer. Brown, a native of Madison who prepped at Memorial H.S., redshirted her freshman year but then embarked on a stellar career for the UW with the 1996 season. One of the most honored defenders in Wisconsin history, Brown started all 65 games her final three seasons. As a senior in 1998, the tough, speedy and agile Brown became one of the Big Ten's strongest and most feared defenders. She dished out game-winning assists against Michigan State, Iowa and Northern Illinois. Brown was picked as a second-team All-American, a first-team NSCAA Academic All-American and a second-team GTE Academic All-American.

1998-99 MEN'S LETTERWINNERS

Basketball
Hennssy Auriantal
Jon Bryant
David Burkemper
Ty Calderwood
Travon Davis
Duany Duany
Erik Faust
Mike Kelley
Andrew Kowske
Maurice Linton
Sean Mason
John Moriarty
Maurice Sessoms
Mark Vershaw
Charlie Wills

Crew
Scott Alwin
Kevin Anderson
Brian Bauer
Joel Berger
Dylan Cappel
John Cummings
Mark Danahy
Matt Fischer
Alan Geweke
Zachary Gutt
Kristian Knutsen
Jeff Maples
James Moody
Matt Noordsij-Jones
Zachery Pollack
Gabriel Rudert
Mike Seelen
Ira Simpson
Matt Smith
Paul Tegan
Ryan Westergard
Jeremy Witish

Cross Country
Jared Cordes
Kevin Cullen
Matt Downin
Jay Schoenfelder
Nate Uselding
Jason Vanderhoof
Jason Weppler

Golf
Todd Anderson
C.J. Brock
John Carlson
Matt Gerlach
Ryan Helminen
Jim Lemon

Hockey
Craig Anderson
Dan Bjornlie
Alex Brooks
Mike Cerniglia
Kent Davyduke
Jeff Dessner
Matt Doman
Kevin Granato
Luke Gruden
Yuri Gusak
Dave Hergert
David Hukalo
Matt Hussey
Dustin Kuk
Graham Melanson
T.R. Moreau
Matt Murray
Steve Reinprecht
Tim Rothering
Niki Siren
Jake Soper
Rick Spooner
Chad Stauffacher
Dave Tanabe
Rob Vega
Andy Wheeler

Soccer
Valentine Anozie
Moriba Baker
Erich Bertsche
Abraham Bull
Matt Burkert
Tim Caprez
Bram Dorresteyn
Leron Gabriel
Tamba Johnson
Salil Kenkre
Adam Kowalski
Scott Krajewski
Erik Lindstrom
Evan Odim
Christian Poppert
Scott Repa
Yuichiro Sakai
Sean Simmons
Steve Sorenson

Swimming & Diving
Troy Blanton
Adam Byars
Brink Ciferri
Brendan Coyne
Aaron Forgy
Eric Godsman
Anders Holm
Ted Krueger
Cory Miller
Brian Neumann
Dan Patee
Neil Pfeiffer
Andrew Tainter
Russell Zuckerman
Matt Zuiderhof

Tennis
Justin Baker
David Chang
Bobby Croll
Jason Gonzaga
Mark Loughrin
Stefan Reist
David Sacks
Adam Schumacher
Danny Westerman

Track & Field
James Berger
Ashley Bronk
Mark Clauss
Jared Cordes
Joshua Dickerson
Matt Downin
Benny Gill
Lenton Herring
Clayton Hiemke
Steve Holzbauer
Ross Kolodziej
Adam Kress
Tim Kulinski
Eric Leicht
Cecil Martin
Nic Matack
Brad Mohns
Bobby Myers
Lance Neely
Jabari Pride
Matt Rodgers
Brody Rose
Scott Synold
Jason Vanderhoof
Chris Van Tassel
Jason Weppler
Scott Wick
Christian Williams
Gordon Zietlow

Wrestling
Steve Alf
Kevin Black
Kole Clauson
Brady Cudd
P.J. Dowling
Grant Hoerr
Koy Kosek
Ryan LaGrange
Cory McNellis
David Moore
Dave Neumyer
Jason Pernat
Don Pritzlaff
Joe Terrill
Mark Trinitapoli
Cory Wallman

1998-99 WOMEN'S LETTERWINNERS

Basketball
Krista Bird
Kyle Black
Tanisha Boston
Christine Cleary
Judy Ebeling
Sarah Jirovec
Rachel Klongland
Missy Konieczny
Tamara Moore
Dee Dee Pate
Kelley Paulus
Erin Schmidt
LaTonya Sims
Jessie Stomski
Amy Wiersma

Lightweight Rowing
Sara Borchardt
Jenny Churus
Sharone Cohen
Dusty Darley
Kirstin Holbeck
Angela Lay
Sara Lyng
Angela Mattern
Tamara Miller
Maura O'Donnell
Anna Vaughn
Sara Webb

Cross Country
Erin AufderHeide
Bethany Brewster
Jenelle Deatherage
Emily Free
Laura Joyce
Erica Palmer
Stephanie Pesch
Avrie Watlers
Jenni Westphal

Golf
Allie Blomquist
Patty Frohna
Andrea Meeker
Heidi Njoes
Kathleen Prieve
Kelly Trapp

Soccer
Jamie Barbian
Shannon Brown
Ana Christianson
Maria De Giovanni
Megan Dobesh
Emily Gassert
Elizabeth Grum
Michelle Hawkins
Lindsay Hoelter
Shelby Johnson
Jamie Keller
Kelly Kundert
Shana Little
Mara Miller
Wynter Pero
heather Priester
Natalie Roedler
Allie Rogosheske
Briget Schwarting
Kathryn Spillane
Emily Stevens
Allison Wagner
Heidi Wegleitner
Jennifer Wright

Softball
Melinda Barth
Amanda Berg
Julie Borchard
Jen Cummings
Meredith Farmer
Ashley Fauser
Jennifer Girard
Jade Gosse
Jennifer Grill
Kerry Hagen
Jennifer Hartmann
Tara Hoff
Jocelyn Lepinski
Sarah Lippert
Sarah Mayer
Keri McGee
Jaime Prickett
Chrissy Swartout

Swimming & Diving
Jamie Belfor
Gianna Bova
Lindsey Chamberlain
Courtney Coleman
Caroline DiSalle
Holly Johannsen
Megan Kernan
Siobhan Kernan
Gina Loechl
Christy Mullinanx
Amy Munz
Gina Panighetti
Jocelyn Plcl
Erin Pohle
Jennifer Rushfeldt
Ellen Stonebraker
Abby Tesch
Andrea Wanezek

Tennis
Dena Baritot
Katie Dougherty
Katie Dow
Rebecca Ebin
April Gabler
Andrea Nathan
Vanessa Rauh
Debbie Reynolds
Mindy Sheppard
Roz Sweeney
Barbara Urbanska

Track & Field
Erin AufderHeide
Christine Baudry
April Beard
Bethany Brewster
Tara Clack
Jenelle Deatherage
Rose Douglas
Lisa Flak
Andrea Geurtsen
Jessica Karnowski
Lisa Kincaid
Sho Kroeger
Shana Martin
Anneli Melin
Susie Motl
Erica Palmer
Stephanie Pesch
Cathy Ross
Stacey Sawtelle
Quinn Scott
Becky Tuma
Avrie Watlers
Janet Westphal
Jenni Westphal

Volleyball
Pauline Bresky
Lindsey Buswell
Julia D'Alo
Lizzy Fitzgerald
Jamie Gardner
Haley Jones
Kelly Kennedy
Sherisa Livingston
Jenny Maastricht
Marisa Mackey
Marie Meyer
Colleen Neels
Allyson Ross
Keylee Wright

1999-2000

MEN'S
CROSS COUNTRY: 1ST (2ND, NCAA)
coached by Jerry Schumacher
FOOTBALL: 1ST
coached by Barry Alvarez
SOCCER: 5TH (TIE)
coached by Kalekeni Banda
BASKETBALL: 6TH (FINAL FOUR)
coached by Dick Bennett
ICE HOCKEY: 1ST, WCHA
coached by Jeff Sauer
SWIMMING: 5TH
coached by Eric Hansen
WRESTLING: 7TH
coached by Barry Davis
INDOOR TRACK: 1ST
coached by Ed Nuttycombe
GOLF: 6TH
coached by Dennis Tiziani
ROWING
coached by Chris Clark
TENNIS: 8TH
coached by Pat Klingelhoets
OUTDOOR TRACK: 1ST
coached by Ed Nuttycombe

WOMEN'S
CROSS COUNTRY: 1ST (4TH, NCAA)
coached by Peter Tegen
BASKETBALL: 6TH (1ST, WOMEN'S NIT)
coached by Jane Albright
SOCCER: 8TH (TIE)
coached by Dean Duerst
SWIMMING: 5TH
coached by Eric Hansen
INDOOR TRACK: 2ND
coached by Peter Tegen
VOLLEYBALL: 3RD
coached by Peter Waite
GOLF: 4TH
coached by Dennis Tiziani
SOFTBALL: 5TH
coached by Karen Gallagher
ROWING: 4TH
coached by Mary Browning
LIGHTWEIGHT ROWING
coached by Maren Watson
TENNIS: 9TH
coached by Patti Henderson
OUTDOOR TRACK: 3RD
coached by Peter Tegen

Big Ten champ Badgers win second consecutive Rose Bowl

Wisconsin's 17-9 Rose Bowl win over Stanford on Jan. 1, 2000, cemented the Badgers' place in history as the first Big Ten team to win the "granddaddy of all bowl games" in back-to-back seasons.

The New Year's Day game was the culmination of a remarkable four-year cycle for the '99 seniors, Wisconsin's all-time winningest group. Its legacy for future Badger squads: a 37-13 record, four bowl berths, two Big Ten championships and three bowl game victories.

Coach Barry Alvarez's 1999 Badgers, who finished fourth in both the coaches' and media polls, won the school's first undisputed Big Ten title in 37 years; recorded 10 wins for the second most victories in UW history; ended the season with eight straight wins; defeated five nationally ranked teams; became just the third team since 1982 to lead the Big Ten in scoring offense and scoring defense; and became the only school to win three Rose Bowls in the 1990s.

The Rose Bowl game itself was somewhat of a surprise in that two high-scoring offenses never really got untracked and battled through a defensive struggle.

After a scoreless first quarter, Stanford scored first on a 28-yard field goal. Vitaly Pisetsky knotted the game at 3-3 on a 31-yard field goal three minutes later. Stanford took the lead at 2:03 of the second quarter on a one-yard run by Kerry Carter.

Wisconsin Time Line

1999: Erica Palmer becomes the third Wisconsin woman to win a national cross country title, taking the NCAA individual championship on her 20th birthday, Nov. 22, 1999.

2000: Wisconsin's men's basketball team is ranked 11th by the Associated Press, the school's highest national ranking since it was rated seventh on Dec. 10, 1962.

Wisconsin romps to an easy victory in the 100th Big Ten men's outdoor track and field championship May 19-21 in Iowa City. UW coach Ed Nuttycombe is named Big Ten Coach of the Year.

WISCONSIN HEADLINER

Dayne wins Heisman Trophy, leads Badgers to Big Ten title, Rose Bowl

The "Great Dayne" was great indeed for Wisconsin in 1999.

Running back Ron Dayne became the second Badger to win the Heisman Trophy, symbolic of college football's best player, with 586 first-place votes and 2,042 points in the balloting for the 65th annual award presented by the Downtown Athletic Club in New York. Fullback Alan Ameche won the 1954 Heisman for the UW.

Dayne outdistanced Georgia Tech quarterback Joe Hamilton, who had 994 points in the voting. Dayne was the top vote-getter in all six regions.

Prior to winning the Heisman, Dayne had won nearly every other award he was up for, including the AP College Player of the Year, the Walter Camp, Maxwell and Doak Walker awards. He also was named MVP of the Rose Bowl for the second straight year, as he rushed for 200 yards and scored one touchdown in his final game as a Badger.

In 1999, Dayne became college football's career rushing leader with 6,397 yards when he ran for 31 yards in the second quarter against Iowa on Nov. 13. He's the only player in the history of college football to rush for more than 7,000 yards (including postseason play). Dayne ended his career with 7,125 yards in 47 games for a 151.6 per game average. He's one of only four players in history to have four seasons of 1,000 rushing yards or more and is the first three-time rushing champion in the annals of the Big Ten.

Dayne personally outrushed the opposition in 29 of his 43 starts and averaged 120.3 yards rushing against nationally ranked opponents during his career. He also tied an NCAA record with 11 career games of 200 yards or more.

Dayne by game in 1999

Opponent	Attempts	Yards	Average	TDs
Murray State	20	135	6.8	3
Ball State	31	158	5.1	1
Cincinnati	28	231	8.3	1
Michigan	22	88	4.0	1
Ohio State	32	161	5.0	4
Minnesota	25	80	3.2	1
Indiana	17	167	9.8	2
Michigan State	34	214	6.3	2
Northwestern	35	162	4.6	2
Purdue	32	222	6.9	1
Iowa	27	216	8.0	1
Stanford	34	200	5.9	1
Totals	337	2,034	6.0	20

Dayne's career yardage

Year	YAC*	Yards	Pct.
1996	1,066	2,109	50.5
1997	699	1,457	48.0
1998	704	1,525	46.1
1999	1,098	2,034	50.1
Totals	3,567	7,125	50.1

*It was rare for Dayne to get a carry without contact. His yards after contact (YAC) total alone would be enough to rank him among the top eight in UW history.

Surprising Badgers advance to NCAA Final Four

No one, even the most loyal and optimistic of the Badger faithful, would have predicted the UW men's basketball team would have been playing on April 1.

Or, for that matter, on March 25 or March 18, either.

But play, the Badgers did, and well, through a remarkable run in the NCAA Tournament that culminated in Wisconsin's first appearance in an NCAA Final Four since the magical championship season of 1941.

That Wisconsin's improbable run at the NCAA championship ended with a 53-41 loss to eventual NCAA kingpin Michigan State—which beat the Badgers four times in the UW's final 14 games and was the only team to stop Wisconsin during the span—in no way diminished the season's accomplishments.

And those were legion. The 1999-2000 squad matched the previous year's group for most wins in Wisconsin history with 22.

Wisconsin started the season well enough, beating Missouri 66-55 in its opener and posting a 6-2 mark after eight games. Losses at South Florida and Northern Illinois slowed the Badgers somewhat, but wins over Marquette and Temple set the stage for Big Ten play.

Wisconsin's lone Big Ten win in its first five league games came at home over Illinois, but then Wisconsin surged a bit, taking seven of its final 11 games heading into the Big Ten Tournament, including a 56-53 season-ending win over Indiana at the Kohl Center to perhaps clinch an NCAA Tournament berth. Victories over Northwestern (51-41) and Purdue (78-66) set the stage for the Badgers' semifinal loss to MSU.

In NCAA play, Wisconsin became one of the stories—if not *the* story of the tournament. Oblivious to records or rankings, the Badgers' tenacious defense shredded Fresno State 66-56 in the opening round, followed in the next by a systematic taking-apart of No. 1-seed Arizona, 66-59, and a berth in the Sweet 16. A 61-48 upset win over LSU put the UW into the Elite Eight against Purdue, which Wisconsin had already beaten in two of three games. The 64-60 win in the regional finals sent Wisconsin to Indianapolis.

Defense was again the Badgers' forte, as it has always been with Dick Bennett-coached teams. The Badgers allowed only 55.8 points per game.

Mark Vershaw led the UW in scoring at 11.8 ppg and also had 118 assists to become only the third forward in school history to reach the 100-assist mark.

Wisconsin wins women's NIT

After finishing in a fifth-place tie at 8-8 in the Big Ten standings, Coach Jane Albright's women's basketball squad found the Women's NIT to its liking.

The Badgers culminated their five-game championship run with a 75-74 victory over Florida in the championship game at the Kohl Center. All five Badger wins came on their home court, the last attended by 13,006.

The UW notched its 21st victory with the championship, equaling the school mark achieved three times previously. It was Wisconsin's fourth 20-victory season in the past six years under Albright.

It also marked the Badgers' second successive appearance in the WNIT final. Wisconsin lost to Arkansas 67-64 in Fayetteville in 1999.

The Badgers almost blew a 15-point lead but hung on for the win behind tournament MVP Tamara Moore, who scored 25 points on 9-for-13 shooting. Moore also had a game-high seven assists, five rebounds and four steals. Moore and LaTonya Sims, who had nine points and six rebounds, were also named to the WNIT all-tournament team.

Sims averaged a double-double in WNIT play with 17 points and 10.2 rebounds in the five games. She had a season-high 28 points and 16 rebounds in the Badgers' 77-45 quarterfinal win over Michigan State.

Jessie Stomski averaged 13.2 points and 6.8 rebounds per game, while Moore averaged 14 points, 4.8 rebounds, 4.2 assists and 3.2 steals. Kelley Paulus added 9.5 ppg.

Wisconsin tied its own WNIT record for largest margin of victory (37) with its 83-46 opening-round win over Fairfield. As a team, the UW averaged 79 points per game to their opponents' 60 and pulled down an average 44.2 rebounds a game to their foes' 37.6. The Badgers shot at a .472 clip from the field in the tourney and held the opposition to .352 shooting.

Following its opening win over Fairfield, Wisconsin defeated DePaul 82-76 before beating MSU for the second time in their three meetings. A 78-60 win over Colorado State in the semis set the stage for the Badgers' championship heroics.

Wisconsin finished the season 21-12.

WISCONSIN HEADLINER

Steve Reinprecht
Hockey

Steve Reinprecht, a first-team All-America selection at forward, was the top scorer for a UW hockey team that posted a 31-9-1 mark and ranked first in the nation through much of the latter part of the season. Reinprecht, a native of Edmonton, Alberta, scored 26 goals and had 40 assists, with his 1.78 points-per-game average helping him to the runner-up spot in balloting for the Hobey Baker Award, collegiate hockey's most prestigious individual honor. The WCHA's Player of the Year, he became the first player in Wisconsin history to lead the Badgers in scoring three straight years. His 15 career game-winning goals tie him for fourth all time at the UW. Reinprecht was named the WCHA Offensive Player of the Week twice in 1999-2000, the sixth and seventh times he was so honored by the league. Following the collegiate season, he played for the Los Angeles Kings of the National Hockey League.

WISCONSIN HEADLINER

Erica Palmer
Cross Country

Erica Palmer gave herself quite a present for her 20th birthday on Nov. 22, 1999: an NCAA cross country championship. The Wisconsin sophomore out of Gilsum, New Hampshire, became Wisconsin's third NCAA cross country champion by running a personal best 16:39.5 for the 5,000-meter course at Indiana University. She's the youngest NCAA harrier champ in four years. Although some "experts" may not have expected the 5'3" Palmer to win over some better known and more experienced rivals, her seasonal performances clearly set her up as a major contender. Palmer became the UW's 11th Big Ten individual champ Oct. 30 at Penn State, winning in a then personal best 16:46.93, almost 20 seconds ahead of teammate Erin AufderHeide. And two weeks later, Palmer became Wisconsin's seventh regional champ, setting a course record of 16:52.2 as she cruised to a 23-second victory. So Nov. 22 offered no real surprise to anyone who had seen Palmer run all season. The best news for Badger cross country fans is that she's back for two more seasons.

WISCONSIN HEADLINER

Don Pritzlaff
Wrestling

Junior 165-pounder Don Pritzlaff became the 12th Badger to win a national collegiate wrestling title in March 2000, beating top-ranked Joe Heskett of Iowa State 4-2 in overtime at the NCAA championships in St. Louis. Ironically, it was the second time in the season that Pritzlaff had defeated Heskett by the same score and in overtime. His win was the 16th NCAA wrestling crown for a Wisconsin athlete and helped propel the Badgers into a ninth-place tie, their best finish in eight years. Pritzlaff, a native of Lyndhurst, New Jersey, had won his second consecutive Big Ten title a couple weeks earlier. Pritzlaff has earned All-America honors in each of his first three seasons at Wisconsin. He finished his junior year with a 36-2 overall record and an 8-0 Big Ten mark.

WISCONSIN HEADLINER

Ellen Stonebraker
Swimming

Nine-time All-American Ellen Stonebraker won just about every honor that a UW swimmer could garner. The Naperville, Illinois, native earned All-America honors nine times for the Badgers from 1997-2000. Stonebraker holds Big Ten records for the 200-yard freestyle (1:45.78), the 500-yard freestyle (4:41.26), the 1,650-yard freestyle (16:11.42) and as a member of the American record-holding 800-yard free relay (7:09.07). Stonebraker was first in the 500 free and third in the 200 free and 1,650 free at the Big Ten championships, earning her Swimmer of the Championship honors. She also won four other Big Ten titles during her career and was a three-time All-Big Ten selection. The 1999 and 2000 UW MVP, Stonebraker also was an Academic All-Big Ten pick for those seasons. She was a member of the 1999 U.S. national team at the Pan-Pacific Games in Australia, where she won a gold in the 800 free relay and bronze medals in the 800 free and 200 free.

WISCONSIN HEADLINER

Mike Kelley
Men's Basketball

Guard Mike Kelley became the consummate thief during the Badgers' run to the NCAA Final Four in March 2000. His 19 steals in the NCAA Tournament were the most by any player in the tourney and tied for second–most ever in NCAA tourney play. The junior from Menomonee Falls has recorded at least five steals in a game 10 times during his career. And as goes Kelley, so go the Badgers–Wisconsin is 16-1 in games in which he had at least four steals. He's the school's career steals leader with 215, and tied for sixth best in Big Ten history with his senior season upcoming. Kelley's 95 steals led the Big Ten and were second-most ever by a conference player. He also led the Big Ten in assist-to-turnover ratio (3.26 to 1). Kelley, the 1998-99 Big Ten Defensive Player of the Year, as selected by the coaches, has started 87 games, eighth most in UW history, and has never missed a game during his career (99 straight).

LEADING THE WAY

Jerry Schumacher
Men's Cross Country Coach

In only two seasons as Wisconsin's men's cross country coach, former UW standout Jerry Schumacher has more than lived up to the expectations for success that his predecessors have created among Badger cross country fans. In 1999, his second season at the helm, the Waukesha native–himself a former three-time cross country All-American and track All-American at 1,500 meters–guided the Badgers to second in the NCAA championships, the team's best finish since 1992. Behind two-time All-Americans Matt Downin and Jay Schoenfelder, the Badgers also won the Big Ten title, their first since 1996. For his efforts, Schumacher was named Big Ten and Great Lakes Regional Coach of the Year and was a finalist for national Coach of the Year honors. That followed his rookie season in which the Badgers placed third in the Big Ten and sixth in the NCAA.

A W first

Women's ice hockey debuts

It's no surprise that women's ice hockey would be a success at Wisconsin.

The UW completed its first season of the sport with a 19-14-2 overall mark and a 15-8-1 record in Western Collegiate Hockey Association play.

First-year coach Julie Sasner's Badgers finished third in WCHA regular-season play and fourth in the tournament. Highlights of the season were the Badgers' 4-4 tie with 10th-ranked Princeton and Wisconsin's top-10 rankings in two polls. The UW was rated as high as ninth in the *American Hockey Magazine* poll and 10th in the U.S. College Hockey Online poll.

Six players earned WCHA awards. Defenseman Sis Paulsen and goaltender Jackie MacMillan made the All-WCHA first team, while defenseman Kerry Weiland was a second-team pick. Bridget Buchholz, Michelle Sikich and Leslie Toner made the WCHA All-Academic team.

The List

Road to the championships

Badger men's NCAA Tournament games

- First round: #8 UW 66, #9 Fresno State 56
- Second round: #8 UW 66, #1 Arizona 59
- Regional semis: #8 UW 61, #4 LSU 48
- Regional final: #8 UW 64, #6 Purdue 60
- National semis: #1 Michigan State 53, #8 UW 41

Badger women's NIT games

- UW 83, Fairfield 46
- UW 82, DePaul 76
- UW 77, Michigan State 45
- UW 78, Colorado State 60
- Championship: UW 75, Florida 74

1999-2000 MEN'S LETTERWINNERS

Basketball
Roy Boone
Jon Bryant
Travon Davis
Duany Duany
Erik Faust
Mike Kelley
Andy Kowske
Maurice Linton
Kirk Penney
Robert Smith
Julian Swartz
Mark Vershaw
Charlie Wills

Cross Country
Jared Cordes
Matt Downin
Jim Marshalek
Jay Schoenfelder
Jason Vanderhoof
Jason Weppler
Nick Winkel

Football
Mark Anelli
Clint Bakken
Michael Bennett
Erik Bickerstaff
Joey Boese
Brooks Bollinger
David Braun
Demetrius Brown
Wendell Bryant
P.J. Cannon
Marcus Carpenter
Chris Chambers
Carlease Clark
David Costa
Nick Davis
Ron Dayne
Jason Doering
T.J. Dooley (Mgr.)
Mark Downing
Mike Echols
Lee Evans
Eddie Faulker
John Favret
Bill Ferrario
Jamar Fletcher
Chris Ghidorzi
Nick Greisen
Ben Herbert
Devery Hughes
Josh Jakubowski
Chris Janek
Al Johnson
Ben Johnson
Jason Jowers
Scott Kavanagh
Roger Knight
Phil Koch
Russ Kolodziej
Chad Kuhns
Brian Lamont
Dan Lisowski
Eric Mahlik
Ryan Marks
Delante McGrew
Chris McIntosh
Ahmad Merritt
Sam Mueller
Bobby Myers
Rick Nelson (Mgr.)
Nick Neumuth (Mgr.)
Vitaly Pisetsky
George Pratt
Casey Rabach
Dague Retzalff
Rob Roell
Tim Rosga
Jason Schick
John Sigmund
Charlie Smith
Mike Solwold
Jake Sprague
Teddy Stanton (Mgr.)
Kevin Stemke
Mark Tauscher
Bryson Thompson
Donnel Thompson
Jeff Topel (Mgr.)
B.J. Tucker
Andy Ulery (Mgr.)
Matt Unertl
Mike Weyer (Mgr.)
Conroy Whyte

Golf
Todd Anderson
C.J. Brock
John Carlson
Jim Lemon
Jon Turcott

Hockey
Mark Baranczyk
Dan Bjornlie
Alex Brooks
Mike Cerniglia
Kent Davyduke
Jeff Dessner
Matt Doman
Brian Fahey
Kevin Granato
Dan Guenther
Dany Heathley
Dave Hergert
David Hukalo
Matt Hussey
Mark Jackson
Erik Jensen
Scott Kabotoff
Dustin Kuk
Graham Melanson
Matt Murray
Steve Reinprecht
Niki Siren
Rick Spooner
Rob Vega
Andy Wheeler
Brad Winchester

Soccer
Valentin Anozie
Phil Ayoub
Moriba Atiba Baker
Abraham Bull
Matt Burkert
Tim Caprez
Matthew Carroll
Bram Dorrestyn
Justin Engelhardt
Mike Epp
Narciso Fernandes
Brian Feyrer
Tamba Johnson
Mark Jones
Salil Kenkre
Aaron Lauber
Christian Poppert
Michale Romenesko
Aymar Sinaise
Perry Smith
Steve Sorensen
Scott Repa
Scott Wood

Swimming & Diving
Troy Blanton
Adam Byars
Brink Ciferri
Brendan Coyne
Aaron Forgy
Eric Godsman
Anders Holm
Ted Krueger
Cory Miller
Brian Neuman
Dan Patee
Neil Peiffer
Andrew Tainter
Russell Zuckerman
Matt Zuiderhof

Tennis
Justin Baker
David Chang
Bobby Croll
Dustin Friedman
Jason Gonzaga
Stefan Reist
Scott Rutherford
Adam Schumacher
Danny Westerman

Track & Field
Michael Bennett
James Berger
Pat Bremer
Clint Chapman
Jared Cordes
Josh Dickerson
Matt Downin
Nathan Fields
Benny Gill
Len Herring
Clayton Hiemke
Anders Holstrom
Steve Holzbauer
Steve Jones
Ross Kolodziej
Adam Kress
Eric Leicht
Pierre Leinbach
Brad Mohns
Jon Mungen
Bobby Myers
T.J. Nelson
Jabari Pride
Tom Ridge
Matt Rogers
Fiatala Salamo
Jay Schoenfelder
Ryan Tremeling
Nate Uselding
Jason Vanderhoof
Chris Van Tassel
Baigeh Tucker
Jason Weppler
Scott Wick
Christian Williams
Nick Winkel
Gordon Zietlow

Wrestling
Steve Alf
Tony Black
Kole Clauson
Brady Cudd
P.J. Dowling
Grant Hoerr
Brad Marte
Corey McNellis
Brad Owens
Jason Pernat
Don Pritzlaff
Justin Staebler
Joe Terrill
Ryan Turner
Cory Wallman

1999-2000 WOMEN'S LETTERWINNERS

Basketball
Krista Bird
Kyle Black
Judy Ebeling
Leah Hefte
Sarah Jirovec
Rachel Klongland
Missy Konieczny
Tamara Moore
Dee Dee Pate
Kelley Paulus
Erin Schmidt
Kristi Seeger
LaTonya Sims
Candas Smith
Nina Smith
Jessie Stomski

Crew (Lightweight)
Dusty Darley
Alison Frohberg
Lindsay Gorsuch
Marisa Hoffman
Kirstin Holbeck
Stacey Langenecker
Angela Lay
Sara Lyng
Nicole Moen
Maura O'Donnell
Karin Swanson
Noelle Vitone
Sara Webb

Cross Country
Erin AufderHeide
Bethany Brewster
Jaime Kulbel
Laura Martin
Susie Motl
Erica Palmer
Stephanie Pesch
Liz Reusser
Lisa Weltzer

Golf
Allie Blomquist
Katie Connelly
Carli Gregorin
Allison Hoggarth
Andrea Meeker
Katie Prieve
Kelly Trapp

Hockey
Gretchen Anderson
Kendra Antony
Bridget Buchholz
Annie Chamberlain
Christine Gehrke
Theresa Hilleman
Elizabeth Jankowski
Janelle Johnson
Kelly Kegley
Jackie McMillan
Jennifer Mead
Roseann Meyer
Jennifer Neary
Abbey Olson
Julia Ortenzio
Shari Paulsen
Melanie Schmitt
Natascha Sherman
Roberta Schufeldt
Michelle Sikich
Leslie Toner
Kerry Weiland

Soccer
Jamie Barbian
Kelly Conway
Megan Dobesh
Camile Flenniken
Elizabeth Grum
Amy Hanna
Kyndra Hesse
Michelle Hawkins
Shelby Johnson
Jamie Keller
Kelly Kundert
Emily Lubcke
Wynter Pero
Alissa Peterson
Heather Priester
Natalie Roedler
Allie Rogosheske
Lauren Schmidt
Kathryn Spillane
Emily Stevens
Allison Wagner
Heidi Wegleitner
Jessica Wolff
Jennifer Wright

Softball
Lindy Barth
Amanda Berg
Jennifer Cummings
Jennifer Girard
Jade Gosse
Jennifer Grill
Kerry Hagen
Anna Jones
Andrea Kirchberg
Sarah Lippert
Sarah Mayer
Theresa Mendez
Kristy Sacknoff
Nicki Starry
Chrissy Swartout

Swimming & Diving
Jamie Belfor
Gianna Bova
Caroline DiSalle
Betsy Hassebroek
Megan Kernan
Siobhan Kernan
Gina Loechl
Jenny Lyman
Sarah McCauley
Christy Mullinanx
Amy Munz
Gina Panighetti
Jocelyn Plcl
Erin Pohle
Jennifer Rushfeldt
Lara Skoog
Ellen Stonebraker
Abby Tesch
Andrea Wanezek
Sara Wiezorek

Tennis
Dena Baritot
Katie Dougherty
Rebecca Ebin
April Gabler
Shana McElroy
Linde Mues
Vanessa Rauh
Mindy Sheppard
Kristen Van Dernoot
Lara Vojnov

Track & Field
Erin AufderHeide
Christine Baudry
April Beard
Bethany Brewster
Tara Clack
Lisa Flak
Andrea Geurtsen
Lisa Kincaid
Jaime Kulbel
Abby Kwapil
Laura Martin
Shana Martin
Susie Motl
Erica Palmer
Stephanie Pesch
Liz Reusser
Catherine Ross
Stacy Sawtelle
Quinn Scott
Julie Stefan
Becky Tuma

Volleyball
Erin Byrd
Julia D'Alo
Lizzy Fitzgerald
Jamie Gardner
Kelly Kennedy
Sherisa Livingston
Jenny Maastricht
Marie Meyer
Lori Rittenhouse
Allyson Ross
Morgan Shields

2000-01

BADGER BIG TEN FINISHES...

TM

MEN'S
CROSS COUNTRY: 1st (5th, NCAA)
coached by Jerry Schumacher
FOOTBALL: 3rd (tie)
coached by Barry Alvarez
SOCCER: 4th
coached by Kalekeni Banda
BASKETBALL: 5th
coached by Dick Bennett & Brad Soderberg
ICE HOCKEY: 5th (WCHA)
coached by Jeff Sauer
SWIMMING: 4th
coached by Eric Hansen
INDOOR TRACK: 1st
coached by Ed Nuttycombe
WRESTLING: 9th
coached by Barry Davis
GOLF: 7th (tie)
coached by Dennis Tiziani
ROWING: Ten Eyck Trophy winners
coached by Chris Clark
TENNIS: 6th (tie)
coached by Pat Klingelhoets
OUTDOOR TRACK: 1st
coached by Ed Nuttycombe

WOMEN'S
CROSS COUNTRY: 1st (8th, NCAA)
coached by Peter Tegen
SOCCER: 2nd
coached by Dean Duerst
VOLLEYBALL: 1st (2nd, NCAA)
coached by Peter Waite
BASKETBALL: 2nd
coached by Jane Albright
ICE HOCKEY: 3rd, WCHA
coached by Julie Sasner
SWIMMING: 5th
coached by Eric Hansen
INDOOR TRACK: 6th
coached by Peter Tegen
GOLF: 8th
coached by Dennis Tiziani
ROWING: 4th
coached by Mary Browning
LIGHTWEIGHT ROWING (2nd, nationals)
coached by Maren Watson
SOFTBALL: 5th (tie)
coached by Karen Gallagher
TENNIS: 8th
coached by Patti Henderson
OUTDOOR TRACK: 6th
coached by Peter Tegen

Bennett quits; Soderberg leads UW to NCAA; Ryan named coach

Dick Bennett

To say it was a sad year for the Wisconsin men's basketball program would be correct. To call it a winning year would also be correct. And to call it an unusual and memorable year would be an understatement. It was the year of three coaches.

It was sad because veteran mentor Dick Bennett, who had led the Badgers to the NCAA Final Four in March 2000, and entertained the notion of calling it a career following that great season, finally said enough was enough when he resigned as head coach Nov. 30, three games into the season and with the Badgers at 2-1.

Brad Soderberg

It was a winning year, too. Assistant Brad Soderberg was immediately elevated to the head job on an acting basis, and the Badgers responded with a season that—in almost any other year at Wisconsin—would have been one for the ages.

Nonetheless, Wisconsin was 18-11 and 9-7 in the Big Ten, good for fifth in the nation's best conference. The Badgers then took a No. 6 seed into the West region of the NCAA Tournament, losing 50-49 to Georgia State in the first round.

Bo Ryan

Then, on March 29, the Bo Ryan era began at Wisconsin when the former UW assistant returned to Madison after 17 years as head coach at UW-Platteville and UW-Milwaukee. Ryan's Platteville teams won four NCAA Division III titles in the 1990s. Over a 12-year stretch, Ryan's teams were 314-37, won eight conference titles, never won fewer than 23 games in a season and were the winningest NCAA men's team of the decade with a 266-26 record.

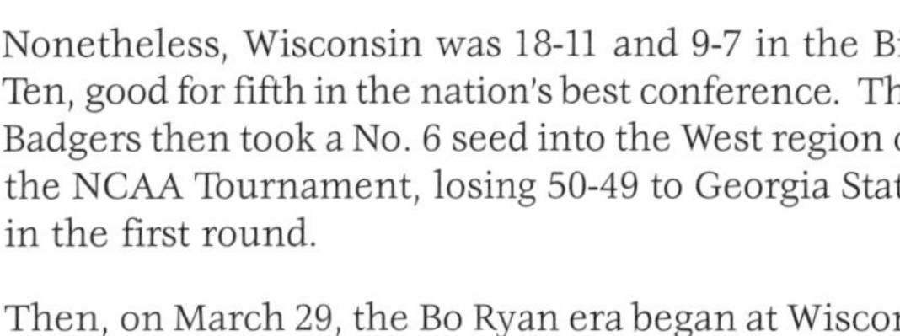

WISCONSIN TIME LINE

2000: The fourth-ranked Wisconsin football team opens its season with three straight victories—19-7 over Western Michigan, 27-23 over Oregon and 28-25 (OT) over Cincinnati. The UW defeats UCLA 21-20 in the Sun Bowl.

2001: Wisconsin's men's ice hockey program leads the nation in attendance for the third straight year, with 229,219 fans watching the Badgers at the Kohl Center, an average of 11,461.

Golfer Allie Blomquist and basketball player Mike Kelley are named Wisconsin's 2000-2001 winners of the Big Ten Medal of Honor, presented to a student in the graduating class who has demonstrated proficiency in scholarship and athletics.

A W first

UW claims Big Ten all-sports title

Wisconsin won Big Ten championships in men's and women's cross country, men's indoor and outdoor track and women's volleyball to lead the conference's all-sports standings for 2000-01. The UW has finished first three times and second five times since the 1990-91 season and was third in 1999-2000 behind Minnesota and Michigan. The standings are not officially recognized by the Big Ten but offer a good barometer of the success of the league's athletic programs. The Badgers averaged 7.50 points in 21 sports to finish just ahead of Michigan, which averaged 7.48 points for its 25-sport program. Like Wisconsin, Michigan won five championships. The 2000-01 Big Ten all-sports standings follow:

Rank	School	Total Points	Sports	Average
1	Wisconsin	157.5	21	7.50
2	Michigan	187	25	7.48
3	Ohio State	185	25	7.40
4	Minnesota	160.5	23	6.98
5	Penn State	163.5	25	6.54
6	Purdue	129.5	20	6.48
7	Indiana	134	23	5.83
8	Northwestern	98	17	5.76
9	Illinois	120.5	21	5.74
10	Iowa	125	24	5.21
11	Michigan State	128.5	25	5.14

WISCONSIN HEADLINER

Allie Blomquist
Women's Golf

Wisconsin golfer Allie Blomquist proved in 2001 that she's as far under par on the links as she is above par in the classroom. She was Wisconsin's female winner of the 2000-01 Big Ten Medal of Honor, awarded to the graduating student who has demonstrated proficiency in scholarship and athletics. Blomquist capped her senior season in fine fashion as the most accomplished woman golfer in UW history. She finished tied for sixth in the Big Ten Tournament, carding a 306 off rounds of 72, 75, 82 and 77, and then became Wisconsin's first NCAA qualifier. She tied for 18th in the national tourney. The Afton, Minnesota, native holds every scoring record at Wisconsin, including a 69 for 18 holes, 142 for 36, 216 for 54 and 296 for 72. She broke her own record for lowest scoring average this season with a 76.67 mark, and her career average of 77.48 is first in the UW record book. Blomquist is also a four-time All-Big Ten academic honoree and four-time National Golf Coaches Association Academic All-American. She was a first-team Verizon/CoSIDA Academic All-America honoree as both a junior and a senior.

WISCONSIN HEADLINER

Len Herring
Track & Field

With one outdoor season remaining, Len Herring has already established himself as one of the top horizontal jumpers in Big Ten history. At the 2001 outdoor meet, the Hawthorne, Florida, native won his fourth straight Big Ten long jump title, as the Badgers won their second consecutive conference "triple crown" with cross country, indoor and outdoor track championships. An injury prevented him from going for a title in the triple jump, the event in which he had qualified for the 2000 Olympic Trials. Three times an All-American in the triple jump, Herring has a best in the event of 54'4" and a best in the long jump of 25'9 $^{1}/_{2}$". He ranks second on the UW all-time list in both events.

BADGER MOMENT

UW posts another winning season and bowl victory

The UW's 2000 football season was a roller-coaster one of sorts, with ups like a five-game, season-ending winning streak and downs like two overtime losses. On balance, however, it was another highly successful one for the Badgers, with a 9-4 record highlighted by a 21-20 win over UCLA in the Sun Bowl. Coach Barry Alvarez's team had to overcome more than its share of injuries, the suspensions of 27 players and the country's toughest schedule. It did, becoming the third straight Badger squad to win nine games. Wisconsin also won four road games; claimed the Paul Bunyan Axe for the sixth straight season; equaled the school mark with 10 academic All-Big Ten picks; and had the winners of the Jim Thorpe Award (Jamar Fletcher) and the Ray Guy Award (Kevin Stemke).

2000-01 MEN'S LETTERWINNERS

Basketball
Roy Boone
Richard Bower
Travon Davis
Kyle Grusczynski
Mike Kelley
Andy Kowske
Maurice Linton
David Mader
Lawrence Owens
Kirk Penney
Peter Schmit
Ike Ukawuba
Mark Vershaw
Charles Wills

Crew
Nathan Altfeather
Scott Alwin
Brian Bauer
Paul Daniels
Alan Geweke
Peter Giese
Ed Golding
Zachary Gutt
Ben Hoopman
Nick Kitowski
Eric Knecht
Reed Kuehn
Brian McDonough
Sam McLennan
Daniel Mueller
Peter Nagle
Dirk Peters
Ken Price
John Remington
Mike Seelen
John Taylor

Cross Country
Jared Cordes
Joe Eckerly
Kyle Fraser
Drew Hohensee
Tim Keller
Nate Uselding
Jason Vanderhoof
Adam Wallace

Football
Ryan Aiello
Mark Anelli
Michael Bennett
Eric Bickerstaff
Joe Boese
Brooks Bollinger
David Braun
Michael Broussard
Wendell Bryant
Bret Burlingame
Chris Chambers
Carlease Clark
David Costa
Nick Davis
Jason Doering
Mark Downing
Jeremy Dox
Michael Echols
Lee Evans
Edgar Faulkner
John Favret
Bill Ferrario
Jamar Fletcher
Nick Greisen
Aaron Habermann
Benjamin Herbert
Devery Hughes
Joshua Hunt
Josh Jakubowski
Allen Johnson
Ben Johnson
Darius Jones
Jason Jowers
Roger Knight
Ross Kolodziej
Chad Kuhns
Brian Lamont
Jeffery Mack
Eric Mahlik
Ryan Marks
Delante McGrew
Nick Mueller
Vitaly Pisetsky
Casey Rabach
Dague Retzlaff
Jason Schick
John Sigmund
Ryan Simmons
Charlie Smith
Michael Solwold
James Sorgi
Jacob Sprague
Kevin Stemke
Bryson Thompson
B.J. Tucker
Matt Unertl
Chris Wagner
Conroy Whyte
Broderick Williams

Golf
Todd Anderson
John Carlson
James Lemon
Joel Rechlicz
Larry Tiziani
Jonathan Turcott

Hockey
Mark Baranczyk
Daniel Boeser
Rene Bourque
Alex Brooks
Mike Cerniglia
Kent Davyduke
Jeff Dessner
Matt Doman
John Eichelberger
Brian Fahey
Kevin Granato
Dan Heatley
Jakob Heisler
David Hergert
David Hukalo
Matt Hussey
Mark Jackson
Erik Jensen
Scott Kabotoff
Jo Krall
David Melanson
Matt Murray
Richard Spooner
Robert Vega
Andrew Wheeler
Brad Winchester

Soccer
Valentine Anozie
Phillip Ayoub
Moriba Baker
Abraham Bull
Timothy Caprez
Mathew Carroll
Bran Dorresteyn
Michael Epp
Narcisco Fernandes
Brian Feyrer
Leron Gabriel
Tamba Johnson
Mark Jones
Salil Kenkre
Aaron Lauber
Christian Poppert
Scott Repa
Michael Romenesko
Aymar Sinaise
Perry Smith
Stephan Sorensen
Scott Wood

Swimming
Chris Anderson
Troy Blanton
Adam Byars
Brink Ciferri
Brendan Coyne
Kevin Engholdt
Aaron Forgy
Anders Holm
Keelan Holman
Lance Jones
Matt Marshall
Manuel Martin

2000-01 MEN'S LETTERWINNERS—CONT.

Brian Neuman
Dale Rogers
Andrew Tainter
Patrick Torpey
Matt Zuiderhof

Tennis

Justin Baker
Blake Baratz
Robert Croll
Dustin Friedman
Jason Gonzaga
Scott Green
David Hippee
Stefan Reist
Scott Rutherford
Dustin Taylor
Daniel Westerman

Wrestling

Kevin Black
Tony Black
Ralph DeNisco
P.J. Dowling
Grant Hoerr
Jareck Horton
Ryan Lewis
Corey McNellis
Don Pritzlaff
Justin Staebler
Nate Erdman
Dave Neumyer
Jason Pernat
Joe Terrill
Mark Trinitapoli
Ryan Turner
Adam Turner

Track & Field

James Berger
Pat Bremer
Jared Cordes
Michael Echols
Joe Eckerly
Ashraf Fadel
Isiah Festa
Benny Gill
Len Herring
Drew Hohensee
Steve Jones
Ross Kolodziej
Adam Kress
Pierre Leinbach
Jon Mungen
Dan Murray
T.J. Nelson
Jabari Pride
Ryan Ridge
Matt Rodgers
Ricardo Rodriguez
Robert Salamo
Spencer Schumacher
Jason Shonkwiler
Ryan Tremelling
B.J. Tucker
Nate Uselding
Chris Van Tassel
Jason Vanderhoof
Adam Wallace
Scott Wick
Brandon Williams
Christian Williams
Nick Winkel

2000-01 WOMEN'S LETTERWINNERS

Basketball
Emily Ashbaugh
Krista Bird
Kyle Black
Judy Ebeling
Leah Hefte
Sarah Jirovec
Rachel Klongland
Jessica Liegel
Tamara Moore
Kristina Seeger
Abigail Simmons
La Tonya Sims
Candas Smith
Nina Smith
Jessica Stomski

Cross Country
Bethany Brewster
Hilary Edmondson
Sarah Kolpin
Michelle Lilienthal
Erica Palmer
Leslie Patterson
Elizabeth Reusser

Golf
Allison Blomquist
Kathleen Connelly
Carli Gregorin
Allison Hoggarth
Heidi Njoes
Anna Temple

Ice Hockey
Gretchen Anderson
Kendra Antony
Stephanie Boeckmann
Kathryn Greaves
Meghan Hunter
Elizabeth Jankowski
Kelly Kegley
Jackie MacMillan
Jennifer Mead
Stephanie Millar
Jennifer Neary
Julia Ortenzio
Shari Paulsen
Karen Rickard
Melanie Schmitt
Natascha Sherman
Roberta Shufeldt
Michelle Sikich
Jaime Thibodeaux
Nicole Uliasz
James Wayne
Kerry Weiland

Soccer
Lindsay Chavez
Kelly Conway
Venetia Dale
Megan Dobesh
Camil Flenniken
Michelle Hawkins
Bethany Heine
Lisa Himrod
Shelby Johnson
Jennifer Jurkowski
Antoinette Koram
Jennnifer Kundert
Kelly Kundert
Emily Lubcke
Franziska Nickel
Wynter Pero
Natalie Roedler
Valerie Rogosheske
Lauren Schmidt
Kathryn Spillane
Allison Wagner
Heidi Wegleitner
Jessica Wolff
Jodi Zilinski

Lightweight Rowing
Alexandra Endress
Leah Hanson
Jadrian Brueckner
Cortney Cowie
Dusty Darley
Rebecca Flood
Alison Frohberg
Lindsay Gorsuch
Marisa Hoffman
Kirstin Holbeck
Stacey Langenecker
Angela Lay
Kathryn O'Donnell
Eileen Ruzicka
Kathryn Shea
Noelle Vitone
Joni Wiebelhaus

Openweight Rowing
Meredith Blair
Jennifer Broerman
Alana Burny
Erin Bye
Carrie Byron
Kathleen Edwards
Alyssa Elver
Tara Gedman
Erin Gladding
Juliann Hertz
Bridgid Myers
Althea Neel
Karolyn Oetjen
Emily Peterson
Jennifer Pofahl
Molly Rennebohm
Sara Stahlman
Tiffany Suda
Annie Trimberger
Mariana Waters

Swimming & Diving
Jamie Belfor
Molly Buhrandt
Kristin Bunnell
Elizabeth Hassebroek
Megan Kernan
Siobahn Kernan
Gina Loechl
Jennifer Lyman
Sarah McCauley
Christy Mullinax
Calyn Patzer
Bethany Pendleton
Emily Pisula
Melissa Ramsey
Jennifer Rushfeldt
Ellen Stonebraker
Andrea Wanezek
Sara Wiezorek

Tennis
Katherine Dougherty
April Gabler
Teresa Gonzaga
Heidi Maskas
Linde Mues
Vanessa Rauh
Mindy Sheppard
Kristen Van Dernoot
Lara Vojnov

Track
Erin AufderHeide
Christine Baudry
Courtney Bauer
Magaret Bauer
Bethany Brewster
Tara Clack
Hilary Edmondson
Sarah Foster
Bree Fuqua
Andrea Geurtsen0
Heidi Hansen
Kimberly Hubing
Jessica Karnowski
Lisa Kincaid
Angela Kolanko
Sarah Kolpin
Abby Kwapil
Michelle Lilienthal
Katie Malcore
Shana Martin
Christine Muenzenberger
Erica Palmer
Chrissy Pasell
Leslie Patterson
Yael Peled
Elizabeth Reusser
Stacey Sawtelle
Quinn Scott
Julie Stefan
Briana Stott-Messick
Rebecca Turna
Amanda Weihert

Volleyball
Erin Byrd
Elizabeth Fitzgerald
Jamie Gardner
Korie Gardner
Meggan Kohnen
Sherisa Livingston
Jennifer Maastricht
Jill Maier
Marie Meyer
Lori Rittenhouse
Claudia Rodriguez-Audelo
Angie Sanger
Morgan Shields
Sara Urbanek
Lisa Zukowski, Lisa

ABOUT THE AUTHORS

DON KOPRIVA, a longtime observer of Big Ten athletics, grew to love Wisconsin during his tenure as sports information director at UW-Parkside (1971-82). As a track-and-field writer and official, he's seen every Badger track or cross country performer over the past 30 years. A 1971 Michigan State graduate, Kopriva served as manager of the main press center for the 1984 Los Angeles Olympics and became assistant managing editor of the *Chicago Sun-Times*. Now editor of *The Business Ledger*, an Oak Brook, Illinois-based business newspaper, Don remains involved with Big Ten sports. He lives in Lisle, Illinois.

JIM MOTT has spent a lifetime in Madison. The retired Wisconsin sports information director (1966-90) is knowledgeable on all things Wisconsin and has used his remarkable recall of Badger athletic events and athletes to help him with this book. A 1954 graduate of Wisconsin, Mott was assistant sports information director for 12 years before becoming SID. Well respected by his peers, Mott was named to the College Sports Information Directors Hall of Fame in 1979. No less respected and revered in Madison, Mott was inducted into the UW Athletic Hall of Fame in 1990. Jim and his wife, Dorothy, are the parents of three adult sons and still reside in Madison.